Mike Meyers'
CompTIA Network+®
Guide to Managing and
Troubleshooting Networks
Lab Manual

Fifth Edition

(Exam N10-007)

About the Authors

Mike Meyers, lovingly called the "AlphaGeek" by those who know him, is the industry's leading authority on CompTIA Network+ certification. He is the president and co-founder of Total Seminars, LLC, a provider of PC and network repair seminars, books, videos, and courseware for thousands of organizations throughout the world. Mike has been involved in the computer and network repair industry since 1977 as a technician, instructor, author, consultant, and speaker. Author of numerous popular PC books and videos, including the best-selling *CompTIA Network+ Certification All-in-One Exam Guide,* Mike is also the series editor for the highly successful *Mike Meyers' Certification Passport* series, the *Mike Meyers' Computer Skills* series, and the *Mike Meyers' Guide To* series, all published by McGraw-Hill Education. As well as writing, Mike has personally taught (and continues to teach) thousands of students, including U.S. senators; U.S. Supreme Court justices; members of the United Nations; every branch of the U.S. Armed Forces; most branches of the U.S. Department of Justice; and hundreds of corporate clients, academic students at every level, prisoners, and pensioners.

Jonathan S. Weissman is a tenured associate professor and IT program coordinator (Department of Computing Sciences) at Finger Lakes Community College, where he designed the Networking Lab. He is also a senior lecturer (Department of Computing Security) at Rochester Institute of Technology, where he was awarded the RIT Outstanding Teaching Award in 2014, as well as the RIT GCCIS Outstanding Educator Award in 2018. Jonathan developed and teaches three courses for the edX RITx Cybersecurity MicroMasters® program to more than 50,000 students worldwide. In addition to his two full-time teaching appointments, Jonathan teaches part-time at Syracuse University (Department of Electrical Engineering and Computer Science) and Nazareth College (School of Management).

Jonathan is also the co-author of the *Mike Meyers' CompTIA Network+ Certification Passport, Sixth Edition* and serves as technical editor for many industry textbooks. In addition, he is a networking and cybersecurity consultant for local businesses and individuals.

Jonathan has a master's degree in Computer Science from Brooklyn College and holds 34 industry certifications, including CCNP® Routing and Switching, CCNA® Security, CompTIA Security+®, CompTIA Network+, CompTIA A+®, EC-Council Certified Ethical Hacker™, EC-Council Computer Hacking Forensic Investigator™, and IPv6 Forum Certified Network Engineer (Gold), among many others.

Follow Jonathan on LinkedIn at www.linkedin.com/in/jonathan-s-weissman-058b649b and Twitter at https://twitter.com/cscprof.

About the Technical Editor

Troy McMillan is a product developer and technical editor for Kaplan IT Training, as well as a full-time trainer. He became a professional trainer over 15 years ago, teaching Cisco, Microsoft, CompTIA, and wireless classes.

Troy has contributed to and written certification exam prep guides and practice tests, technically edited and authored books, and appeared in training videos for various topics including CCNA, Network+, Security+, Cloud+®, CISSP®, Windows administration, and VMware virtualization.

Mike Meyers' CompTIA Network+® Guide to Managing and Troubleshooting Networks Lab Manual

Fifth Edition

(Exam N10-007)

Mike Meyers
Jonathan S. Weissman

Mc
Graw
Hill
Education

New York   Chicago   San Francisco
Athens   London   Madrid   Mexico City
Milan   New Delhi   Singapore   Sydney   Toronto

Cataloging-in-Publication Data is on file with the Library of Congress

McGraw-Hill Education books are available at special quantity discounts to use as premiums and sales promotions, or for use in corporate training programs. To contact a representative, please visit the Contact Us pages at www.mhprofessional.com.

Mike Meyers' CompTIA Network+® Guide to Managing and Troubleshooting
Networks Lab Manual, Fifth Edition (Exam N10-007)

1 2 3 4 5 6 7 8 9   QVS   21 20 19 18

ISBN   978-1-260-12120-9
MHID   1-260-12120-8

Sponsoring Editor	**Technical Editor**	**Production Supervisor**
Amy Stonebraker	Troy McMillian	James Kussow
Editorial Supervisor	**Copy Editor**	**Composition**
Janet Walden	Lisa McCoy	Cenveo® Publishing Services
Project Editor	**Proofreader**	**Illustration**
Laura Stone	Rick Camp	Cenveo® Publishing Services
Acquisitions Coordinator	**Indexer**	**Art Director, Cover**
Claire Yee	Ted Laux	Jeff Weeks

Contents at a Glance

Contents

Acknowledgments

Many great people worked together to make this book happen.

Our sponsoring editor at McGraw-Hill Education, Amy Stonebraker, set the entire book in motion and provided valuable guiding hands. Thanks, Amy!

Our acquisitions coordinator, Claire Yee; our editorial supervisor, Janet Walden; and our project editor, Laura Stone, helped us keep it all on track and did an outstanding job managing this book through the many phases of development.

At Total Seminars, CEO Dudley Lehmer was a great support, creating an environment for getting projects done. Scott Jernigan performed his usual magic as Editor in Chief. Shannon Murdoch, Dave Rush, and Michael Smyer assisted with photographs, illustrations, and as technical sounding boards.

Our technical editor, Troy McMillian, provided a helpful pair of eyes.

To the copy editor, Lisa McCoy, and the proofreader, Rick Camp—thank you for your excellent work!

Additional Resources for Teachers

The answer keys to the lab manual activities in this book are provided along with resources for teachers using the *Mike Meyers' CompTIA Network+® Guide to Managing and Troubleshooting Networks, Fifth Edition (Exam N10-007)* textbook (available separately). Instructors who have adopted these books for a course can access the materials identified next. Contact your McGraw-Hill Education sales representative for details on how to access the materials.

Instructor Materials

A companion web site provides resources for teachers in a format that follows the organization of the textbook. This site includes the following:

- Answer keys to the Mike Meyers' Lab Manual activities

- Answer keys to the end-of-chapter activities in the textbook

- Instructor's Manual that contains learning objectives, classroom preparation notes, instructor tips, and a lecture outline for each chapter

- Engaging PowerPoint slides on the lecture topics that include full-color artwork from the textbook

- Access to test bank files and software that allow you to generate a wide array of paper- or network-based tests, and that feature automatic grading. The test bank includes:

  - Hundreds of practice questions and a wide variety of question types and difficulty levels, enabling you to customize each test to maximize student progress

  - Test bank files available for Blackboard, Respondus, and Moodle, and other formats may also be available upon request

Please contact your McGraw-Hill Education sales representative for details.

Chapter 1

Network Models

Lab Exercises

Congratulations! You have decided to tackle the prestigious CompTIA Network+ certification. Whether you are a seasoned network engineer pursuing certification to further your career or a relative novice building your fundamental skills in networking, you're in the right place. The fact that you've got the *Mike Meyers' CompTIA Network+® Guide to Managing and Troubleshooting Networks* textbook and this Lab Manual in your hands shows that you're serious about earning that certification. That's a smart move!

As discussed in the textbook, the term *networking* describes a vast field of study, far too large for any single certification book, training course, or for that matter, lab manual to cover. However, armed with the textbook and this Lab Manual, you have the tools not only to pass the certification exam, but also to exercise the skills you will need to develop and grow as a networking professional. Ask any veteran network tech, and they will tell you that the key to being a good tech is working through the installation, configuration, management, and troubleshooting of network devices, cabling, protocols, and applications. That's where this Lab Manual is invaluable. It will take you through hands-on exercises with cabling, switches, routers, and servers. You'll configure protocols and services such as TCP/IP, DNS, DHCP, QoS, VPNs, and many more. If some of these abbreviations are new to you, don't worry; you will learn them all!

Another skill required by network techs is the ability to find information regarding network devices, protocols, and applications and their interoperability quickly and efficiently. Many times when you run into problems, it's not necessarily a failure of one specific device, protocol, or application but a combination of the configuration parameters and interaction between those devices, protocols, and applications. Many of the labs will have you practice the art of researching information on these devices, protocols, and services as if your job depended on it. It just might!

To help you grasp these networking concepts, the following scenario is used throughout this Lab Manual. You are a newly hired desktop support specialist in a mid-sized IT consulting firm, JSW. JSW has clients of all sizes scattered all over the country. Client networks can be as small as a single insurance office with 15 computers to a financial institution with 1500 computers and dozens of servers.

You are CompTIA A+ certified, but are immediately encouraged to pursue the CompTIA Network+ certification. Jonathan, your boss, offers to mentor you. He believes that achieving the CompTIA Network+ certification will strengthen your fundamental understanding of networking and will really help when communicating with both customers and your supervisor, Scott. You respect his advice and dive right in to a CompTIA Network+ training course—this course!

This chapter starts you off with network models, network hardware, and the data delivery process. Ladies and gentlemen, start your engines!

In 1983, the International Organization for Standardization (ISO, derived from the Greek word *isos*, meaning "equal") developed the Open Systems Interconnection (OSI) model. That's right, the ISO OSI model! This model provided a multiprotocol, prescriptive template for network hardware manufacturers and network software developers to use so that products from different manufacturers and developers would work together. This template, the OSI seven-layer model, is still in great use today.

As you study to pass the CompTIA Network+ exam and work to be a better network tech, you should develop an understanding of the OSI model.

Delivering data across a network is a process both elegant in its simplicity and mind-boggling in its complexity. For one thing, data files don't move across the network intact. Instead, computers break any kind of data transfer into smaller chunks and then package, address, and send those chunks across the network. This applies to any kind of data, whether you browse the Web, copy files to a co-worker's computer, or stream music across the Internet. Computers on the receiving end reassemble all the pieces upon receipt. Every computer network—regardless of the operating system, protocols, or network media—works this way.

To appreciate and define the process using the OSI model, you have to understand a few important things. First, you should understand what kind of hardware and software a computer needs to connect to a network. You also need to know how a computer sends and retrieves data using a network. Finally, you need to understand the rules that govern the structure of Ethernet networks and how data moves across these networks. In this lab, I'll talk about these concepts, applying examples of the activity taking place at the various layers of the OSI model, to help you develop a greater understanding of the big networking picture.

There's no time like the present to get started!

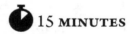 15 **MINUTES**

Lab Exercise 1.01: Exploring Network Hardware

In the OSI model, the Physical, Data Link, and Network layers define the operation of network hardware. Cables and wireless signals work at Layer 1, the Physical layer (hubs, long obsolete, operated at this layer too).

Layer 2, the Data Link layer, is where the physical address comes into play. The various devices that utilize the MAC address, such as NICs (network interface cards, which also function at the Physical layer because they transmit and receive signals) and switches, devices that connect nodes of the same network together, function at Layer 2. *Ethernet* defines all Layer 1 and 2 aspects of wired networks, while 802.11 standards define all Layer 1 and 2 aspects of wireless networks.

Layer 3, the Network layer, handles IP addressing and routing. Routers, devices that connect different networks together, operate at Layer 3.

Network connectivity starts with the network connection—the physical link between the PC and the network media. A good network tech can quickly locate and identify the network cabling and network hardware installed on a PC and determine the PC's state of connectivity. The tech should also be able to identify the protocols used by the NIC to communicate on the network, as well as the PC's unique logical address and physical address. You're about to take a look at the steps to accomplish these goals.

Learning Objectives

In this lab exercise, you'll explore the hardware and software components of a networked PC. At the end of this exercise, you'll be able to

- Identify the network interface, network cabling, and network connectors

- Determine which protocols the NIC uses

- Record the PC's MAC and IP addresses

Lab Materials and Setup

The materials you'll need for this lab exercise are

- *Mike Meyers' CompTIA Network+ Guide to Managing and Troubleshooting Networks* textbook

- Windows 10 machine with a wired or wireless NIC (network interface card)

- Connection to a network

Getting Down to Business

Your company, JSW, has three locations in Upstate New York. All of the offices have multiple computers, servers, and printers, all connected via the LAN (local area network) in each office. The offices can communicate with each other and the outside world via the Internet.

When you speak with your boss, Jonathan, he recommends that you start your study by examining the home office's network connections, devices, and addressing. He asks if you have learned about the OSI model yet and adds that you might want to define at which layers the various devices, protocols, and addresses belong.

Step 1 Locate the NIC (network interface card) of your computer. This interface will most likely be integrated onto the motherboard. Older machines may have a physical NIC installed in an expansion slot. What type of NIC does your PC have? At what layer(s) of the OSI model does the NIC operate?

_____

_____

Step 2   If your NIC is a wired NIC, identify the type of network cabling and network connector that plugs into the NIC. At what layer of the OSI model do cabling and connectors operate?

_____

_____

Step 3   Identify the network protocols installed for the NIC. On a Windows 10 machine, in the search box on the taskbar at the bottom, type **sharing**, and then select Manage Advanced Sharing Settings. In the title bar of the Advanced Sharing settings window, click Network and Sharing Center. In the left pane of the new window, click Change Adapter Settings. Last, right-click the Local Area Connection or Wi-Fi icon, and click the Properties menu item. You should see a screen similar to Figure 1-1.

What items are listed in the This Connection Uses The Following Items: section?

_____

_____

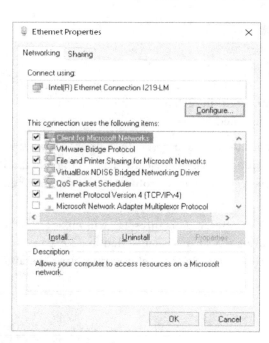

FIGURE 1-1 Windows 10 Local Area Connections Properties sheet

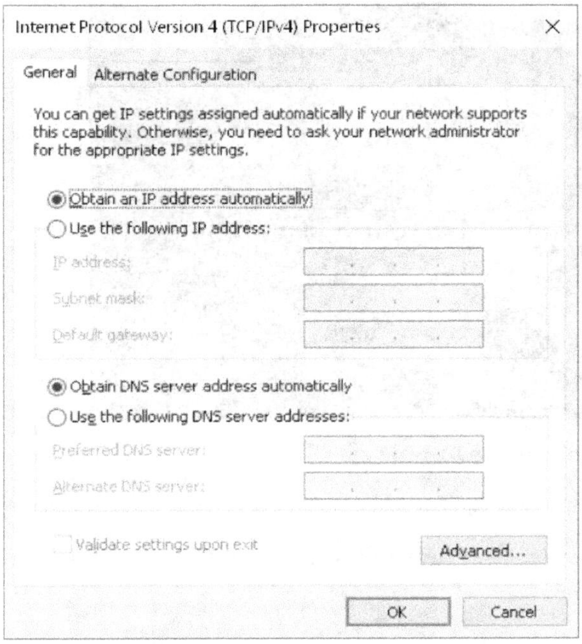

FIGURE 1-2 Windows 10 Internet Protocol Version 4 (TCP/IPv4) Properties sheet

Step 4   Highlight the Internet Protocol Version 4 (TCP/IPv4) item and click the Properties button. See Figure 1-2.

How is the NIC configured to receive an address?

_____

_____

Step 5   If the NIC is configured to obtain an IP address automatically, you will need to determine the IP address elsewhere. In the search bar, type **cmd** and press the ENTER key. This will bring up a command prompt. Type `ipconfig /all` and press ENTER. Find your NIC's physical address (MAC address) and IPv4 address. My system's information is shown in Figure 1-3.

What layer of the OSI model is a MAC address associated with? What about an IP address?

_____

_____

```
Ethernet adapter Ethernet:

   Connection-specific DNS Suffix  . :
   Description . . . . . . . . . . . : Intel(R) Ethernet Connection I219-LM
   Physical Address. . . . . . . . . : 54-EE-75-D8-63-89
   DHCP Enabled. . . . . . . . . . . : Yes
   Autoconfiguration Enabled . . . . : Yes
   Link-local IPv6 Address . . . . . : fe80::ddfe:6b25:2589:16a5%4(Preferred)
   IPv4 Address. . . . . . . . . . . : 10.80.100.2(Preferred)
   Subnet Mask . . . . . . . . . . . : 255.255.255.0
   Lease Obtained. . . . . . . . . . : Thursday, March 8, 2018 8:03:02 AM
   Lease Expires . . . . . . . . . . : Thursday, March 8, 2018 10:03:02 AM
   Default Gateway . . . . . . . . . : 10.80.100.254
   DHCP Server . . . . . . . . . . . : 10.200.200.1
   DHCPv6 IAID . . . . . . . . . . . : 39120501
   DHCPv6 Client DUID. . . . . . . . : 00-01-00-01-21-11-F7-C8-54-EE-75-D8-63-89

   DNS Servers . . . . . . . . . . . : 10.200.200.1
                                       10.200.200.2
   NetBIOS over Tcpip. . . . . . . . : Disabled
```

FIGURE 1-3 Partial results of running the `ipconfig /all` utility

Step 6   What networking device allows the devices on your network to communicate with each other? At what layer of the OSI model does this device operate?

_____

_____

Step 7   What device allows your network to communicate with devices on other networks? At what layer of the OSI model does this device operate?

_____

_____

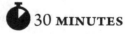 30 MINUTES

Lab Exercise 1.02: Understanding the Data Delivery Process

Often the network tech's role as installer and administrator takes a back seat to the tech's role as educator. Many clients, and certainly your bosses, want to know what you're doing when they see you stringing cables from hither to yon or when you're gazing at some obscure-looking string of numbers in a command-line window. The good network tech is able to explain not just practical, nuts-and-bolts configuration tasks but also the "fuzzier" conceptual topics that describe the functions of a network.

Learning Objectives

In this lab, you'll examine the process of data delivery on a network. You will also identify the components involved in transferring data between two computers on a network. At the end of this lab, you will be able to

- Identify the parts of an Ethernet frame

- Examine the process of data delivery

- List the number of active sessions on a computer

Lab Materials and Setup

- *Mike Meyers' CompTIA Network+ Guide to Managing and Troubleshooting Networks* textbook

- Windows 10 machine with network access

- Pen or pencil

- Paper

Getting Down to Business

You've examined your office and determined that most of the PCs and physical offices are fairly up to date. Most of the devices are connected through 1000BaseT interfaces over Cat 6A UTP cabling through Cisco 1000BaseT switches. Your supervisor, Scott, noticing that you have spent most of your lunch hour inspecting the office connections, asks you to provide a quick explanation of how data moves from one PC to another on the network.

Step 1   List and define the parts of an Ethernet frame.

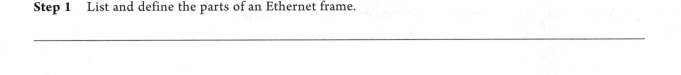

Step 2   Briefly describe the process of data delivery from one machine to another machine on the same network. Use the concept of frames, the OSI model (see Figure 1-4), switches, and the NIC's functionality to formulate your answer.

Step 3   Scott is impressed with your response and introduces you to a utility that enables you to explore the connections between networked computers. To generate some network traffic, he has you launch your browser and access the CompTIA Web site. He then has you bring up a command prompt and type the following line:

```
netstat -a
```

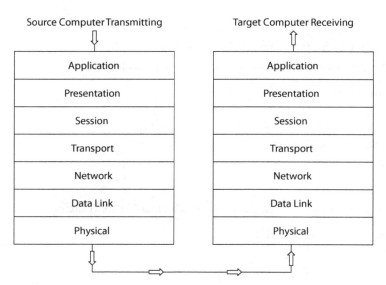

FIGURE 1-4 Data going down OSI on the source and up OSI on the destination

The output should be similar to Figure 1-5.

For now, don't worry about all of the information you see, but take notice of your computer name and the number of connections. How many connections are there?

_____

With which layer of the OSI model are these connections associated?

_____

_____

Notice each connection is represented by a local and foreign socket (the column headers use the term "address"). A socket is an endpoint in network communication (on each of the two communicating sides) represented by an IP address and port number (written in a concatenated form with a colon in the middle). The local socket is on the machine you're using, while the remote socket is on the machine you're connected to and communicating with.

We'll learn a lot more about ports in a future chapter, but for now, let's say that they are endpoints of specific programs or services and are represented by numbers, which, in turn, represent a way into and out of a program or service running on a machine.

```
      Command Prompt

C:\Users\jswics>netstat -a

Active Connections

   Proto   Local Address            Foreign Address          State
   TCP     0.0.0.0:21               jweissman:0              LISTENING
   TCP     0.0.0.0:135              jweissman:0              LISTENING
   TCP     0.0.0.0:445              jweissman:0              LISTENING
   TCP     0.0.0.0:5357             jweissman:0              LISTENING
   TCP     0.0.0.0:5985             jweissman:0              LISTENING
   TCP     0.0.0.0:47001            jweissman:0              LISTENING
   TCP     0.0.0.0:49664            jweissman:0              LISTENING
   TCP     0.0.0.0:49665            jweissman:0              LISTENING
   TCP     0.0.0.0:49666            jweissman:0              LISTENING
   TCP     0.0.0.0:49667            jweissman:0              LISTENING
   TCP     0.0.0.0:49673            jweissman:0              LISTENING
   TCP     0.0.0.0:49677            jweissman:0              LISTENING
   TCP     10.80.100.3:5040         jweissman:0              LISTENING
   TCP     10.80.100.3:49670        13.89.185.175:https      ESTABLISHED
   TCP     10.80.100.3:49712        13.89.188.5:https        ESTABLISHED
   TCP     10.80.100.3:49718        65.55.44.109:https       TIME_WAIT
   TCP     127.0.0.1:14147          jweissman:0              LISTENING
   TCP     127.0.0.1:49682          jweissman:4243           SYN_SENT
   TCP     127.0.0.1:49693          jweissman:62522          ESTABLISHED
   TCP     127.0.0.1:62522          jweissman:0              LISTENING
   TCP     127.0.0.1:62522          jweissman:49693          ESTABLISHED
   TCP     [::]:21                  jweissman:0              LISTENING
   TCP     [::]:135                 jweissman:0              LISTENING
   TCP     [::]:445                 jweissman:0              LISTENING
   TCP     [::]:5357                jweissman:0              LISTENING
   TCP     [::]:5985                jweissman:0              LISTENING
   TCP     [::]:47001               jweissman:0              LISTENING
   TCP     [::]:49664               jweissman:0              LISTENING
   TCP     [::]:49665               jweissman:0              LISTENING
   TCP     [::]:49666               jweissman:0              LISTENING
   TCP     [::]:49667               jweissman:0              LISTENING
   TCP     [::]:49673               jweissman:0              LISTENING
   TCP     [::]:49677               jweissman:0              LISTENING
   TCP     [::1]:14147              jweissman:0              LISTENING
   UDP     0.0.0.0:500              *:*
   UDP     0.0.0.0:3702             *:*
   UDP     0.0.0.0:3702             *:*
   UDP     0.0.0.0:4500             *:*
   UDP     0.0.0.0:5050             *:*
   UDP     0.0.0.0:5353             *:*
   UDP     0.0.0.0:5355             *:*
   UDP     0.0.0.0:60633            *:*
```

FIGURE 1-5 Output of running the `netstat -a` command

For example, if you have an FTP (File Transfer Protocol) server and Web server running on the same machine, they both will be accessible by the same IP address. How does the traffic for the FTP server go to the FTP server and traffic for the Web server go to the Web server? Ports! FTP servers listen for control traffic on and send traffic out of port 21, while Web servers listen for traffic on and send traffic out of port 80 (HTTP, unencrypted) or 443 (SSL/TLS, encrypted).

If the NIC represents the way the ones and zeros enter and exit a machine physically, ports are the way the data enters and exits a machine logically.

We've already seen MAC addresses in Layer 2 frames and IP addresses in Layer 3 packets. Well, ports are one more form of addressing and are found in Layer 4 TCP segments or UDP datagrams, which we also will explore more in a future chapter.

Since we entered `netstat -a`, the output showed all connections and listening ports. Because we didn't add the `-n` option (`netstat -an` would be the command) for the Foreign Address column, the output used computer names/FQDNs (fully qualified domain names) for IP addresses (your computer name instead of 127.0.0.1, for example) and protocol names for their corresponding port numbers (https instead of 443, for example) when possible.

What are some ports that you observe in the netstat output from the Local Address column?

_____

_____

Go to a few different Web sites and then execute `netstat -an`. What are some ports that you observe in the netstat output from the Foreign Address column?

_____

_____

 30 MINUTES

Lab Exercise 1.03: Examining the Layers of the OSI Seven-Layer Model

Given that the OSI seven-layer model's functions are largely hidden from our eyes, it's sometimes difficult to appreciate how each discrete level performs a necessary step of the data delivery process. Nonetheless, it's important for you to understand just how the OSI seven-layer model operates. Understanding the OSI seven-layer model is one of the keys to understanding modern networking technology.

Learning Objectives

In this lab, you'll examine the layers of the OSI seven-layer model. When you've completed the lab, you will be able to

- Identify and define the seven layers of the OSI seven-layer model

- Recognize the functions of each layer in the OSI seven-layer model

Lab Materials and Setup

The materials you'll need for this lab exercise are

- *Mike Meyers' CompTIA Network+ Guide to Managing and Troubleshooting Networks* textbook

- Pen or pencil

- Paper

Getting Down to Business

Using the *Mike Meyers' CompTIA Network+ Guide to Managing and Troubleshooting Networks* textbook and the previous labs, work through the following steps to further examine the details of network data delivery using the OSI seven-layer model.

Step 1   Label the OSI network model layers listed here and arrange them in their proper order from top to bottom:

Data Link   _____

Application   _____

Physical   _____

Session   _____

Presentation   _____

Network   _____

Transport   _____

✔ **Hint**

Remember that the OSI model is diagrammed with the seventh layer at the top and the first layer at the bottom. As noted in the textbook, many students will develop mnemonics to remember the layers and their order. A popular mnemonic is, from the top down, All People Seem To Need Data Processing.

Step 2   Read the following descriptions and fill in the appropriate OSI network model layer.

Description	OSI Network Model Layer
The topmost layer. At this layer, programs access network services using APIs (application programming interfaces).	
This layer enables computers to establish, maintain, and terminate connections.	
This layer includes either TCP segments or UDP datagrams and port numbers.	
This layer features compression/decompression, encryption/decryption, and formatting.	
This layer is where frames are created.	
This layer is responsible for transmitting and receiving signals.	
This layer adds IP addresses and encapsulates segments or datagrams in packets.	

 1 HOUR

Lab Exercise 1.04: Preparing a Presentation of the OSI Seven-Layer Model

As discussed in Lab Exercise 1.02, sometimes the network tech's role as installer and administrator takes a back seat to the tech's role as educator. There is a second benefit to the latter role. One of the best ways to learn the concepts of networking is to teach those concepts to others. This helps you review the concepts and reinforce them in your memory. Scott knows that you have just finished learning about the OSI seven-layer model and asks you to prepare a brief presentation for the other desktop support technicians.

You should plan on preparing enough material for a 15- to 20-minute presentation and leave about 10 minutes for a question-and-answer session. If things keep going this well at work, you may have that new pay grade in conjunction with your CompTIA Network+ certification.

Learning Objectives

In this lab, you'll research the OSI model and develop a Microsoft PowerPoint presentation to teach the concepts and layers of the OSI model. Finally, you will teach this information to your peers. At the conclusion of this lab, you will be able to

- Introduce the OSI model

- Define the layers of the OSI model

- Teach the concepts and functions of networking based on the OSI model

- Prepare and deliver a professional presentation

Lab Materials and Setup

The materials you'll need for this lab exercise are

- *Mike Meyers' CompTIA Network+ Guide to Managing and Troubleshooting Networks* textbook

- Microsoft PowerPoint or Google Slides

- Optionally, a projector or large display to facilitate the presentation

Getting Down to Business

A good presentation begins with an introduction of what you plan to present. The body of the presentation will cover the actual material—in this case, the OSI seven-layer model. For a strong finish, the conclusion to the presentation should include a review of what you just presented. The following lab steps will walk you through setting up an informative presentation on the OSI seven-layer model.

→ **Note**

> **If you are in an instructor-led class, you may be assigned to a group and instructed to focus on only one or two of the layers for your presentation. Given this situation, work with your team members to develop a comprehensive introduction and concise summary review of the entire OSI model. You may then spend the remaining time developing the details of your assigned layers.**

Step 1   Using the textbook and prior labs, review the OSI seven-layer model.

Step 2   Using Microsoft PowerPoint or Google Slides, begin your presentation by developing an outline of the number of slides and subject of each slide. Two slides per layer is fine, so plan on your presentation being around 16 to 18 slides, including an introduction and conclusion.

Step 3   Develop an introduction based on the overview of the OSI model.

Step 4   For each of the layers, include details on the function, protocols, addressing, and, where applicable, the hardware associated with the layer. Building the model from either the bottom up or the top down is acceptable as long as you remain consistent. You may want to integrate a block diagram of the model as it unfolds.

Step 5   Conclude the presentation with a summary review of the OSI model.

Step 6   Deliver the presentation to an audience of your peers.

Lab Analysis

1. Jonathan wants to see if you know why the function of the NIC can be said to exist in both the Data Link layer and the Physical layer of the OSI seven-layer model. How would you explain it to him?

    _____

    _____

2. Eva keeps hearing the term "frames" when discussing networking with fellow techs. What are the basic components of a frame?

    _____

    _____

3. Noah wants to know what information can be seen from the output of `ipconfig /all`, and Jacob wants to know what the output from `netstat` will show. Can you help them out?

    _____

    _____

4. Draw a block diagram of the OSI seven-layer model in the proper sequence and label the numbers of the layers. Can you add any sublayer information?

Key Term Quiz

Use the vocabulary terms from the following list to complete the sentences that follow.

IP address

```
ipconfig /all
```

MAC address

```
netstat
```

port

1. The _____ command will show you information about endpoints in network communications.

2. Running the _____ command on a Windows computer will display the MAC and IP addresses.

3. The _____ is a Layer 3 logical address bound to a NIC.

4. A program or service listens for incoming traffic on a certain _____.

5. A physical address is another name for the _____ of a NIC.

Chapter 2

Cabling and Topology

Lab Exercises

Most of JSW's clients' users never give a moment's thought to the mechanics of how their particular workstation ties into their corporate network. They just want to know that their data gets where it's supposed to go when they click the *Send* button in their e-mail program or that they can get to important sites on the Internet. As a network technician, you're the one who has to make sure that your network users' data can get from here to there, and vice versa. You've already learned about the concepts and models that serve as a basis for modern networks. Now it's time to look at the base hardware that makes a network a network.

First, you will explore the network's physical and logical layout—the topology. Next, you'll examine the needs of a new building project and recommend the different types of physical network media, or cabling. You'll then explore a number of the governing bodies that handle the management and configuration of the networking standards. You have already met the ISO organization; now meet ANSI, TIA/EIA, and IEEE. Lastly, you will further explore the IEEE specifications that define the different network standards.

 15 MINUTES

Lab Exercise 2.01: Identifying Network Topologies

A network's physical topology defines the physical layout of network cabling, switches, routers, patch panels, and other hardware that carries the network's data. Some network topologies define how wireless networking devices such as wireless network adapters and wireless access points transfer data between computers. In this lab, you'll explore network topologies.

If you're setting up a network from scratch, start with your topology design. You won't always have this luxury, of course. If you're walking into a situation where a network is already in place, for example, evaluating the topology design is a top priority. Identifying the current network topology is the key to determining the type of network cabling and hardware or wireless communication technology that you'll be using.

Good network techs document everything about their network, listing the location of every network cable (usually called a *cable run* or *drop*) and all WAPs (wireless access points). They make sure to describe the type of cabling used and give details about the associated network hardware (brand and model of each network switch, router, etc.). Unfortunately, not all network techs take the time to create this documentation or update it when they make changes, so you may wind up having to gather this information on your own. This is where your knowledge of the different network topologies, network cabling, and network hardware pays off.

✖ Cross-Reference

When network techs or, more importantly, professional cable installers plan a new network installation or upgrade existing network installations, they will utilize much more formal techniques to organize and document the install. These techniques include a formal site survey in which the installer will identify and document the location of demarcs (demarcation points), MDFs (main distribution frames), IDFs (intermediate distribution frames), and punchdown blocks. You will further explore these components in Chapter 5 of the *Mike Meyers' CompTIA Network+ Guide to Managing and Troubleshooting Networks* textbook as well as the Lab Exercises in Chapter 5 of this manual.

Learning Objectives

In this lab, you'll examine several network topologies. When you've completed the lab, you will be able to

- Identify and describe the different standard network physical topologies
- Identify the advantages and disadvantages of selected topologies
- Suggest an appropriate topology solution

Lab Materials and Setup

The materials you'll need for this lab exercise are

- *Mike Meyers' CompTIA Network+ Guide to Managing and Troubleshooting Networks* textbook
- Pen or pencil
- Paper

Getting Down to Business

You are studying network topologies at the end of the day, when your boss, Jonathan, stops by. You explain to him that you have a handle on the old network topologies like bus and ring, but you are trying to better understand the more current network topologies such as hybrid star-bus, mesh, and point-to-multipoint. Making a little bit of time in his busy schedule (one of JSW's clients is rolling out new Internet cafés at rest stops along the freeways), he offers to help.

Jonathan comes up with the excellent idea of describing various network installations he has been involved with. He will detail cabling, hardware components, and, where applicable, wireless components and technologies. Using this information, he asks you to define the network topology employed in the scenario.

✖ **Cross-Reference**

To review the various network topologies, refer to the "Network Topologies" section of Chapter 2 of the *Mike Meyers' CompTIA Network+ Guide to Managing and Troubleshooting Networks* textbook.

Step 1   Jonathan starts you off with a story of an after-work, impromptu LAN party at one of your coworker's houses. Everybody brought their laptops, and rather than setting up everybody on his wireless access point (he is using MAC address filtering), the host configured an ad hoc SSID of CraftonAve. The whole crew joined the network, and the members started gaming against each other. When a number of computers are communicating without an access point (as they do in an infrastructure topology/mode), what is this topology/mode called?

_____

_____

Step 2   Jonathan is really excited about this new project: equipping freeway rest stops with wireless Internet connectivity. Each location will have a high-speed Internet connection with a wireless access point. When travelers visit, they will be able to sign on to the network using devices with wireless network adapters. What does this tell you about the topology?

_____

_____

Step 3   To finish up, Jonathan recommends that you take a look at the network installation in your own office. You begin by examining the computer in your cubicle. A Cat 6A, unshielded twisted pair (UTP) cable runs from the back of your computer to a wall jack. It appears to use RJ-45 connectors. You then walk down the hall to the wiring closet, observing a mass of cables (also UTP) terminating in a number of patch panels. Patch cables are then connected from the patch panel to an equal number of gigabit switches that are all connected together in a daisy chain fashion. What topology does this depict?

_____

_____

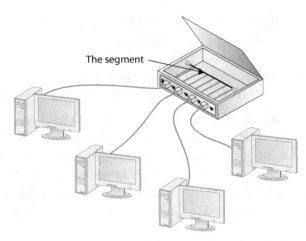

FIGURE 2-1 Diagram of the internal workings of a hybrid star-bus switch

Step 4   When analyzing the various topologies, what conclusions can you draw concerning the most prevalent wired network topologies, and the most prevalent wireless network topologies?

_____

_____

Step 5   When discussing topologies, there is a difference between a logical topology and a physical topology. Using the hybrid star-bus topology as an example, define a logical topology versus a physical topology; see Figure 2-1.

_____

_____

 30 MINUTES

Lab Exercise 2.02: Determining Network Cabling Requirements

One of JSW's larger clients, the Department of Transportation, is building a new regional Department of Motor Vehicles (DMV) complex consisting of two physical buildings. One building will house all of the administrative departments (licensing, title, tags, and registration). The other building, located approximately

900 feet away from the administrative building, will be a large, garage-like structure, where the physical inspection of the automobiles will be conducted. Along with designing the overall network infrastructure, JSW has been asked to make recommendations regarding the physical cabling for the two buildings, as well as the connection between the two buildings. You have been invited to work with the team to make these cabling recommendations. Professional installers will be hired, so you may even get to review some of the proposals.

You have two choices when it comes to network cabling: glass-cored fiber optics or good old-fashioned copper wire. UTP copper cable is currently used in most network installations, from small to gigantic. UTP cabling is differentiated by characteristics such as cost, bandwidth, and fire ratings. Fiber-optic cable provides high speed, the ability to travel long distances, and a high degree of security. To make informed decisions about what kind of network cabling best suits a given network installation, you have to examine the features, functions, and limitations of different network cabling media as applied to various networking applications.

Learning Objectives

In this lab, you'll practice researching the characteristics, typical application, and overall cost of network cables. When you've completed this lab, you will be able to

- Identify the various network cabling options

- Recommend specific cabling based on application

- Compare the function, speed, and maximum data transfer distance of each cable

- Suggest the cabling solutions with the best price/performance ratio

Lab Materials and Setup

The materials you'll need for this lab exercise are

- *Mike Meyers' CompTIA Network+ Guide to Managing and Troubleshooting Networks* textbook

- Internet access

- Pen or pencil

- Paper

Getting Down to Business

When you're designing a new building plan, one of the major expenses can be the network infrastructure, and a portion of that is the physical cabling. It is imperative that the design implemented meet a price/performance balance along with future-proofing for technological improvements. The cabling installation can be broken down into two distinct applications. Cabling will need to be purchased for the two buildings—the main administrative building and the inspection garage—and the backbone between the two buildings.

Step 1   You'll start the cabling layout with the administrative building and the inspection garage. The team determines that approximately 11,500 feet of cabling will be required. The cabling will have to meet the strict fire codes for office buildings and should meet the specifications allowing for future technology improvements.

What grade of cable would you recommend to meet the city's building codes?

_____

What category cable would you recommend to future-proof this cable installation?

_____

Step 2   Now launch your browser and navigate to www.primuscable.com/store/c/829-CAT6A-Bulk-Cables.aspx. Record the bulk cost of 1000 feet of the following categories and grades of cable.

Category 6A, Riser: US$_____

Category 6A, Plenum: US$_____

Based on your recommendations, what are the final specifications and total cost for the 11,500 feet of internal cabling for the two buildings?

_____

_____

Step 3   The run between the two buildings, as stated previously, is approximately 900 feet. You'll want to select cabling that will handle the distance in one run, require the least amount of maintenance, and provide for future technological improvements. It will probably be buried, so it will be very difficult and expensive to upgrade in the future.

What type of cable would you recommend for the run between the two buildings?

_____

Step 4   Fire up your browser again and visit www.l-com.com (that's a lowercase "L"). Select Products | Fiber Optic from the menu bar on the top, then click Bulk Cable from either the expanded menu on the left or the main pane, and locate the various types of cable. Use the links, and either this site or a search engine, to answer the following questions.

What are the differences between the four levels of Optical Multimode (OM): OM1, OM2, OM3, and OM4? Which one would you recommend for this project?

OM1:   US$_____

OM2:   US$_____

OM3:   US$_____

OM4:   US$_____

_____

_____

What's the difference between breakout style and distribution style? Which one would you recommend for this project?

_____

_____

List a pro and con for using single-mode fiber for this project, instead of multimode fiber.

_____

_____

Based on your recommendations, what are the final specifications and total cost of the cabling for the run between the two buildings? Remember, you want the cable to provide for improvements for years to come, so you'll want to select the highest-performance cable you can purchase today.

_____

_____

Step 5   Fill in the following chart.

Cat Rating	Maximum Frequency	Maximum Bandwidth
Cat 6		
Cat 6A		

Step 6   After working with the team on the prior cabling project, Jonathan informs you that a number of the remote offices of the Department of Transportation are scheduled for network upgrades. The offices are currently using Cat 5e UTP, and the office space is roughly 2000 square feet. There are approximately 15 computers and two servers at each office.

Based on this information, he asks what type of network cabling you would recommend for this network upgrade. Give your recommendation and list your reasons.

_____

_____

 20 MINUTES

Lab Exercise 2.03: Governing Bodies, Part 1

One of the amazing aspects of networking in general is that thousands of hardware manufacturers and software developers can create devices and applications that allow computers to communicate with each other, and it all works! Part of the reason that it works is that there are established organizations that set the standards for development and manufacturing of these components and devices. These organizations define the international standards so that when you try to access a Web site in Japan from a computer in the United States, you can connect.

You have already encountered the International Organization for Standardization (ISO), but there are other organizations that are just as important to the successful communication of digital data. You're going to research a little about each of these organizations, starting with the groups that work with cabling, devices, and technologies like Ethernet. Later in this book, after you have traveled further up the OSI model, you'll explore some of the organizations that handle TCP/IP, the Internet, and the World Wide Web.

Learning Objectives

In this lab, you'll explore various organizations that are responsible for the development and management of international standards. By the end of this lab, you will be able to

- Describe the purpose of the governing bodies, the organizations that define the standards for networking

- Detail some of the features of the governing bodies

Lab Materials and Setup

The materials you'll need for this lab exercise are

- Internet access
- Pen or pencil
- Paper

Getting Down to Business

If you have ever been a member of a *World of Warcraft* guild, you have probably teamed up with people from all over the world. When your avatar and theirs are on the same quest, have you ever thought about the fact that their computer is connected to some switch in some distant country, yet here they are virtually, standing next to you? Thank goodness for standards!

Step 1   You're going to start with the granddaddy of all the organizations, the International Organization for Standardization (ISO). Launch your Web browser and enter this URL: www.iso.org/iso/about-us.html. Now just take a few notes on who ISO is, where it's located, how long it's been around, and its general purpose.

———

———

Step 2   Navigate to this Web site: www.ansi.org/about_ansi/overview/overview.aspx?menuid=1. This is the American National Standards Institute (ANSI), which is both the official U.S. representative of ISO and a major international player. Review the page and capture the same information as you did in Step 1.

———

———

Step 3   ANSI has the responsibility of checking the standards and accrediting other groups, such as the Telecommunications Industry Association (TIA). A related organization that was also accredited by ANSI, the Electronics Industries Alliance (EIA), ceased operations on February 28, 2011.

Read about TIA at www.tiaonline.org/about-tia/. What are their credentials?

———

———

Step 4   As a precursor to the last lab exercise, check out the Institute of Electrical and Electronics Engineers (IEEE), often pronounced as I-triple-E. The URL is www.ieee.org/about/index.html. What pertinent information can you find about the IEEE?

_____

_____

 20 MINUTES

Lab Exercise 2.04: Industry Standards

You have just learned about various organizations that drive the standards for just about every technological industry. One of these organizations, the IEEE, formed a committee known as the 802 committee. The name 802 comes from the timeframe when this committee was established, 80 referring to 1980, and 2 to February. The 802 committee sets the standards that all modern networking hardware must meet in order to function with other networking hardware. The 802 committee is divided into a number of subcommittees, each responsible for defining the standards and methods by which different networking devices are governed. Among these are the subcommittees that have established the 802.2, 802.3, and 802.11 networking standards.

Before wrapping up this chapter, you'll review these important IEEE standards and definitions.

Learning Objectives

In this lab, you'll identify the function of each of the important IEEE 802 subcommittees. By the end of this lab, you will be able to

- Describe the IEEE subcommittees responsible for defining the standards of the most popular network technology implementations

Lab Materials and Setup

The materials you'll need for this lab exercise are

- _Mike Meyers' CompTIA Network+ Guide to Managing and Troubleshooting Networks_ textbook

- Pen or pencil

- Paper

Getting Down to Business

Having studied network topologies and the physical cabling that is usually employed to realize them, you wonder how all of these components are designed to be compatible with each other. You'll soon determine that all modern networking equipment conforms to the same standards, and therefore compatibility is not an issue.

Step 1   Utilizing the textbook, fill in the function of each of the most common IEEE 802 subcommittees listed.

Subcommittee Designation	Description
802.1s	
802.1w	
802.1X	
802.3	
802.11	

Step 2   Explain why compliance with these IEEE standards is important.

_____

_____

Lab Analysis

1. Diagram a mesh topology configured with five computers. What is the total number of separate connections that are needed to complete the design? What is the formula?

_____

_____

_____

_____

2. Explain the physical design of a star-bus topology and the advantage of this topology.

    _____

    _____

3. When designing a cable installation, what is the primary grade of cabling that should be used for horizontal runs in the ceilings and walls? Why?

    _____

    _____

4. What are the most common categories and speeds of UTP cabling?

    _____

    _____

5. Which IEEE 802 subcommittee represents the Ethernet standard?

    _____

    _____

Key Term Quiz

Using the vocabulary terms from the list provided, complete the sentences that follow.

ANSI

Cat 6

Cat 6A

fiber-optic

hybrid star-bus topology

LC

SC

ST

1. When you're planning a new local area network infrastructure, the most common type of network cable implemented would be either _____ or _____ cable.

2. _____ describes a network in which all the computers connect to a central wiring point, which creates a logical bus topology.

3. _____ is responsible for accrediting other groups.

4. _____ cables transmit light for distances up to 10 kilometers.

5. When you're working with fiber-optic cabling, there are three prominent connector types used: the _____, the _____, and the _____.

Chapter 3
Ethernet Basics

Lab Exercises

Ethernet is the infrastructure used by all wired LANs. For this reason, it's important for network techs to understand Ethernet's functions and features as defined by the IEEE 802.3 standards. These include such things as how Ethernet network nodes build data frames, how they access the network media, and how they send and receive data.

Even though Ethernet speeds have increased exponentially over the years—primarily by increasing the bandwidth of the media (cables) and hardware (NICs and switches)—the core technology remains the same. Network nodes identify each other by MAC address, and data is transferred between machines using Ethernet frames. The basics you explore here still apply to the higher-speed implementations, which you will explore in later chapters.

In these labs, you'll examine the IEEE 802.3 working group and standards, review the bits and pieces of Ethernet data frame construction and media access methods, look at the physical characteristics of Ethernet networks using unshielded twisted pair cabling, talk about how you enhance the performance of Ethernet, and define the Spanning Tree Protocol.

On your marks, get set, GO!

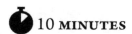 10 MINUTES

Lab Exercise 3.01: The 802.3 Working Group and Standards

In the early 1970s, Xerox developed a set of standards to facilitate the exchange of data between computers. These standards, Ethernet, have gone on to become the dominant industry standard. Over the years, the control of these standards has changed hands a few times. In the late 1970s, Xerox joined forces with Digital Equipment Corporation (DEC) and Intel to propagate the standard. Today, the Institute of Electrical and Electronics Engineers (IEEE) has the responsibility of controlling and updating the Ethernet standards. The IEEE formed a special 802.3 working group to manage these standards.

As a competent network technician, you should have a basic understanding of how Ethernet operates. Visiting the IEEE 802.3 working group is a great place to start.

Learning Objectives

At the completion of this lab, you will be able to

- Utilize Internet resources for research

- Identify and record key components of the Ethernet standard

Lab Materials and Setup

The materials you'll need for this lab exercise are

- *Mike Meyers' CompTIA Network+ Guide to Managing and Troubleshooting Networks* textbook

- Internet access

- Pen or pencil

- Paper

Getting Down to Business

According to their Web site, the IEEE 802 LAN/MAN Standards Committee "develops and maintains networking standards and recommended practices" for network communication and hardware. The IEEE 802.3 working group specifically manages the standards for Ethernet. You're going to visit the IEEE Web site, download specific Ethernet standards, and then answer some questions based on the information contained within these documents.

Step 1   Open a browser and navigate over to www.ieee802.org. What are the stated objectives of the IEEE 802 LAN/MAN Standards Committee?

Step 2   Now head to http://standards.ieee.org. Mouse over About Us, and then click GET Program. Now click the GET 802(R) Standards link. Next, click IEEE 802.3: Ethernet and then 802.3-2015.

A direct link is provided here: http://ieeexplore.ieee.org/servlet/opac?punumber=7428774

At the top, in the blue box, click Online Access Provided At No Cost By The IEEE Get Program™. Follow the prompts to create an account, then come back to the same blue box and fill out the additional required information. The text in the blue box will change to View Document. When you click it, you'll be sent to the Download PDF Link lower down on the page. Click it.

What is the publication date of this document?

_____

_____

➜ **Note**

Due to the dynamic nature of the content available on the Internet, Web sites, pages, and hyperlinks change often. If one of the sites, pages, or links referenced in the lab steps is no longer available, with a little investigation, you should be able to find the appropriate information.

Step 3   Within the introduction, scroll down to the paragraphs defining the contents of each section (Page 21). What are some of the key points covered in Section One?

_____

_____

What are some of the key points covered in Section Three?

_____

_____

Step 4   Locate Clause 3.1.1, "Packet format" (Page 108). Note the diagram of the Ethernet frame. How does this diagram compare to the diagram of the Ethernet frame in Figure 3.1 of the textbook? List and explain the purpose of each of the fields of an Ethernet frame.

_____

_____

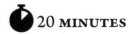 20 MINUTES

Lab Exercise 3.02: CSMA/CD—Past and Present

Originally, with half-duplex Ethernet, where nodes could transmit and receive—but not at the same time—just a single node could access any given network segment at a time. When two or more PCs tried to send data on the network at the same time, the data frames collided, causing the frames to become corrupted.

Therefore, the designers of Ethernet had to devise a method for the network nodes to access the network media without stepping on each other's frames. This network access method was called *carrier sense multiple access/collision detection*, or CSMA/CD. The CSMA part of CSMA/CD defined the method by which multiple network nodes monitored the network media to determine if any other nodes were currently transmitting data. The CD part defined how the network nodes dealt with collisions when they occurred. In this lab, you'll discuss how CSMA/CD went from always used to never used on modern networks.

Learning Objectives

In this lab, you'll review the carrier sense multiple access/collision detection function of Ethernet. At the end of this lab, you will be able to

- Explain why half-duplex used CSMA/CD, while full-duplex doesn't.

Lab Materials and Setup

The materials you'll need for this lab exercise are

- *Mike Meyers' CompTIA Network+ Guide to Managing and Troubleshooting Networks* textbook

- Internet access

- Pen or pencil

- Paper

Getting Down to Business

It has been some time since Scott studied for and passed the CompTIA Network+ exam. He asks you to explain why half-duplex communications always used CSMA/CD, while full-duplex communications don't use it at all.

Step 1   In the PDF you downloaded in the previous exercise, locate Clause 1.1.2.1 Half duplex operation (Page 55). Explain why half-duplex communications always used CSMA/CD.

_____

_____

Step 2   In the PDF you downloaded in the previous exercise, locate Clause 1.1.2.2 Full duplex operation (Page 55). Explain why full-duplex communications never use CSMA/CD.

_____

_____

 35 MINUTES

Lab Exercise 3.03: Building an Ethernet Patch Cable

In Chapter 2, "Cabling and Topology," you learned about Cat 6A UTP cable, which is now the dominant cabling media for wired networks. This is due to the fact that Ethernet has become the dominant networking technology, and Ethernet uses UTP cabling to electrically transmit the data frames. To ensure that these data frames are transmitted and received correctly requires that these UTP cables are wired to exacting specifications. The Telecommunications Industry Association/Electronics Industries Alliance (TIA/EIA) defines the industry standard for wiring Ethernet UTP cables.

Installing the cabling infrastructure when a facility is being built or upgrading the cabling infrastructure of an existing building is largely left to professional cable installers (though you will assemble a small structured cabling installation in the Lab Exercises for Chapter 5). However, when it comes to connecting devices, computers, and printers to the network jack in the wall, or patching the switches in a wiring closet, this job falls squarely on the shoulders (or in the hands) of the network tech. The common patch cable is a length of UTP cable with RJ-45 connectors on each end wired to the specifications of the TIA/EIA 568A or 568B standards.

Typical IT departments will have several lengths of premade patch cables on hand to be used as needed. Nonetheless, a well-versed network tech should have a good command of assembling and testing UTP patch cables. Some folks refer to building UTP patch cables as an "art." It requires stripping the insulation, arranging the wires to meet the TIA/EIA standards, and crimping RJ-45 connectors onto the ends of the wire.

Learning Objectives

In this lab, you'll assemble a TIA/EIA 568B patch cable. When you've completed this lab, you will be able to

- Identify proper orientation of RJ-45 connectors

- Identify the wire pairs of a UTP patch cable according to the specification of the TIA/EIA 568A and 568B standards

- Successfully crimp an RJ-45 connector to the end of a UTP cable

- Verify proper wiring of a completed patch cable using a commercial cable tester

Lab Materials and Setup

The materials you'll need for this lab exercise are

- Internet access

- Cut length of Cat 6A UTP cable

- RJ-45 connectors

- Wire strippers

- Wire snips

- Crimping tool

- TIA/EIA 568B color codes

- Cable tester

- Pen or pencil

- Paper

Getting Down to Business

The TIA/EIA 568A and 568B standards define the arrangement of 4-pair UTP cabling into RJ-45 connectors. In purchasing commercial, premade cables, the emerging default standard is TIA/EIA 568B. For the purposes of this lab, you will adhere to the default industry standard of TIA/EIA 568B.

You'll find that once you develop some technique, you will enjoy making patch cables. As mentioned earlier, in the eyes of some, this is an "art," and any skill that you become better at with practice holds an attractive quality for many. I want to caution you against spending too much time making cables and, therefore, spending too much time completing this lab exercise. The skill you develop will not be tested on the CompTIA Network+ examination, and even in the field, making cables will not be the prime example of your skills as a network tech.

That said, you will want to spend enough time to know the basics so that you will not look like a novice when it comes to whipping up a few patch cables.

Step 1 You'll begin with a cut length of UTP cable. Your instructor may define the lengths based on actual implementation. Shorter, 2- to 5-foot cables may be made to patch in a new switch or router, and medium lengths of 14 to 25 feet may be used to connect computers and printers to wall jacks. What lengths of cable will you be using?

_____

_____

Step 2   Using the Internet, conduct a search for TIA/EIA 568A and 568B wiring diagrams. There are many sites that offer color-coded diagrams of the standards for wiring both straight-through and crossover patch cables. I found a nice diagram on the Web site of the Alberta, Canada Internet service provider The Internet Centre at www.incentre.net/tech-support/other-support/ethernet-cable-color-coding-diagram/. I have also included here (Figure 3-1) the wiring diagram from the *Mike Meyers' CompTIA Network+ Guide to Managing and Troubleshooting Networks* textbook (see Figure 3.7 in the textbook: The TIA/EIA 568A and 568B standards).

✖ Cross-Reference

The textbook is in FULL COLOR! Take a look at Figures 3.3 through 3.7 in Chapter 3 of *Mike Meyers' CompTIA Network+ Guide to Managing and Troubleshooting Networks.*

Using either the provided diagram or one of the diagrams you have found, record the proper color wire for each of the pins of the RJ-45 modular connector when assembled using the TIA/EIA 568B standard.

Pin 1:   _____

Pin 2:   _____

Pin 3:   _____

Pin 4:   _____

Pin 5:   _____

Pin 6:   _____

Pin 7:   _____

Pin 8:   _____

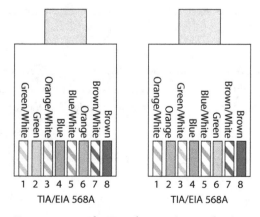

FIGURE 3-1 The TIA/EIA 568A and 568B standards

Step 3 Using wire strippers (often the crimping tool has wire strippers and snips built in), carefully remove approximately 0.5 inch of the outer insulating jacket of each end of the UTP cable.

→ **Note**

> After removing the outer insulating sheathing, look for any damaged or cut wires. This is a very delicate procedure, so finesse is required. If any of the eight wires have been damaged, use the wire snips to cut off the entire end (all eight wires and insulation) and repeat Step 3.

Step 4 Separate each pair of wires and align them in the correct sequence according to the TIA/EIA 568B standards defined in Step 2. Step 5, where you insert the wires into the RJ-45 connector, will go more smoothly if you take your time during this procedure. Once the sequence is correct, grasp the wires firmly between your thumb and forefinger and carefully snip the edges of the wires to make them even, as shown in Figure 3-2.

Step 5 With the pins of the RJ-45 connector facing up and away from you, slide the wires all the way into the connector. The outer insulating sheath should be just past the first crimping point in the connector, and you should be able to see the copper of all eight wires if you look at the head of the RJ-45 connector, as shown in Figure 3-3.

Step 6 Place the RJ-45 connector into the crimping tool. Firmly squeeze the handle of the tool until the wires are crimped into place. The crimp should bind each of the wires tightly, and the connector should bind the outer jacket. If any of the wires can be pulled from the connector with a gentle tug, the connection is incorrect. If that is the case, snip the RJ-45 connector off and return to Step 3.

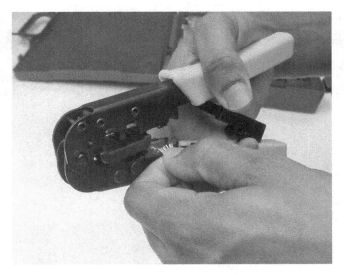

FIGURE 3-2 Aligning the wires and evening the ends

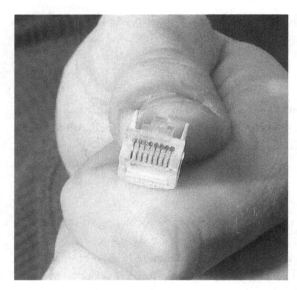

FIGURE 3-3 Head of an RJ-45 connector showing all eight wires firmly inserted

Step 7 To complete the assembly of the patch cable, repeat Steps 3–6 to add a connector to the other end of the cable.

Step 8 Now you will verify the construction of the UTP patch cable using a commercial cable tester. Most testers come with a remote end and a master module. Plug each of the RJ-45 plugs into the jacks on the cable tester. Following the directions provided with the cable tester, verify the performance of the UTP patch cable. Record your results in the following table:

TIA/EIA 568 Pair	Connection	Results (Good/Bad)
Wire Pair 1	Pin 5 to Pin 5	
	Pin 4 to Pin 4	
Wire Pair 2	Pin 1 to Pin 1	
	Pin 2 to Pin 2	
Wire Pair 3	Pin 3 to Pin 3	
	Pin 6 to Pin 6	
Wire Pair 4	Pin 7 to Pin 7	
	Pin 8 to Pin 8	

Lab Exercise 3.03 Alternate Ending: Building an Ethernet Crossover Cable

Sometimes when troubleshooting a networking problem, it is a timesaver to be able to just connect two computers directly together. This bypasses any complications from the horizontal cabling or switches of the structured network. To accomplish this, all you need to do is construct a crossover cable to connect directly between the two machines. Crossover cables are also used to connect other devices of the same type together, for instance, switch to switch and router to router.

To build a crossover cable, simply follow the instructions in Lab Exercise 3.03: Building an Ethernet Patch Cable above. Perform Steps 1–6 just as instructed, discarding and redoing steps if you make mistakes.

In Step 7, instead of completing the cable with a TIA/EIA 568B termination, substitute a TIA/EIA 568A termination. This will create a cable with a 568B termination on one end of the cable and a 568A termination on the other end of the cable. From one end of the cable to the other, the White-Orange/Orange and White-Green/Green pairs will swap, creating the Ethernet crossover cable.

When you perform Step 8 and test the crossover cable, depending on your cable tester, you should be able to confirm that all of the four pairs are properly connected. Most cable testers will indicate that there are crossed connections, though some may not indicate that the proper pairs are crossed. Use the following table to verify the crossover cable.

TIA/EIA 568 Pair	Connection	Results (Good/Bad)
Wire Pair 1	Pin 5 to Pin 5	
	Pin 4 to Pin 4	
Wire Pair 2	Pin 1 to Pin 3	
	Pin 2 to Pin 6	
Wire Pair 3	Pin 3 to Pin 1	
	Pin 6 to Pin 2	
Wire Pair 4	Pin 7 to Pin 7	
	Pin 8 to Pin 8	

You can perform a quick check of the crossover cable simply by inserting it directly between the NICs of two working, networked computers. You may have to alter some of the network configuration settings to allow the machines to communicate with each other, but you should be able to share a folder or copy a file.

 20 MINUTES

Lab Exercise 3.04: Understanding the Differences Between Cat 5e and Cat 6/6A

New installations should always be done with an eye to the future, not the past. While many installations for Cat 5 and Cat 5e are still in place in many businesses and homes, to be scalable for the future, all new installations should use nothing lower than Cat 6.

This lab helps you understand why future-proofing is a major consideration when selecting network cable types.

Learning Objectives

At the completion of this lab, you will be able to

- Understand what scalability and future-proofing are, in terms of cable installation
- Select the appropriate cable for future installations

Lab Materials and Setup

The materials you'll need for this lab exercise are

- Internet access
- Pen or pencil
- Paper

Getting Down to Business

You're going to visit Web sites, and then answer some questions.

Step 1   Head on over to www.broadbandutopia.com/caandcaco.html. What are some reasons to use Cat 6/6A for future installations, instead of Cat 5e?

_____

_____

Step 2 In terms of future-proofing your network, why isn't it advised to spend less money on Cat 5e now, but rather to go right to Cat 6/6A for all new installations?

_____

_____

Step 3 If the bandwidth of Cat 6/6A seems to be more than you'd ever need, should you instead install Cat 5e?

_____

_____

Step 4 How, in the home specifically, can Cat 6/6A benefit users?

_____

_____

Step 5 Why aren't Cat 7, 7A, and 8 discussed as viable replacements for Cat 6/6A?

_____

_____

 20 MINUTES

Lab Exercise 3.05: Enhancing the Performance of Ethernet Networks

The specifications for Ethernet, such as the number of supported network nodes and the length of network cable runs, require some thought on the part of the network tech when physically designing the network. How can you stretch the network cabling beyond the stated distance limits? How do you configure a network to support more network nodes? How do you achieve bandwidth at close to rated speeds as the number of network nodes grows?

As you learned in Chapter 2, the dominant network topology is the hybrid star-bus topology. Even the early 10-Mbps networks implemented this topology using UTP cable and a central device to facilitate communication between network nodes. Originally, multiport repeaters known as Ethernet hubs were the primary central devices. Later, Ethernet switches were incorporated to improve bandwidth utilization.

In this lab, you'll explore the basic functions of switches. You'll configure a simple multiswitch network.

Learning Objectives

Upon the completion of this lab, you will be able to

- Define the configuration and characteristics of a multiswitch Ethernet network

- Recommend a hardware solution to achieve optimal bandwidth performance

Lab Materials and Setup

The materials you'll need for this lab exercise are

- *Mike Meyers' CompTIA Network+ Guide to Managing and Troubleshooting Networks* textbook

- Three Ethernet switches

- Two working computers with Ethernet NICs

- Two UTP straight-through cables

- Two UTP crossover cables

- Pen or pencil

- Paper

Getting Down to Business

Using the lab materials, you will build a simple multiswitch network. You will then review the characteristics of switches, summarizing their basic features and limitations.

✖ Cross-Reference

To refresh your understanding of the function of Ethernet switches, refer to the "Enhancing and Extending Ethernet Networks" section of Chapter 3 of *Mike Meyers' CompTIA Network+ Guide to Managing and Troubleshooting Networks*.

Step 1   Using the switches, configure a switched network with a central switch and two second-level switches. Connect one of the computers to one of the second-level switches, and the other to the other second-level switch. Confirm connectivity between the two machines. Document your configuration.

_____

_____

Step 2   In the space that follows, describe the function of a switch.

_____

_____

Step 3   Describe why switches have replaced hubs as the central device that all nodes connect to.

_____

_____

 15 MINUTES

Lab Exercise 3.06: Exploring the Spanning Tree Protocol (STP)

As you finish up your study of Ethernet switches (at least for now), it would be a good time to discuss a situation that sometimes happens when you are interconnecting multiple switches. Whether by design or by accident, if you connect a number of switches so that one or more can connect back into themselves, you will create what is known as a *switching loop*. Left unchecked, this can cause a packet storm, basically flooding the network with packets and bringing the network to a crawl.

Enter Spanning Tree Protocol (STP), designed to detect and block bridging loops. This protocol was developed in the early 1980s by DEC, but is now defined by the IEEE 802.1D and 802.1w (Rapid Spanning Tree Protocol) standards.

Learning Objectives

At the completion of this lab, you will be able to

- Utilize Internet resources for research
- Summarize the Spanning Tree Protocol

Lab Materials and Setup

The materials you'll need for this lab exercise are

- Internet access
- Pen or pencil
- Paper

Getting Down to Business

As you have already learned, the IEEE 802 committee develops and maintains the standards for network communication and hardware. The IEEE 802.1D committee specifically manages the standards for MAC bridges. An independent vendor, Cisco, is renowned for its implementation of switches and routers. You're going to visit both the IEEE 802 Web site and the Cisco Web site to gather some information and summarize the Spanning Tree Protocol.

Step 1   Now head to http://standards.ieee.org. Mouse over About Us, and then click GET Program. Now click the GET 802(R) Standards link. Next, click IEEE 802.1™: Bridging and Management and then 802.1D-2004.

A direct link is provided here: http://ieeexplore.ieee.org/document/1309630/

At the top, in the blue box, click Online Access Provided At No Cost By The IEEE Get Program™. Follow the prompts to log in to the account you created earlier. The text in the blue box will change to View Document. When you click it, you'll be sent to the Download PDF Link lower down on the page. Click it.

Navigate to Clause 17 of this document. What is the title of this clause?

_____

_____

➜ **Note**

> Due to the dynamic nature of the content available on the Internet, Web sites, pages, and hyperlinks change often. If one of the sites, pages, or links referenced in the lab steps is no longer available, with a little investigation, you should be able to find the appropriate information.

Step 2   Now pop over to the Cisco Web site and search for information on Spanning Tree Protocol. Your instructor can help with the search if you get stuck. Document one or two of the URLs that the search directs you toward.

_____

_____

Step 3   Given the information from the textbook, the IEEE 802 standards, and the Cisco implementation, write a short summary of the Spanning Tree Protocol.

_____

_____

Lab Analysis

1.   What's the difference between half-duplex and full duplex?

_____

_____

2.   What is the basic function of the FCS (frame check sequence) in an Ethernet frame? What algorithm is used for the FCS?

_____

_____

3.   Alex created an Ethernet crossover cable. What pins are connected to each other on the RJ-45 connector? How does this facilitate communication between two switches?

_____

_____

4. Which addresses are found in Ethernet frames?

   _____

   _____

5. Bruce is throwing a LAN party this weekend and needs to whip up a few extra Ethernet patch cables for his guests. He already has the cable and the connectors. What tools would you recommend he use to build and test the cables?

   _____

   _____

Key Term Quiz

Use the vocabulary terms from the list below to complete the sentences that follow.

   crossover cable

   full-duplex

   IEEE 802.3 working group

   STP (Spanning Tree Protocol)

   straight-through cable

   TIA/EIA 568A

   TIA/EIA 568B

1. You'd connect a PC to a switch with a(n) _____.

2. _____ prevents switches that have been mistakenly connected back into themselves, forming a bridging loop, from flooding the network with damaged packets.

3. A(n) _____ is created when you construct a UTP cable using the _____ standard for one end of the cable, and the other _____ standard for the other end of the cable.

4. The Ethernet standard developed by Xerox was eventually handed over to the _____, who continue to manage the standard today.

5. Ethernet no longer needs to use CSMA/CD, because modern devices use a method called _____, which allows simultaneous bidirectional communication between two sides of a connection.

Chapter 4
Modern Ethernet

Lab Exercises

Ethernet has gone through a number of evolutionary changes to bring us to where we are today. Modern Ethernet networks are based on the same technologies and standards that you learned about in the previous chapter. The newer versions continue to improve the bandwidth, but they use the same frame types, access methods, and so on—even the connectors, NICs, and switches have relatively the same form factor. Modern Ethernet enables network techs to build larger, faster, more reliable networks!

In this lab, you'll examine the specifications and hardware that make up Ethernet standards, look at design aspects to keep in mind when planning a modern switched Ethernet network, and then explore the Ethernet developments that take us beyond Gigabit Ethernet.

 30 MINUTES

Lab Exercise 4.01: Understanding Ethernet Standards

Ethernet networks have evolved over the last 20 years or so from the early 10-Mbps implementations to today's speeds of 100 Mbps, 1 Gbps, 10 Gbps, and now the latest and greatest 40/100 Gbps, for which standards were ratified in 2010. Wired networks utilize either copper wire or fiber-optic cabling to physically transmit the Ethernet frames from device to device. You explored the basics of Ethernet in Chapter 3, "Ethernet Basics," learning that no matter what speed Ethernet performs at, the fundamentals of the technology remain the same.

100BaseTX (copper wire) and 100BaseFX (fiber-optic cabling) Ethernet provide 100-Mbps performance. Both technologies have a large installed base, utilizing hybrid star-bus topology with central switches. You'll still need to familiarize yourself with their characteristics to provide quality network support for existing installations. However, the current trend when installing or upgrading wired networks is 1000BaseT utilizing Cat 6A UTP copper cabling and gigabit NICs and switches. Cat 5e was the first standard to support Gigabit Ethernet. In addition, many backbones are implementing either 1000BaseSX multimode fiber or 1000BaseLX single-mode fiber, depending on distance.

With this in mind, you're going to spend some time exploring the characteristics of Gigabit Ethernet and gather some information on Gigabit Ethernet NICs. In the next lab exercise, you will examine Gigabit Ethernet switches.

Learning Objectives

In this lab, you'll examine the standards and technology of 1000BaseT, 1000BaseSX, and 1000BaseLX Ethernet. When you have completed this lab, you will be able to

- Define the 1000BaseT Ethernet specifications, requirements, and limitations

- Define the 1000BaseSX and 1000BaseLX Ethernet specifications, requirements, and limitations

- Recommend Gigabit Ethernet NICs

- Determine appropriate use of fiber-optic Ethernet based on application

Lab Materials and Setup

The materials you'll need for this lab exercise are

- *Mike Meyers' CompTIA Network+ Guide to Managing and Troubleshooting Networks* textbook

- Internet access

- Pen or pencil

- Paper

Getting Down to Business

Recalling the cabling scenario from Chapter 2, your client, the Department of Transportation, is building a new regional Department of Motor Vehicles (DMV) complex consisting of two physical buildings. One building will house all of the administrative departments (licensing, title, tags, and registration). The other building, located approximately 900 feet away from the administrative building, will be a large, garage-like structure where the physical inspection of the automobiles will be conducted. The professional installers have submitted a proposal that has been accepted, outlining the following parameters:

- The proposed cabling for the internal office space of the administrative building is Category 6A UTP. The administrative network will need to support 75 to 100 devices (servers, computers, and printers).

- The proposed cabling for the internal area of the inspection building is Category 6A UTP. The network in the inspection building will need to support 25 to 40 devices (computers and printers).

- For the backbone between the two buildings, the proposal is single-mode 12-fiber optic cabling.

Using this general information, follow Steps 1 through 7 to develop an implementation plan for the new site. The design should take advantage of the Gigabit Ethernet technology.

Step 1   Utilizing online resources, research and document the following information for 100BaseT Ethernet:

    Speed: _____

    Distance: _____

    Cabling: _____

    Connectors: _____

Step 2   Utilizing the textbook and online resources, research and document the following information for 1000BaseT Ethernet:

    Speed: _____

    Distance: _____

    Cabling: _____

    Connectors: _____

Step 3   Utilizing the textbook and online resources, research and document the following information for 1000BaseLX Ethernet:

    Speed: _____

    Distance: _____

    Cabling: _____

    Connectors: _____

Step 4   Utilizing the textbook and online resources, research and document the following information for 1000BaseSX Ethernet:

    Speed: _____

    Distance: _____

    Cabling: _____

    Connectors: _____

Step 5   Utilizing online resources, research and document the following information for 10GBaseT Ethernet:

    Speed: _____

    Distance: _____

    Cabling: _____

    Connectors: _____

Step 6   As discussed in the scenario, the new facility will have approximately 100 to 140 network devices (computers and printers). In order to implement Gigabit Ethernet throughout the organization, each device will need a gigabit NIC. Launch your browser and research the current pricing for Gigabit Ethernet NICs. Document your findings in the following space:

_____

_____

→ **Note**

Commercial computer vendors, like Dell, will provide Gigabit Ethernet NICs on the ATX motherboards of new machines. For the purposes of this lab step, assume that you are purchasing NICs for 100 new computers not coming from a commercial computer vendor.

Step 7   Ethernet networks using 1000BaseSX and 1000BaseLX fiber-optic hardware and cabling share most of the qualities of 1000BaseT networks, but they are considerably more expensive to implement. What are the circumstances under which 1000BaseSX or 1000BaseLX would be preferable to 1000BaseT?

_____

_____

Step 8   Which technology would you recommend for the 900-foot backbone run between the administrative building and the inspection building?

_____

_____

 30 MINUTES

Lab Exercise 4.02: Ethernet Network Design: Implementing Switches

Continuing with the installation of the Department of Transportation regional DMV complex, you have determined that the administrative building will need to support 75 to 100 network devices, and the inspection building will need to support 25 to 40 network devices. The professional cable installers will calculate the horizontal runs and cable drops needed from the telecommunications room(s) to each node.

Now it is your turn! You will need to research Gigabit Ethernet switching technology to provide recommendations regarding make and model, quantity, and specific solutions based on application.

Learning Objectives

In this lab, you'll explore Ethernet switch technology.

By the end of this lab, you will be able to

- Research and recommend Ethernet switches to meet specific applications

- Define solutions to implement high-speed backbone ports

- Design a simple network using Gigabit Ethernet switches

- Define full-duplex operation

Lab Materials and Setup

The materials you'll need for this lab exercise are

- *Mike Meyers' CompTIA Network+ Guide to Managing and Troubleshooting Networks* textbook

- Internet access

- Pen or pencil

- Paper

Getting Down to Business

The physical layout of the buildings and proposed location of telecommunications rooms, cubicles, computers, and printers is complete. The cable installers have provided 100 drops in the correct locations throughout the administrative building, and 40 drops in the inspection garage. The design of the network will have to meet the following criteria:

- A total of 82 network devices will be installed in Phase 1 of the administrative building.

- A total of 30 network devices will be installed during Phase 1 in the inspection garage.

- In the administrative building, there are two areas where clusters of computers will outnumber the wall jacks in close physical proximity. It has been recommended that desktop switches be employed in these two areas.

- The cable installers have qualified the single-mode fiber-optic backbone and have terminated a pair of the cables with LC connectors on each end. Each termination is fed into the telecommunications room of both the administrative building and the inspection garage.

In the following steps, you will research and select the switches to meet the design specifications of the campus and define the quantity and location(s) of each switch. You'll also explore some of the modular interface options to connect LAN and WAN backbones. Better get to work!

Step 1 With the current layout of the facilities and total number of network nodes (devices), you will need to provide anywhere from 100 to 140 network connections throughout the two physical buildings. Each NIC ultimately connects to a port on a switch.

Depending on the application of the switch, you may have to make some decisions, such as whether to install economical, desktop switches or enterprise, fully managed switches, and whether you will provide power to downstream devices through the Ethernet cabling known as Power over Ethernet (PoE). You'll also want to plan on having one switch in each physical building that will provide fiber-optic ports to tie in the backbone between the two buildings.

✖ Cross-Reference

You will study and perform other exercises with Ethernet switches later in Chapter 5 and Chapter 11. If you would like to familiarize yourself with managed and unmanaged switches or multilayer switches, you can jump ahead and read the sections "Virtual LANs" and "Multilayer Switches" in Chapter 11. You do not need detailed understanding of these switching technologies to complete this lab exercise step, but you will want to understand these technologies before taking the CompTIA Network+ Certification Exam.

Using the Internet, explore the various gigabit switches available today, and price out a configuration to meet the needs of this facility. You should document the following varieties at various price points:

a. Economical, desktop switches:

_____

_____

b. Managed switches supporting PoE:

_____

_____

c. To implement the fiber-optic backbone, almost every mid- to high-end switch offers some type of small form factor (SFF) port. Most manufacturers are offering a modular design with either small form-factor pluggable (SFP) or gigabit interface converter (GBIC) transceivers to support multiple technologies and connections without replacing the switch. Explore the offerings for 1000BaseLX SFP transceivers to enable these switches for the single-mode fiber-optic backbone connection between the buildings:

_____

_____

✔ Hint

You can learn a lot about switches and switching technology from the manufacturers' product descriptions. Take some time while you are researching the following models to explore the various applications and options presented in the online documentation. You will also find that you may have to visit multiple Web sites of manufacturers and resellers to uncover aspects of specifications, options, and pricing.

Here are some keywords to help you in your search: Gigabit Ethernet switch, Cisco, D-Link, NETGEAR, Linksys, SFP LC, GBIC, and 1000BaseLX SFP transceivers.

Step 2   Now it is time to configure the telecommunications rooms and workgroups to enable the network. Using the information you have gathered in Step 1, describe the switch configuration you will be using to support the regional DMV.

a. The administrative building will initially implement 82 of the 100 cable drops available throughout the building. Remember that you will need to configure the interface for the fiber-optic connection between the two buildings. What quantity and configuration of switches do you recommend to meet the requirements of the network design?

_____

_____

b. There will be two workgroups located in areas that will not support the total number of network devices that the workgroups will be using (only one or two drops in these areas). What is your recommendation to accommodate the additional network devices?

_____

_____

c. The inspection garage will initially implement 30 of the 40 cable drops available throughout the building. Remember that you will need to configure the interface for the fiber-optic connection between the two buildings. What quantity and configuration of switches do you recommend to meet the requirements of the network design?

✖ Cross-Reference

To refresh your understanding of half-duplex versus full-duplex, refer to the "Full-Duplex Ethernet" section of Chapter 4, "Modern Ethernet," in the *Mike Meyers' CompTIA Network+ Guide to Managing and Troubleshooting Networks* textbook.

 30 MINUTES

Lab Exercise 4.03: Beyond Gigabit Ethernet: 10 Gigabit Ethernet

Gigabit Ethernet is becoming the standard for new installs right to the desktop! In other words, 1000-Mbps NICs and switches are reaching a price point where they can be implemented cost-effectively throughout an organization. As you learned in previous labs, many gigabit NICs and switches are available to complement the design of modern organizational networks.

10 Gigabit Ethernet (10 GbE), providing 10 gigabits of data per second over copper or fiber-optic connections, is still comparatively pricy and therefore relegated to high-demand, high-speed applications: high-demand servers, campus backbones, and WAN communications. In this lab, you'll explore some of the aspects of 10 GbE.

Learning Objectives

In this lab, you will examine 10 GbE options for modern network environments. When you've completed this lab, you will be able to

- Describe the 10GBaseT, 10GBaseSR/SW, 10GBaseLR/LW, and 10GBaseER/EW Ethernet specifications, requirements, and limitations

- Examine 10 GbE NICs

- Determine appropriate switching interfaces to implement 10 GbE backbones

Lab Materials and Setup

The materials you'll need for this lab exercise are

- *Mike Meyers' CompTIA Network+ Guide to Managing and Troubleshooting Networks* textbook
- Internet access
- Pen or pencil
- Paper

Getting Down to Business

One of the benefits of the network design the team has implemented for the regional DMV is known as *future-proofing*. Throughout the design and install, the highest-performance cabling has been used (Category 6A UTP, 10 GbE single-mode fiber-optic), and switches in the telecommunications room utilize modular SFP interfaces that can be upgraded as well. Running 10 GbE to the desktop is still cost-prohibitive, but implementing 10 GbE for the communication on the high-traffic servers and the backbone between the administrative building and the inspection garage may be feasible.

Jonathan asks Scott to research 10 GbE solutions and to prepare a presentation of his findings, including interfaces and pricing, to the network design team. Scott asks if it would be okay to have you assist, so the two of you set off to prepare your report.

Step 1   Using various resources such as the textbook and the Internet, research and document the following implementations of 10 GbE:

1. 10GBaseT

    Cabling: _____

    Cable Details: _____

    Connectors: _____

    Length: _____

2. 10GBaseSR/SW

    Cabling: _____

    Cable Details: _____

    Connectors: _____

    Length: _____

3. 10GBaseLR/LW

Cabling: _____

Cable Details: _____

Connectors: _____

Length: _____

4. 10GBaseER/EW

Cabling: _____

Cable Details: _____

Connectors: _____

Length: _____

Step 2   The high-traffic servers are located in the telecommunications room, so copper or fiber-optic solutions are feasible. Research the current availability of network interface cards supporting 10 GbE technology. Document some of the makes and models, characteristics, and pricing:

_____

_____

What do you recommend: copper or fiber-optic technology? Why?

_____

_____

Step 3   Using online manufacturers' and resellers' Web sites, explore the various SFF 10 GbE interfaces available. Document the make, model, characteristics, and pricing as if you are shopping for the modular transceivers for the switches to implement the link between the administrative building and the inspection garage:

_____

_____

→ **Note**

In keeping with the scenario presented, the fiber-optic cabling you choose between the administrative building and the inspection garage may be specified to support 10 gigabit multimode fiber (MMF) (10GBaseSR). However, the total distance recommended for 10GBaseSR is only 26–300 meters (about 85–980 feet), so the distance of 900 feet could push the specifications for 10 GbE performance. In this case, higher-performance single-mode cable would be the better choice to implement 10 GbE. For the purposes of this lab exercise, provide the results of both 10GBaseSR and 10GBaseLR.

You will also have to be careful when physically implementing 10 GbE transceivers due to the various form factors of both the modular interfaces and the cable interfaces. Currently there are SFP+, XENPAK, X2, and XFP modules available, utilizing SC, LC, and various other fiber-optic cable terminations.

✔ **Hint**

Here is a great Cisco page that covers all of the versions of modular transceiver they currently support. Cisco 10 Gigabit Ethernet Transceiver Modules Compatibility Matrix: www.cisco.com/en/US/docs/interfaces_modules/transceiver_modules/compatibility/matrix/OL_6974.html

 30 MINUTES

Lab Exercise 4.04: Beyond 10 Gigabit Ethernet: 40/100 Gigabit Ethernet

You thought we were done with Ethernet speed improvements after learning about the 10 Gigabit Ethernet used by servers in data centers and WAN connections? Well, think again! In 2010, the latest and greatest standard of Ethernet was defined. It was the first standard to include two different speeds for Ethernet, 40 Gbps and 100 Gbps, and is referred to as 40/100 Gigabit Ethernet (40/100 GbE).

Why in the world would we need Ethernet to go that fast? Why in the world were two speeds included in the same standard? You'll answer those questions and more in this lab.

Learning Objectives

In this lab, you will delve into 40/100 GbE. When you've completed this lab, you will be able to

- Describe the motivations for this standard

- Explain the different parts of this standard

- Look toward the potential successor of 40/100 GbE

Lab Materials and Setup

The materials you'll need for this lab exercise are

- *Mike Meyers' CompTIA Network+ Guide to Managing and Troubleshooting Networks* textbook

- Internet access

- Pen or pencil

- Paper

Getting Down to Business

Before you run to your computer store and ask for a 40/100 Gbps NIC for your laptop, you need to understand that the standard isn't concerned with Local Area Networks. When a speed limit from a highway is raised, it has nothing to do with the speed limits on the local streets. Furthermore, certain types of vehicles on the road, like police cars, fire trucks, and ambulances, are authorized to move quicker than the general public. Think of the highway as a Wide Area Network, and think of special vehicles as servers as you answer the following questions.

Step 1   Using an Internet search engine, find the motivation for each of the two new speeds of Ethernet.

40 Gbps: _____

100 Gbps: _____

Step 2   What is IEEE P802.3ba, and what were its objectives?

_____

_____

_____

_____

Step 3   40GBaseKR4 and 100GBASE-KP4 are two of the many standards used for 40/100 GbE. What are the others?

_____

_____

_____

_____

Step 4   On December 6, 2017, Terabit Ethernet (400 Gigabit Ethernet and 200 Gigabit Ethernet) was standardized. Read about it at www.ieee802.org/3/bs/ and https://en.wikipedia.org/wiki/Terabit_ Ethernet.

Who are these technologies for? What are some reasons these technologies are needed?

_____

_____

_____

_____

Lab Analysis

1. Dave has decided to install Cat 6A UTP cabling in a small office so that they may upgrade to 10GBaseT in the future without having to "pull" cable again. Are there any concerns you would voice to Dave before he installs the Cat 6A cable?

_____

_____

2. Jeff is going to implement Gigabit Ethernet for a small office, home office (SOHO) campus. What kind of network cabling is necessary to implement Gigabit Ethernet?

    _____

    _____

3. Aaron is studying fiber-optic technology and asks what the major differences are between 10GBaseSR and 10GBaseLR. Can you explain the difference?

    _____

    _____

4. Will understands that high data-throughput speeds and longer throughput distances are two advantages of fiber-optic cabling over copper cabling. He doesn't understand why the cable installers are recommending the use of fiber-optic cable for the machine shop of a local high school. Can you describe two other advantages that fiber-optic cabling offers over copper wire that would help him understand?

    _____

    _____

Key Term Quiz

Use the vocabulary terms from the list below to complete the sentences that follow.

1000BaseLX

1000BaseSX

1000BaseT

400

GBIC (gigabit interface converter)

modular transceivers

SFP (small form-factor pluggable)

1. _____ uses multimode fiber.

2. _____ uses single-mode fiber.

3. The fastest-rated speed of Ethernet is _____ Gbps.

4. To implement _____, Cat 5e or higher, UTP cabling must be installed, although new installs should use either Cat 6 or Cat 6A.

5. Many Gigabit Ethernet switches support _____ to allow support of the ever-increasing speeds. The two dominant forms of these devices are _____ and _____.

Chapter 5

Installing a Physical Network

Lab Exercises

Now that you're familiar with the major network types, topologies, and technologies that network techs have at their disposal, it's time to dive into the physical aspects of network implementation. These include installing the network media and network hardware that tie your network together, installing the switches that form the central communication point of the physical network, configuring the network adapters (commonly known as NICs, or network interface cards) that connect your network nodes (PC workstations, servers, printers, and so on) to the network, testing network connections, and troubleshooting any ensuing network errors.

As discussed in the textbook and defined in the CompTIA Network+ Certification Exam Objectives, you are not expected to be as knowledgeable as a professional network designer or cable installer when it comes to the actual implementation of the physical network. However, you will need to be familiar with the concepts! Working with the cable, hardware, devices, installation tools, and troubleshooting tools is a great way to learn the concepts, so this is a good place to start practicing.

 20 MINUTES

Lab Exercise 5.01: Examining Structured Network Cabling

One of the proposals that your client received for the installation of the Department of Motor Vehicles (DMV) complex was from an inexperienced firm. The professional cable installers calculated the horizontal runs and cable drops needed from the telecommunications room to each node, the methods to install the cable runs in the inspection garage, the type of UTP cabling to implement, and the outfitting of the telecommunications room. Scott asks for your assistance to double-check the proposal.

Learning Objectives

In this lab, you will examine the principles that lead to a successful structured network cabling installation. When you have completed this lab, you will be able to

- Understand the proper planning issues that go into a network deployment
- Make informed recommendations for a network installation

Lab Materials and Setup

The materials you'll need for this lab exercise are

- *Mike Meyers' CompTIA Network+ Guide to Managing and Troubleshooting Networks* textbook

- Small length of Cat 6A plenum-grade, solid-core cable

- Small length of Cat 6A stranded copper patch cable

- Pen or pencil

- Paper

Getting Down to Business

When planning a building project these days, almost all designs will take into account the design of the network infrastructure. The professional network designers will work hand in hand with the architects to include one or more telecommunications rooms right from the initial design. If it is a new build, as the DMV project is, network cable will be strung along with electrical and telephone cabling during the building process, saving the cable installers from the tedious task of "pulling cable" after the building is in place.

Examine the following steps as if they were components of the proposal from the professional cable installers and network infrastructure design team.

✖ **Cross-Reference**

You may want to review the "Understanding Structured Cabling" section of Chapter 5, "Installing a Physical Network," in the *Mike Meyers' CompTIA Network+ Guide to Managing and Troubleshooting Networks* textbook. Also review the specifics of CompTIA Network+ Exam Objectives in Domain 5.2—Given a scenario, use the appropriate tool.

Step 1   The administration building will have 100 cable runs. You are examining the network cabling installation proposal that was submitted by the inexperienced professional cable installers. The following is a sample of some of the runs, shortest to longest, that the proposal calls out:

Location	Distance
MDF Telecommunications Room Patch Panel to Network Node A	48 meters (157 feet)
MDF Telecommunications Room Patch Panel to Network Node B	55 meters (180 feet)
MDF Telecommunications Room Patch Panel to Network Node C	60 meters (197 feet)
MDF Telecommunications Room Patch Panel to Network Node D	68 meters (223 feet)
MDF Telecommunications Room Patch Panel to Network Node E	75 meters (246 feet)
MDF Telecommunications Room Patch Panel to Network Node F	84 meters (275 feet)

Location	Distance
MDF Telecommunications Room Patch Panel to Network Node G	91 meters (300 feet)
MDF Telecommunications Room Patch Panel to Network Node H	102 meters (334 feet)
MDF Telecommunications Room Patch Panel to Network Node I	113 meters (371 feet)
MDF Telecommunications Room Patch Panel to Network Node J	122 meters (400 feet)
MDF Telecommunications Room Patch Panel to Network Node K	125 meters (410 feet)

The proposal calls for using Cat 6A UTP network cabling. Which, if any, of the network cabling runs are outside the limits for that type of cabling? Does your answer change if you are running 10 GbE equipment? What solutions can you offer to overcome any limit violations?

_____

_____

Step 2   Many of the runs in the inspection garage will be terminated at inspection stations right on the garage floor. These stations will be unfinished areas of the garage (no office walls or cubicles). The walls of this area are concrete. What is the best way to install the network cable drops in this area?

_____

_____

Step 3   As you have learned, the horizontal cable runs will most likely be snaking through walls and ceilings of public offices. Because of this, the proper type of cabling should be used for the horizontal runs. Closely examine a small length of UTP cable recommended for horizontal use. Look for information printed right on the outer insulation of the cable and then strip a length off one end and examine the copper wires. Document some of the features of the cable.

_____

_____

There will also be patch cables between the wall jack and the network devices as well as the patch panels and switches. Closely examine a small length of UTP patch cable. Look for information printed right on the outer insulation of the cable and then strip a length off one end and examine the copper wires. Document some of the features of the cable.

_____

_____

Step 4   List at least four requirements for the telecommunications room(s) that will house rack-mounted patch panels, a stack of switches, and at least one file server.

_____

_____

 1 HOUR

Lab Exercise 5.02: Implementing a Small Network Infrastructure

Installing the cabling that carries data frames from one network node to another (affectionately called "pulling cable") is the most physically demanding task in a network installation and is typically left to professional cable installers. Believe me, once you've got your network cabling installed, you don't want to have to go back into the walls and pull it out again! Tasks include planning the installation, pulling the cabling, connecting network access jacks, and, finally, testing the connections to ensure that your installation is successful.

Though full-blown corporate cable installs are left to the professionals, many network techs have been called upon to wire a room, upgrade a floor, or punch down a new patch panel. You'll want to be familiar with the basic skills of pulling cable through a ceiling, punching down a patch panel, and connecting the wall jack (also known as a _keystone_). This will not only help you in the field; it will also clarify key concepts you will see on the CompTIA Network+ exam.

Learning Objectives

In this lab, you'll practice the art of installing network cabling, hardware, and devices.

When you have completed this lab, you will be able to

- Pull a length of cable through a ceiling (or raceway)

- Use a punchdown tool and terminate UTP cabling into a rack-mounted patch panel

- Drop a cable through a wall and terminate the cable drop with an RJ-45 keystone

- Mount a wall plate

- Verify the run using a cable tester

Lab Materials and Setup

The materials you'll need for this lab exercise are

- Bulk UTP cabling (Cat 6A)

- Nylon pull rope

- 24- to 48-port rack-mounted patch panel

- RJ-45 wall jack keystone (quantity 2 to 4)

- Low-voltage mounting bracket and faceplate (quantity 2 to 4)

- Drywall saw

- Wire snips

- 110-punchdown tool

- Cable tester

- Label maker

- Pen or pencil

- Paper

→ **Note**

It would really help to have an actual wall and equipment rack to perform this lab. There are commercial practice walls that are sold just for this purpose. However, over the years I have actually built my own practice wall with a handful of drywall screws, a number of 2 × 4 studs, and a couple of sheets of drywall (see Figure 5-1). It doesn't have to be pretty, just functional. You can even get some cable trays to form a false ceiling for the cables to run over. Worst case, just get the cable, hardware, and devices and complete all of the punchdowns on a lab bench. You should still be able to demonstrate connectivity.

FIGURE 5-1   Do-it-yourself wall

Getting Down to Business

Installing structured network cabling begins with planning. You should physically survey the site and examine the site's floor plan for any hazards that you may not be able to spot visually. Then you can examine the logistics of your planned installation, such as the methods that you will use to deploy and install the horizontal cabling, network outlet drop locations, and so on. You also need to select the most appropriate type of cabling for the job, making sure to comply with any applicable codes and regulations. Then you should document your plans and note any discrepancies during installation. Remember to label your runs and outlets while you're at it. Finally, you need to test your network cabling for continuity and troubleshoot any problems that arise. These are the basic steps that apply to any network cabling installation, from the small office/home office (SOHO) environment with only a few workstations to the large enterprise with thousands of clients.

In the following steps, you will "pull cable," drop it through a small practice wall, punch down one end to a rack-mounted patch panel, punch down the other end to an RJ-45 keystone, and then fix the RJ-45 keystone into a wall-mounted faceplate. You will repeat this a second time, providing two cable drops. Later, in Lab Exercise 5.03, you will install and verify the configuration of a couple of NICs, add a switch, connect the two computers, and then, voilà, you have a small network! You have a lot of work to do, so let's get going!

Step 1 Start with the placement of the wall jack. Using a pencil and tape measure, choose the location along the wall for the wall jack and mark the wall 18 inches off the floor. Depending on the style of low-voltage mounting bracket you are using, use the drywall saw to cut an appropriate-size hole to mount the bracket. See Figures 5-2 and 5-3 for an example of cutting the drywall and mounting a bracket, respectively.

FIGURE 5-2 Cutting a hole

FIGURE 5-3 Installing a low-voltage mounting bracket

✖ Cross-Reference

Consult the "Installing Structured Cabling" section of Chapter 5 in the *Mike Meyers' CompTIA Network+ Guide to Managing and Troubleshooting Networks* textbook.

Step 2   Using the tape measure, measure the lateral distance between the proposed cable drop and the telecommunications room. This will be the basis for the length of cable you will need for this run. Remember, you will typically be "pulling" this cable through the drop ceiling and using either cable hangers or trays to keep it suspended off the ceiling tiles. Be sure to include in the total length of cable that you will cut the distance for the height of the ceiling and the cable hangers or trays to the wall outlet and the patch panel.

➔ Note

Professional cable installers typically pull one or more cables at a time from the telecommunications room through the walls and ceilings to the cable drop location. They leave the cable on the spool as they pull it through the ceiling and walls, rolling out the amount needed plus some slack before snipping the cable from the spool. Since you are most likely using a smaller practice wall, you may not follow this exact technique.

What is the total length of cable that you have calculated?

_____

_____

Step 3   Starting at the telecommunications room (where you have located your equipment rack and patch panel), attach a nylon pull rope to the UTP cable and begin to pull the cable through the cable hangers or cable trays until you reach the cable drop location. Be careful to ease the cable through any snags or twists—you do not want to break the internal cables, rendering the run useless.

At the point of the cable drop, fasten a small weight to the end of the nylon pull rope and, using some finesse, drop the pull rope through the wall to the hole created for the wall jack (see Figure 5-4). The cable should be long enough that you have 6 to 12 inches of spare cable at each end. One end will be terminated to the patch panel; the other will be terminated to the RJ-45 keystone.

FIGURE 5-4 Dropping the cable

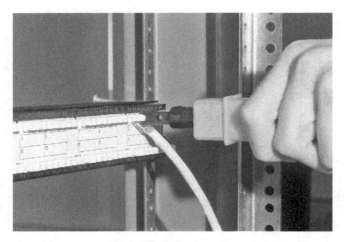

FIGURE 5-5 Punching down the patch panel

Step 4   While located at the equipment rack, strip approximately 1 inch of the outer insulation from the UTP cable and slightly untwist the four pairs. Following the labeling or color code guide on the patch panel, use the 110-punchdown tool to fasten the cables to the block for port 1 of the patch panel (see Figure 5-5).

Step 5   While you're at the wall jack, feed the cable through the low-voltage mounting bracket and fasten the bracket to the wall. Strip approximately one inch of the outer insulation from the UTP cable and slightly untwist the four pairs. Following the labeling or color code guide on the RJ-45 keystone, use the 110-punchdown tool to fasten the cables to the block (see Figure 5-6).

FIGURE 5-6 Punching down the RJ-45 keystone

→ **Note**

RJ-45 keystones come in many styles, incorporating different methods to connect the wires to the pins of the RJ-45 jack. Most use a small 110-punchdown block to facilitate this connection. Follow the instructions for the style of RJ-45 keystone you are working with.

Step 6   Insert the keystone into the faceplate, and fasten the faceplate to the low-voltage mounting bracket (see Figure 5-7).

Step 7   Verify the cable run using a commercial cable tester.

→ **Note**

Professional cable installers will use much more complex, and expensive, cable certifiers to verify not only connectivity but attenuation, near-end crosstalk (NEXT), and far-end crosstalk (FEXT) of the cable run. For the purposes of this lab exercise, only the connectivity of the cable run will be verified. If you have access to a high-end cable certifier, by all means, examine the attenuation, NEXT, and FEXT.

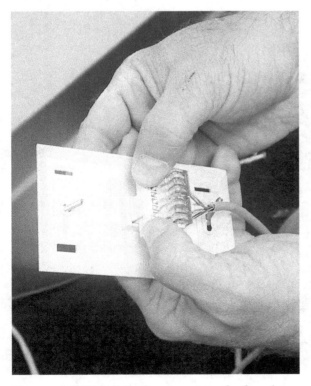

FIGURE 5-7   Fitting the keystone into the faceplate

Most testers come with a remote end and a master module. Using a known-good patch cable, connect the master module to port 1 of the patch panel. Using a second known-good patch cable, connect the remote end to the RJ-45 connector in the wall jack. Following the directions provided with the cable tester, verify the connectivity of the cable run. Record your result in the following table:

TIA/EIA 568 Pair	Connection	Result (Good/Bad)
Wire Pair 1	Pin 5 to Pin 5	
	Pin 4 to Pin 4	
Wire Pair 2	Pin 1 to Pin 1	
	Pin 2 to Pin 2	
Wire Pair 3	Pin 3 to Pin 3	
	Pin 6 to Pin 6	
Wire Pair 4	Pin 7 to Pin 7	
	Pin 8 to Pin 8	

Step 8   Don't forget to label both the patch panel and the wall jack (see Figures 5-8 and 5-9). After all of the runs are in place, you will save hours of troubleshooting time with properly labeled patch panels and wall jacks!

FIGURE 5-8 A labeled patch panel

FIGURE 5-9 Properly labeled
wall jack

Step 9 Create a second run and drop, following Steps 1 through 8. In Step 4, use the second port of
the patch panel.

 30 MINUTES

Lab Exercise 5.03: Installing Switches, Network Adapters, and PCs

In the prior exercise, you completed the installation of the physical wiring of the network and verified that you
had connectivity from the patch panel to the wall jack. Now you are going to explore and install the devices
that allow PCs to use that physical network to communicate: Ethernet switches and network interface cards.

Switches form the central meeting point for all of the cable runs and provide smooth communication
between all of the devices attached to those cable runs. The telecommunications room is the gathering place
for patch panels and switches. Each run that is terminated at the patch panel will be "patched" into the switch
to provide connectivity to all the other devices on the network.

Your PC's physical link to the network is the network adapter. You're probably used to hearing this piece
of equipment referred to simply as a network interface card (NIC), because historically, this device was only
available as an add-on peripheral card. With the worldwide application of networking, most notably the
Internet, modern PC manufacturers have adopted the practice of integrating the network adapter (electronics
and connector) right on the motherboard.

→ **Note**

NICs haven't gone away; they are just utilized slightly differently these days. Often, an older machine can be upgraded with higher-speed copper, fiber-optic, or wireless adapters. Sometimes USB adapters are used to facilitate connectivity (especially for wireless and Bluetooth). You will still see ExpressCard network adapters being used on laptops, but even laptop manufactures are incorporating wired and wireless interfaces into the onboard electronics. Installing and configuring switches, network adapters, and PCs is a task that many network techs do so often it becomes second nature. In later chapters you will study more complex configuration components and practices for both switches and network interfaces. Currently, I want you to focus on the physical aspects of the installation and configuration; that is, connecting and communicating from one PC to another over your physical installation.

Learning Objectives

You'll begin this lab by installing and patching the Ethernet switch into the rack. You will then install and/or configure a network interface. This may include an integrated network interface, or an add-on device such as an internal NIC or USB network adapter, on your PC. You'll finish up by verifying proper operation through the device and configuration tools included with the operating system and establishing connectivity between two machines. By the end of this lab, you will be able to

- Install a rack-mount switch and correctly cable it to a patch panel
- Properly install and configure a network interface
- Verify connectivity between two PCs

Lab Materials and Setup

The materials you'll need for this lab exercise are

- Rack-mount Ethernet switch
- Minimum four (4) Cat 6A straight-through patch cables
- Two PCs with either integrated network interfaces or expansion card NICs (PCIe)
- Windows 10 operating systems installed
- Phillips-head screwdriver
- Pen or pencil
- Paper

Getting Down to Business

With the fine art of pulling cable, terminating connections, and verifying continuity of the structured cabling complete, it's time to get the telecommunications room and the work area up to par. This is where the network tech is responsible for the connectivity! The network tech must be able to connect and verify switches, servers, and wide area network devices in the telecommunications room, and guarantee that all of the PCs can communicate with the servers and the outside world.

Using the mock wall from the previous exercise, you are now going to install a rack-mount switch, and two PCs (with network interfaces) to complete a small working office network.

Step 1   Starting in the telecommunications room (the equipment rack between your two mock walls), mount the Ethernet switch.

Step 2   Using two of the straight-through patch cables, connect ports 1 and 2 of the patch panel to two of the open ports on the switch.

Step 3   Now moving to the work area (the two PCs you are going to use near the two wall jacks), examine the physical PCs and determine if there are integrated network interfaces. If the systems are equipped with onboard interfaces, you may skip to Step 8. If a NIC needs to be installed in either of the machines, use the following guidelines (Steps 4 through 7) to install the NIC.

Step 4   To install a NIC in a Windows 10 machine, turn the PC off. Once the PC is completely powered down, unplug all cables, including the power cable, from the power supply.

→ **Note**

> As recommended by CompTIA A+ certified techs the world over, be sure to follow all proper anti-static procedures when working inside your PC case. Use an anti-static mat and anti-static wrist strap if you have them. If you lack these components, the next best thing is to discharge any static electricity in your body by touching a grounded metal component on the PC case (such as the power supply casing). Before you start poking around inside the PC case, remove any rings, bracelets, watches, or any other items that may snag on exposed components.

Step 5   Place the PC case on an anti-static mat and attach your anti-static wrist strap (aka nerd bracelet), and then remove the PC case cover to expose the interior.

Step 6   Using the NIC provided by your instructor (PCIe), locate an available expansion bus slot. Remove the slot cover, and then insert the NIC into the slot. Be sure to handle the NIC only by its edges, and firmly press the card straight down into the slot. Once the NIC is properly seated in the slot, make sure it is secure by applying whichever locking mechanism the expansion card uses.

Step 7   Replace the PC case cover and reattach all cables to the PC, including the power cable, then start the PC and log on when the desktop appears. Windows 10 have built-in support for many NICs, so assuming you're running one of these operating systems, plug and play kicks in, detects the card, installs Windows' built-in drivers, and alerts you that the NIC is ready to use, as shown in Figure 5-10. In most cases, the Windows NIC driver works fine, but it's usually a good idea to use the latest driver provided by the NIC manufacturer.

Step 8   Open the Windows Device Manager and expand the list of installed NICs. Double-click the NIC's icon to open its Properties dialog box, as shown in Figure 5-11. Record the make and model of the NIC. Is the NIC functional? What are the details of the driver that is installed?

_____

_____

_____

Step 9   Once the systems have been verified to have working network interfaces, place each system in proximity of each wall jack. Using the patch cables, connect each machine to the respective wall jack.

✔ **Hint**

> **At this point in your studies, you are not expected to perform the configuration of the network operating system and protocols. The next two steps will go much more smoothly if the computers have been preconfigured for network connectivity. If any of the results seem incorrect, please consult with your instructor to troubleshoot and diagnose the connectivity issues.**

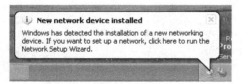

FIGURE 5-10 The New Network Device Installed alert

FIGURE 5-11 The NIC Properties dialog box

Step 10   Power up the Ethernet switch and the two PCs. With a little effort, you should be able to determine if the network has basic connectivity. Are there any visual indicators that the systems are connected to the switch?

_____

_____

Step 11   Log on to the systems and experiment with Explorer to see if you can see each system from the other. Can you share or copy files from machine to machine? Are there any additional visual clues that the systems are communicating over the network?

_____

_____

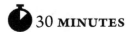 30 MINUTES

Lab Exercise 5.04: Diagnostics and Troubleshooting

Network connectivity issues come in many shapes and sizes. Just like networks themselves, these issues can range from the simple to the complex. In this exercise, you'll walk through some simple diagnostic and troubleshooting steps to ensure that the physical network is in tip-top shape. Network adapter hardware is fairly foolproof, assuming that it has been installed and configured correctly. A couple of quick tests confirm whether a lack of network connectivity lies with the network adapter hardware or somewhere else.

Once installed, network cabling doesn't suffer from a lot of wear and tear—after all, there are no moving parts, and the voltage carried is very low. Nonetheless, network cabling is subject to physical damage and interference, so it's important for you to be able to diagnose and repair this type of failure. Locating breaks in the cable is particularly frustrating, so having a time domain reflectometer (TDR) really comes in handy.

Even well-meaning, organized network techs can have a telecommunications room become a nightmare of snaked, unlabeled patch cables and runs. A toner is invaluable in this situation and will allow the network tech to get organized!

Basic Ethernet switches are fairly robust and normally provide for auto-sensing multispeed communications. It is not uncommon to have legacy devices on a gigabit network operating at 100 Mbps or even 10 Mbps. It is important that you be able to quickly verify that the switch is indeed communicating with legacy devices.

Learning Objectives

In this lab, you will go through some basic network connectivity troubleshooting scenarios, so by the time you complete this lab, you'll be able to

- Troubleshoot simple, physical network connectivity issues

Lab Materials and Setup

The materials you'll need for this lab exercise are

- The two networked Windows PCs from the previous exercise
- Length of patch cable that can be cut in half
- 10/100/1000 Ethernet switch
- Time domain reflectometer (TDR)
- Toner unit
- Access to the telecommunications room and patch panel from the previous exercise
- Pen or pencil
- Paper

Getting Down to Business

The first symptom of a network connectivity issue usually manifests itself as a loud screeching noise! Oddly enough, the noise is not coming from the network hardware or fancy test equipment, but from the frustrated user. Typically, this noise will be accompanied by a vocal error message, such as "I can't get on the Internet!" or "I can't get my e-mail!" "Great, the network is down!" is also pretty common. In most cases, network connectivity problems are simple in nature. Accordingly, you should begin your diagnosis and troubleshooting with simple solutions.

Assume for a moment that one of your network users is unable to access network resources. In the following steps, you'll go through a simple diagnostic and troubleshooting scenario.

✖ **Cross-Reference**

> Additional information may be found in the "Testing the Cable Runs," "Link Lights," and "Diagnostics and Repair of Physical Cabling" sections of Chapter 5 in the *Mike Meyers' CompTIA Network+ Guide to Managing and Troubleshooting Networks* textbook.

Step 1   Your first step is to determine whether or not the PC has a network connection, and then determine the state of the connection. The obvious place to start is with the physical connection. Locate the PC's network adapter. Is the RJ-45 connector of the Ethernet cable plugged into the network adapter?

If so, check the status lights. What is the result?

_____

_____

Step 2   If you have physical connectivity, your next step is to determine if the operating system recognizes the connection. Windows provides a couple of methods to determine the network connection state quickly. First, look in the Notification area of the taskbar. Is there a Local Area Connection Status icon? If so, click Open Network And Sharing Center. (See Figure 5-12.) Now click Connections: Local Area Connection to bring up the Local Area Connection Status dialog box as shown in Figure 5-13.

Fill in the following information. If no icon is visible, skip to Step 3.

IPv4 Connectivity: _____

IPv6 Connectivity: _____

Media State: _____

Duration: _____

Speed: _____

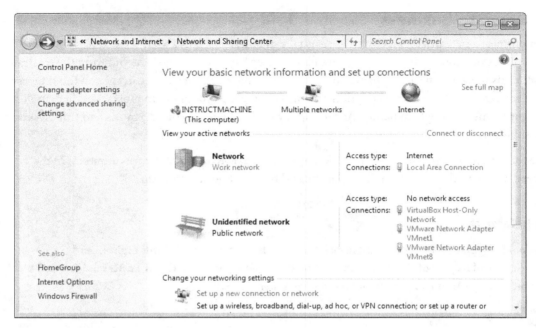

FIGURE 5-12 Network and Sharing Center

FIGURE 5-13 Local Area Connection Status

Step 3   An alternate path to the Status window in Windows 10 is as follows: Choose Start | Control Panel, select the Network And Sharing Center icon (if you're in the icon view), and then click Change Adapter Settings on the side menu.

Right-click the Local Area Connection icon and select Status from the pop-up menu to bring up the network connection's status dialog box. Are the reported results for the IPv4 Connectivity, IPv6 Connectivity, Media State, Duration, and Speed the same as in the previous Status report?

_____

_____

✔ **Hint**

> **Within Windows 10, it is possible to configure the Local Area Connection Status icon so that it is visible or hidden in the Notification area. Open Control Panel, select Notification Area Icons (in the icon view), then click the drop-down arrow next to Network and choose to show or hide icons and notifications as shown in Figure 5-14.**

Step 4   Disconnect the PC's network cable from the network adapter. What are the results?

_____

_____

Step 5   Using a loose patch cable, possibly with a partial slice or a missing RJ-45 connector, connect the cable to a TDR. What are the results?

_____

_____

Step 6   Using the mock wall with the equipment rack and the patch panel, attach the tone generator unit from a network toner to an active network drop wall outlet. Then go to the patch panel and use the tone probe unit to locate the patch panel cable that corresponds to the network outlet. What are the results?

_____

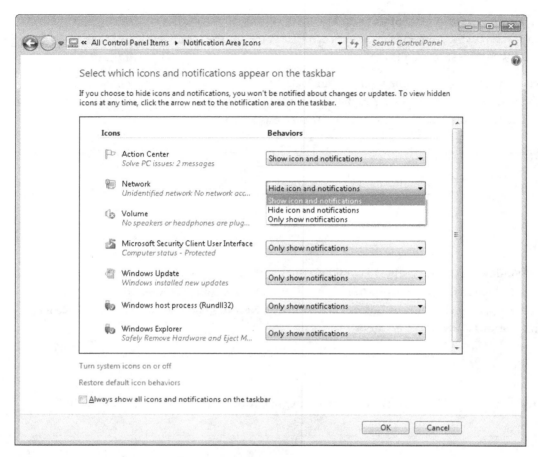

FIGURE 5-14 Notification Area Icons

Step 7   Most gigabit switches support auto-sensing, multispeed performance enabling 10-Mbps, 100-Mbps, and 1000-Mbps devices to connect and communicate through the same switch. Often, these switches will even have status lights (LEDs) that indicate the operating speed of the attached device.

Using a 10/100/1000 Ethernet switch, configure a small network with devices using a mixture of 100BaseT NICs and 1000BaseT NICs. Include a device with a 10BaseT NIC, if one is available, just to see what happens. Document the results of the status lights on the switch. Can all of the devices communicate with each other?

_____

_____

→ **Note**

A simple five-port or eight-port workgroup 10/100/1000 Ethernet switch will work fine for this exercise. Different switches may or may not support status indicator lights for multispeed operation, so the only confirmation of the operation of the switch with different speed NICs will be successful communication. You may also need to work with the network configuration of the devices (computers or printers) to implement network communication. Please consult with your instructor for further directions.

 OPEN

Lab Exercise 5.05: Field Trip: A Visit with the IT Department

You have spent the first part of this class studying the physical components of computer networking. Classroom exercises involving topologies, technologies, the OSI model, Ethernet, and devices have strengthened your understanding of these components. Now it is time to go see these components in a real-world environment!

Just about every organization has some collection of information technology, and often, the IT department is more than happy to show off their implementation of the technology to meet their users' needs. If you are attending a CompTIA Network+ class, the facility or the school where you are taking the class is a great place to request a tour of the IT department and the telecommunications room(s). Talk with your instructor, make a few inquiries, and set up a visit with the IT department of an organization in your community.

Learning Objectives

This lab is actually more of a recommended activity. When you have completed this lab, you will be able to

- Explore the real-world implementation of the physical network
- Establish communication with local IT department personnel

Lab Materials and Setup

The materials you'll need for this lab exercise are

- Invitation to tour an organization's facilities and telecommunications room(s)
- Pen or pencil
- Paper

Getting Down to Business

It is important to establish a rapport with the personnel that you will be spending time with. Obviously, it is not their primary responsibility to be ushering around a small class of students through their facilities and discussing their physical network with you. However, you will find that if you are courteous, many network techs enjoy talking about their network infrastructure solutions.

If you are in an instructor-led class, you will most likely be invited to visit a location of the instructor's choosing. This can be very informative as the instructor usually will have established a rapport with the techs prior to your visit, which means they will probably be very agreeable to entertaining your questions. Plan on asking a bunch!

Step 1   When visiting a physical location, it would be beneficial if you could examine a copy of the floor plans. However, with the need for heightened security at every level, viewing the floor plans will probably not be an option. Work through the following scenario even if your answers do not pertain to an actual physical location. The steps will still reinforce your understanding of the physical layout of a network.

The blueprints will offer a visual indication of all of the important areas of the facility including the main distribution frame (MDF), any intermediate distribution frames (IDFs), the demarc, and all of the cable drops to wall outlets. Study the floor plan and prepare a detailed description of the facility, including the following points:

  a.   Identify and note the approximate location of the MDF.

  _____

  b.   Identify the IDF(s). How many are implemented in this facility? What is the approximate location of each compared to the MDF?

  _____

  c.   Is the demarc identified in the floor plans? Is it located in the MDF or is it located in a completely isolated part of the building?

  _____

  d.   What is the approximate total number of drops (wall outlets) for this facility? The network administrator may be able to help you with this one, as opposed to your counting all of the cable drops in the floor plan!

  _____

Step 2   Ask if it is possible to get a tour of the facilities. One area of interest would be the MDF telecommunications room. Most likely this is where the foundation of the network infrastructure has been established. You might use some of the following questions as openers for further discussion about the facilities:

a.   Are there any special conditions that have been set up in the telecommunications room (that is, air conditioning, electrical service, and so on)?

_____

b.   Is most of the equipment (UPSs, switches, patch panels, and servers) rack-mounted? What are the approximate quantities of equipment (racks, patch panels, switches, servers, and so on)?

_____

c.   Note the labeling technique. Are most of the important components and runs labeled?

_____

d.   What category of cable is used throughout the facility?

_____

e.   What are the common speeds of switches and NICs?

_____

f.   Are there any fiber-optic technologies implemented in this facility?

_____

Step 3   What complement of test equipment do the network techs employ to verify the connectivity of the network?

cable tester   _____

time domain reflectometer   _____

cable certifier   _____

toner   _____

Lab Analysis

1. Tyler complains that he cannot get on your corporate network. You discover that he moved his desk and PC to another part of his office, and in doing so forcibly pulled the Cat 6A patch cable out of its wall outlet. A quick visual inspection doesn't reveal any obvious damage to the patch cable. How do you determine if the patch cable is damaged?

    _____

    _____

2. Nathan has been asked to patch in a new install. What specialized equipment will he use to connect the endpoint of a cable run to a patch panel?

    _____

    _____

3. The cable installers have been working all day and have now completed the internal wiring for 48 wall outlets. Sarah asks if she can use the leftover cabling to create the patch cables for some of the workstations. You explain to Sarah that this would not be a good idea. Why?

    _____

    _____

4. Laura was talking with Jonathan. She asked why you would always defer to professional cable installers to guarantee cable runs, and why the higher-bandwidth cabling and connections needed more precise placement and termination when installed. How do you think Jonathan responded to these questions?

    _____

    _____

5. Renee has upgraded a small 25-node network with cabling and switches to operate at 1000BaseT. She has a few old HP LaserJet 4100n printers with 100BaseT JetDirect cards. She is concerned that they will have to be upgraded as well. What do you recommend?

    _____

    _____

Key Term Quiz

Use the vocabulary terms from the list provided to complete the sentences that follow.

auto-sensing

demarc

link light

multispeed

time domain reflectometer (TDR)

tone generator

tone probe

1. Phillip has determined that his connectivity problem is between the patch panel and the wall outlet. He uses a(n) _____ to pinpoint the exact location of the cable break.

2. Use a(n) _____ and _____ to trace network cabling between a wall outlet and a patch panel.

3. In a facility, the point where responsibility of the physical cabling shifts from the ISP to the organization is known as the _____.

4. Practically all modern Ethernet switches and NICs are _____ and _____.

5. The simplest test of network connectivity is to check the NIC's _____.

Chapter 6

TCP/IP Basics

Lab Exercises

The TCP/IP (Transmission Control Protocol/Internet Protocol) suite can trace its beginnings all the way back to the late 1960s, when the first four network nodes were connected to the Advanced Research Project Agency Network (ARPANET). This enabled communication between host computers at UCLA, Stanford Research Center, UC Santa Barbara, and the University of Utah. Over the next decade, a group of scholars and engineers contributed specifications for the initial protocols that make up the TCP/IP suite, which was officially "launched" on January 1, 1983.

While other networking protocols and suites have come and gone, TCP/IP has stood the test of time, and is the only protocol suite used by the Internet today. Many factors have contributed to this popularity. If you send or receive an e-mail, research information, or play an online role-playing game with thousands of people from around the world, you're using the TCP/IP suite to communicate. Also, the TCP/IP suite was placed in the public domain, ensuring that companies could design network software using it. All of the major operating systems—Windows, Unix, Linux, and macOS—provide network communications and services via TCP/IP. Another important contribution to TCP/IP's popularity is that it is built on a set of dynamic specifications that are constantly modified and updated through a process known as request for comments (RFCs). RFCs ensure that TCP/IP is relevant to the networking technologies and methodologies now and in the future. You may peruse the thousands of RFCs at www.ietf.org/rfc.html.

In this chapter, you'll explore and configure the basics of IPv4 addressing and subnet masks. You'll examine how a network node—or, as they're usually called when discussing TCP/IP, a network host—determines whether an IP address is local or remote, and you'll set up the parameters that will enable your system to communicate with hosts on remote networks. This chapter will focus on IPv4. Later, in Chapter 12, you'll dive into IPv6.

Wireshark, a free and open source packet analyzer, will enable you to view the contents of Ethernet frames, IP packets, TCP segments, UDP datagrams, and more. You'll use Wireshark to examine how IP addresses (the logical addresses) are resolved to MAC addresses (the physical addresses). Remember, Ethernet ultimately uses the MAC addresses to get the frames from machine to machine. You'll configure both static and dynamic IP addressing, and then finish with a review of Automatic Private IP Addressing (APIPA).

As you develop the skill sets required of a network technician and study to pass the CompTIA Network+ certification exam, it is imperative that you comprehend the finer details of the TCP/IP suite. There is a lot to cover in this chapter, and at times it will be pretty intense, but I know you have what it takes to see it through.

 45 MINUTES

Lab Exercise 6.01: Diagramming the IP Address and Subnet Mask

There are two key components to all IP addresses: the IP address itself and the corresponding subnet mask. The IP host addresses follow defined rules that specify whether they are valid IP addresses, which network they belong to, and their unique computer address on that network. The subnet mask is used to identify which part of the IP address is the network ID, shared by all hosts on the network, and which portion of the IP address is the host ID, unique to each network host.

You should appreciate that a network host's IP address and subnet mask, both displayed in dotted decimal notation, are simply numeric representations of the binary values. It's these binary values that identify each node on the TCP/IP network. Finally, you should recognize that there are defined IP address classes and that each of those classes comes with its own default subnet mask.

Valid IP addresses must follow a specific format. Knowing the rules for valid IP addresses is particularly important when you must manually configure a network node's IP address. Configuring an IP address in the wrong format means that your PC won't communicate on the network.

There's a famous joke that reads, "There are only 10 types of people in the world: Those who understand binary, and those who don't." It's good for a laugh for anyone who understands the basics of IP addressing. As a network tech, you should be able to perform simple decimal-to-binary and binary-to-decimal conversions.

Learning Objectives

In this lab, you will review the basic rules of IP addressing. When you've completed this lab, you will be able to

- Convert IP addresses and subnet masks from dotted decimal notation to binary values
- Identify IP address class ranges
- Name default subnet masks
- Define network IDs and host IDs
- Validate IP addresses and subnet masks for a given network

Lab Materials and Setup

The materials you'll need for this lab exercise are

- Windows 10 system with Internet connectivity
- Pen or pencil
- Paper

Getting Down to Business

Jonathan has appropriated some funds to set up a small networking lab in one of the spare offices at JSW. It will consist of six Windows 10 machines, three Linux machines (Ubuntu, Kali, CentOS), and a server running Windows Server 2016. For the time being, he has provided a couple of simple eight-port switches and a SOHO router.

Scott recommends that you head up the group to assemble and configure the network. Before working with the hardware, you'll work through the basic configuration of IP addressing. Follow these steps to strengthen your prowess in IP addressing.

Step 1   Scott explains that every TCP/IP network must have a valid network ID and that each device (host) on the network must have a unique host ID on that network. He starts you off with the following network ID and subnet mask.

Network ID	192.	168.	5.	0
Subnet Mask	255.	255.	255.	0

You'll start this exercise by converting the network ID and subnet mask to their binary equivalents. The built-in Windows calculator is an invaluable tool for configuring and converting network IDs, IP addresses, and subnet masks into their rudimentary binary format.

In Windows 10, type **calc** in the Windows Search Box, select Calculator, and press ENTER. Once the Calculator program is up and running, select View from the menu bar and click Programmer to change the view to programmer mode.

By default, the decimal number system is selected. To convert a value from decimal, simply enter the value in decimal, and notice that the number is automatically listed in HEX (hexadecimal, base 16), DEC (decimal, base 10), OCT (octal, base 8), and BIN (binary, base 2), below the textbox, as shown in Figure 6-1.

✔ **Hint**

For accurate results, convert each decimal value one octet at a time rather than entering the entire string of the IP address's digits all at once. Note also that smaller decimal values will generate fewer than eight digits when converted to binary. This is simply the Windows Calculator leaving off the leading zeroes of the binary octet. When this happens, simply "pad" the binary value with enough leading zeroes to bring the total number of digits to eight. For example, the decimal value 46, converted to binary in the Windows Calculator, displays a six-digit binary value of 101110. To bring this value "up to code," add two zeroes at the beginning for a result of 00101110.

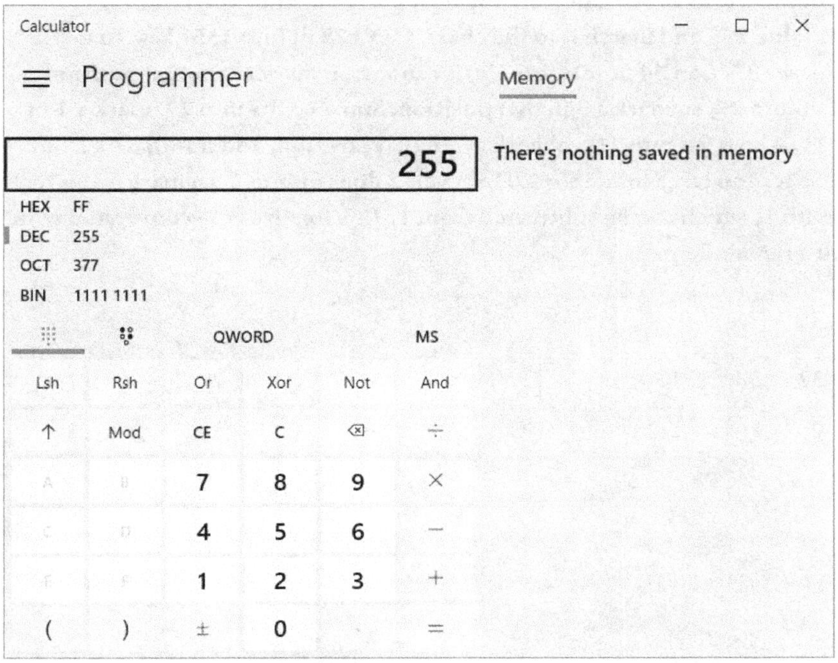

FIGURE 6-1 Converting 255 to other number systems

Network ID	Dotted Decimal Notation	192.	168.	5.	0
	Binary Equivalent				
Subnet Mask	Dotted Decimal Notation	255.	255.	255.	0
	Binary Equivalent				

Step 2   Now close the Windows Calculator and use the following chart to convert the network IDs and subnet masks into binary values the "old-fashioned" way.

2^7	2^6	2^5	2^4	2^3	2^2	2^1	2^0
128	64	32	16	8	4	2	1

✔ **Hint**

The binary system, also referred to as the "base 2 numbering system," is based on powers of 2, just as the decimal system is based on powers of 10. Each digit in this conversion table can be turned "on," represented by a value of 1, or "off," represented by a value of 0, to complete the eight digits contained in a binary octet.

To convert a decimal value to binary using this table, start with 128 and work your way to the right, marking a 1 in each position where your decimal value "fits" and subtracting that value from the decimal total. Then move to the next position, and the next position, until you arrive at 0. For example, take the decimal value 155 and match it to the chart. Can 128 fit into 155? Yes, so mark a 1 in that position. That leaves 27. Can 64 fit into 27? No, it cannot, so mark a 0 in that position. Same for 32—it does not fit into 27, so mark a 0 in that position. Since 16 fits into 27, mark a 1 in that position. This leaves 11. And 8 fits into 11, so mark a 1 in that position. You now have a 3 left. The 4 position gets a 0 since it's too large to fit into 3. However, 2 does fit into 3, so mark a 1 in that position. This leaves you with 1, which can be subtracted from 1. This finalizes the conversion with a 1 in the last position and a remainder of 0.

128	64	32	16	8	4	2	1
1	0	0	1	1	0	1	1

Network ID	Dotted Decimal Notation	10.	0.	0.	0
	Binary Equivalent				
Subnet Mask	Dotted Decimal Notation	255.	0.	0.	0
	Binary Equivalent				
Network ID	Dotted Decimal Notation	172.	16.	0.	0
	Binary Equivalent				
Subnet Mask	Dotted Decimal Notation	255.	255.	0.	0
	Binary Equivalent				

Step 3   Scott wants you to understand how classless addressing works today. Classless addressing, introduced in 1993, replaced the classful addressing that was in place for the previous 10 years, when the world switched to TCP/IP. Scott explains that in order to understand how classless addressing works today, you must understand how classful addressing worked.

Using Google, research the IP address ranges defined by each of the default address classes. In the following table, fill in the appropriate address ranges for each IP address class and identify the private address reserved for that class.

✱ Cross-Reference

Additional information may be found in the "IP Addresses" and "Class IDs" sections of Chapter 6 in the *Mike Meyers' CompTIA Network+ Guide to Managing and Troubleshooting Networks* textbook.

IP Address Class	Public IP Address Range	Private IP Address Range
Class A		
Class B		
Class C		
Class D		
Class E		

Step 4   The IP address classes skip the entire 127.0.0.0–127.255.255.255 range. This is a special range reserved for testing the configuration of TCP/IP on the local machine. 127.0.0.1 is referred to as the loopback address. Open a command prompt and type ping 127.0.0.1. What are the results?

_____

_____

Step 5   Before closing the command prompt, type `ipconfig /all`. What are your PC's IP address and subnet mask? What IP address class would it fit into if classful addressing was used today?

_____

_____

Step 6   Define the function of a subnet mask.

_____

_____

Step 7   In the following table, fill in the appropriate default subnet mask for each IP address class:

IP Address Class	Default Subnet Mask
Class A	
Class B	
Class C	

Step 8   Based on the default subnet masks for the preceding classes, identify the class, network IDs, and host IDs for the following IP address examples:

IP Address	IP Address Class	Network ID	Host ID
131.194.192.3			
45.200.49.201			
194.39.110.183			
208.154.191.9			
126.9.54.172			

Step 9   Classful addressing created networks of different sizes: small, medium, and large.

The default Class A subnet mask is 255.0.0.0, which means the first octet is a network octet (shared by all hosts on the network), and the last three octets are host octets (unique to each host).

Since all Class A networks need to have a first octet value of 1–126, the first octet, in binary, must start with a 0 in binary (the 128s column): 0xxxxxxx. If the other 7 bits in the octet are 0s, that's the value of 0, which is not valid. If the other 7 bits in the octet are 1s, that's 127, which, as mentioned earlier, is reserved. Therefore, we can say that if there are 8 bits in a Class A address that are network bits but the first one is locked in as a 0, there are 7 bits that can vary. The formula for determining how many Class A networks there are is $2^7 = 128$. After throwing away the two invalid numbers (0 and 127), we get 126, which is how many Class A networks there are. On a related note, you won't have to "throw away" any invalid values for Class B or Class C networks.

To figure out how many hosts there can be on a Class A network, we have to raise base 2 to the power of the number of host bits. In this case, it would be $2^{24} = 16,777,216$. Then we throw away two of these addresses, because they can't all be 0s (that's the network ID), and they can't all be 1s (that's the broadcast address), leaving us with 16,777,214.

You wouldn't dream of putting anything close to that number of hosts on a network, but this massive number allows for more flexibility when subnetting (covered later).

Fill in the chart for the corresponding information for Class B and Class C networks.

IP Address Class	Number of Networks	Number of Hosts per Network
Class A	126	16,777,214
Class B		
Class C		

Step 10 Classless Inter-Domain Routing (CIDR) was introduced in 1993 to solve the following three problems, as listed in RFC 1519:

1. Exhaustion of the class B network address space. One fundamental cause of this problem is the lack of a network class of a size which is appropriate for mid-sized organization; class C, with a maximum of 254 host addresses, is too small, while class B, which allows up to 65,534 addresses, is too large for most organizations.

2. Growth of routing tables in Internet routers beyond the ability of current software, hardware, and people to effectively manage.

3. Eventual exhaustion of the 32-bit IP address space. (Fuller, V., Li, T., Yu, J., and K. Varadhan, "Classless Inter-Domain Routing (CIDR): An Address Assignment and Aggregation Strategy", RFC 1519, https://tools.ietf.org/html/rfc1519)

The first problem was solved with concepts known as *subnetting* and *variable-length subnet masking* (*VLSM*). The second problem was solved with a concept known as *supernetting*, and the third problem was solved with a new protocol known as *IPv6*.

Why do you think CIDR was needed so soon (ten years is not a lot of time) after classful addressing was implemented?

_____

_____

Step 11   Explain what is meant by using CIDR notation (for example, /24) following an IP address. For example, what does the value 201.23.45.123/24 represent?

_____

_____

Step 12   Now that you have explored IP addresses and subnet masks, Scott asks you to take a look at some of the network IDs he has configured for the lab network.

The network ID is 192.168.5.0/24.

He asks you to determine if they are valid addresses and, if not, to explain why.

IP Address	Valid/Invalid
192.168.5.10/24	
192.168.6.10/24	
192.168.5.10/24 (again)	
192.168.5.11/26	
192.168.7.12/24	
192.168.5.13/24	
192.168.5.255/24	
172.16.5.15/16	
10.168.5.16/8	
192.168.5.0/24	

 30 MINUTES

Lab Exercise 6.02: Configuring IP Addresses and Subnet Masks

Having now spent some time working through the concepts of IP addressing and subnet masks, it is time to build and configure the lab network. The addressing scheme will vary from one network administrator to another, but all will have some logic to the class range and assignment that they use. Jonathan has already provided the network ID and subnet mask of 192.168.5.0/24. Now it is up to you to choose how to assign individual host addresses. You will work through planning the address scheme, connecting the hardware, and then configuring each machine's TCP/IP properties to communicate on the network.

Learning Objectives

In this lab, you will configure the IP addresses and subnet masks for a small lab network. When you've completed this lab, you will be able to

- Assemble the hardware (computers, cabling, and switches) in a small network environment

- Determine an addressing scheme for the 192.168.5.0/24 network you have been provided

- Configure IP addresses and subnet masks

- Confirm connectivity between machines on the specified network

Lab Materials and Setup

The materials you'll need for this lab exercise are

- Two Windows 10 systems

- Ethernet switch and eight UTP straight-through cables

- Pen or pencil

- Paper

→ **Note**

For the purposes of this lab exercise, students may build a lab setup similar to the lab setup described in the JSW scenario or apply the steps to the classroom lab setup as directed by the instructor. The speed of the switches and NICs and the category of UTP cabling are not critical as long as connectivity can be established.

Getting Down to Business

You will begin this exercise with the assembly of a small lab network using a switch and two Windows 10 computers. You will then calculate the range of host addresses that you will assign to the computers.

When network administrators plan out their network addressing scheme, they always work to have expansion planned into the design. Typically, a range of addresses will be set aside for routers, servers, and printers. Over the years, depending on the overall population of the network, I have used a methodology in which the first 10 addresses are reserved for routers, the last 20 to 50 addresses for servers, and 10 to 20 addresses below the servers for printers.

For example, the network of 192.168.5.0/24 might be distributed as follows:

Routers: 192.168.5.1–192.168.5.10

Clients: 192.168.5.11–192.168.5.212

Printers: 192.168.5.213–192.168.5.232

Servers: 192.168.5.233–192.168.5.254

However, there is no requirement to assign any device any specific host address. That's completely up to you.

After planning the network addressing scheme, you'll configure each machine with an appropriate static address and subnet mask and then test the connectivity.

Step 1   Utilizing the lab hardware provided by your instructor, assemble the computers into a small network connected via UTP straight-through cables to the Ethernet switch. Alternatively, the instructor may have students utilize the existing classroom computers and network to facilitate the lab exercises.

Step 2   Now calculate the IP addresses and subnet masks for each of the host computers on this network. The network administrator has reserved the addresses from 192.168.5.1/24 through 192.168.5.10/24 for routers, 192.168.5.220/24 through 192.168.5.229/24 for printers, and 192.168.5.230/24 through 192.168.5.254/24 for servers.

Pay careful attention to these reserved addresses, and avoid assigning duplicate addresses, as they will create TCP/IP conflicts on the network.

Host Computer	IP Address	Subnet Mask
Windows 10 Computer A		
Windows 10 Computer B		

Step 3 With your documentation in hand, go through the following substeps:

   a. Open up the first Windows 10 machine.

   b. In the Windows search box, type **sharing**.

   c. Click Manage Advanced Sharing Settings, which will appear as the top choice, in the dynamically generated menu.

   d. In the address bar at the top, click Network And Sharing Center.

   e. In the pane at the left, click Change Adapter Settings.

   f. Right-click Ethernet and select Properties.

   g. Select Internet Protocol Version 4 (TCP/IPv4) and click the Properties button.

   h. In the General tab, which will open by default, change the radio button selection to Use The Following IP Address. Configure the Windows 10 machine with the IP address and subnet mask that you determined in the previous step. Set the Default Gateway IP Address to **192.168.5.1** (set it even though we don't have a router in place).

   i. In the next section on the dialog box, make sure Use The Following DNS Server Addresses is also selected. Assign **9.9.9.9** as the Preferred DNS Server, and **8.8.8.8** as the Alternate DNS Server.

   j. Click the OK button, and then click the next OK button.

See Figure 6-2 to see how your configuration should look.

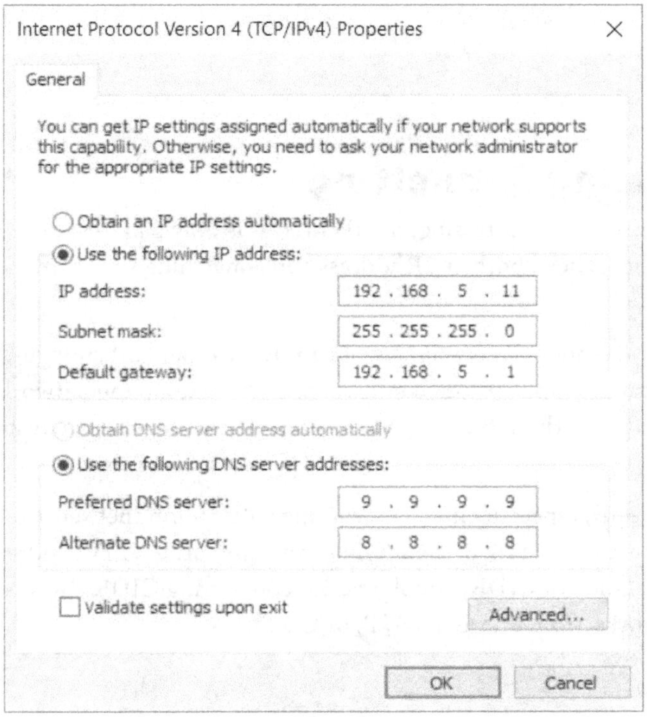

FIGURE 6-2 Configuration of Windows 10 Computer A

Step 4   Repeat the configuration steps with Windows 10 Computer B.

Step 5   Open up a command prompt on the first Windows 10 machine. Type ping followed by the IP address of the second Windows 10 machine, and press ENTER (for example, ping 192.168.1.12). Now, send a ping from the second Windows 10 machine to the first Windows 10 machine. Were the pings successful?

You might have to disable firewalls on the machines to let the pings through, by typing **Firewall** into the Windows search box, selecting Windows Defender Firewall, clicking Turn Windows Defender Firewall On Or Off, and clicking all radio buttons next to Turn Off Windows Defender Firewall (Not Recommended). These machines are not connected to the Internet, so it's fine. Furthermore, in Chapter 19, "Protecting Your Network," we'll see how to add rules that let pings through, instead of disabling the firewall altogether, which is obviously a better approach.

The ping utility is a great diagnostic tool that allows a network host to ask another device "Can you hear me?" by sending ICMP (Internet Control Message Protocol) Echo request packets. If the pinged device can hear the pings, it replies with "Yes, I can hear you" by sending ICMP Echo reply packets. Much more on ping and ICMP itself will be discussed later.

_____

_____

 45 MINUTES

Lab Exercise 6.03: Configuring Subnetting

As you learned in Lab Exercise 6.01, when it comes to IP addressing, the IP address is only half the story. The other component is the subnet mask. Network hosts need both an IP address and a matching subnet mask in order to communicate on a network.

Up to now, you have only explored IP addresses and subnet masks that conform to standard configurations for each major IP address class. Network techs can also use custom configurations that extend the network ID portion of the subnet mask into the host ID portion of the subnet mask, creating what are affectionately known as *subnets*.

Depending on your particular IP network needs, especially if you're working with an Internet service provider (ISP), you will need to become familiar with the task of identifying and configuring CIDR addresses and subnet masks. To develop a deeper understanding of CIDR, you'll practice configuring CIDR addresses and subnet masks, which create additional networks, from one Class A, B, or C address.

Learning Objectives

In this lab, you will explore CIDR. When you've completed this lab, you will be able to

- Define a custom subnet mask
- Calculate custom subnet masks and the total number of network IDs and host IDs they define for each IP address class
- Define a CIDR address to provide a specific number of networks for future lab exercises

Lab Materials and Setup

The materials you'll need for this lab exercise are

- Pen or pencil
- Paper

Getting Down to Business

While working on the configuration of the lab machines in the previous exercise, you may have noticed that all of the addresses are on the same network. You know that in the near future, you would like to expand to additional networks, separated by routers, but Jonathan has provided only the Class C network ID of 192.168.5.0/24.

Scott would like you to explore using subnetting to create multiple networks from the one Class C address, dividing the lab network into several subnets.

✖ Cross-Reference

To prepare for the following lab steps, review the "CIDR and Subnetting" section of Chapter 6 of the *Mike Meyers' Network+ Guide to Managing and Troubleshooting Networks* textbook. As a brief review, CIDR and subnetting are virtually the same thing. Subnetting is done by an organization—it is given a block of addresses and then breaks the single block of addresses into multiple subnets. CIDR is done by an ISP—it is given a block of addresses, subnets the block into multiple subnets, and then passes out the smaller individual subnets to customers.

Step 1   What is the motivation behind using a custom subnet mask versus a default subnet mask?

_____

_____

Step 2   To get you started with some calculations, Scott presents you with the Class B network ID of 165.1.0.0/16. How many hosts can this network support?

_____

_____

✔ **Hint**

To determine the number of hosts supported by a network (or subnet), convert the 32-bit subnet value to binary, and separate the network portion from the host portion. Count the number of bits in the 0 ("off") position in the host portion of the subnet mask. Then use the formula $2^x - 2$, with x being the number of bits. Using a default Class C subnet mask as an example, note that there are 8 bits in the 0 position in the host portion, so $2^8 - 2 = 254$ possible hosts. We always subtract 2, because all host bits can't be 0 (that represents the Network ID) and all host bits can't be 1 (that represents a broadcast address for that subnet).

Step 3   Using the same address of 165.1.0.0/16, subdivide the network into at least five subnets. You need to configure the subnet mask to create an extension of the network ID, allowing for additional subnets. How many bits of the host portion of the subnet mask do you need to "borrow"? What will the resultant subnet mask be in decimal value? How many hosts will each subnet support?

_____

✔ **Hint**

To determine the number of bits to borrow from the host portion of the subnet mask, first convert the subnet mask into binary. Then separate the network portion from the host portion. Using the formula 2^y = number of subnets, calculate the number of bits you will have to borrow from the host portion in order to support the number of subnets that are needed.

For example, to define at least 12 subnets for a Class C network using the default subnet mask of 255.255.255.0, convert the subnet mask to binary: 11111111.11111111.11111111.0000 0000. Separate the network portion (11111111.11111111.11111111) from the host portion (00000000). Now calculate the number of bits to borrow. Using the formula 2^y, plug in successive numbers of bits until you arrive at the number that provides 12 or more subnets. Using 2^4, you will arrive at 16 subnets.

The host portion of the subnet mask is now 11110000 in binary. To determine the decimal value of the subnet mask, add together the numeric value of each borrowed binary bit. With the first four bits of the host portion of the subnet mask borrowed, add 128 + 64 + 32 + 16 for a decimal value of 240. Append the default subnet mask with this value (that is, 255.255.255.240).

Step 4 Using the techniques practiced in the preceding steps, create a table of the custom subnet masks. Include the appropriate values for both the binary and decimal representations; number of subnets; and the number of Class A, Class B, and Class C hosts for each subnet mask. The first two subnets have been calculated already as examples.

Subnet Mask Host Portion With:	Binary and Decimal Value of Subnet	# Subnets	# Class A Hosts	# Class B Hosts	# Class C Hosts
No bits borrowed	.0 (00000000)	$1(2^0)$	16,777,214 $(2^{24} - 2)$	65,534 $(2^{16} - 2)$	254 $(2^8 - 2)$
One bit borrowed	.128 (10000000)	$2(2^1)$	8,388,606 $(2^{23} - 2)$	32,766 $(2^{15} - 2)$	126 $(2^7 - 2)$
Two bits borrowed					
Three bits borrowed					
Four bits borrowed					
Five bits borrowed					
Six bits borrowed					
Seven bits borrowed					
Eight bits borrowed					

Step 5 Take the original network ID of 192.168.5.0/24 and calculate the custom subnet mask to produce at least five subnets for the lab network.

Document the total number of bits "masked" for the network ID and record the subnet mask for this custom subnet mask.

_____

_____

✔ **Hint**

To define the network ID, host address range, and broadcast address for each subnet, you first must determine something known as the multiplier, spacing, and magic number. It's just the column of the furthermost right one bit. This defines the spacing between each subnet. Begin with the original network ID (this example uses 192.168.5.0/26) and convert the subnet mask into binary as follows:

Dotted Decimal Notation	255.	255.	255.	192
Binary Equivalent	11111111.	11111111.	11111111.	1100000000

Now identify the furthermost right one bit and convert it to its decimal equivalent, in this case, 64. This is the number you will use to increment each network. This produces the following table of subnets:

Subnet ID	First Host Address	Last Host Address	Broadcast Address
192.168.5.0/26	192.168.5.1	192.168.5.62	192.168.5.63
192.168.5.64/26	192.168.5.65	192.168.5.126	192.168.5.127
192.168.5.128/26	192.168.5.129	192.168.5.190	192.168.5.191
192.168.5.192/26	192.168.5.193	192.168.5.254	192.168.5.255

Now take the network ID and subnet mask you defined earlier to produce at least five subnets. Using the method just described, define the subnet, host address range, and broadcast address of each subnet and record it in the following table:

Subnet ID	First Host Address	Last Host Address	Broadcast Address

 45 MINUTES

Lab Exercise 6.04: Local vs. Remote IP Addresses: The Function of the Default Gateway

So far, so good! You just finished configuring two computers in a small LAN and validated that they can communicate using IP addresses. Now it is time to expand your horizons, so to speak, and facilitate communication beyond the LAN. Wise network techs, after plowing through the "bits" and pieces of configuring IP addresses and subnet masks, inevitably ask themselves, "Why am I doing this again?" It's a valid question, because when your brain is overheating from converting decimal to binary and calculating subnet network IDs and host IDs, it's easy to lose sight of the real purpose behind all of these mathematical gymnastics. The answer is deceptively simple: to distinguish between local and remote network addresses!

That's right. The whole point of all the previous ciphering and decimal-to-binary flip-flopping is to tell the network host how to distinguish between packets meant for the LAN and those meant to go beyond the LAN. In the following exercises, you'll review how a network host uses the IP address and subnet mask to determine if a packet is meant for the local or remote network and how packets that are meant for remote networks get there. Then, with the help of your instructor, you'll add a router to your lab and configure PCs on both sides to enable communication between the different networks.

Learning Objectives

In this lab, you will examine how computers communicate beyond the local area network and configure a router to implement that communication. When you've completed this lab, you will be able to

- Define how a network host distinguishes between local and remote addresses

- Describe the function of a default gateway

- Configure PCs on different networks to communicate through a router

Lab Materials and Setup

The materials you'll need for this lab exercise are

- Two Windows 10 systems

- The Ethernet switch from Lab Exercise 6.02 and a second Ethernet switch

- Wired or wireless router

- UTP straight-through cables to connect the PCs to the switches and the switches to the router

- Pen or pencil

- Paper

✖ **Cross-Reference**

To complete the steps contained in this lab, students may expand on the lab setup from Lab Exercise 6.02 or apply the steps to the classroom lab setup as directed by the instructor. The router can be a simple wireless router from Linksys or NETGEAR (currently, you'll only be using the wired interfaces on the router) or a fully functional Cisco Systems or Juniper Networks router. The router may be configured by the instructor, or you may want to jump ahead to Lab Exercise 7.02, where you will practice the configuration of routers.

Getting Down to Business

It's time to expand your lab's LAN beyond itself, with the introduction of a router and a remote network. Before you assemble the hardware, cabling, and additional machines, you'll calculate how computers on one network know whether data is for them or for a different network. You will then explore how computers on different networks send data to each other. Finally, you'll set up an addressing scheme for the remote network and configure the router and hosts.

Step 1   Describe the process that a network host uses to determine whether a packet is local or remote. Provide an example using the following IP addresses:

- Source IP address 188.254.200.13/28
- Destination IP address 188.254.157.9/28

_____

_____

✔ **Hint**

To determine if an IP address is local or remote, you must first convert the IP addresses and subnet masks to their binary values. You then perform the logic AND operation on the IP addresses and subnet masks for each of the nodes and compare the results. If the results are the same (all 1s and 0s match), the hosts are on the same network. If the results do not match, the hosts are on different networks.

The actual ANDing operation to determine if a destination host is local or remote is performed internally in the sending host. It is a complex process involving ANDing the destination host's IP address against entries in the sending host's routing table. This example is an extremely simplified method and is included for educational purposes only.

In the logical AND operation, 0 AND 0 = 0, 1 AND 0 = 0, 0 AND 1 = 0, and 1 AND 1 = 1.
For example:

Host IP Address (192.168.5.98)	11000000.10101000.00000101.01100010
Host Subnet Mask (255.255.255.224)	11111111.11111111.11111111.11100000
ANDed Result	11000000.10101000.00000101.01100000

Data Packet Destination IP Address (192.168.5.131)	11000000.10101000.00000101.10000011
Host Subnet Mask (255.255.255.224)	11111111.11111111.11111111.11100000
ANDed Result	11000000.10101000.00000101.10000000

Host ANDed Result	11000000.10101000.00000101.01100000
Destination ANDed Result	11000000.10101000.00000101.10000000
Result	Results do not match = remote address

Step 2   Compare the following IP addresses and determine whether they are local or remote:

Host IP Address	Host Subnet Mask	Destination IP Address	Local or Remote?
a) 210.145.149.123	255.255.255.0	210.145.253.199	
b) 192.168.4.189	255.255.255.224	192.168.1.107	
c) 10.154.187.89	255.192.0.0	10.152.179.88	
d) 132.100.45.5	255.255.252.0	132.100.45.45	
e) 151.251.100.101	255.255.0.0	166.200.110.10	

✔ **Hint**

A good online subnet calculator is available here:
www.subnetonline.com/pages/subnet-calculators/ip-subnet-calculator.php

Step 3   When a network host determines that a packet is intended for a remote network, what does it do with the packet?

_____

_____

Step 4   Name two ways that a network host can be configured with the IP address of its default gateway.

_____

_____

Step 5   What is the function of the default gateway?

_____

_____

Step 6   The goal of the new setup is to have Windows 10 Machine A plugged into a switch, which will be connected into a router interface, and Windows 10 Machine B plugged into a different switch, which will be plugged into a different router interface on the same router.

If you're using a SOHO router (which has a built-in switch), plug one of the switches into the port marked WAN or Internet, and the other switch into any other port (which will be a switch port).

Step 7   Jonathan has established the following network IDs:

Network 1: 192.168.5.32/27

Network 2: 192.168.5.96/27

He has also reserved the first address in each range for the IP address of each network's default gateway. The Network 1 default gateway IP address is 192.168.5.33/27, and the Network 2 default gateway IP address is 192.168.5.97/27. Now he would like you to configure each machine on each network with an appropriate IP address, subnet mask, and default gateway.

As in Lab Exercise 6.02, pay careful attention to reserved addresses (such as the router interfaces) and avoid assigning duplicate addresses, as they will create TCP/IP conflicts on the network.

How did you configure each machine on each network?

_____

_____

_____

_____

Step 8   Have each machine ping the other machine (on the remote network) as well as its default gateway. Were the pings successful?

_____

_____

Step 9   On each of the Windows 10 machines, open a command prompt and type `ipconfig /all`. What is the IP address of each machine's default gateway?

_____

_____

 30 **MINUTES**

Lab Exercise 6.05: Packet Sniffing; IP Addresses and MAC Addresses Working Together

Some people like to sniff glue. Some people like to sniff paint. Some professors like to sniff whiteboard markers! Some people like to sniff…other things. What about me? Well, there's something that I love to sniff more than anything else in the whole world—packets!

Of course, IP packets, which exist at Layer 3 of the OSI model, are encapsulated inside of Layer 2 frames. On wired LANs, they are Ethernet frames. On wireless LANs, they are 802.11 frames. In the context of capturing and analyzing network traffic, though, even though the lowest unit to analyze is the frame, it's still called packet sniffing.

Wouldn't it be nice if we knew about every single detail about every little thing that entered and exited our body? Every liquid, solid, or gas. Every molecule. Every atom. Well, in the wonderful world of digital networking, we can do the equivalent! Every single bit, all the 1s and 0s that go in and out of an NIC (Network Interface Card), can be seen and analyzed. There is an option to see them in true binary, even hexadecimal, but as humans, we prefer a format that is more intuitive. A packet sniffer, implemented in software or hardware, will not only intercept and log all the 1s and 0s moving in and out of a NIC, but show it to us humans in a human-readable format in addition to binary and hexadecimal. All of the fields of every single frame, packet, segment, datagram, and upper-layer data will be shown with their names, along with their corresponding data values. For example, in the IP packet, you'll see the source IP address with a value like 192.168.1.113, and the destination IP address with a value like 192.168.1.107. You'll see the content as it's listed in the RFC or other specifications.

Packet sniffers can provide so much insight to network traffic. This impressive list of functions of packet sniffers can be found on Wikipedia:

- Analyze network problems

- Detect network intrusion attempts

- Detect network misuse by internal and external users

- Documenting regulatory compliance through logging all perimeter and endpoint traffic

- Gain information for effecting a network intrusion

- Isolate exploited systems

- Monitor WAN bandwidth utilization

- Monitor network usage (including internal and external users and systems)

- Monitor data-in-motion

- Monitor WAN and endpoint security status

- Gather and report network statistics

- Filter suspect content from network traffic

- Serve as primary data source for day-to-day network monitoring and management

- Spy on other network users and collect sensitive information such as login details or users cookies (depending on any content encryption methods that may be in use)

- Reverse engineer proprietary protocols used over the network

- Debug client/server communications

- Debug network protocol implementations

- Verify adds, moves, and changes

- Verify internal control system effectiveness (firewalls, access control, Web filter, spam filter, proxy) (Wikipedia, "Packet analyzer" entry, https://en.wikipedia.org/wiki/Packet_analyzer)

While there are a few dozen packet sniffers, some with specialized purposes, there is one that stands above the rest. From Wireshark's Web site:

> Wireshark is the world's foremost and widely-used network protocol analyzer. It lets you see what's happening on your network at a microscopic level and is the de facto (and often de jure) standard across many commercial and non-profit enterprises, government agencies, and educational institutions. Wireshark development thrives thanks to the volunteer contributions of networking experts around the globe and is the continuation of a project started by Gerald Combs in 1998.

I agree!

✔ **Tech Tip**

The terms *frame* and *packet* are often used interchangeably. However, this is incorrect. Frames are found at Layer 2, while packets are found at Layer 3. You should use the proper terms!

Learning Objectives

In this lab, you'll install and run the Wireshark packet sniffer application, use it to capture data from your network, and examine the captured data. When you've completed this lab, you will be able to

- Perform a live capture of network traffic
- Examine the captured data to view each frame's contents, specifically focusing on ARP and ICMP

Lab Materials and Setup

The materials you'll need for this lab are

- Windows 10 system with Internet connectivity

Getting Down to Business

The source of traffic knows its MAC address and IP address, but before any traffic can be sent, that host needs to have a destination MAC address and a destination IP address to send traffic to. The host will know the destination's IP address. It will either just have that IP address or DNS (Domain Name System), coming up in Chapter 9, will resolve an FQDN (fully qualified domain name) into its corresponding IP address. Getting the destination MAC address, though, is a different story, made possible by a protocol called ARP (Address Resolution Protocol). In fact, the process differs for local communication (meant for a device on the same network) and remote communication (meant for a device on a different network).

In this lab exercise, you will explore the mechanics of ARP (Address Resolution Protocol) and ICMP (Internet Control Message Protocol) and dissect network traffic to fully understand the relationship between IP addresses and MAC addresses.

To make a detailed analysis of network traffic, you must install Wireshark on one of the networked PCs.

Step 1   Follow these steps to download and install Wireshark:

    a.   Go to www.wireshark.org and click on the Download Get Started Now button.

    b.   On the Download Wireshark page, click the link for the 64-bit Windows Installer.

    c.   Download the Wireshark executable installation file (the current version at the time of this writing is 2.4.5) to your Downloads folder.

    d.   Double-click the Wireshark installation file to start the installation wizard, and follow the prompts, accepting all defaults, to complete the installation.

Step 2   Start the Wireshark packet sniffer by typing **Wireshark** into the Windows search box and clicking on Wireshark. All you have to do to start sniffing is to double-click on the NIC you want to capture traffic from, as shown in Figure 6-3.

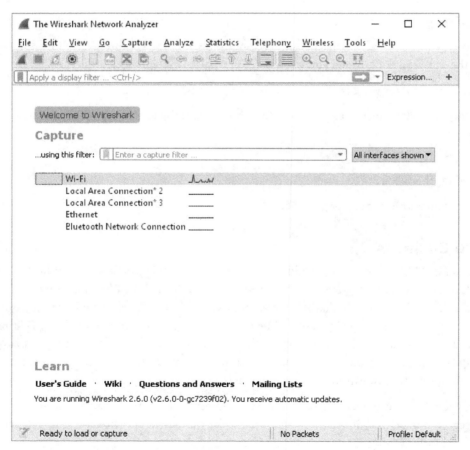

FIGURE 6-3 Welcome to Wireshark!

Step 3 Notice the Wireshark window is divided into three panes. The top section is the Packet List pane, which lists a summary of each frame captured. The middle section is the Packet Details pane, which displays details of each captured frame. The bottom section is the Packet Bytes pane, which shows hexadecimal values of captured data. The right side of the bottom section will show the ASCII/Unicode values for the hex values, even if the hex values are not meant to be translated into ASCII/Unicode. When you see a dot, it means that there is no ASCII/Unicode equivalent. Other times you'll see ASCII/Unicode translations that make no sense because they weren't meant to be translated.

Step 4 Computers and devices generate a large amount of network traffic just establishing communications. To clear away some of these packets from the view of your capture, you are going to apply a filter. In the display filter on the toolbar, enter the following string: **arp or icmp** (this is case-sensitive, use only lowercase letters) and press ENTER (or click the Apply button). This will filter out all other traffic except ARP frames (ARP exists at Layer 2) or ICMP packets (ICMP exists at Layer 3) from the displayed traffic, although Wireshark will continue to capture everything.

Step 5 Now to see a concrete example of a capture, stop the running capture by clicking the red square (second icon from left), and then click the blue shark fin (first icon from the left) to start a new capture. Click the Continue Without Saving button.

Now, open a command prompt, type `ping`, followed by a space, and the hostname or IP address of a PC on your network. To ping a PC with the host name bob, for example, type `ping  bob` and press the ENTER key. The following text shows sample output from the `ping` command:

```
C:\>ping bob
Pinging bob [192.168.5.13] with 32 bytes of data:
Reply from 192.168.5.13: bytes=32 time=110ms TTL=48
Reply from 192.168.5.13: bytes=32 time=115ms TTL=48
Reply from 192.168.5.13: bytes=32 time=107ms TTL=48
Reply from 192.168.5.13: bytes=32 time=111ms TTL=48
Ping statistics for 192.168.5.13:
        Packets: Sent = 4, Received = 4, Lost = 0 (0% loss)
Approximate round trip times in milli-seconds:
        Minimum = 107ms, Maximum = 115ms, Average = 110ms
```

Since you probably don't have DNS set up at this point, ping another machine on your network by its IP address. What are the results of your ping operation?

_____

_____

_____

_____

Step 6   Close the command-line window by typing `exit` at the prompt. In Wireshark, click the Stop button (the red square, second from the left on the toolbar) to stop the capture. Now it's time to analyze the captured traffic for the ping operation you just ran.

Step 7   Packet sniffers can capture hundreds of frames in just a matter of seconds, especially if left in promiscuous mode, so applying the **arp or icmp** filter should help you to easily identify the traffic you want to analyze. The important information you are interested in for this Lab Exercise are the frames containing ARP (Address Resolution Protocol). There should be two lines of ARP frames displaying IP addresses and the MAC addresses to which they resolve, followed by eight lines of ICMP packets showing the results of the ping (see Figure 6-4, which has the answer to the question, highlighted). Did you get similar results?

_____

_____

_____

_____

If, when you display the capture information, no ARP frames are displayed, it may be caused by one of two situations. First, if you have been communicating with the target machine prior to the capture, there may be entries in the ARP cache. Open a command prompt and run the following command to see all (`-a` stands for all) entries in the ARP cache.

```
C:\>arp -a
```

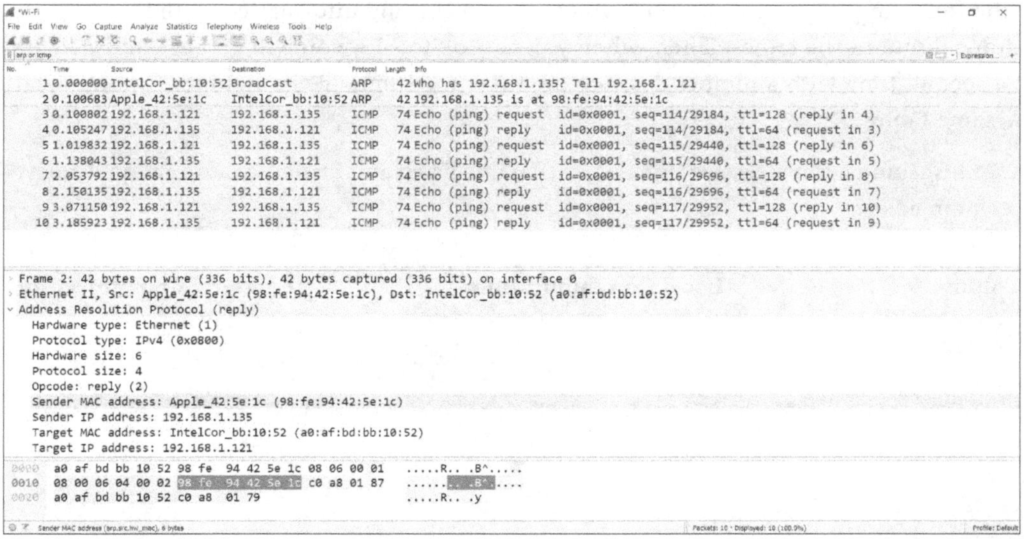

FIGURE 6-4 ARPs and ICMPs

If the following information (or similar with the IP address of your target machine) is displayed, you have an entry in the ARP cache:

```
Interface: 192.168.5.12 --- 0x3
Internet Address          Physical Address
192.168.5.12              00-0e-28-92-ac-b7
```

Once two machines have communicated, they will place entries into the ARP cache to avoid generating broadcast traffic. The entries can remain anywhere from 2 to 20 minutes depending on the operating system. In this Lab Exercise, you want to create ARP broadcast traffic to capture, so you'll want to delete (-d stands for delete) the entries in the ARP cache. To clear the ARP cache entries, use the following command. You will need to run the command prompt in elevated mode (as Administrator). When opening the command prompt, right-click cmd.exe and select Run As Administrator from the drop-down menu.

```
C:\>arp -d
```

To verify the ARP cache is cleared, type arp -a once again. Your results should match the following output:

```
C:\>arp -a
No ARP Entries Found
```

The second situation could be an incorrectly entered filter setting in Wireshark. Open Wireshark and examine both the Capture and Display filters. Confirm that the **arp or icmp** filter has been selected in the display filter.

Step 8   For the following steps up to Step 12, you will be recording information in the Local Communication column in the tables. Then, when you get to Step 13, you will go back and perform Steps 5 to 12 a second time with a remote destination, this time filling in the Remote Communication column in the same tables.

In the Packet List summary pane, select the first ARP frame listed and fill in the information displayed in the following column fields:

Packet List Column	Local Communication	Remote Communication
No. (Number)		
Time		
Source		
Destination		
Protocol		
Length		
Info		

Step 9   In the Packet Details pane, you'll see a wealth of information, including the Ethernet frame that contains some of the information that you viewed in Step 9 in the Packet List pane. Clicking the small plus sign (+) at the beginning of each line expands it into a Packet Details showing details. Expand the Frame (summary information from Wireshark), Ethernet II (the actual Ethernet frame), and Address Resolution Protocol (Request) tree listings (ARP is encapsulated inside the Ethernet frame at Layer 2).

Look at the fields in the Address Resolution Protocol (request) section. The Hardware type is Ethernet. This might strike you as odd if you captured on a wireless device, especially when you notice in the capture that the ARP frame is encapsulated inside of an Ethernet frame. This is explained on the Wireshark Wiki page:

> 802.11 adapters often transform 802.11 data packets into fake Ethernet packets before supplying them to the host, and, even if they don't, the drivers for the adapters often do so before supplying the packets to the operating system's networking stack and packet capture mechanism.

> This means that if you capture on an 802.11 network, the packets will look like Ethernet packets, and you won't be able to see all the fields in the 802.11 header. (Wireshark Wiki, "Packet Types," https://wiki .wireshark.org/CaptureSetup/WLAN#Packet_Types)

The Protocol type field lists IPv4.

Hardware size (6) and Protocol size (4) list how long MAC addresses (hardware) and IP addresses (protocol) are.

The Opcode for a request is 1, while the Opcode for a reply is 2.

Using the other fields in the ARP frame, fill in the following information:

ARP Row Field	Local Communication	Remote Communication
Sender MAC address		
Sender IP address		
Target MAC address		
Target IP address		

Now look just above the Address Resolution Protocol (Request) section, and you'll notice the Ethernet II section. This is the actual Ethernet frame. Fill in the information displayed in the following row fields:

Ethernet II Row Field	Local Communication	Remote Communication
Destination		
Source		
Type		

What's the difference between Target MAC address in the ARP section and Destination in the Ethernet header? Why is this so?

_____

_____

Step 10 In the Packet List summary pane, select the very next ARP frame listed (which should be an ARP reply to the ARP request) and fill in the information displayed in the following column fields:

Packet List Column	Local Communication	Remote Communication
No. (Number)		
Time		
Source		
Destination		
Protocol		
Length		
Info		

Step 11   In the Packet Details pane, expand the Frame (summary information from Wireshark), Ethernet II (the actual Ethernet frame), and Address Resolution Protocol (Reply) tree listings (ARP is encapsulated inside the Ethernet frame at Layer 2).

Look at the fields in the Address Resolution Protocol (Reply) section, and fill in the information displayed in the following row fields:

ARP Row Field	Local Communication	Remote Communication
Sender MAC address		
Sender IP address		
Target MAC address		
Target IP address		

Now look just above the Address Resolution Protocol (Request) section, and you'll notice the Ethernet II section. This is the actual Ethernet frame. Fill in the information displayed in the following row fields:

Ethernet II Row Field	Local Communication	Remote Communication
Destination		
Source		
Type		

What's the difference again between Target MAC address in the ARP section and Destination in the Ethernet header? Why is this so?

_____

_____

Step 12   In the Packet List section, directly underneath the ARP request and ARP reply, you should see the four sets of ICMP Echo requests and ICMP Echo replies. In the Info section they are listed as Echo (ping) request and Echo (ping) reply.

In the Packet Details section, you'll notice that, unlike before (with the ARPs), there is now an IP header inside of the Ethernet frame. Inside the IP header is the ICMP header and the ICMP data.

For now, just look at the gray section headers, without expanding the small plus signs (+). If you expanded them and they are now small minus signs (−), you'll can click the minus signs to collapse them back, or just view the gray section headers with the fields expanded.

The purpose of ARP (and of this exercise up until now) was to find the MAC address for the IP address that we wanted to contact. Now, while the ICMP Echo request is selected, using the information in the Ethernet II frame header and the Internet Protocol Version 4 header, fill in the following information:

Ethernet II	Local Communication	Remote Communication
Destination		
Source		
Type		

Internet Protocol Version 4	Local Communication	Remote Communication
Source		
Destination		

Step 13   Now you are going to repeat Steps 3 through 12. However, this time you will use the address of a computer on a remote network. Fill in the previous tables again, but this time use the Remote Communication column. If you don't have another network with a router set up, you can ping a Web server, like www.yahoo.com or www.google.com.

To make sure you see the ARPs, this time, make sure to start the capture first, then type arp -d, and immediately after type ping www.google.com. This is necessary, because some routers are configured to send gratuitous ARPs every two seconds (to prevent an attack called ARP spoofing and ARP cache poisoning). If that ARP gets to your machine after you clear your ARP cache but before you send the ping to the remote host, your machine will not send an ARP, because it will already have the gateway's MAC address from the gratuitous ARP. Another way to do this would be to make a batch file by typing notepad pinger.bat at the command prompt. When Notepad opens up, add the following two lines:

```
arp -d
ping www.google.com
```

Save the file and exit Notepad.

Now, from the command prompt, type pinger (with or without the .bat extension, it makes no difference). This is a guaranteed way to capture the relevant ARPs!

Compare your results to the data you captured for the ping to the machine on the local network. What are the differences?

_____

_____

_____

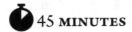45 MINUTES

Lab Exercise 6.06: Static IP Addressing vs. Dynamic IP Addressing

One of the reasons that TCP/IP is so widely adopted is that it's extremely flexible. The TCP/IP protocol suite not only works on any number of computer platforms and applications but also interfaces with a variety of advanced network services. One of these important services is the Dynamic Host Configuration Protocol (DHCP) IP addressing service. DHCP provides valuable functions that make your job as a network tech easier. In this lab exercise, you will take a look at what DHCP does, how you configure your host to use DHCP, and how DHCP actually works. You will then examine what happens if the DHCP server goes down or becomes unavailable.

Learning Objectives

In this lab, you will explore and configure the various components of the DHCP client. When you have completed this lab, you will be able to

- Describe the functions of the DHCP service

- Configure PCs to use DHCP

- Diagram how DHCP works between a DHCP client and DHCP server

- Customize a Windows client to use DHCP and static IP information for unique situations

- Recognize some typical DHCP problems and know how to deal with them

Lab Materials and Setup

The materials you will need for this lab are

- Windows 10 system

- DHCP server (the service running on a router or a Windows Server)

- Pen or pencil

- Paper

✖ Cross-Reference

These steps again utilize the lab setup from Lab Exercise 6.02. As before, you may perform these steps on the classroom network as directed by the instructor. The DHCP server services may be enabled on the router, or a server may be added to the network (for example, Windows Server 2016). For the purposes of this lab, DHCP need only be enabled on the LAN network. The instructor should configure the DHCP server for proper operation.

Getting Down to Business

Up to now, you have configured all of the IP addresses, subnet masks, and default gateways manually. This is known as *static IP addressing*. Imagine, though, if instead of ten computers on a two-subnet network, you were responsible for managing thousands of devices (computers, servers, printers, tablets, mobile devices, and so on) on hundreds of networks. The documentation alone would be staggering! DHCP to the rescue!

Jonathan stops by to see how the network lab is shaping up just as you are setting up for some DHCP exercises. He conveys to you that the inspection facilities are actually experiencing problems that seem to be related to DHCP. Some of the systems are intermittently receiving APIPA (Automatic Private IP Addressing) addresses, signifying no connection to a DHCP server. He also states that some of the systems are being assigned IP addresses with the wrong network ID! Jonathan compliments you on the progress with the network lab and asks you to run a few tests to see if you can re-create the problems over at the inspection facilities.

Step 1   Describe the function of the DHCP service on a TCP/IP network.

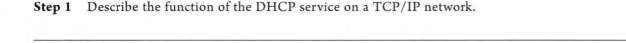

Step 2   With the assistance of your instructor, enable the DHCP service on the router. Optionally, you may add a Windows server and enable the DHCP role on the physical server.

Step 3   Perform the following substeps to configure a Windows 10 system for DHCP:

   a.   Open up the first Windows 10 machine.

   b.   In the Windows search box, type **sharing**.

   c.   Click Manage Advanced Sharing Settings, which will appear as the top choice, in the dynamically generated menu.

   d.   In the address bar at the top, click Network And Sharing Center.

   e.   In the pane at the left, click Change Adapter Settings.

   f.   Right-click Ethernet and select Properties.

   g.   Select Internet Protocol Version 4 (TCP/IPv4) and click the Properties button.

   h.   In the General tab, which will open by default, change the radio button selection to Obtain An IP Address Automatically.

   i.   In the next section on the dialog box, make sure Obtain DNS Server Address Automatically is also selected.

   j.   Click the OK button, and then click the next OK button.

Step 4   To view your PC's TCP/IP configuration, including advanced settings such as its DHCP server IP address, type `ipconfig /all` at the command prompt. What is the IP address of your DHCP server?

_____

_____

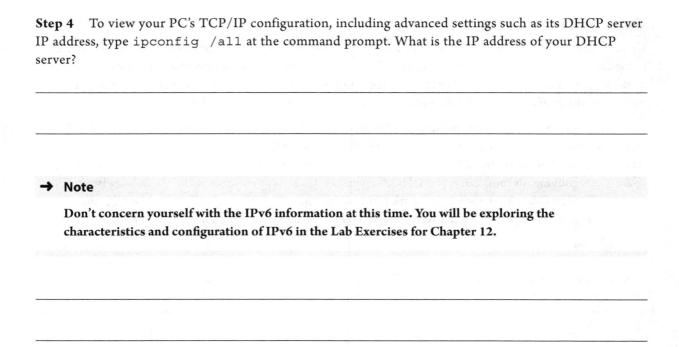

→ **Note**

> Don't concern yourself with the IPv6 information at this time. You will be exploring the characteristics and configuration of IPv6 in the Lab Exercises for Chapter 12.

_____

_____

Step 5   Network techs sometimes must manually refresh a network host's DHCP lease, such as when a major change has been made to the network's configuration. To release and renew a network host's DHCP lease manually, you must execute two commands. The first is `ipconfig /release`, which, when typed at the command prompt, releases the IP address back into the pool of addresses. The second command is `ipconfig /renew`. When you type this at the command prompt, it causes the host to obtain a new DHCP lease. You will now use Wireshark to capture DHCP traffic while you obtain an IP address from a DHCP server.

Step 6   Run Wireshark on one of the DHCP client systems, but do not start capturing yet. Open a command prompt and run `ipconfig /release`. Go back to Wireshark and start capturing. As in the previous lab exercise, you are going to use a filter to isolate DHCP traffic. Use the following display filter: **bootp**.

Return to your command prompt and run `ipconfig /renew`. When the renewal is successful, stop capturing frames.

✔ **Tech Tip**

> In the preceding step, you added a filter by using bootp. Bootstrap Protocol (BOOTP) was the predecessor to DHCP, and is the protocol that DHCP is based on. The fields are the same, except for an additional Option 53, which distinguishes between BOOTP and DHCP. Even though BOOTP is obsolete and never used anymore, the Wireshark display filter requires bootp, and not dhcp.

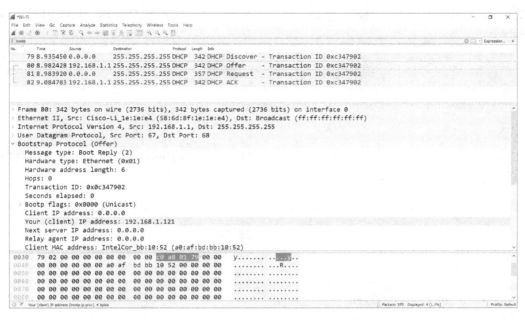

FIGURE 6-5 DHCP's DORA in action

Step 7   You should see four frames labeled DHCP under the Protocol column, as shown in Figure 6-5 (with the offer highlighted in the DHCP Offer): DHCP Discover, DHCP Offer, DHCP Request, and DHCP ACK. This process, where a client gets a lease, is therefore known as the DORA (Discover, Offer, Request, ACK) process.

Step 8   Examine the DHCP Discover. What is the source IP address? What is the destination IP address? What do you think is the significance of this destination address? What port does a DHCP client use? What port does a DHCP server use? Go into the Bootstrap Protocol details. Did your system request a particular IP address? If so, why do you think it did so?

_____

_____

Step 9   Next, examine the DHCP Offer. What IP address did this come from? Go into the Bootstrap Protocol details. What is the IP address the DHCP server is offering? What other IP information is being offered by the DHCP server?

_____

_____

Step 10   Now examine the DHCP Request, which is almost identical to DHCP Discover. What's the purpose of this step?

_____

_____

Step 11   The DORA process concludes with a DHCP ACK, which is almost identical to the DHCP Offer. What's the purpose of this step?

_____

_____

Step 12   Now disable the DHCP server.

➜ **Note**

> If you're in a lab without the ability to disable the DHCP server, but you do have available switches, there is an alternative to this step. Take the Ethernet cable out of a data port (which leads to the DHCP server) and plug it into a switch that's not connected to anything.

Open up the command prompt once again and type `ipconfig /release`. After a moment, type `ipconfig /renew`. What are the results?

_____

_____

 45 MINUTES

Lab Exercise 6.07: Configuring and Testing a DHCP Client and a DHCP Server

After a great look at how DHCP works from the client side, it's now time to get some valuable hands-on experience with how DHCP servers work.

Learning Objectives

In this lab, you will explore and configure both a DHCP client and a DHCP server. At the end of the lab, you will be able to

- Configure a DHCP client

- Configure a DHCP server

- Create a DHCP scope

- Analyze, test, and debug DHCP traffic

Lab Materials and Setup

The materials you'll need for this lab exercise are

- Windows 10 system

- Windows Server 2016 system

- Pen or pencil

- Paper

Getting Down to Business

In previous steps, you might have used the DHCP service in a box that we just call a router, but this lab requires use of a stand-alone, dedicated DHCP server.

Step 1   Perform the following substeps to configure the DHCP client:

a.   Open up the first Windows 10 machine.

b.   In the Windows search box, type **sharing**.

c.   Click Manage Advanced Sharing Settings, which will appear as the top choice, in the dynamically generated menu.

d.   In the address bar at the top, click Network And Sharing Center.

e.   In the pane at the left, click Change Adapter Settings.

f.   Right-click Ethernet and select Properties.

g.   Select Internet Protocol Version 4 (TCP/IPv4) and click the Properties button.

h.   In the General tab, which will open by default, change the radio button selection to Obtain An IP Address Automatically.

i.   In the next section on the dialog box, make sure Obtain DNS Server Address Automatically is also selected.

j.   Click the OK button, and then click the next OK button.

Step 2   Perform the following substeps to configure the DHCP server:

   a.   Using the same steps as provided earlier, assign the Windows Server 2016 machine the following information:

   IP address: **10.0.0.52**

   Subnet mask: **255.0.0.0**

   Default gateway: (leave blank)

   Preferred DNS server: **127.0.0.1** (even though we don't have this set up)

   b.   Let's also give the server a host name instead of using the long awkward one that was generated. Right-click the This PC icon on the desktop and select Properties.

   c.   In the Computer Name, Domain, And Workgroup Settings section, click Change Settings. Click the Change button toward the middle of the dialog box. Enter any name for your computer and then click OK. Then click OK, Close, and Restart Now. Your server will now reboot.

Step 3   Perform the following substeps to install the DHCP role on the server:

   a.   The Server Manager window should be opened. If not, click the Start button and then Server Manager.

   b.   Click the Add Roles And Features link. Click Next until the Select Server Roles page is displayed.

   c.   Select the DHCP Server check box. On the Add Roles And Features Wizard dialog box, click Add Features.

   d.   The Select Server Roles page returns with the DHCP Server role check box selected. Click Next.

   e.   Complete the installation process.

Step 4   Perform the following substeps to install the DHCP role on the server:

   a.   On the Server Manager console, click Tools, and then click DHCP.

   b.   On the DHCP console, expand your server name.

   c.   Now create a new DHCP scope to specify the IP address ranges for your DHCP server. To do so, select and right-click IPv4 and then select New Scope.

   d.   On the welcome page of the New Scope Wizard, click Next.

   e.   On the Scope Name page, specify a DHCP scope name (anything, really), and then click Next.

f. On the IP Address Range page, specify the start and end IP addresses from which the DHCP server will allocate the IP addresses to the clients. We will use the following information:

Start IP address: **10.0.0.1**

End IP address: **10.0.0.99**

Length: **8**

Subnet mask: **255.0.0.0**

g. Click Next.

h. On the Add Exclusions And Delay page, exclude the IP addresses that you want to be not distributed by the DHCP server. For example, we will exclude the server's IP address this way:

Start IP address: **10.0.0.52**

End IP address: **10.0.0.52**

i. Click Add, and then click Next. On the Lease Duration page, review the default lease duration limit, and then click Next.

j. On the Configure DHCP Options page, make sure that the Yes, I Want To Configure These Options Now radio button is selected and then click Next.

k. On the Router (Default Gateway) page, in the IP Address text box, type the address of your router. We will use **10.0.0.200** as a default gateway for the DHCP clients. Note that we have no router set up; this is just for display purposes.

l. Click Add, and then click Next. On the Domain Name And DNS Servers page, enter the IP address of this machine, which will later become the DNS server as well: **10.0.0.52** and then click Next.

m. On the WINS Servers page (WINS is old and obsolete), leave it as is and click Next.

n. On the Activate Scope page, make sure that the Yes, I Want To Activate This Scope Now radio button is selected. Click Next and complete the wizard.

o. Refresh the DHCP console. Make sure that the IPv4 node is marked with the green color. Now your DHCP server is configured and ready to allocate TCP/IP settings to the DHCP clients.

Step 5 Perform the following substeps to initiate the DORA process and watch it in Wireshark:

a. On the Windows 10 machine, open up a command-line interface and type the command `ipconfig /release`, which will release the lease your machine should have already.

b. Open up Wireshark, and start capturing network traffic.

   c.   In the filter box type **bootp** and press ENTER. Since DHCP is modeled after its predecessor, BOOTP, Wireshark requires you to use that as the filter for DHCP traffic.

   d.   In the command-line interface of the Windows 10 machine, type `ipconfig /renew`; when the action completes, stop the Wireshark capture and examine the DHCPDISCOVER, DHCPOFFER, DHCPREQUEST, and DHCPACK messages. Type `ipconfig /all` in the command-line interface of the Windows 10 machine to see the configuration information given to it by the DHCP server.

Lab Analysis

1.   Tegan works for an ISP and has been asked to set up the IP addressing scheme for a new region of the city they are providing with Internet service. She is provided the Class B address of 141.27.0.0/16 as a starting point and needs at least 25 subnets. What is the custom subnet mask for this, how many networks does this allow for, and how many hosts will be available on each subnet?

_____

_____

2.   Describe the function of private IP addresses, and list the private IP address ranges for Class A, B, and C IP networks.

_____

_____

3.   Alexis arrived at work this morning, logged on to her Windows 10 machine, and found that she has no Internet access. You respond to her network support call. All of the obvious hardware and configuration settings check out, so you run `ipconfig /all`. The IP address is 169.254.113.97/16. What do you think the problem could be? What might you check next?

_____

_____

4.   Garret is troubleshooting a network connectivity problem. He tries pinging 127.0.0.1, but the command is unsuccessful. What might this indicate?

_____

_____

5. Matthew is trying to determine if Workstation A and Workstation B are on the same network. Workstation A has an IP address of 172.16.33.1/20 and Workstation B has an IP address of 172.16.45.254/20. Are they on the same network?

    _____

    _____

Key Term Quiz

Use the IP addresses and vocabulary terms from the list provided to complete the sentences that follow.

`arp -a`

default gateway

DHCP ACK

DHCP Discover

DHCP Offer

DHCP Request

`ipconfig`

`ipconfig /all`

packet sniffer

Wireshark

1. Many utilities are available, both software based and hardware based, that enable you to capture frames and analyze the contents. The generic name for these utilities is a(n) _____, and an excellent free and open source version is _____.

2. When a PC communicates with another PC over a TCP/IP network, the IP address must be resolved to the MAC address in order for the communication to take place. After the communication is established, the system stores the resolved address in a cache. The command to view this cache is

    _____.

3. To determine the IP address, subnet mask, and default gateway on a Windows PC, type _____ at a command prompt. To display even more information, type

    _____.

4.   The _____ is the IP address of a router that takes traffic off the LAN to other networks and brings traffic from other networks onto your LAN.

5.   When a client is negotiating with a DHCP server to obtain an address, the sequence of transmissions is as follows: The client will broadcast a(n) _____ to the LAN. All of the DHCP servers will respond with a(n) _____. The client will select one DHCP server and then send a formal _____ informing all of the DHCP servers that an address has been obtained. Finally, the DHCP server selected will send a(n) _____ confirming the address to the client.

Chapter 7

Routing

Lab Exercises

As you learned in Chapter 6, TCP/IP is built on a set of dynamic specifications that are constantly modified and updated through documents known as request for comments (RFC). There is an RFC for every component of the TCP/IP protocol suite, so you can imagine how many are associated with routing. As a precursor to working with routers, you will explore the organizations that deal with the TCP/IP protocol suite, as well as RFCs.

Taking communications off the LAN and moving them out to other networks and ultimately the Internet requires a reexamination of a number of concepts, components, and software you have already worked with. For example, you've configured client computers to communicate with other computers on the local area network, as well as computers on remote networks, using the default gateway. Now, you need to look at routing from the perspective of the router itself, to learn how to configure the routers to make those connections beyond the local network possible.

In addition, you will work with some important components that really enhance IP routing—in particular, Network Address Translation (NAT) and dynamic routing. These two technologies are critical for communication over the Internet and the protection of any private network you want to connect to the Internet. In this chapter, you'll explore some additional organizations and then you'll install and configure routers, NAT, and dynamic routing protocols to see how they work in the real world.

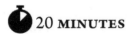 20 MINUTES

Lab Exercise 7.01: Governing Bodies, Part 2

The TCP/IP suite is so important to modern networking that both the textbook and Lab Manual devote multiple chapters to the various components of TCP/IP. These chapters cover in detail IPv4 and IPv6 addressing, IP routing, DNS, DHCP, VPNs, and VLANs. In almost every chapter, you will work with various TCP/IP utilities.

Just as there are organizations that handle the specifications and management of Ethernet and cabling, so too are there organizations that handle the specifications and management of the TCP/IP protocol suite. Before starting your journey through the wonderful world of routing, it is a good time to introduce you to some of these organizations.

Learning Objectives

In this lab, you'll explore various organizations that are responsible for the development and management of standards for TCP/IP, the Internet, and the World Wide Web. By the end of this lab, you will be able to

- Describe the purpose and detail some of the features of the organizations responsible for the TCP/IP standards, Internet addressing, and domain naming

- Research and report on some of the paramount RFCs

Lab Materials and Setup

The materials you'll need for this lab exercise are

- Internet access

- Pen or pencil

- Paper

Getting Down to Business

Imagine for a moment you are working for a large company that wants to have their own pool of public IP addresses. Or perhaps you have decided to launch your own Web site discussing, trading, and selling vintage guitars, and you want a great domain name, also known as a Uniform Resource Locator (URL), like www.vintageguitars.com. Who knows? You might decide to write the next all-encompassing dynamic routing protocol. All of these situations are administered by official organizations that help to manage the TCP/IP protocol suite. In the next few steps you will explore these organizations and document some of the information you uncover.

Step 1 Similar to the International Organization for Standardization (ISO), the Internet Corporation for Assigned Names and Numbers (ICANN) owns and operates some of the other key organizations responsible for TCP/IP and the Internet. Open your Web browser and enter this URL: **www.icann.org**. Record who ICANN is, how long it's been around, and its mission statement.

_____

_____

Step 2   Navigate to the Web site www.iana.org/about/ to learn about the Internet Assigned Numbers Authority (IANA). Write a short summary of this organization, when it was founded, and what its main responsibilities are.

_____

_____

Step 3   IANA works closely with the Internet Society (ISOC). Record some of the facts you learn about ISOC at www.internetsociety.org.

_____

_____

Step 4   There are numerous organizations responsible for steering the Internet. Yet another of these organizations is the Internet Engineering Task Force (IETF). What are some of the characteristics of the IETF? Check them out at www.ietf.org/about.

_____

_____

Step 5   One of the most important contributions of the IETF is the stewardship of the RFC database. The RFCs are the open source recommendations and standards for the Internet (more specifically, TCP/IP is defined by RFCs). The main repository for the RFCs is the RFC Editor, which can be found at www.rfc-editor.org. Once there, use the search box in the upper-right corner of the screen to find major protocols, technologies, and strategies listed in the RFCs listed next:

RFC 826   _____

RFC 894   _____

RFC 791   _____

RFC 4632   _____

RFC 2460   _____

RFC 792   _____

RFC 793   _____

RFC 768   _____

RFC 2328 _____

RFC 1034 _____

RFC 2131 _____

As you progress through the rest of the lab exercises in this Lab Manual, you may find it interesting and beneficial to consult the RFCs as you learn about the application of the protocols of the TCP/IP protocol suite.

Can you find a pattern in the order the RFCs were listed above?

_____

_____

 45 MINUTES

Lab Exercise 7.02: Installing and Configuring Routers

In the previous chapter, you learned that in order to move packets from a machine on the local area network (LAN) to a machine on a remote, wide area network (WAN), like the Internet , you need to use a router. Until now, you have only been responsible for configuring a PC to use the default gateway to send packets destined for remote networks to the near port of the router. The router then handles the delivery of these packets from the local network to the remote network.

Now it is time to explore the fine details of installing and configuring routers. You will begin with this lab exercise, where you will install and configure one router, creating two networks. In Lab Exercise 7.03, you will add additional routers (creating additional networks), emulating the router configuration and management that an enterprise network technician would be responsible for.

✔ **Tech Tip**

The following routing labs were designed to utilize the excellent capabilities of inexpensive home routers that are also wireless access points (WAPs). For the lab exercises in this chapter, an inexpensive router will route packets between two networks, enable the configuration of NAT and port forwarding, and create dynamic routing tables.

If you have access to Cisco or Juniper routers, such as the Cisco 2600 series routers or the Juniper J-series routers, they will obviously meet the requirements of the following labs. The full configuration of these routers, though, is beyond the scope of these lab exercises (as well as the objectives for the CompTIA Network+ exam).

Learning Objectives

When you have completed this lab exercise, you will be able to

- Design and implement a routed, two-network infrastructure

- Physically install router hardware

- Configure multiple interfaces on Ethernet routers

- Implement static routes in routers

Lab Materials and Setup

Preferably, you will have access to the small "network lab" you assembled in the previous chapter's exercises. The materials you'll need for this lab exercise are

- Two or more PCs

- One router

- Two eight-port Ethernet switches

- Appropriate UTP cabling

- Pen or pencil

- Paper

Getting Down to Business

Jonathan stops by the Network Lab to see how you are progressing. He finds that you not only have the small network up and running, but also have configured both static and dynamic IP addressing. You demonstrate the communication between the two networks over the router using the ping utility. Packets are successfully sent to one of the machines on the remote network, which successfully replies to one of the machines on the local network.

He is duly impressed and asks if you are up for experimenting with the configuration of the router. You respond with "You bet!" and begin to disassemble the Network Lab. Jonathan stops you and says that you won't need to disassemble the physical setup, but he is going to give you new network IDs that you'll need to configure.

Network 1 (LAN):   192.168.10.0/24

Network 2 (WAN):   192.168.20.0/24

Step 1   Based on these network IDs for the two networks, complete the following table, filling in the appropriate IP addresses for each router interface and each computer. Remember, as you learned in Chapter 7, to plan out your network addressing scheme. Typically, a range of addresses will be set aside for network routers, servers, and network printers.

Network 1	IP Address	Subnet Mask	Default Gateway
Router Interface (LAN)			
Computer A			
Computer B			

Network 2	IP Address	Subnet Mask	Default Gateway
Router Interface (WAN)			
Computer A			
Computer B			

Step 2   Verify the configuration of the physical setup as follows using Figure 7-1.

Step 3   Armed with your addresses for the LAN and WAN interfaces, launch your browser and open the router configuration utility. Consult the user's manual or the Internet to determine the correct information for the specific model you are using. The default address is commonly 192.168.1.1. It's also common for the default username to be "admin" and the default password to be the never-secure "password." You should arrive at the main setup screen, similar to Figure 7-2.

Step 4   You will begin by configuring the IP addresses of the WAN interface and the LAN interface. Start by giving the WAN interface a static IP address. Configure the IP address, subnet mask, and default gateway for the WAN interface. For the default gateway, enter an IP address for the second router interface on the same network (in our Network Lab, this is 192.168.20.2). Next, configure the LAN interface IP address and subnet mask. Disable DHCP. Save your changes.

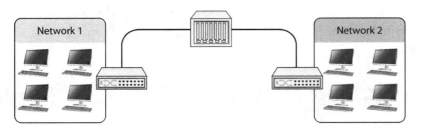

FIGURE 7-1   **Physical layout of the network for Lab Exercise 7.01**

FIGURE 7-2 Router configuration utility

✔ **Hint**

Since you have just changed the IP address of the router's WAN and LAN interfaces, you have effectively changed the IP address for the Setup Web page. In order to re-enter the router setup utility, you will need to configure the computer from which you are accessing it to be on the correct network and use the new IP address for the router. If the IP addresses were improperly configured, you would have to reset the router. There is a small recessed button on the back of most routers. Pressing the reset button for 15 seconds or so will reset the router to default values. Use the default values to once again enter the Setup page and reconfigure the lab exercise settings.

Step 5   Next, find the advanced routing settings, and disable Network Address Translation (NAT). Usually, selecting "Router" instead of "Gateway" does the trick, and allows properly routed packets to travel freely between the two networks. Be sure to save your changes.

Then, display your routing table. This is a simple static routing table that is created when you configure the LAN and WAN interfaces. Note the destination network, subnet mask, gateway, hop count (metric), and interfaces for each entry. See Figure 7-3.

Destination LAN IP	Subnet Mask	Gateway	Hop Count	Interface

Routing Table Entry List   [Refresh]

Destination LAN IP	Subnet Mask	Gateway	Hop Count	Interface
192.168.20.0	255.255.255.0	0.0.0.0	1	WAN (Internet)
192.168.10.0	255.255.255.0	0.0.0.0	1	LAN & Wireless
0.0.0.0	0.0.0.0	192.168.20.2	1	WAN (Internet)

[Close]

FIGURE 7-3 Routing table for the router in the Network Lab

✖ Cross-Reference

Review the "Routing Tables" section of Chapter 7 in the *Mike Meyers' CompTIA Network+ Guide to Managing and Troubleshooting Networks* textbook. This will help you better understand the details of the specific entries in the preceding table.

Step 6 Find the security settings and disable the firewall. You would never do this if you were using the router to access the Internet (you'd add rules instead), but these two LANs are private and will be isolated from the Internet. Save your changes.

Step 7 Now configure each of the computers on both Network 1 and Network 2. Remember to use the router's IP address for the network you are configuring as the default gateway for each of the systems on that network. You will also want to disable the Windows firewall on each machine. Again, you'd never do this if the machines were connected to the Internet (you'd add rules instead).

Step 8 On one of the computers on Network 2 (WAN), open a command prompt, and using the `ping` utility, record the results of testing the communication with the following interfaces:

Interface	IP Address	Result
Loopback address		
This computer		
Another computer on Network 2		
The "near" router interface (router interface for Network 2)		
The "far" router interface (router interface for Network 1)		
One of the computers on Network 1		

If any or all of the prior communication tests fail, try to isolate the problem (individual computer, router, or switch). Depending on your findings, check the cabling, review the configurations of the PCs, or review the configuration of the router. If everything checks out, congratulations! You have a routed internetwork.

45 MINUTES

Lab Exercise 7.03: Exploring NAT and Port Forwarding

Network Address Translation (NAT) is a powerful technology that enables many network clients on a TCP/ IP network to share a single Internet connection. The inside hosts use their own unique private IP addresses internally, but out on the Internet, all hosts from within that network use/share the same single public IP address. Most popular Internet gateway routers and home network routers on the market have built-in NAT functionality. While there are many different flavors of NAT, the one most often being referred to simply as NAT is PAT (Port Address Translation), which maps an inside socket (private inside IP address and local source port) to a remote socket (shared public outside IP address with a LAN unique source port).

NAT was designed for one reason and one reason only: to slow down the depletion of IPv4 addresses. NAT was not designed for any form of security. Thinking NAT is security is an example of "security through obscurity," relying on something being kept secret for security and letting your guard down to secure any possible vulnerabilities.

If NAT was, in fact, essential network security, why are so many devices in homes around the world infected with malware? The following Web sites explain this in greater detail:

https://blog.webernetz.net/why-nat-has-nothing-to-do-with-security/

http://blog.ipspace.net/2011/12/is-nat-security-feature.html

www.internetsociety.org/blog/2015/01/ipv6-security-myth-3-no-ipv6-nat-means-less-security/

Even though NAT blocks unsolicited direct access from computers on the Internet to computers on a private network behind NAT, phishing attacks involving malicious links and files, as well as simply visiting malicious sites, will invite the attackers in. While it is difficult for a malicious program to attack your computer based solely on the private IP address, devices behind a NAT regularly invite hackers inside.

But what if you want to host a game or a Web site? Nobody would be able to directly access your computer with NAT enabled, since state is established with packets leaving your private inside network, you will configure port forwarding. When servers on the private inside network must be accessed from the outside world directly—for example, Web servers, mail servers, and terminal servers—port forwarding is the way it's done.

In this lab, you will explore both NAT and port forwarding.

Learning Objectives

In this lab, you will explain the function of NAT. When you have completed this lab, you will be able to

- Define the versions of NAT

- Implement NAT on a SOHO router

- Configure port forwarding to allow applications to pass through the router from the outside world

Lab Materials and Setup

The materials you'll need for this lab exercise are

- *Mike Meyers' CompTIA Network+ Guide to Managing and Troubleshooting Networks* textbook

- Internet access

- The basic one-router, two-switch, four-computer lab network from the prior lab exercise

- Pen or pencil

- Paper

Getting Down to Business

It's time to get some hands-on experience with both NAT and port forwarding. Jonathan wants you to report what you learned to Scott, so it's time to get cracking.

Step 1 Go back to the router configuration utility you were using earlier (remember to use the new IP address since the router no longer has the default settings). Find the advanced routing settings and enable Network Address Translation (NAT). Usually, selecting "Gateway" instead of "Router" will do the trick. Save your settings.

_____

_____

_____

_____

Step 2 Try to ping any of the computers on Network 1 from one of the computers on Network 2. Try to ping any of the computers on Network 2 from one of the computers on Network 1. How do the results differ?

_____

_____

_____

_____

Step 3   Now, once again, send a ping from Network 1 to Network 2. This time, sniff with Wireshark on both machines involved in the pings. What difference in IP addresses can you spot between the two captures?

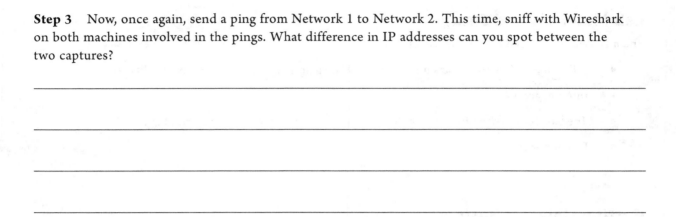

Step 4   Now, you're going to conduct a simple experiment to test our port forwarding. In your router's configuration utility, find the screen that allows you to configure port forwarding. For example, see Figure 7-4.

Configure the following:

External Port **80**

Internal Port **80**

Protocol **TCP**

To IP Address <IP Address of one of the machines on Network 1>

Enabled (check the box).

Save your changes.

This will take any unsolicited traffic from Network 2 with a destination IP address of the outside router IP address (from Network 1's perspective) and send it to the host on the inside, whose IP address you listed in the previous step.

On that Network 1 computer, start sniffing with Wireshark.

Now, from a computer on Network 2, open up a browser and, in the URL bar, type the IP address of the computer on Network 1. This will get the computer on Network 2 to send HTTP traffic to the computer on Network 1. By default, HTTP uses port 80. There is no Web server running on the computer on Network 1; however, you should see the HTTP GET request in Wireshark, proving that the machine behind a NAT was able to receive unsolicited traffic. What do you observe?

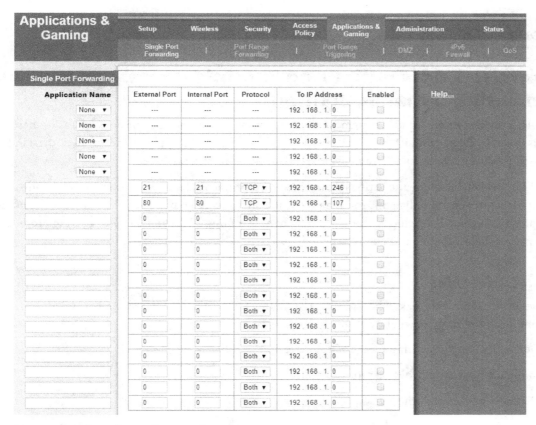

FIGURE 7-4 Port forwarding configuration

1 HOUR

Lab Exercise 7.04: Configuring Multiple Routers and Implementing Dynamic Routing

Routing tables provide routers the ability to move data successfully from one node or network to another as efficiently as possible. Being comfortable reading and understanding routing tables is the key to understanding exactly how IP packets move around large networks, including the Internet.

In this exercise, you'll explore the various dynamic routing protocols; configure a small, routed, four-network infrastructure; enable a dynamic routing protocol; confirm connectivity; and document your findings. From this information, you'll develop an understanding of how routing tables and dynamic routing protocols operate from the simplest to the most complex networks.

Learning Objectives

In this lab, you will examine the basic characteristics of routing tables and dynamic routing protocols. When you have completed this lab, you will be able to

- Define the individual components of a generic routing table

- Implement a dynamic routing protocol

- Diagnose and correct routing issues

Lab Materials and Setup

Preferably, you will have access to the small network lab you assembled in the previous chapter's exercises. The materials you'll need for this lab exercise are

- *Mike Meyers' CompTIA Network+ Guide to Managing and Troubleshooting Networks* textbook

- Internet access

- Four or more PCs

- Three routers

- Four 8-port Ethernet switches

- Appropriate UTP cabling

- Pen or pencil

- Paper

Getting Down to Business

Jonathan has one last set of experiments he would like you to conduct with the routing lab. He leaves the room and returns with a few more switches and two additional routers. Then, Jonathan requests that you configure a four-network infrastructure using the multiple switches and routers that are now available to you. As before, he provides you with the network IDs for each of the networks, but leaves the addressing scheme up to you. The diagram in Figure 7-5 defines the basic setup.

Step 1 Using the assembled hardware, build and configure the physical network based on the network diagram in Figure 7-5. Document the IP address configuration for the computers and router interfaces on each network:

✔ Hint

> On each of the three routers, remember to disable DHCP, NAT, and the firewall to allow packets to move freely from both the LAN interface to the WAN interface and vice versa.

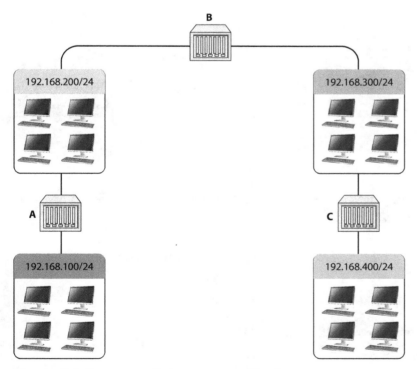

FIGURE 7-5 Four networks interconnected by three routers

Network 1 192.168.10.0/24	IP Address	Subnet Mask	Default Gateway
Router A Interface (LAN)			
Windows Computer A			

Network 2 192.168.20.0/24	IP Address	Subnet Mask	Default Gateway
Router A Interface (WAN)			
Router B Interface (LAN)			
Windows Computer B			

Network 3 192.168.30.0/24	IP Address	Subnet Mask	Default Gateway
Router B Interface (WAN)			
Router C Interface (LAN)			
Windows Computer C			

Network 4 192.168.40.0/24	IP Address	Subnet Mask	Default Gateway
Router C Interface (WAN)			
Windows Computer D			

Step 2   After completing the configuration in Step 1, log on to a computer on Network 1. Use the ping utility to verify connectivity with the following addresses:

Interface	IP Address	Result
Loopback address		
Computer A		
The "near" interface for Router A on Network 1 (192.168.10.0/24)		
The "far" interface for Router A on Network 2 (192.168.20.0/24)		

Computer B		
The "near" interface for Router B on Network 2 (192.168.20.0/24)		
The "far" interface for Router B on Network 3 (192.168.30.0/24)		
Computer C		
The "near" interface for Router C on Network 3 (192.168.30.0/24)		
The "far" interface for Router C on Network 4 (192.168.40.0/24)		
Computer D		

Try This!

You may be using SOHO wireless routers for this lab exercise, so the Internet (WAN) interface may actually have an entry that configures the gateway address for that network. If your configuration uses the preceding table, where each LAN interface is the "near" interface and each WAN interface is the "far" interface, this effectively creates a routing table entry for this interface. When you ping from a computer on Network 1, the partial routing table on each of the routers may allow packets to complete additional hops.

To fully test connectivity, log on to a computer on Network 4 (possibly Computer D), open a command prompt, and ping Computer A. What are the results?

_____

_____

Step 3   In Step 2, what do you think contributed to some of the connections not being able to communicate?

_____

_____

Step 4   In the following steps you will enable a dynamic routing protocol to automatically configure the routing tables on each router. This will facilitate the communication of computers on all four networks

Starting with Router A, launch the setup utility and find the advanced routing settings. Before you change any of the settings, show the routing table. Refer back to Figure 7-3 in Lab Exercise 7.02 for an example of a default static routing table. Record the results in the following table:

Destination LAN IP	Subnet Mask	Gateway	Hop Count	Interface

You may notice that the table has only information on Networks 1 and 2. There is no information on how packets travel to Network 3 or Network 4. How can this situation be remedied?

_____

_____

Step 5   Now close the Routing Table information and enable a dynamic routing protocol. Many home routers, unfortunately, allow you to use the old, obsolete RIP. Use it if you have to. Alternatively, if your router supports OSPF, use it. OSPF is the world's #1 interior gateway protocol.

Save your changes. Repeat this step on both Router B and Router C.

Wait a minute or so to allow convergence of the routing tables, and then on Router A, launch the setup utility once again. Find the routing table. See Figure 7-6.

Record the results in the following table:

Destination LAN IP	Subnet Mask	Gateway	Hop Count	Interface

Routing Table Entry List [Refresh]

Destination LAN IP	Subnet Mask	Gateway	Hop Count	Interface
192.168.20.0	255.255.255.0	0.0.0.0	1	WAN (Internet)
192.168.30.0	255.255.255.0	192.168.20.2	2	WAN (Internet)
192.168.10.0	255.255.255.0	0.0.0.0	1	LAN & Wireless
192.168.40.0	255.255.255.0	192.168.20.2	3	WAN (Internet)
0.0.0.0	0.0.0.0	192.168.20.2	1	WAN (Internet)

[Close]

FIGURE 7-6 Routing table for Router A after implementing RIP

Step 6 Log on to Computer A on Network 1. Use the `ping` utility to verify connectivity with the following addresses:

Interface	IP Address	Result
Loopback address		
Computer A		
The "near" interface for Router A on Network 1 (192.168.10.0/24)		
The "far" interface for Router A on Network 2 (192.168.20.0/24)		
Computer B		
The "near" interface for Router B on Network 2 (192.168.20.0/24)		
The "far" interface for Router B on Network 3 (192.168.30.0/24)		
Computer C		
The "near" interface for Router C on Network 3 (192.168.30.0/24)		
The "far" interface for Router C on Network 4 (192.168.40.0/24)		
Computer D		

To fully test connectivity, log on to a computer on Network 4 (Computer D, for example), open a command prompt, and ping Computer A. What are the results?

_____

_____

Step 7 You're going to finish up this lab exercise with another TCP/IP utility known as traceroute (tracert in Windows). Tracert will allow you to record the number of "hops" or routers a packet has to pass through to get from a source computer to a destination computer (usually on a far-removed remote network).

```
C:\Windows\system32>tracert 192.168.40.104

Tracing route to CETECH-27B5F5DD [192.168.40.104]
over a maximum of 30 hops:

  1    <1 ms    <1 ms    <1 ms  192.168.10.1
  2     1 ms    <1 ms    <1 ms  192.168.20.2
  3     2 ms     1 ms     1 ms  192.168.30.3
  4     1 ms     1 ms     1 ms  CETECH-27B5F5DD [192.168.40.104]

Trace complete.

C:\Windows\system32>
```

FIGURE 7-7   Tracing the route from Computer A to Computer D

Log on to Computer A and open a command prompt. Type `tracert 192.168.40.XX`, where XX is the address of your computer on Network 4. See Figure 7-7. Record the results in the following space:

_____

_____

_____

_____

Lab Analysis

1. Neelufer has just manually edited the routing table on an internal Cisco 2651 router. She knows that these routes will remain fairly constant, but wants to know why you would configure a dynamic routing protocol. Can you explain it to her?

_____

_____

_____

_____

2. Roshni overheard your conversation about dynamic routing protocols and wants to know when manually configuring static routes makes more sense than running a dynamic routing protocol. Can you help her out?

_____

_____

_____

_____

3. Kevin has just installed two new internal routers to configure separate networks for the marketing department and the sales department of his organization. Now the sales team is having trouble reaching the Internet. Using ping, what troubleshooting sequence should he follow to determine where the connectivity issues are located?

_____

_____

_____

_____

4. Meet would like to see an example of a routing table but currently does not have access to a router. Show him how to use the route print command on any Windows computer and record some of the entries listed in the routing table.

_____

_____

_____

_____

5. Sarosh has heard you mention the terms "distance vector" and "link state" when you were discussing dynamic routing protocols. He would like you to explain the difference between these two types of dynamic routing protocols in more detail.

_____

_____

_____

_____

Key Term Quiz

Use the vocabulary terms from the list provided to complete the sentences that follow.

convergence

Open Shortest Path First (OSPF)

Port Address Translation (PAT)

Routing Information Protocol (RIP)

`tracert`

1. _____ enables the use of one public address for a network of private addresses that connect to the Internet.

2. The original routing protocol used was _____.

3. The _____ dynamic routing protocol is the most commonly used one within autonomous systems.

4. The command-line utility that allows you to follow the path that a packet takes as it travels over networks and through routers is _____.

5. _____ is the point when all of the routers have used a dynamic protocol and all of the routing tables on all of the routers are up to date.

Chapter 8

TCP/IP Applications

Lab Exercises

Obviously, one of the reasons you are spending all of this time and effort studying the minute details of the network infrastructure, besides the fact that it's fun, is to better provide networking services to users. The most popular applications—World Wide Web, e-mail, streaming audio and video, file transfers, Voice over IP, and so on—all require the configuration of specific components of the TCP/IP suite of protocols.

At Layer 7, protocols like DNS, DHCP, FTP, SSH, HTTP, SSL/TLS, SMTP, and more can be found. At Layer 4, either TCP or UDP will be chosen. Layer 3 protocols include IP, ICMP, and IGMP.

To effectively perform the management of even the smallest network, administrators must develop a strong command of the network applications and the mechanisms they use to communicate over TCP/IP.

 30 MINUTES

Lab Exercise 8.01: Transport Layer and Network Layer Protocols

All of the Layer 7 upper-layer data communications that take place over the TCP/IP protocol suite will be encapsulated at the Transport layer inside of either TCP segments or UDP datagrams. At the Network layer, two specialized protocols, ICMP and IGMP, provide for low-level messaging and management communication. In this lab exercise, you will explore the TCP, UDP, ICMP, and IGMP protocols. Chapter 6 already covered IP in great depth.

Learning Objectives

In this lab, you will research and define the important characteristics of the Transport and Network layer protocols. By the end of this lab, you will be able to

- Define TCP (Transmission Control Protocol)
- Define UDP (User Datagram Protocol)
- Define ICMP (Internet Control Message Protocol)
- Define IGMP (Internet Group Management Protocol)

Lab Materials and Setup

The materials you'll need for this lab exercise are

- *Mike Meyers' CompTIA Network+ Guide to Managing and Troubleshooting Networks* textbook

- Internet access

- Pen or pencil

- Paper

Getting Down to Business

Jonathan notices that you have been aggressively studying the configuration of IP addressing and routing. After some discussion, he agrees that you are really getting a handle on the IP component of the TCP/IP protocol suite. He thinks it would be an excellent time to delve into the other protocols that enable the TCP/IP protocol suite to successfully deliver packets between hosts.

You agree, fire up your favorite browser, and dive into some research on the protocols that work hand in hand with IP to communicate information from one machine to another over the network.

> ✖ **Cross-Reference**
>
> **For further information on TCP, UDP, ICMP, and IGMP, review the "TCP," "UDP," "ICMP," and "IGMP" sections in Chapter 8 of the *Mike Meyers' CompTIA Network+ Guide to Managing and Troubleshooting Networks* textbook.**

Step 1   Research TCP (Transmission Control Protocol) and provide a short summary of its features. Make sure to include discussion regarding the OSI model. Define the communication method used (such as connection-oriented or connectionless, reliable or unreliable), and some of the Application layer protocols that require it for their functionality.

_____

_____

_____

_____

Step 2   Research UDP (User Datagram Protocol) and provide a short summary of its features. Make sure to include discussion regarding the OSI model. Define the communication method used (such as connection-oriented or connectionless, reliable or unreliable), and some of the Application layer protocols that require it for their functionality.

_____

_____

_____

_____

Step 3   Research ICMP (Internet Control Message Protocol) and provide a short summary of its features. Make sure to include discussion regarding the OSI model. Describe some of the applications that take advantage of its functionality.

✔ **Hint**

Refer to Chapter 6, "TCP/IP Basics," and review Lab Exercise 6.02: Configuring IP Addresses and Subnet Masks, and Lab Exercise 6.05: Packet Sniffing, IP Addresses, and MAC Addresses: Working Together, to see ICMP in action. Pay special attention to the Tech Tips and the output of the Wireshark utility.

_____

_____

_____

_____

Step 4   Research IGMP (Internet Group Management Protocol) and provide a short summary of its features. Make sure to include discussion regarding the OSI model. Describe some of the applications that take advantage of its functionality.

_____

_____

_____

_____

 30 MINUTES

Lab Exercise 8.02: Analyzing TCP/IP Ports and Associations

By this point, you should appreciate the complexity of the TCP/IP suite's many network functions. To the novice technician, it might seem as if these many capabilities could spill over into one another, but TCP/IP does a great job of keeping its different programs and services separate. It does this by using logical ports.

Learning Objectives

In this lab, you will define the function of TCP/IP logical ports and review the common port number assignments. You'll also use several utilities that will allow you to explore and analyze protocols, ports, and services. When you have completed this lab, you will be able to

- Define the function of TCP/IP logical ports

- List some of the well-known port number assignments

- Explore the various protocols, ports, and services employed in a typical network communication

Lab Materials and Setup

The materials you'll need for this lab exercise are

- PC running Windows 10 with Internet access

- Pen or pencil

- Paper

Getting Down to Business

The way network communication (all those 1s and 0s) goes in and out of a machine physically is through the NIC (network interface card). The way network communication goes in and out of a machine logically, though, is through a program or service. A *service* is a program that runs in the background, independent of a logon, that provides functionalities to a system.

Windows client machines, for instance, have a Workstation service that runs in the background and enables connections to remote network resources. It's not tied to a single user logon, and is always running in the background. As another example, when you turn on a Web server, you're starting a specific server service that isn't tied to a specific user logon. In the world of Linux, services are known as *daemons*.

Well, then, how does network communication go in and out of a program or service?

Let's say a single machine is running both an FTP (File Transfer Protocol) server, like FileZilla, and a Web (HTTP) server, like Apache. If both are accessible by the same IP address, how does the traffic for the FTP server get to the FTP server, and the traffic for the Web server get to the Web server? The way into and out of a program or service is through a *port*, which is an endpoint in communication, represented by a logical number.

So, in addition to source and destination MAC addresses and source and destination IP addresses, there are source and destination ports. MAC addresses are found in frames at Layer 2 of the OSI model. IP addresses are found in packets at Layer 3. Port numbers are found in either TCP segments or UDP datagrams at Layer 4.

Based on the destination port, the destination machine knows which program or service to send the data to. This is like a postal carrier bringing mail for tenants of an apartment building. The tenants all live at the same street address (like an FTP server and a Web server share the same IP address). However, the postal carrier knows to put the mail for Frank Thomas Peterson (FTP), who lives in Apartment 21, in the box for Apartment 21, and the mail for Helen Theresa Thomasina Parker (HTTP), who lives in Apartment 80, in the box for Apartment 80.

Step 1   In your own words, explain the purpose of a logical port.

_____

_____

_____

_____

Step 2   Fill in the protocols/services associated with these commonly used ports. If you need some help, check out www.iana.org/assignments/port-numbers.

Port	Protocol/Service
21	
22	
25	
53	
67/68	
80	
88	
143	
389	
443	
3389	

✔ **Hint**

> Windows lists all of the well-known ports and protocol services that are associated with them in a file without an extension, simply named "services." This file is more than just a list, though. It is used by Windows to map port numbers to services, and can be tweaked to modify a default port that a service is associated with. Access this list in Windows 10 by opening Notepad (Start | All Programs | Accessories | Notepad) and navigating to c:\windows\system32\drivers\etc. Change the view from "Text Documents (*.txt)" to "All Documents (*.*)" to view and open the services file. If you want to edit this file, you have to open Notepad as an Administrator. Other network operating systems maintain an equivalent document of port-to-service mappings. Linux, for example, also uses a file named "services" located in the /etc directory.

Step 3   You can view a listing of the active ports using the netstat command-line utility. We took a brief look at this utility in Chapter 1, but now we're going to go deeper into its capabilities.

With `netstat`, you have a number of options/switches to customize the output of the list. Run the `netstat /?` command, and provide a description of the following switches:

    `netstat -a`

_____

    `netstat -b`

_____

    `netstat -n`

_____

    `netstat -o`

_____

When you want to run multiple options/switches at a time, you don't need to specify a new - for each one. For example, `netstat -b -a -n -o` can simply be written as `netstat -bano`.

→ **Note**

> **You'll be making heavy use of the help function of utilities throughout the rest of the Lab Manual in order to use more advanced features of each utility. When in doubt, type the command and then add a space and /? to the end of the command. For example, type `ping /?` to explore the ping options.**

Step 4   Scott calls you over to see a system that he suspects may have a Trojan horse. Before running your company's standard anti-malware program, he wants you to run `netstat`. Why would he want you to do this?

_____

_____

On your lab system, run `netstat` without any switches. Are there any established connections?

You'll recall that each Session layer connection is represented by a local and foreign socket (the column headers use the term "address"). A socket is an endpoint in network communication (on each of the two communicating sides), represented by an IP address and port number (written in a concatenated form with a colon in the middle). The local socket is on the machine you're using, while the remote socket is on the machine you're connected to and communicating with. The last column in the netstat output deals with TCP connection states and is explained more here: www.tcpipguide.com/free/t_TCPOperationalOverviewandtheTCPFiniteStateMachineF-2.htm

Now launch a Web browser, navigate to www.flcc.edu, and run netstat -bano (note that -b requires you to run the Windows command-line interface as Administrator). Record some of the connection information.

Step 5 After waiting for a few moments, if you run netstat -bano once again, you will find that the status of some of the connections will change or disappear. To have netstat run itself repeatedly, put a number after netstat that represents an interval of seconds for netstat to rerun itself. For example, netstat 15 -bano, will automatically run the command every 15 seconds. To stop it, press CTRL-C.

 1 HOUR

Lab Exercise 8.03: HTTP and Ports

In essence, most people mistakenly equate the World Wide Web with the Internet! In reality, the Internet is the infrastructure of connected networks, while the World Wide Web is the multimedia content with hyperlinks. They probably make this mistake because the World Wide Web, using HTTP (Hypertext Transfer Protocol) and SSL/TLS (Secure Sockets Layer/Transport Layer Security), is the most widely used TCP/IP application. That said, one of the best ways to develop and practice the skills needed to support TCP/IP applications is to install and configure a server to support an Internet or intranet Web server.

There are really two important components associated with hosting a Web site. The first, and the one that you will be concerned with the most as a network support technician, is the installation, configuration, and management of the Web server itself. A close second would be the development and layout of the actual content (the Web pages), as a Web designer. To configure the Web server, you will work with the world's single most popular Web server, Apache HTTP Server.

Learning Objectives

In this lab, you will install and configure Apache HTTP Server. When you have completed this lab, you will be able to

- Install and configure server-side and client-side networking applications

- Configure TCP/IP addressing and ports

- Troubleshoot TCP/IP applications

Lab Materials and Setup

The materials you'll need for this lab exercise are

- Two Windows 10 systems

- Pen or pencil

- Paper

Getting Down to Business

WampServer is an environment for developing Web applications for Windows. The *W* in "Wamp" stands for Windows, the operating system that this platform is run on. (Alternatively, there is LAMP for Linux and MAMP for Mac.) The *a* stands for Apache, the world's most used Web server. The *m* stands for MySQL, the world's most used open source relational database management system (second to Oracle Database for market share, when including proprietary systems). The *p* stands for PHP, the world's most used server-side scripting language. Bundling these applications together in one environment is of great benefit for Web developers.

Step 1   On one machine, go to https://sourceforge.net/projects/wampserver/files/ and click WampServer 2, then WampServer 2.5, and then "wampserver2.5-Apache-2.4.9-Mysql-5.6.17-php5.5.12-64b.exe" (the 64-bit Windows executable installer). WampServer 3 on Windows 10 has some bugs and issues, so we're going to use WampServer 2.5 instead.

Run the executable from the Downloads folder, accept the agreement, keep all subsequent default selections, and open up the program.

FIGURE 8-1 Starting services

Step 2   If you have Skype running, stop it at this time. In the Notification Area, click the orange WampServer icon "(a stylized *W*)" and select Start All Services (see Figure 8-1). The orange icon will change to green. Skype uses port 80 (in a non-standard usage of that port) and will prevent the Web server from listening on the same port.

Step 3   Click the green WampServer icon. Select Apache | Service and click Test Port 80 (see Figure 8-2). You should see a message that the port is being used by the Apache Web server (see Figure 8-3).

Step 4   Open a Windows command-line interface, type `netstat  -an`, and then press ENTER. You should now see an entry, possibly at the very top, that looks like this:

```
Proto   Local Address          Foreign Address        State
TCP     0.0.0.0:80             0.0.0.0:0              LISTENING
```

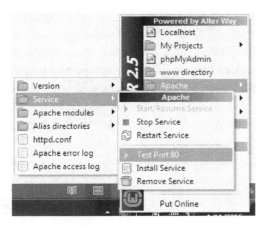

FIGURE 8-2 Testing port 80

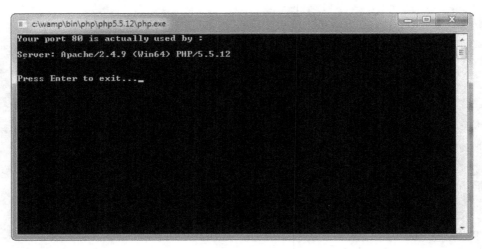

FIGURE 8-3 Apache using port 80

What does all of this mean?

_____

_____

Step 5   What is the difference between the following IP addresses found in the Local Address column: 0.0.0.0, 127.0.0.1, and the actual IP address bound to your NIC?

_____

_____

_____

Step 6   Why does the output of `netstat  -an` show asterisks instead of an IP address and port in the Foreign Address column and nothing in the State column for UDP?

_____

_____

_____

Step 7   Click the green WampServer icon. Click www directory to bring you to the root folder for the Web server. In the menu bar, click the View tab, and make sure there is a check in the box marked File Name Extensions.

To create a default Web page, right-click a blank area inside the root folder, mouse over New, and then select Text Document. Change the filename and extension to **index.html** (make sure you don't call it index.html.txt, and click Yes in the rename pop-up), which will be the default page that loads for your Web site. Right-click the file and select Open With | Choose Another App | Notepad. Type **Hello, World!** in the file, save it, and then exit Notepad.

Step 8   To allow access into the Web server from other machines, click the green WAMP icon and then Put Online at the very bottom. (If you see Put Offline, your server is already online.)

Step 9   On the second machine, open up a browser. In the address bar, type the IP address of the machine that's running the Web server, followed by the name of the file you just created (for example, 192.168.1.86/index.html). You should see the simple Web page you just made. (On the machine running the Web server, you might need to disable the firewall or write a rule to allow the unsolicited incoming traffic.)

Quickly enter `netstat -n` on both machines. Were you able to see the connection's sockets listed in the output from the command?

In this step, what is the Web client and what is the Web server?

_____

_____

_____

_____

_____

_____

_____

Step 10   Click the green WampServer icon. Select Apache | Service and click Stop Service. The WampServer icon should now turn orange, which means, in this case, that the Web server component of WampServer has been stopped, although the MySQL service (which was started earlier too) is still running. Can you spot the MySQL service's port in the output of `netstat -an`?

_____

_____

_____

Step 11   Click the orange WampServer icon. Select Apache | Service and click Test Port 80. You should see a message indicating that port 80 is not being used by any application.

Step 12   Open a Windows command-line interface, type `netstat -an`, and then press ENTER. The entry seen earlier

```
Proto   Local Address          Foreign Address        State
TCP     0.0.0.0:80             0.0.0.0:0              LISTENING
```

should no longer be present. Why do you think this is the case? What is the difference between an open port and a closed port? Do firewalls open and close ports?

_____

_____

_____

 30 MINUTES

Lab Exercise 8.04: FTP and Ports

Transferring files between computers is a very important process that all networks require. Whether files from the Web designer's computer are being sent to the Web server or an Internet file server is acting as a repository for files, the underlying protocol is FTP (File Transfer Protocol), which was designed for the uploading and downloading of files between computers.

FTP is a major protocol in the TCP/IP suite, and this lab walks you through the entire process of transferring files with a free, open source program called FileZilla.

Learning Objectives

In this lab, you will set up both an FTP client and an FTP server. Then, you will transfer data between the two. By the end of this lab, you will be able to

- Install, configure, and manage an FTP server

- Install an FTP client, and transfer files.

Lab Materials and Setup

The materials you'll need for this lab exercise are

- Two Windows 10 systems

- Pen or pencil

- Paper

Getting Down to Business

There are three ways that you can use FTP: a command-line interface, a Web browser, and a third-party application. This lab uses one of the simplest third-party FTP applications for Windows, especially for those "let me put up an FTP server so you guys can get a copy" type of situations. Let's get started with FileZilla!

Step 1 Go to https://filezilla-project.org/download.php?show_all=1 and then download, install, and run the FileZilla FTP Client on one machine. Be sure to decline all additional requested packages.

Go to https://filezilla-project.org/download.php?type=server and then download, install, and run the FileZilla FTP Server on the other machine. Stop when you see the Connect To Server dialog box.

The default admin port for the FileZilla FTP Server is 14147. After you start the server, `netstat -an` will show the following output:

```
TCP     127.0.0.1:14147          0.0.0.0:0              LISTENING
```

Why does the source socket start with an IP address of 127.0.0.1 and not 0.0.0.0 in this case (compared to what was seen earlier with the Web server)?

_____

_____

Step 2   On the machine on which you installed the FileZilla FTP Server, in the Connect To Server dialog box, click OK. In the menu bar at the top, select Edit | Users, and then click the Add button on the right side of the dialog box. Type **bob** for the username, and then click OK. Put a check in the check box Password: under Account settings, and type **bob** into the Password text box (see Figure 8-4). Click Shared Folders on the left side of the dialog box. Minimize FileZilla, and using Windows Explorer, create a folder called **bobftp** off of the root of the C:\ drive. Go back to the FileZilla window. Click Add and then browse to the bobftp folder, check all unchecked check boxes in the Files section (Write, Delete, Append) and all unchecked check boxes in the Directories section (Create, Delete), and click OK (see Figure 8-5).

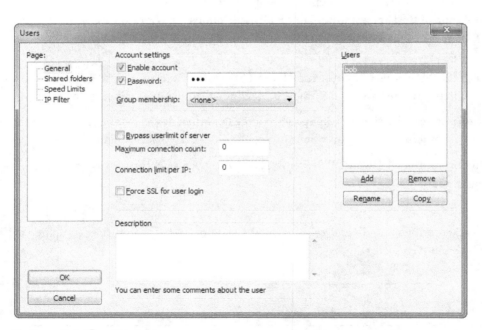

FIGURE 8-4 Creating a user account

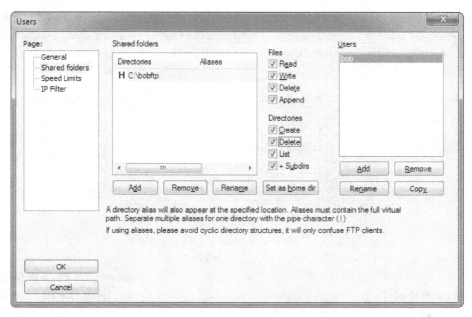

FIGURE 8-5 Setting up the shared folder

Step 3 Start sniffing with Wireshark on the FTP server. Use the display filter of **ftp || ftp-data** to restrict the output to related packets. You may have to allow FTP through the firewall on this machine. To do so, follow these steps:

a. In the Windows Search Box, type **firewall** and select Windows Defender Firewall.

b. In the pane at the left, select Allow An App Or Feature Through Windows Defender Firewall.

c. Click the Allow Another App button.

d. Click the Browse button.

e. Browse to the C:\Program Files (x86)\FileZilla Server folder.

f. Double-click FileZilla Server.exe.

g. Click the Add button.

h. Verify that FileZilla Server.exe has been added to the Allowed Apps And Features list.

i. Make sure there are checks in the boxes for Public and Private for FileZilla Server.exe.

j. Click OK to close the window.

k. Close the Windows Defender Firewall by clicking the X in the top right.

l. Open a command-line interface with administrative rights and execute the following command:

```
netsh advfirewall set global StatefulFTP disable
```

On the machine on which you installed the FileZilla FTP Client, type in the IP address of the FTP server in the Host box. Provide the username of **bob** and password of **bob** in the Username and Password boxes. Leave the Port box blank, and FTP will use its default port for establishing the connection (see the top of Figure 8-6).

What do you see in Wireshark on the server related to the bob account? What port is being used by the FTP server?

_____

_____

Step 4   With Wireshark still running on the FTP server, on the FTP client, create a text file called **bobsfile** on the desktop, and type a sentence into that file. In the FileZilla FTP Client on the same machine, in the Local Site: pane, browse to the desktop. From the pane below, where you can see the files on the desktop, drag and drop bobsfile.txt to the pane to its right, which represents the FTP server's directory for the user bob (see the middle of Figure 8-6).

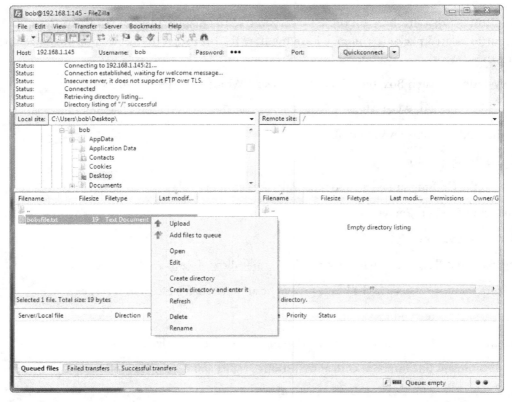

FIGURE 8-6 FileZilla FTP Client

On the FTP server, use Windows Explorer to browse and open the file that was just uploaded to the server. Then open a command-line interface and run netstat -an. What ports are relevant to this lab? What are represented by the local address and foreign address values?

_____

_____

Step 5   What port was used for the data transfer in the previous step? Why wasn't port 20 used? Use this link as a reference: http://slacksite.com/other/ftp.html.

_____

_____

30 **MINUTES**

Lab Exercise 8.05: The TCP Three-Way Handshake in Action

You've heard much about the TCP three-way handshake up to this point, but now it's time to actually see it in action. In order to form a bidirectional line of communication at Layer 4 with the sequencing, acknowledging, connection-oriented features, and guaranteed delivery of TCP, each host needs to acknowledge a TCP segment sent from the other side.

Learning Objectives

In this lab, you will analyze the TCP three-way handshake with Wireshark. Seeing the sequence and acknowledgement numbers will solidify your knowledge of the steps involved. By the completion of the lab you should be able to

- Establish a connection between two hosts
- Observe and record the TCP flags
- Observe and record the sequence and acknowledgement numbers

Lab Materials and Setup

The materials you'll need for this lab exercise are

- *Mike Meyers' CompTIA Network+ Guide to Managing and Troubleshooting Networks* textbook
- Windows 10 system
- Pen or pencil
- Paper

Getting Down to Business

Before starting this lab, it would be a great idea to review the "TCP" section in Chapter 8 of the *Mike Meyers' CompTIA Network+ Guide to Managing and Troubleshooting Networks* textbook; it contains a great look at the TCP three-way handshake.

Step 1   Open Wireshark, and start capturing packets. Add a display filter of **ip.addr==75.126.29.106**, which will limit the display to packets to and from the Total Seminars Web server, and press ENTER. Open a browser, and head to www.totalsem.com. After the page loads, stop the Wireshark capture.

Step 2   Look at the first three rows in the Wireshark capture (see Figure 8-7). What TCP flags are set for each of those segments?

_____

_____

_____

_____

_____

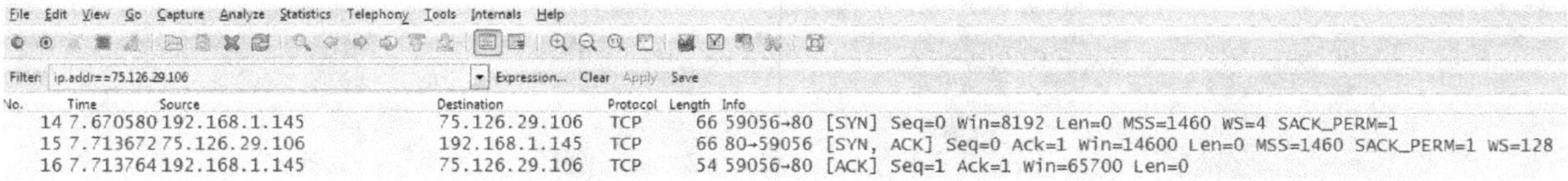

| File | Edit | View | Go | Capture | Analyze | Statistics | Telephony | Tools | Internals | Help |

Filter: ip.addr==75.126.29.106   ▼ Expression... Clear Apply Save

No.	Time	Source	Destination	Protocol	Length	Info
14	7.670580	192.168.1.145	75.126.29.106	TCP	66	59056→80 [SYN] Seq=0 Win=8192 Len=0 MSS=1460 WS=4 SACK_PERM=1
15	7.713672	75.126.29.106	192.168.1.145	TCP	66	80→59056 [SYN, ACK] Seq=0 Ack=1 Win=14600 Len=0 MSS=1460 SACK_PERM=1 WS=128
16	7.713764	192.168.1.145	75.126.29.106	TCP	54	59056→80 [ACK] Seq=1 Ack=1 Win=65700 Len=0

FIGURE 8-7 The TCP three-way handshake

Step 3 Select the first row in the Packet List pane. In the Packet Details pane, expand the TCP segment fields, and click the Sequence Number field. Look in the Packet Bytes pane to see the actual sequence number (see Figure 8-8). Record that number, represented by eight hex characters, here.

_____

_____

Step 4 Select the second row in the Packet List pane. In the Packet Details pane, expand the TCP segment fields, and click the Sequence Number field. Look in the Packet Bytes pane to see the actual sequence number. Record the number, represented by eight hex characters, here. Then, click the field called Acknowledgement Number. Record the number, represented by eight hex characters, here as well.

_____

_____

Step 5 Select the third row in the Packet List pane. In the Packet Details pane, expand the TCP segment fields, and click the Acknowledgement Number field. Look in the Packet Bytes pane to see the actual acknowledgement number. Record that number, represented by eight hex characters, here.

_____

_____

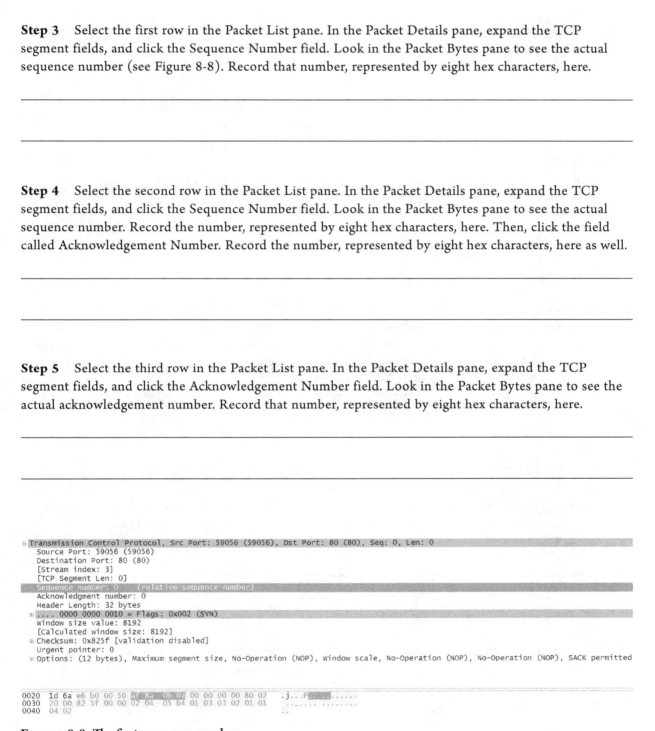

FIGURE 8-8 The first sequence number

Step 6　Explain how the four numbers you captured prove that a TCP three-way handshake occurred.

_____

_____

Lab Analysis

1.　Scott asks you to explain the main operational difference between TCP and UDP. How does this difference affect which services use TCP or UDP?

_____

_____

2.　Ann has configured Apache HTTP Server to host an equipment sign-out application. Students who use the university video cameras and accessories to complete assignments in their film class will complete the online form. She has configured the server to use an alternative port of 8080 as opposed to the well-known port of 80 for HTTP. Why would Ann choose to configure the application in this manner?

_____

_____

3.　After working with FileZilla, Harrison notices that sometimes protocols use different ports in different situations. Passive FTP doesn't use port 20, in this case. Shortly thereafter, while setting up e-mail, Harrison is instructed to use port 993 for IMAP, and port 587 for SMTP. Use the Web to find out why you would you use these port numbers, instead of the well-known port numbers of 143 for IMAP, and 25 for SMTP?

_____

_____

4.　While capturing packets with Wireshark, Meir pings one of the other computers on his network. He examines the output of the capture and finds the section relating to the ping activity. What is the underlying protocol you would expect Meir to observe?

_____

_____

Key Term Quiz

Use the vocabulary terms from the following list to complete the sentences that follow.

21

Apache HTTP server

ICMP (Internet Control Message Protocol)

IGMP (Internet Group Management Protocol)

IMAP (Internet Message Access Protocol)

netstat -b

SMTP (Simple Mail Transfer Protocol)

TCP (Transmission Control Protocol)

UDP (User Datagram Protocol)

1. A command that will allow you to explore all of the current connections and the associated program or service involved with the connection is _____.

2. _____ and _____ are defined at the Transport layer of the OSI model, whereas _____ and _____ are defined at the Network layer of the OSI model.

3. When working with e-mail, _____ is associated with sending e-mail and _____ is associated with receiving e-mail.

4. _____ listens on port 80.

5. FTP servers listen on port _____.

Chapter 9

Network Naming

Lab Exercises

As demonstrated in the last few chapters, you can cable some systems together and manually configure their IP addresses, subnet masks, and default gateways to create a very basic TCP/IP network. Over this network, users can send information to and receive information from each other. You can even add a Web server to this small network and host some information for the clients to access. However, without the addition of some sort of naming convention and resolution, you'll soon find that the use and management of this network becomes fairly tedious.

If you use only the basic configuration, you'll be stuck using IP addresses for everything. Instead of typing something like www.totalsem.com into your Web browser, you'll need to enter the IP address of the totalsem.com Web server. The answer to resolving this issue is the powerful protocol, DNS (Domain Name System). In the following labs, you will gain valuable hands-on experience with DNS.

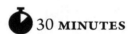 30 **MINUTES**

Lab Exercise 9.01: DNS Resolver Cache

As a network tech, and in subsequent lab exercises, you will utilize and configure DNS to resolve host names to IP addresses.

Learning Objectives

In this lab, you will review the DNS hierarchical steps and explore how the DNS Resolver Cache works on a client. When you have completed this lab, you will be able to

- Describe the DNS hierarchal process

- Explain how the DNS Resolver Cache works

Lab Materials and Setup

The materials you will need for this lab exercise are

- *Mike Meyers' CompTIA Network+ Guide to Managing and Troubleshooting Networks* textbook
- Windows 10 system with Internet access
- Pencil or pen
- Paper

Getting Down to Business

Having recently finished Chapter 9 on network naming in the *Mike Meyers' CompTIA Network+ Guide to Managing and Troubleshooting Networks* textbook, you know that you are going to have to implement DNS on the JSW Network Lab's systems. You want to get a jump on the setup, so you set out to review the order of queries and response in the hierarchical process of DNS.

Step 1   Place the following steps in order, from first to last, in the DNS hierarchical process.

____ Authoritative TLD DNS server gives a referral to the destination domain's authoritative DNS server.

____ DNS client adds the response to its DNS Resolver Cache.

____ Local DNS server queries an authoritative TLD DNS server.

____ Destination domain's authoritative DNS server gives the DNS response to the local DNS server.

____ Root server gives a referral to an authoritative TLD DNS server.

____ DNS client queries its local DNS server.

____ Local DNS server queries the destination domain's authoritative DNS server.

____ DNS client checks its DNS Resolver Cache.

____ Local DNS server gives the DNS response to the DNS client.

____ Local DNS server queries one of the 13 root servers.

Step 2   To view your PC's TCP/IP configuration, including IP addresses of the DNS servers, type `ipconfig /all` at a command prompt. What are the IP addresses of your DNS servers?

_____

_____

→ **Note**

> For all the commands in this chapter, press ENTER after every command.

Step 3   A PC's DNS Resolver Cache in RAM stores recently resolved entries received from its DNS servers. To view a display of resolved addresses cached on your PC, open a command prompt, and type `ipconfig /displaydns`. You should see a list of results similar to what's shown in Figure 9-1. What are your results?

_____

_____

Step 4   Manually clear the DNS Resolver Cache by typing `ipconfig /flushdns` into the command prompt. Start sniffing with Wireshark, using a display filter of **dns**. Now, open a browser and go to www.flcc.edu. After the page loads, stop the capture.

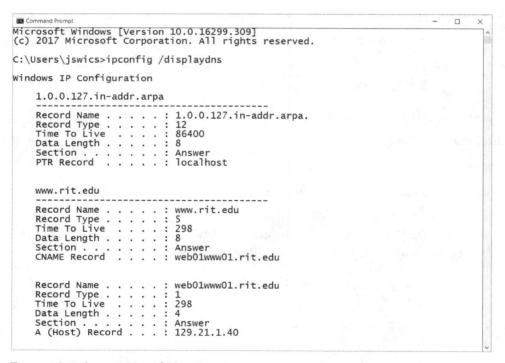

FIGURE 9-1 `ipconfig /displaydns` output

In the Packet List pane, find and select the DNS query response for the A record of www.flcc.edu (see Figure 9-2). In the Packet Details pane, expand the UDP datagram. Referring to the OSI model, DNS, at Layer 7, is in the UDP datagram at Layer 4. The data is then encapsulated by a Layer 3 IP packet. Finally, the IP packet is encapsulated by a Layer 2 frame.

Why do you think DNS uses UDP for DNS queries and replies (aside from something called a zone transfer, where a DNS server sends a copy of its DNS records to another DNS server for that domain, which uses TCP)?

_____

_____

→ **Note**

Loading a page like this will cause other DNS queries and DNS responses for other parts of the page. You want to find the specific query and response for www.flcc.edu. Filtering by dns, therefore, might still give you lots of other related DNS traffic. To search for a string in Wireshark, click Edit | Find Packet, change the display filter to string, type www.flcc.edu in the search box, and click the Find button. Now you should clearly see the query and response for www.flcc.edu.

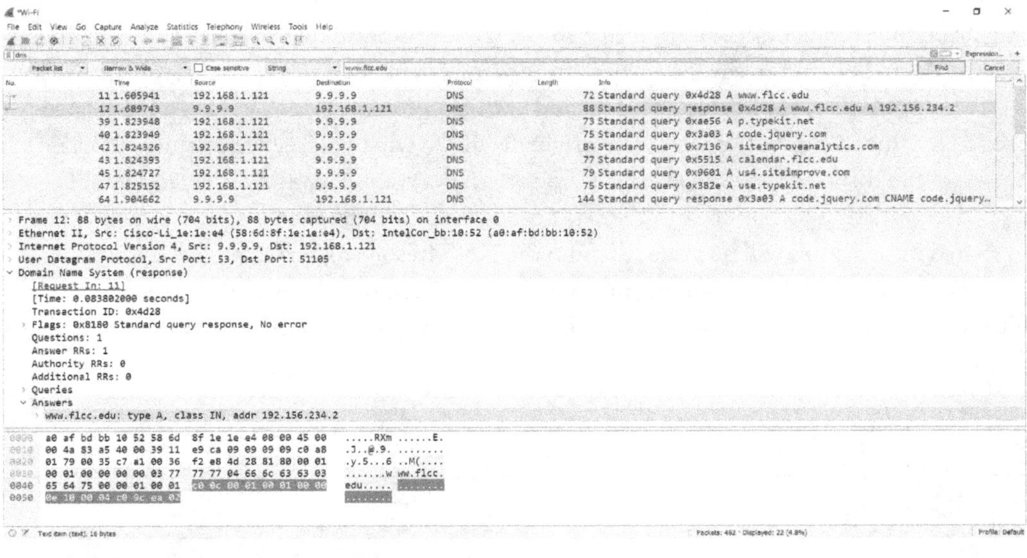

FIGURE 9-2 Wireshark capture showing a DNS query and a DNS response

Step 5   Go through both the DNS query and DNS response in detail and answer the following questions. What port do DNS servers use? What ports do DNS clients use? What is the answer to the query, "What's the IP address of www.flcc.edu?"

_____

_____

Step 6   Back at the command prompt, type `ipconfig /displaydns`. How do the results compare to the previous step?

_____

_____

Step 7   Earlier, you saw how DNS kicks in when you go to a Web site by typing its FQDN (fully qualified domain name) into the address bar of a browser. DNS also kicks in when you ping by FQDN.

Close the browser, and start sniffing with Wireshark, using a display filter of **dns or icmp**. In the command prompt, clear the DNS Resolver Cache by typing `ipconfig /flushdns`, and then type `ping www.syr.edu`. You should see the DNS query and response in Wireshark, followed by the ICMP Echo request and replies.

You'll notice from the command-line output that the FQDN is resolved into its corresponding IP address. Type `ipconfig /displaydns` to see the records from www.syr.edu in the DNS Resolver Cache. You should notice a TTL (Time To Live) of around 50 seconds, which means your PC will keep the related information cached for this amount of time. (It was originally 60, so what you see for a value will be how quickly after the ping you displayed the cache.) Type `ipconfig /displaydns` again, and you'll notice the TTL is decrementing with each second. Try it again, and it will be even lower, as it ticks down to 0, when the related information will be removed from the DNS Resolver Cache. In fact, if you type `ping www.syr.edu` again, while still sniffing in Wireshark, you'll notice the ICMPs again, but you will not see the DNS query and response. When will you see the DNS query and response related to this ping again?

_____

_____

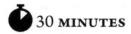 30 MINUTES

Lab Exercise 9.02: Using the hosts File for Name Resolution

Before DNS hit the networking scene in 1984, a text file called hosts.txt was manually maintained and shared by Stanford Research Institute for the ARPANET (Advanced Research Projects Agency Network). The file mapped networks, gateways, and host names to IP addresses for member organizations. An amazing repository of actual hosts files has been collected through the years and it can be located here: https://emaillab.jp/dns/hosts/.

Operating systems today have a text file called hosts that maps host names, or FQDNs (fully qualified domain names), to IP addresses. This file might seem like a relic of the past, since DNS seems to do the same thing today. However, believe it or not, the hosts file is used by both malware and anti-virus software.

Learning Objectives

In this lab, you will explore common, modern uses of the hosts file. When you have completed this lab, you'll be able to

- Examine and configure entries in a hosts file
- Protect your system with the hosts file

Lab Materials and Setup

The materials you'll need for this lab exercise are

- *Mike Meyers' CompTIA Network+ Guide to Managing and Troubleshooting Networks* textbook
- Windows 10 system
- Pencil or pen
- Paper

Step 1   Open up Notepad as an Administrator by typing **Notepad** into the Windows search box, right-clicking on Notepad, and selecting Run As Administrator. From Notepad, click File | Open, and browse to c:\windows\system32\drivers\etc. Change the dropdown at the bottom from Text Documents (*.txt) to All Files (*.*). You should see hosts. Yes, this file, even on Windows, has no extension. Double-click on hosts to open it.

Everything in this file is commented out with the pound sign. There is nothing in play. In the file, add on its own line: **129.21.1.40 www.jonathanscottweissman.edu**. Save the file by pressing CTRL-S.

Step 2   Open up a command prompt and type `ipconfig /flushdns`. There are two ways entries are added to the host DNS Resolver Cache The first, and obvious, way, is replies to DNS queries. When the host sends a DNS query to its DNS server, the DNS server, after doing some querying on the client's behalf, will give back the answer to the client. The second way entries get added to the client's DNS Resolver Cache is the hosts file.

Type `ipconfig /displaydns`. The entry in the hosts file has been re-added to the DNS Resolver Cache, with a TTL of zero seconds. This TTL, though, doesn't decrement like a TTL from a DNS response would. It's just a dummy placeholder value. Entries from the hosts file are always going to be in the DNS Resolver Cache.

You'll notice two records here. The first, an A (Address record), maps a name into its corresponding IPv4 address. The second, a PTR (Pointer record), maps an address shown here in DNS reverse lookup format into its corresponding name.

Open up a browser and enter **www.jonathanscottweissman.edu**.

What do you see and why? Was a DNS query issued? Why or why not?

_____

_____

Step 3   Based on what was illustrated in the previous step, how might malware use the hosts file?

_____

_____

Step 4   In the hosts file, add this entry underneath the previous one: **127.0.0.1 www.naz.edu**. Remember, 127.0.0.1 is the loopback address of your computer. Open up a browser and go to www.naz.edu. What do you see, and why? Now, remove this entry and the one from earlier and go to www.naz.edu. What do you see and why?

_____

_____

Step 5   Based on what was illustrated in the previous step, how might malware use the hosts file (differently than your answer in Step 3)?

_____

_____

_____

Step 6   Open up a browser and visit someonewhocares.org/hosts/. Scroll and read through the various categories of sites listed. Copy the text from this site and paste it into your hosts file, and then save your hosts file. How can this protect your machine?

_____

_____

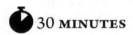 30 MINUTES

Lab Exercise 9.03: nslookup

Now it's time to look at a great utility, nslookup (name server lookup). There are times when you'll need this tool to troubleshoot and diagnose situations.

Learning Objectives

In this lab, you will learn how to use the nslookup utility to

- Troubleshoot DNS issues
- Diagnose DNS problems

Lab Materials and Setup

The materials you'll need for this lab exercise are

- *Mike Meyers' CompTIA Network+ Guide to Managing and Troubleshooting Networks* textbook
- Windows 10 system with Internet connectivity
- Pencil or pen
- Paper

Getting Down to Business

Users complain about not being able to access a Web site. You have an idea what the problem is, and you decide to run a few diagnostic tests to see if they will provide answers to this riddle and get the network running at optimum performance!

Step 1 Start sniffing with Wireshark, using a display filter of **dns**. As you go through each step, notice the DNS queries and DNS responses in Wireshark.

Open a command prompt and type nslookup, which will run the utility in interactive mode. To break out of this mode, press CTRL-C.

→ **Note**

You can also run nslookup in non-interactive mode by typing in the rest of the command after nslookup.

You'll notice the FQDN and IP address of your default server and a > prompt. At the > prompt type set q=ns, which will set the query type to NS, the name server DNS resource record type. Now, just type . and press ENTER (see Figure 9-3). What do you see as output?

_____

_____

```
Command Prompt - nslookup                                          —  □  ×
Microsoft Windows [Version 10.0.16299.309]
(c) 2017 Microsoft Corporation. All rights reserved.

C:\Users\jswics>nslookup
Default Server:  dns.quad9.net
Address:  9.9.9.9

> set q=ns
> .
Server:  dns.quad9.net
Address:  9.9.9.9

Non-authoritative answer:
(root)  nameserver = j.root-servers.net
(root)  nameserver = k.root-servers.net
(root)  nameserver = l.root-servers.net
(root)  nameserver = m.root-servers.net
(root)  nameserver = a.root-servers.net
(root)  nameserver = b.root-servers.net
(root)  nameserver = c.root-servers.net
(root)  nameserver = d.root-servers.net
(root)  nameserver = e.root-servers.net
(root)  nameserver = f.root-servers.net
(root)  nameserver = g.root-servers.net
(root)  nameserver = h.root-servers.net
(root)  nameserver = i.root-servers.net
>
```

FIGURE 9-3 nslookup showing the root servers

```
■■ Command Prompt - nslookup                                    —   □   ×
Microsoft Windows [Version 10.0.16299.309]
(c) 2017 Microsoft Corporation. All rights reserved.

C:\Users\jswics>nslookup
Default Server:  dns.quad9.net
Address:  9.9.9.9

> set q=ns
> com.
Server:  dns.quad9.net
Address:  9.9.9.9

Non-authoritative answer:
com      nameserver = d.gtld-servers.net
com      nameserver = c.gtld-servers.net
com      nameserver = i.gtld-servers.net
com      nameserver = e.gtld-servers.net
com      nameserver = h.gtld-servers.net
com      nameserver = f.gtld-servers.net
com      nameserver = m.gtld-servers.net
com      nameserver = a.gtld-servers.net
com      nameserver = g.gtld-servers.net
com      nameserver = b.gtld-servers.net
com      nameserver = j.gtld-servers.net
com      nameserver = l.gtld-servers.net
com      nameserver = k.gtld-servers.net
>
```

FIGURE 9-4 nslookup showing the Authoritative DNS Servers for the .com TLD

Step 2 At the > prompt, type com. Notice, as shown in Figure 9-4, that it's com, followed by . and not .com. This is because the . at the end prevents your system from appending anything after, and it's the proper way to end an FQDN.

In a similar fashion, one at a time, type net., edu., gov., and other top-level domains (TLDs) you can think of. What do you see as output?

_____

_____

Step 3 At the > prompt try the following, one at a time: rit.edu., flcc.edu., naz.edu., and syr.edu.. See Figure 9-5. What do you see as output?

_____

_____

➜ **Note**

You will not get the expected results if you type www (or any hostname) in front of any of the listed domains in this step. nslookup will display the start of authority (SOA) record for the domain instead of the DNS servers. The reason is because NS records are for an entire domain, not a specific machine, like a Web server named www.

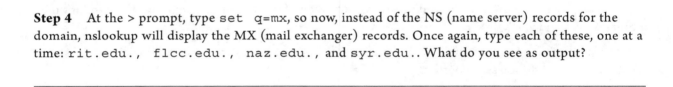

```
Command Prompt - nslookup                                    —   □   ×
Microsoft Windows [Version 10.0.16299.309]
(c) 2017 Microsoft Corporation. All rights reserved.

C:\Users\jswics>nslookup
Default Server:  dns.quad9.net
Address:  9.9.9.9

> set q=ns
> rit.edu.
Server:  dns.quad9.net
Address:  9.9.9.9

Non-authoritative answer:
rit.edu nameserver = accuvax.northwestern.edu
rit.edu nameserver = ns1a.rit.edu
rit.edu nameserver = ns2a.rit.edu
> flcc.edu.
Server:  dns.quad9.net
Address:  9.9.9.9

Non-authoritative answer:
flcc.edu         nameserver = ns.flcc.edu
flcc.edu         nameserver = ns4.flcc.edu
flcc.edu         nameserver = ns7.suny.edu
flcc.edu         nameserver = ns8.suny.edu
flcc.edu         nameserver = ns9.suny.edu
flcc.edu         nameserver = dns3.flcc.edu
>
```

FIGURE 9-5 nslookup showing the Authoritative DNS Servers for the rit.edu and flcc.edu domains

Step 4   At the > prompt, type set q=mx, so now, instead of the NS (name server) records for the domain, nslookup will display the MX (mail exchanger) records. Once again, type each of these, one at a time: rit.edu., flcc.edu., naz.edu., and syr.edu.. What do you see as output?

_____

_____

Step 5   At the > prompt, type set q=a, so now nslookup will show the A (IPv4 address) record(s) for each query. What is the IPv4 address of www.rit.edu? You'll notice the output contains web01www01.rit.edu, and the Wireshark capture shows a CNAME (Canonical Name) record in response with the same FQDN (web01www01.rit.edu). What is the purpose of a CNAME record?

_____

_____

Step 6 At the > prompt, type `set  q=aaaa`, so now nslookup will show the AAAA (IPv6 address) record(s) for each query. What is the IPv6 address of www.rit.edu? IPv6 addresses are four times the length of IPv4 records (32 × 4 = 128), which is why this DNS resource record was named AAAA.

_____

_____

Step 7 With nslookup, you can change the DNS server from your default that the queries go to by simply typing `server` followed either by the IP address or FQDN of another DNS server.

Type `server  8.8.8.8` or `server  8.8.4.4` to have any subsequent queries through nslookup go to one of these Google Public DNS Servers. Then execute a few of the earlier queries (see Figure 9-6). Where can you see proof that the queries went to the new servers in both the command prompt and Wireshark?

_____

_____

```
Microsoft Windows [Version 10.0.16299.309]
(c) 2017 Microsoft Corporation. All rights reserved.

C:\Users\jswics>nslookup
Default Server:  dns.quad9.net
Address:  9.9.9.9

> server 8.8.8.8
Default Server:  google-public-dns-a.google.com
Address:  8.8.8.8

> set q=a
> www.rit.edu.
Server:  google-public-dns-a.google.com
Address:  8.8.8.8

Non-authoritative answer:
Name:    web01www01.rit.edu
Address:  129.21.1.40
Aliases:  www.rit.edu

> set q=mx
> rit.edu.
Server:  google-public-dns-a.google.com
Address:  8.8.8.8

Non-authoritative answer:
rit.edu MX preference = 10, mail exchanger = mx03a-in01r.rit.edu
rit.edu MX preference = 10, mail exchanger = mx03b-in01r.rit.edu
rit.edu MX preference = 5, mail exchanger = mx03c-in01r.rit.edu
rit.edu MX preference = 5, mail exchanger = mx03d-in01r.rit.edu
>
```

FIGURE 9-6 nslookup using a non-default DNS server

 45 MINUTES

Lab Exercise 9.04: DNS Client and DNS Server in Action

If it ended up being your job to configure and maintain a hosts file on every computer that needed to access Web sites by their URLs, just the sheer number of entries would be astounding! Furthermore, IP addresses of servers do change from time to time.

DNS to the rescue! DNS allows a distributed database of name-to-IP-address (and other) mappings, called *zones*, to be stored on dedicated DNS servers and be accessed by clients to resolve those names to IP addresses.

From the Internet DNS root servers to simple intranet DNS servers, the goal is to make access to Web sites as transparent to the end user as possible, while keeping administrative overhead to a minimum. Even entry-level network techs are expected to have some understanding of DNS server configuration and maintenance.

Learning Objectives

In this lab, you will install a DNS server. When you have completed this lab, you'll be able to

- Install and configure a DNS server on a Microsoft Windows Server 2016 system

- Configure DNS server entries to resolve host names to IP addresses

Lab Materials and Setup

The materials you'll need for this lab exercise are

- *Mike Meyers' CompTIA Network+ Guide to Managing and Troubleshooting Networks* textbook

- Windows 10 system

- Pencil or pen

- Paper

- Windows Server 2016 system

- Network switch

- Cabling

Getting Down to Business

Having played with the hosts file, you realize that even for the intranet Web site, you will not want a network tech or administrator tied up with configuring hosts files on all of the client systems. You have to learn about DNS servers anyway, so you dive in and begin configuring the Windows Server 2016 machine to provide DNS services. You hope to have this up and running before Scott returns to check on your progress!

Step 1   Perform the following substeps to configure the DNS client:

   a.   Open up the Windows 10 machine.

   b.   In the Windows search box, type **sharing**.

   c.   Click Manage Advanced Sharing Settings, which will appear as the top choice, in the dynamically generated menu.

   d.   In the address bar at the top, click Network And Sharing Center.

   e.   In the pane at the left, click Change Adapter Settings.

   f.   Right-click Ethernet and select Properties.

   g.   Select Internet Protocol Version 4 (TCP/IPv4) and click the Properties button.

   h.   In the General tab, which will open by default, change the radio button selection to Use The Following IP Address. Use the following information:

       IP address 192.168.1.18

       Subnet mask 255.255.255.0

       Default gateway (leave blank)

       In the next section, make sure Use The Following DNS Server Addresses is also selected. Assign 192.168.1.81 as the Preferred DNS server, and leave the Alternate DNS server field blank.

   i.   Click the OK button, followed by the Close button on the remaining dialog box. Click OK twice and close the Network Connections window.

Step 2   Perform the following substeps to configure the DNS server:

   a.   Using the same steps provided earlier, assign the Windows Server 2016 machine the following information:

       IP address 192.168.1.81

       Subnet mask 255.255.255.0

       Default gateway (leave blank)

       Preferred DNS server 127.0.0.1

   b.   Let's also give the server a host name instead of using the long awkward one that was generated. Right-click the This PC icon on the desktop and select Properties.

    c. In the Computer Name, Domain, And Workgroup Settings section, click Change Settings. Click the Change button toward the middle of the dialog box. Enter any name for your computer and click OK. Then click OK, Close, and Restart Now. Your server will now reboot.

_____

_____

Step 3   Perform the following substeps to install the DNS role on the server:

    a. On the Windows Server 2016 machine, open Server Manager by clicking Start and then clicking Server Manager.

    b. Click the Add Roles And Features link. Click Next until the Select Server Roles page is displayed.

    c. Select the DNS Server check box. On the Add Roles And Features Wizard dialog box, click Add Features.

    d. In the Add Roles Wizard, if the Before You Begin page appears, click Next.

    e. In the Roles list, click DNS Server, and then click Next.

    f. Read the information on the DNS Server page, and then click Next.

    g. On the Confirm Installation Options page, verify that the DNS Server role will be installed, and then click Install.

_____

_____

Step 4   Perform the following substeps to configure the DNS zone on the server:

    a. On the Server Manager console, click Tools and open the DNS Manager console.

    b. Expand Domain Server, select and right-click Forward Lookup Zones, and then select New Zone.

    c. Navigate to the Zone Type page, and make sure that the Primary Zone radio button is selected.

    d. Clear the Store The Zone In Active Directory check box, and then click Next.

    e. On the Zone Name page, type **jonathan.weissman** and then click Next.

    f. Navigate to the Dynamic Update page, make sure that the Do Not Allow Dynamic Updates radio button is selected and then click Next and finish the wizard.

_____

_____

Step 5 Perform the following substeps to add resource records (RRs) to the DNS Forward Lookup Zone:

a. On the DNS Manager console, expand Forward Lookup Zones. Select and right-click the created zone, and then select New Host (A or AAAA).

b. On the New Host dialog box, specify the host name and IP address of your host and then click Add Host. Let's make the following two A records:

professor for the host name and **192.168.1.81** for the IP address (the server's IP address)

rochester for the host name and **192.168.1.99** for the IP address (an IP address that doesn't exist)

c. Click **Done** once you have added the desired hosts.

_____

_____

Step 6 Perform the following substeps to test out the DNS resource records from the client:

a. Open up the Windows 10 machine.

b. Start Wireshark on the client, and filter by **dns**.

c. Disable the firewall on both machines for this experiment.

d. Type `ping professor.jonathan.weissman.` (with the dot at the end). You should see the ping successfully get replies from your server in the command prompt. You should also see the DNS query and DNS reply in Wireshark.

e. Type `ping rochester.jonathan.weissman.` (with the dot at the end). Even though the ping fails, since there is no host at 192.168.1.99, you'll see that the DNS query gets a DNS response in both the command prompt and Wireshark, mapping the name rochester.jonathan.weissman to its corresponding IP address of 192.168.1.99.

_____

_____

Lab Analysis

1. Peter is attempting to access a Web site, but he keeps receiving an error message. Someone told him that there may be a file on his computer that is keeping him from loading the site. He asks you to explain the relationship between the hosts file and DNS, and give an example of how they might conflict.

    _____

    _____

2. Andrew wants to know about DNS root servers. Explain their purpose to him.

    _____

    _____

3. While installing and configuring a DNS server, Evan observes various identifiers for the DNS record entries such as Host (A or AAAA), Alias (CNAME), and Mail Exchanger (MX). What are these identifiers?

    _____

    _____

4. After finally getting a number of systems configured in his SOHO, Michael discovers that one system cannot access the address www.ibm.com. It was able to access this Web site earlier, but now it just returns a message, "The address is not valid." What commands should Michael run, and why would he run them to diagnose the problem?

    _____

    _____

5. What does the company Dyn have to do with DNS? What happened to Dyn in 2016?

    _____

    _____

Key Term Quiz

Use the terms and commands from the list provided to complete the sentences that follow.

A

FQDN (fully qualified domain name)

hosts

`ipconfig /displaydns`

`nslookup`

`ping`

1. When troubleshooting DNS, you could use the _____ command to query the DNS server.

2. The _____ record maps a name to an IPv4 address.

3. You can run the _____ utility with the _____ to test if DNS is configured correctly. If this task returns an error, you can run the command with the IP address to further clarify if there is a problem with DNS.

4. A way to map names to IP addresses without a DNS server is through a file called _____.

5. _____ is the command to see the names and IP addresses that have been resolved for you by your DNS server.

Chapter 10

Securing TCP/IP

Lab Exercises

There are a number of mechanisms, protocols, and utilities that make using the Internet safer for sharing private data and conducting business transactions. In broad terms, this is accomplished by securing the TCP/IP suite of protocols following the guidelines of the CIA model, which looks to secure the confidentiality, integrity, and availability of data.

To accomplish confidentiality, the encryption of data guarantees that only the intended parties will be able to view the data. To accomplish integrity, the hashing of data guarantees that the data received is the same as originally sent. To accomplish availability, fault tolerance and load balancing must be in place, as well as security controls, so that data can be accessed by those authorized to do so. Another important principle is nonrepudiation, which ensures that the sender can't deny having sent a message.

In the following lab exercises, you will work to secure communications with TCP/IP technologies that address confidentiality and integrity (availability is covered in other chapters). You'll explore, install, and configure the components that handle confidentiality, integrity, and nonrepudiation.

 45 MINUTES

Lab Exercise 10.01: Evaluating Digital Signatures

Creating and implementing a public key infrastructure (PKI) to secure the transfer of data can be achieved using various inexpensive encryption applications. This is all well and good, but are you going to trust sending private information, such as credit card numbers or Social Security numbers, to an organization that hasn't verified its integrity? Even if a Web site has implemented security using PKI, you still want verification that the organization is a valid, respectable outfit and that this is really their Web site.

A number of organizations (Comodo, GoDaddy, and DigiCert, to name a few) have established themselves as reputable providers of digitally signed certificates: certificate authorities (CAs). A company that wants to do business over the Internet will apply with one of these organizations for a digital certificate, and after passing a background check, will receive a valid digital certificate for their Web server. This certificate not only provides secure communications through encryption, but it also validates the company's integrity by providing a digital signature from a reputable certificate authority.

Learning Objectives

In this lab, you will examine the solutions provided by various certificate vendors. When you have completed this lab, you will be able to

- Confirm at least three certificate vendors

- Analyze various product offerings from these vendors

- Recommend a specific product based on needs

Lab Materials and Setup

The materials you'll need for this lab exercise are

- *Mike Meyers' CompTIA Network+ Guide to Managing and Troubleshooting Networks* textbook

- Windows 10 machine with Internet access

- Pen or pencil

- Paper

Getting Down to Business

JSW's client, the Department of Transportation (DOT), has decided to add a customer response Web page to its Web site, where commuters can report traffic concerns (such as road hazards/damage) or make suggestions for improvements. To keep the spam and prank comments to a minimum, the DOT has asked JSW to implement a members-only site and require commuters to provide some personal data and create a user name and password. To ensure the security of the commuters' personal data, Jonathan is going to secure the site and assign a PKI certificate to it.

Jonathan asks you to help Scott research at least three certificate providers and put together a report on the costs and benefits of the various products. Due to the public nature of the client, Jonathan recommends that you narrow your research to mid-level and top-of-the-line products.

Step 1 On your Windows 10 machine, open up the Firefox browser. If you don't have Firefox, get it at www.mozilla.org/en-US/firefox/new/.

Click the Open Menu icon (three horizontal lines) at the top right, click Options, click Privacy & Security on the top left, scroll all the way down to the Certificates section, and click the View Certificates button. Scroll through the list and list any names that you recognize. Close the Certificate Manager window when you're done. Figure 10-1 shows Firefox's Certificate Manager.

FIGURE 10-1 Firefox's Certificate Manager

Step 2   Read the following two items:

- "What is a Digital Certificate, and why do you need one?"
  www.comodo.com/resources/small-business/digital-certificates4.php

- "How Extended Validation SSL Can Help Increase Online Transactions and Improve Customer
  Confidence"   www.symantec.com/content/en/us/enterprise/fact_sheets/b-how-ev-ssl-increase-
  online-transactions-improve-confidence_DS.en-us.pdf

What is the difference between an Extended Validation (EV) certificate and a certificate without EV?

_____

_____

_____

_____

Step 3   Compare the following products offered from the following three CAs. Which one would you recommend and why?

- Comodo: https://ssl.comodo.com/

- GoDaddy: www.godaddy.com/web-security/ssl-certificate

- DigiCert: www.digicert.com/order/order-1.php

_____

_____

_____

_____

_____

_____

_____

➜ **Note**

> As discussed throughout this Lab Manual, Web site addresses change from time to time. If any of
> the listed Web sites are not valid, search for the company, and then navigate to the appropriate Web
> page for digital certificates.

Step 4   Let's Encrypt (https://letsencrypt.org) describes itself as "a free, automated, and open
Certificate Authority." On this page, https://letsencrypt.org/about/, they claim: "We give people the
digital certificates they need in order to enable HTTPS (SSL/TLS) for websites, for free, in the most
user-friendly way we can. We do this because we want to create a more secure and privacy-respecting
Web."

That's great, but why would a corporation like a bank never use Let's Encrypt as a CA?

_____

_____

_____

_____

_____

_____

 1 HOUR

Lab Exercise 10.02: Configuring and Using GPG Encryption

GNU Privacy Guard (GPG) is a free implementation of OpenPGP, which is a standard that allows e-mails to be signed and encrypted. The original proprietary version, Pretty Good Privacy (PGP), was created by Phil Zimmerman in 1991.

Encrypting e-mail enforces confidentiality, while signing e-mail enforces both integrity and nonrepudiation.

Learning Objectives

In this lab, you will install, configure, and use GPG. After completion of this lab, you will be able to

- Sign e-mail
- Encrypt e-mail
- Decrypt e-mail

Lab Materials and Setup

The materials you'll need for this lab exercise are

- *Mike Meyers' CompTIA Network+ Guide to Managing and Troubleshooting Networks* textbook
- Windows 10 machine with Internet access

- A partner, who you'll be sending e-mail to and receiving e-mail from

- Pen or pencil

- Paper

Getting Down to Business

There are versions of GPG for many different operating systems, including Windows, macOS, Debian, RPM, Android, VMS, and RISC OS. In this lab, we're going to use Gpg4win, the version of GPG for Microsoft Windows operating systems.

Step 1 Follow these substeps to gain hands-on experience in confidentiality, integrity, and nonrepudiation:

a. Head to www.gpg4win.org/download.html to download and install the latest version of Gpg4win (3.1.1 at the time of this writing). In the installer, uncheck all boxes except GPG.

b. Create a Gmail account by going to www.google.com/gmail and clicking the Create An Account button in the upper-right portion of the page.

c. Head to www.mozilla.org/en-US/thunderbird/download and then download and install the latest version of Thunderbird (52.6.0 at the time of this writing). Accept all default settings. Thunderbird should load after the installation is complete. Click Skip Integration in the System Integration window that pops up.

d. From Thunderbird's menu bar (if you don't see it, press the ALT key), choose File | New | Existing Mail Account. Fill in your information, following all prompts.

e. From Thunderbird's menu bar, choose Tools | Add-Ons | Extensions, type **Enigmail** in the Search All Add-ons search box at the top right of the screen, and then press ENTER. The first item in the results list should be Enigmail. Click the Install button to the far right of the row, and then click Restart Now. Thunderbird will restart.

f. From Thunderbird's menu bar, click Enigmail (which now appears after the previous step) and then Setup Wizard. Continue with the following steps.

    i. Select the radio button for Start Setup Now and click the Next button.

    ii. Select the radio button for I Prefer A Standard Configuration (Recommended For Beginners) and click the Next button.

    iii. Enter and confirm a passphrase (see Figure 10-2) and click the Next button.

    iv. Your key pair will now be generated (see Figure 10-3). Click the Close button and then the Next button.

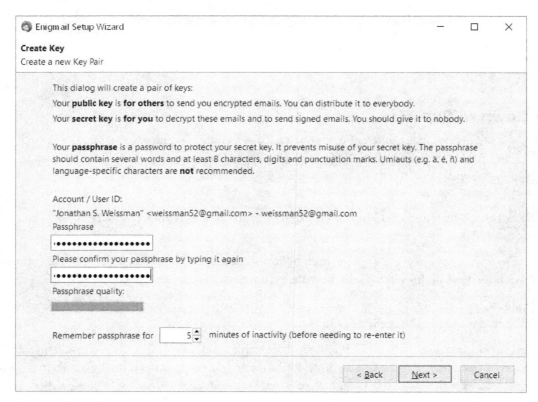

FIGURE 10-2 Entering a passphrase

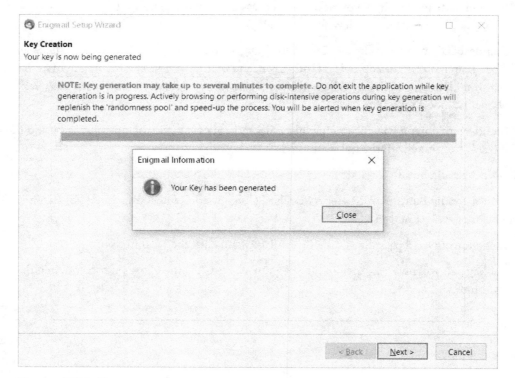

FIGURE 10-3 Key generation

     v. Click the Create Revocation Certificate button, enter your passphrase, and click the OK button. Save the certificate to your Documents folder, as prompted. Click the Close button and then click the Next button.

     vi. Click the Finish button.

  g. Pair up with a classmate. Each partner should send an e-mail, as described here, to the other partner. Click the Write button on the Mail toolbar. In the Write window that pops up, select Enigmail from the menu bar (note that this is not the same menu bar or Enigmail selection in the main Thunderbird window). Select Attach My Public Key. Fill in your partner's e-mail address in the To: field. For the Subject: of the e-mail, type **My public key**. Add a short message in the body of the e-mail, and then click the Send button. At the Enigmail Prompt, click the Leave Subject Unprotected button.

  h. When your partner's e-mail arrives, open it, right-click the attachment on the bottom of the window (with the .asc extension), select Import OpenPGP Key, and then click OK.

  i. Click the Write button on the Mail toolbar (or reply to the e-mail your partner sent you), which will once again open a Write window for an outgoing e-mail. Compose an e-mail to your partner, just like before. This time, however, Enigmail will encrypt the outgoing e-mail with your partner's public key. Verify that this is the case by clicking the Enigmail menu item on the Write window. You'll notice there is a check mark by Encrypt Message (Auto). Select Sign Message (Auto) as well.

  j. Each partner should now open the e-mail sent from the other partner, and Enigmail will decrypt it using the private key of the recipient. You should see a light blue bar at the top of the e-mail with the message "Decrypted message; good signature from" followed by the name and e-mail address of your partner.

  k. Go to www.google.com/gmail and log into your account. Open the e-mail that your partner sent to you.

Step 2 Answer the following questions, regarding your work in Step 1.

  a. How does the e-mail look in the Web browser compared to how it looks in Thunderbird? Why is this the case?

_____

_____

  b. When encrypting the e-mail to your partner, which key did you use?

_____

_____

c.   When your partner decrypted that e-mail, which key did he or she use?

_____

_____

d.   When signing your e-mail to your partner, which key did you use?

_____

_____

e.   When your partner verified your signature, which key did he or she use?

_____

_____

f.   How was confidentiality accomplished?

_____

_____

g.   How was integrity accomplished?

_____

_____

h.   How was nonrepudiation accomplished?

_____

_____

 30 MINUTES

Lab Exercise 10.03: Analyzing Secure TCP/IP Ports and Associations

In Chapter 8, you examined the TCP and UDP ports of various applications, like a Web server and an FTP server. Now that you have been working with secure TCP/IP applications, you will spend some time analyzing the connection between secure applications, their port numbers, and the associated function the secure application provides. Then, you will use Wireshark to see the difference between ports used for unencrypted communications and ports used for encrypted communications.

Learning Objectives

In this lab, you will work with various TCP/IP security components. When you have completed this lab, you will be able to

- Define the function of the various TCP/IP security components

- List some of the well-known port numbers for TCP/IP security protocols

- Explore the results of utilizing some of the secure protocols used in typical network communications

Lab Materials and Setup

The materials you'll need for this lab exercise are

- *Mike Meyers' CompTIA Network+ Guide to Managing and Troubleshooting Networks* textbook

- Windows 10 system with Internet access

- Pen or pencil

- Paper

Getting Down to Business

You want to explore some protocols involved in creating secure connections. While you're at it, go ahead and examine some of the other components that help keep TCP/IP secure, their function, port numbers, and associations.

Step 1   Fill in the secure protocols/services associated with the given ports. Check out www.iana.org/assignments/port-numbers if you need some help.

Port	Protocol/Service
22	
49	
88	
443	
465	
636	
993	
1812, 1813	

Step 2   Start capturing in Wireshark. Open a browser and go to www.rit.edu. After it loads completely, stop the capture. What is the destination port in the TCP segments leaving your machine?

_____

Step 3   Start capturing again in Wireshark. Open a browser and go to https://mycourses.rit.edu. After it loads completely, stop the capture. What is the destination port in the TCP segments leaving your machine?

_____

Step 4   In Firefox, go to https://online.citi.com. Mouse over the Extended Validation (green padlock and green words "Citigroup Inc. (US)") and notice the popup "Verified by: DigiCert Inc." Now click the EV bar, click the arrow at the far right, and at the bottom click More Information. Now click the View Certificate button, and then the Details tab at the top. Examine the fields and values of this digital certificate.

Now visit www.flcc.edu. Does this site offer the same level of security? Why or why not?

_____

_____

_____

_____

Lab Analysis

1. While conducting the research to recommend a certificate authority to your client, Bo notices that CAs are highly recommending Extended Validation (EV). Do a little further investigation and provide a short description of these features to him.

   _____

   _____

2. Yin wants to know exactly how the digital signature of the certificate authority on the digital certificate guarantees integrity. Help her out.

   _____

   _____

3. Your co-worker, Bill, has been using Wireshark to explore packets while running Secure Shell (SSH), Secure File Transfer Protocol (SFTP), and Secure Copy Protocol (SCP) applications. He notices that all of these protocols have a destination port of 22. What explanation can you provide to him regarding this finding?

   _____

   _____

4. Sumita has heard the term "encryption" used throughout the entire lab session and is still not completely sure she understands the meaning or methodology behind the term. Write a short definition of the term "encryption."

   _____

   _____

5. Daryl has decided to purchase a book from amazon.com. He is going to create an account so that he can use his credit card to make the purchase. The browser informs him that he is entering a secure page, but he is still concerned about entering his sensitive information. How can Daryl feel confident that the amazon.com Web site is the real one and that he is indeed on a secure channel?

   _____

   _____

Key Term Quiz

Use the vocabulary terms from the list provided to complete the sentences that follow.

certificate authority (CA)

confidentiality

integrity

nonrepudiation

private key

public key

SSL/TLS (Secure Sockets Layer/Transport Layer Security)

1. When an organization provides secure services over the Internet, they will obtain a certificate from a(n) _____ such as Comodo or DigiCert that verifies the public key is legitimate.

2. When using GPG, you encrypt to your friend with their _____ and they decrypt with their _____.

3. Signing with your private key provides both _____ and _____.

4. Encryption provides _____.

5. Port 443 is used by _____.

Chapter 11

Advanced Networking Devices

Lab Exercises

Working with networks today, you will encounter a number of advanced and specialized network devices. You will still be responsible for troubleshooting clients, servers, and cables, but you will also deal with the detailed configuration of switches and routers.

In this chapter you will explore basic network terms; configure and work with VPNs and VLANs; and examine the properties of intrusion detection systems, intrusion prevention systems, and proxy servers.

 10 **MINUTES**

Lab Exercise 11.01: Exploring Network Terms

As with any discipline, developing an understanding of the terminology of the discipline is almost as important as being able to work with the technology. Network technicians must be very comfortable with their terminology, so that they can talk properly with peers, management, and customers about network-related problems and solutions.

In this lab exercise you will develop clear definitions of popular network terms and network technologies.

Learning Objectives

At the completion of this lab, you will be able to

- Identify advanced networking terms

Lab Materials and Setup

The materials you'll need for this lab exercise are

- *Mike Meyers' CompTIA Network+ Guide to Managing and Troubleshooting Networks* textbook
- Pen or pencil
- Paper

Getting Down to Business

Now that you have been with the company for some time, there actually are some techs who have less experience than you do. One of the junior network technicians is having some trouble understanding terms such as VLANs and VPNs, to name a couple. He asks if you would sit with him and help him identify the purpose of each of the mentioned technologies. You decide to help out by creating definitions of each and asking him to associate the terms with the definitions.

Match the following terms to the appropriate definitions:

A. Multilayer switch	_____ An encrypted tunnel across an unsecured infrastructure.
B. Broadcast domain	_____ A piece of software or a non-inline device that detects suspicious activity, logs the action, sends an alert, and can even notify another device to take corrective action.
C. PuTTY	_____ A switch that operates at both Layer 2 and Layer 3 of the OSI model.
D. Client/server	_____ A group of computers that receive each other's broadcast messages.
E. Peer-to-peer	_____ A VPN protocol that has clients connect to the VPN server using a standard Web browser.
F. VPN	_____ A virtual network that allows hosts to belong to the same network ID, even if they are connected to different network switches that are in different geographical locations.
G. IPsec	_____ A network that has a dedicated server sharing resources and clients that connect to that server to access those resources.
H. SSL	_____ An inline piece of software or a device that detects suspicious activity and then takes corrective action itself.
I. VLAN	_____ Delaying some or all packets, to bring them into compliance with a desired traffic profile. It is a form of rate limiting.
J. Traffic shaping	_____ A VPN protocol that used to be used with L2TP VPNs, but now is a complete VPN solution by itself.
K. IDS	_____ A network in which all systems act as both clients and servers.
L. IPS	_____ A popular SSH client, Telnet client, and terminal emulator.

 30 MINUTES

Lab Exercise 11.02: Encrypting Through a VPN

One of JSW's new clients is a small insurance firm with a number of agents who work from their homes. Jonathan and Scott ask you to use the machines in the network lab to configure and test a virtual private network (VPN) solution using the built-in Routing and Remote Access Services (RRAS) role in Windows Server 2016. You will first create the VPN server, and then you will configure the client systems to access that server using VPN. Good luck!

✖ Cross-Reference

For additional information on VPN technologies, check out the "Virtual Private Networks" section in Chapter 11 of the *Mike Meyers' CompTIA Network+ Guide to Managing and Troubleshooting Networks* textbook.

Learning Objectives

In this lab, you'll configure a Windows VPN server and a Windows VPN client. At the end of this lab, you will be able to

- Configure the RRAS VPN on a Windows Server 2016 system

- Implement and test a Windows VPN

Lab Materials and Setup

The materials you'll need for this lab exercise are

- *Mike Meyers' CompTIA Network+ Guide to Managing and Troubleshooting Networks* textbook

- Windows 10 system

- Windows Server 2016 system

- Switch and appropriate cabling to connect the small network

- Pen or pencil

- Paper

Getting Down to Business

You have really become quite efficient at managing the resources in the Network Lab and are very skilled at reconfiguring the machines and the network to test different scenarios. Jonathan explains that you will need to install and configure the RRAS role on the Server 2016 machine.

Every time you configure these lab exercises, you learn a little more about networking technologies and reinforce the concepts you have been studying. In this lab exercise you will actually build an RRAS server to host your VPN server.

✔ **Tech Tip**

Microsoft allows you to create a VPN server with Windows Server 2016 using RRAS. The RRAS role is installed from the Network Policy and Access Services under Server Roles.

Step 1   To configure the RRAS server for this lab exercise, complete the following substeps:

    a.   Boot up the Windows Server 2016 machine. The Server Manager window should have popped up by default when you got to the desktop. If you closed this window, reopen it by clicking the Server Manager icon in the bottom-left corner of the taskbar.

    b.   In the top-right corner, click Manage and then click Add Roles And Features, and then click the Next button.

    c.   Click Next through the next couple of screens (Installation Type and Server Selection). The next screen should be the Server Roles selection.

    d.   Select Remote Access and click Next (see Figure 11-1).

    e.   Click Next for the next three screens.

    f.   At the Role Services page, put a check mark in the box next to DirectAccess And VPN (RAS). Click the Add Features button in the new window that pops up. Click Next.

    g.   Click Next two more times to accept the defaults in the Web Server Role (IIS) and Role Services screens.

    h.   On the Confirmation screen, put a check in the box next to Restart The Destination Server Automatically If Required, click the Yes button in the new window that pops up, and then click the Install button. When the installation concludes, click the Close button.

    i.   Click the yellow Notifications triangle at the top of the Server Manager window. In the Post-Deployment Configuration section, click Open The Getting Started Wizard.

    j.   In the Configure Remote Access window that pops up, select the Deploy VPN Only option (see Figure 11-2).

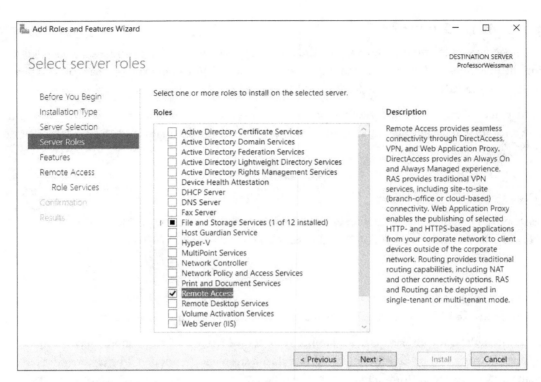

FIGURE 11-1 Selecting the Remote Access role

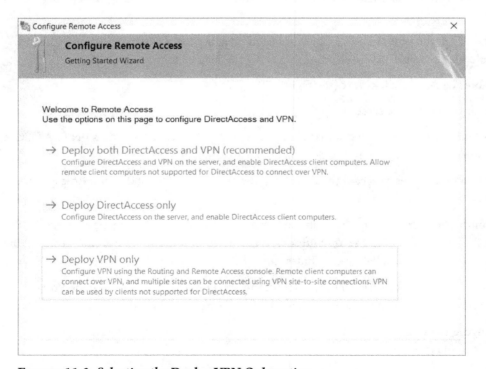

FIGURE 11-2 Selecting the Deploy VPN Only option

k. In the Routing And Remote Access window that pops up, right-click the server and select Configure And Enable Routing And Remote Access. Click the Next button on the following screen. On the next screen, select Custom Configuration and click Next. On the following screen, put a check mark in the box next to VPN Access (see Figure 11-3) and click Next. Then, click Finish and, finally, click Start Service.

Step 2 Now follow the substeps to create and authorize a user for the VPN:

a. Press the WINDOWS key, type **Computer Management**, and click Computer Management.

b. Under Local Users And Groups, select Users, right-click in the middle pane, and select New User.

c. Create a new user with a user name and password.

d. Right-click the user you created and select Properties.

e. Click the Dial-In tab and, under Network Access Permission, select Allow Access.

Step 3 Now follow the substeps to send client traffic through the VPN:

a. Before connecting to the VPN, open Wireshark and start a capture on the client machine. From the client machine, go to www.rit.edu. You should see the HTTP traffic in Wireshark.

b. On your Windows 10 client, open Network And Sharing Center and select Set Up A New Connection Or Network to open the Set Up A Connection Or Network wizard (see Figure 11-4).

c. Select Connect To A Workplace and click Next.

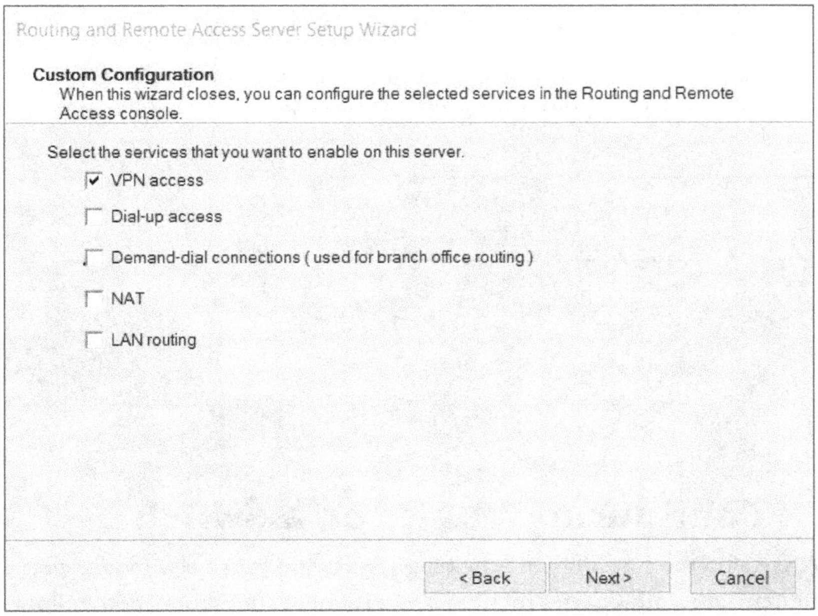

FIGURE 11-3 Enabling VPN access

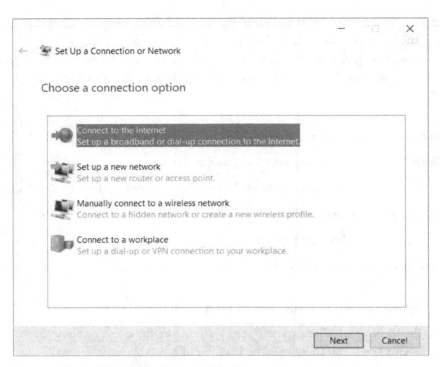

FIGURE 11-4   **Choose a connection option**

d.   When asked how you want to connect, select Use My Internet Connection (VPN).

e.   Enter the IP address of your server and then click Next.

f.   Enter the user name and password of the user you created in the previous step and click Connect.

Now that you are connected to the VPN, start a packet capture using Wireshark on the client and on the server. Go to www.rit.edu again. After the page loads, stop the capture. How is this capture different?

_____

_____

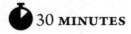 30 MINUTES

Lab Exercise 11.03: Configuring VLANs on a Switch

Virtual local area networks (VLANs) offer the capability of providing security on your network because systems in one VLAN cannot communicate with systems in other VLANs unless the administrator allows routing between the VLANs.

VLANs also offer the capabilities of creating broadcast domains within the switch. When a system in a VLAN broadcasts a message, that broadcast message does not go beyond the VLAN.

Learning Objectives

In this lab, you will create two VLANs on a Cisco multilayer switch. You will then verify that two systems connected to the switch and placed in different VLANs cannot communicate with one another until you enable interVLAN routing. By the end of this lab you should be able to

- Define the function of a VLAN

- Configure VLANs

- Configure interVLAN routing

Lab Materials and Setup

The materials you'll need for this lab exercise are

- *Mike Meyers' CompTIA Network+ Guide to Managing and Troubleshooting Networks* textbook

- Cisco 3560 switch or similar (alternatively, this can be done in Cisco's Packet Tracer simulation)

- Console (rollover) cable

- Two client systems

- Pen or pencil

- Paper

✔ Tech Tip

The Cisco 3560 switch is a multilayer switch providing the capability to create VLANs as well as implement interVLAN routing. There are many manufacturers and models of multilayer switches (sometimes called Layer 3 switches). If you have access to different model switches or only have access to a Layer 2 switch, you may still follow the steps to create two VLANs; however, you will not be able to configure interVLAN routing without a separate external router.

You will also be working with the Cisco command-line interface (CLI) in the Cisco IOS software. Only the commands needed to complete the lab exercise will be introduced.

Many of the commands you will use in this lab exercise will be run from the privileged EXEC mode (Switch#). This mode is normally password protected, and if the password is lost or forgotten, it can be difficult to reset the password. Do an Internet search for Cisco Password Recovery to find the steps.

Getting Down to Business

Erica, one of the network technicians at JSW, is talking with Jonathan and learns that you are working on your CompTIA Network+ certification. Erica is working with a customer who is implementing VLANs and would like to know if you would like to learn how to configure VLANs. As usual, you jump at the chance to work with a mentor, and you invite Erica to use a switch and two computers in the network lab.

Step 1   To set up the small network, power on the switch and then plug the first computer into port number 2. Connect the second computer to port number 8 on the switch.

Step 2   On both systems, disable the Windows Firewall. Configure the first computer (System1) with an IP address of 10.0.0.1/8 and the second computer (System2) with an IP address of 10.0.0.2/8.

Step 3   After configuring the IP addresses, open a command prompt and verify that you can ping from one computer to the other. Can you successfully ping from computer 1 to computer 2?

_____

Step 4   Connect the console cable to the console port on your switch and then to the serial port on System 1. On System 1, launch PuTTY (download from www.chiark.greenend.org.uk/~sgtatham/putty/download.html). In the Basic Options For Your PuTTY Session, verify that the Serial button is selected. Under the Category: pane, click the Serial menu item. Under Options Controlling Local Serial Lines verify the following settings as shown in Figure 11-5:

Serial line to connect to	COM1
Speed (baud)	9600
Data bits	8
Stop bits	1
Parity	None
Flow control	None

Click the Open button. You may have to press ENTER in the PuTTY command-line window before you see a prompt, allowing you to type commands.

Step 5   To display a list of VLANs that currently exist, type show vlan. You should see that there are a few default VLANs for different network architectures—notice that VLAN 1 is named the default VLAN (see Figure 11-6). The far right column shows you which ports are part of the VLAN. Record the ports that are part of the default VLAN:

_____

_____

FIGURE 11-5 PuTTY configuration window with serial settings to manage the Cisco 3560 switch

```
COM1 - PuTTY
Switch>show vlan

VLAN Name                             Status    Ports
---- -------------------------------- --------- -------------------------------
1    default                          active    Fa0/1, Fa0/2, Fa0/3, Fa0/4
                                                 Fa0/5, Fa0/6, Fa0/7, Fa0/8
                                                 Fa0/9, Fa0/10, Fa0/11, Fa0/12
                                                 Fa0/13, Fa0/14, Fa0/15, Fa0/16
                                                 Fa0/17, Fa0/18, Fa0/19, Fa0/20
                                                 Fa0/21, Fa0/22, Fa0/23, Fa0/24
                                                 Gi0/1, Gi0/2
1002 fddi-default                     act/unsup
1003 token-ring-default               act/unsup
1004 fddinet-default                  act/unsup
1005 trnet-default                    act/unsup

VLAN Type  SAID       MTU   Parent RingNo BridgeNo Stp  BrdgMode Trans1 Trans2
---- ----- ---------- ----- ------ ------ -------- ---- -------- ------ ------
1    enet  100001     1500  -      -      -        -    -        0      0
1002 fddi  101002     1500  -      -      -        -    -        0      0
1003 tr    101003     1500  -      -      -        -    -        0      0
1004 fdnet 101004     1500  -      -      -        ieee -        0      0
1005 trnet 101005     1500  -      -      -        ibm  -        0      0
```

FIGURE 11-6 Looking at the default VLANs on a Cisco switch

✔ **Hint**

If you are using a switch that has been in the lab environment, it may already be in some state of configuration as opposed to the default out-of-box state. If you had any trouble pinging between the computers, or there seem to be some VLANs already configured, use the following steps to reset the switch:

a. Press and hold the Mode button for approximately 15 seconds (until the four LEDs turn solid green), and then release the Mode button. The SYST LED should then blink and the terminal should indicate `Reload Requested`.

b. Press ENTER and, when prompted `Would You Like To Terminate Autoinstall?` `[Yes/No]`, type Yes and press ENTER.

c. When prompted `Would You Like To Enter The Initial Configuration Dialog?` `[Yes/No]`, type No and press ENTER.

d. You should now be at the `Switch>` prompt.

e. Type enable and press ENTER. You should now be at the `Switch#` prompt. Type delete vlan.dat and press ENTER. Type reload and then press ENTER. Press y, press ENTER, and boot back into the switch.

Step 6 To create a VLAN named Acct and one called Marketing, type the following commands, pressing ENTER after each command. You'll start at the `Switch>` prompt:

```
enable
```

You should now be at the `Switch#` prompt. Keep going:

```
conf t
```

Now the prompt looks like this: `Switch(config)#`. Keep going:

```
vlan 2
```

Now the prompt looks like this: `Switch(config-vlan)#`. Keep going:

```
name Acct
```

You will return to the `Switch(config-vlan)#` prompt. If you did this correctly, you won't get any feedback. Keep going:

```
exit
```

Now the prompt again looks like this: `Switch(config)#`. Keep going:

```
vlan 3
```

The prompt will change to `Switch(config-vlan)#`. Keep going:

```
name Marketing
```

You will return to the `Switch(config-vlan)#` prompt. If you did this correctly, you won't get any feedback. Keep going:

```
end
```

Step 7 At this point, you should be at the prompt `Switch#`. You might see a log entry appear, saying that the switch configuration has changed. If so, press ENTER to get back to the prompt.

To view the newly created VLANs, type the following commands. Figure 11-7 shows the results.

```
Switch# show vlan
```

Step 8 To place port 2 in the Acct VLAN, type the following commands, and press ENTER after each one. Note that the prompt dialog will change as you move through the commands.

```
Switch# conf t
Switch(config)# interface fa0/2
Switch(config-if)# switchport mode access
Switch(config-if)# switchport access vlan 2
Switch(config-if)# exit
```

Step 9 To place port 8 in the Marketing VLAN, type the following commands:

```
Switch(config)# interface fa0/8
Switch(config-if)# switchport mode access
Switch(config-if)# switchport access vlan 3
Switch(config-if)# end
```

```
COM1 - PuTTY                                                        [_][□][✕]

VLAN Name                             Status    Ports
---- -------------------------------- --------- -------------------------------
1    default                          active    Fa0/1, Fa0/2, Fa0/3, Fa0/4
                                                 Fa0/5, Fa0/6, Fa0/7, Fa0/8
                                                 Fa0/9, Fa0/10, Fa0/11, Fa0/12
                                                 Fa0/13, Fa0/14, Fa0/15, Fa0/16
                                                 Fa0/17, Fa0/18, Fa0/19, Fa0/20
                                                 Fa0/21, Fa0/22, Fa0/23, Fa0/24
                                                 Gi0/1, Gi0/2
2    Acct                             active
3    Marketing                        active
1002 fddi-default                     act/unsup
1003 token-ring-default               act/unsup
1004 fddinet-default                  act/unsup
1005 trnet-default                    act/unsup

VLAN Type  SAID       MTU   Parent RingNo BridgeNo Stp  BrdgMode Trans1 Trans2
---- ----- ---------- ----- ------ ------ -------- ---- -------- ------ ------
1    enet  100001     1500  -      -      -        -    -        0      0
2    enet  100002     1500  -      -      -        -    -        0      0
3    enet  100003     1500  -      -      -        -    -        0      0
1002 fddi  101002     1500  -      -      -        -    -        0      0
 --More--
```

FIGURE 11-7 Looking at the newly created VLANs

```
COM1 - PuTTY                                                      [-][□][×]
Switch>show vlan

VLAN Name                             Status    Ports
---- -------------------------------- --------- ------------------------------
1    default                          active    Fa0/1, Fa0/3, Fa0/4, Fa0/5
                                                Fa0/6, Fa0/7, Fa0/9, Fa0/10
                                                Fa0/11, Fa0/12, Fa0/13, Fa0/14
                                                Fa0/15, Fa0/16, Fa0/17, Fa0/18
                                                Fa0/19, Fa0/20, Fa0/21, Fa0/22
                                                Fa0/23, Fa0/24, Gi0/1, Gi0/2
2    Acct                             active    Fa0/2
3    Marketing                        active    Fa0/8
1002 fddi-default                     act/unsup
1003 token-ring-default               act/unsup
1004 fddinet-default                  act/unsup
1005 trnet-default                    act/unsup
```

FIGURE 11-8 Verifying that ports are assigned to the correct VLANs

Step 10   To verify that the ports are placed in the appropriate VLANs, use the following command to display VLANs. Figure 11-8 shows the results.

```
Switch# show vlan
```

Step 11   Now that you have the ports that each system is connected to in different VLANs, the two systems should not be able to ping one another. The reason is that VLANs are security boundaries and broadcast domains. Unless a Layer 3 device is used, only systems within a single VLAN and IP subnet will be able to communicate with one another, and not with systems in other VLANs or subnets. Furthermore, if two systems in the same IP subnet are configured for different VLANs, they will never be able to communicate under any circumstance, since Layer 3 devices only take traffic off a subnet.

Can you ping from System 1 to System 2? _____

Can you ping from System 2 to System 1? _____

Step 12   Now you will implement interVLAN routing to allow the two separate VLANs to communicate with each other. To enable interVLAN routing, you will assign a router address to each VLAN, and enable routing using the following commands, pressing ENTER after each command. Note that the prompt will change as you move through the commands. Start in privileged EXEC mode (Switch#).

```
Switch# configure terminal
Switch(config)# interface vlan 2
Switch(config-if)# ip address 10.2.0.1 255.255.0.0
Switch(config-if)# no shutdown
Switch(config-if)# exit
Switch(config)# interface vlan 3
Switch(config-if)# ip address 10.3.0.1 255.255.0.0
Switch(config-if)# no shutdown
Switch(config-if)# exit
Switch(config)# ip routing
Switch(config)# end
```

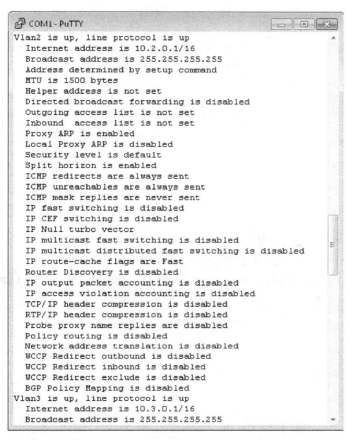

```
COM1 - PuTTY
Vlan2 is up, line protocol is up
  Internet address is 10.2.0.1/16
  Broadcast address is 255.255.255.255
  Address determined by setup command
  MTU is 1500 bytes
  Helper address is not set
  Directed broadcast forwarding is disabled
  Outgoing access list is not set
  Inbound  access list is not set
  Proxy ARP is enabled
  Local Proxy ARP is disabled
  Security level is default
  Split horizon is enabled
  ICMP redirects are always sent
  ICMP unreachables are always sent
  ICMP mask replies are never sent
  IP fast switching is disabled
  IP CEF switching is disabled
  IP Null turbo vector
  IP multicast fast switching is disabled
  IP multicast distributed fast switching is disabled
  IP route-cache flags are Fast
  Router Discovery is disabled
  IP output packet accounting is disabled
  IP access violation accounting is disabled
  TCP/IP header compression is disabled
  RTP/IP header compression is disabled
  Probe proxy name replies are disabled
  Policy routing is disabled
  Network address translation is disabled
  WCCP Redirect outbound is disabled
  WCCP Redirect inbound is disabled
  WCCP Redirect exclude is disabled
  BGP Policy Mapping is disabled
Vlan3 is up, line protocol is up
  Internet address is 10.3.0.1/16
  Broadcast address is 255.255.255.255
```

FIGURE 11-9 Verifying the VLANs and assigned
IP addresses

Step 13   To verify that the IP addresses have been assigned to the appropriate VLANs, use the
following command to display VLANs and IP addresses. Figure 11-9 shows the results.

```
show ip interface
```

Step 14   Now you must place the computer systems in the correct networks. Configure the first
computer (System 1) with an IP address of 10.2.0.11/16 and a default gateway of 10.2.0.1. Configure the
second computer (System 2) with an IP address of 10.3.0.11/16 and a default gateway of 10.3.0.1.

Step 15   Now that you have the VLANs routed, the two systems should be able to ping one another.
The Acct VLAN is network 10.2.0.0/16 and the Marketing VLAN is network 10.3.0.0/16.

Can you ping from System 1 to System 2? _____

Can you ping from System 2 to System 1? _____

✖ **Cross-Reference**

To learn more about advanced switching topics such as VLANs, VLAN Trunking Protocol (VTP), and interVLAN routing, refer to Chapter 11 of the *Mike Meyers' CompTIA Network+ Guide to Managing and Troubleshooting Networks* textbook.

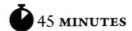 45 MINUTES

Lab Exercise 11.04: Exploring Network Protection

You have installed and configured a VPN and implemented VLANs. Now, to finish your exploration of advanced networking devices, you will explore what Mike terms *network protection*. There are four areas that you will examine:

- Intrusion detection system/intrusion protection system (IDS/IPS)
- Port mirroring
- Proxy serving
- Port authentication

Just as there are manufacturers that provide multilayer switches that are capable of providing VPNs and VLANs, there are manufacturers, developers, and methods that provide network protection. You're going to explore some of these manufacturers, developers, and methods.

Learning Objectives

In this lab, you'll explore a few of the manufacturers, developers, and methods that offer various network protection solutions. By the end of this lab, you will be able to

- Define IDS/IPS and profile one or two of the manufacturers
- Define port mirroring
- Contrast the two types of proxy serving
- Detail port authentication

Lab Materials and Setup

The materials you'll need for this lab exercise are

- *Mike Meyers' CompTIA Network+ Guide to Managing and Troubleshooting Networks* textbook

- Internet access

- Pen or pencil

- Paper

Getting Down to Business

As with any network consulting firm, the staff at JSW work hard to stay informed on the latest networking technologies, especially where network security and protection are concerned! After talking with one of your co-workers about IDS/IPS, you are intrigued and decide to do some further investigation.

Step 1   Beginning with IDS/IPS devices, provide a brief description of each device. Then conduct a Web search to profile one or two manufacturers that offer devices fitting those descriptions.

_____

_____

Step 2   See what you can find out about port mirroring. Record your findings in the following space.

_____

_____

Step 3   You have already read about proxy servers in the textbook. Now compare the features of a physical proxy server (such as the Blue Coat ProxySG 510) and a public proxy server.

_____

_____

Step 4 Finish with a short discussion about port authentication.

_____

_____

Lab Analysis

1. Sara knows that using a VPN allows you to safely connect to computers over the Internet using an encrypted channel. She would like to know the difference between an SSL VPN and an IPsec VPN. Briefly describe the difference for her.

    _____

    _____

2. Marc is about to purchase five new switches that he will be using in a VLAN configuration. What is the benefit of a multilayer switch?

    _____

    _____

3. Robert would like to implement the strongest protection available to prevent unwanted access to the corporate network. What is the difference between an IDS and an IPS? Which device would be considered the strongest protection?

    _____

    _____

4. JSW already implements a robust firewall on their office Internet connection. Why might they want to install a proxy server as well?

    _____

    _____

Key Term Quiz

Use the vocabulary terms from the list provided to complete the sentences that follow.

intrusion detection system (IDS)

port mirroring

Routing and Remote Access Services (RRAS)

tunnel

1. A VPN is used to create an encrypted _____ between the VPN client and the VPN server.

2. The _____ role allows for the capability of a VPN on a server.

3. A(n) _____ will monitor network traffic for suspicious activity.

4. In order to monitor network traffic on your switch, you will need to configure _____ on the switch.

Chapter 12

IPv6

Lab Exercises

Whether you are a seasoned tech, have been in IT for only a few years, or have just begun your journey toward becoming a networking professional, these are exciting times. IPv6 usage is growing more and more each day.

The CompTIA Network+ exam objectives require a networking professional to be familiar with IPv6 addressing concepts and some of the supporting technologies, like tunneling. The labs in this chapter are designed to give you an opportunity to practice what you have learned about IPv6 from the *Mike Meyers' CompTIA Network+ Guide to Managing and Troubleshooting Networks* textbook but go even further.

First, you will learn about great IPv6 facts, figures, and historical dates. Then, you'll review some of the new IPv6 terminology and practice address notation shortcuts. You'll configure machines for IPv6 and send traffic and verify your TCP/IP configuration on a Windows 10 system. Finally, you will experiment with one of the IPv6 tunnel brokers, Hurricane Electric.

 20 MINUTES

Lab Exercise 12.01: IPv6 Facts, Figures, and Dates

To begin your exploration of IPv6, you will examine some of the organizations that are involved with IPv6.

Learning Objectives

In this lab, you'll explore various organizations that are responsible for the development, management, and distribution of IPv6. By the end of this lab, you will be able to

- Describe the purposes and features of the organizations responsible for IPv6 addressing

- List the important dates in the history of IPv6 related to IPv4 address exhaustion

- Research and provide some detail on requests for comment (RFCs) associated with IPv6

- Understand how large the IPv6 address space really is

Lab Materials and Setup

The materials you'll need for this lab exercise are

- Internet access
- Pen or pencil
- Paper

Getting Down to Business

At the very top of the Internet hierarchy is ICANN (Internet Corporation for Assigned Names and Numbers). Just below ICANN is IANA (Internet Assigned Numbers Authority). IANA allocates IP addresses to five RIRs (regional Internet registries) that assign addresses to ISPs (Internet service providers) and large organizations.

Step 1   Start this exploration of IPv6 with a visit to the following Web sites:

www.iana.org/numbers

https://ipv4.potaroo.net

https://en.wikipedia.org/wiki/IPv4_address_exhaustion

Based on these links, answer the following questions.

What happened on January 31, 2011?

_____

_____

What happened on February 3, 2011?

_____

_____

Fill in the requested information in the following chart.

RIR	Area(s) Covered	Exhaustion Date	Remaining Addresses in RIR Pool (/8s)

Step 2   Fill in the missing information, using Slides 39–42 in the following PowerPoint presentation from APNIC: www.apnic.net/wp-content/uploads/global-ipv6-summit/assets/apnic-v6-tutorial-distribution.ppt. Other related information, some not covered by the PowerPoint presentation, has already been filled in.

Entity	Minimum Prefix Length	Provides
RIR	/23	33,554,432 (2^{25}) site addresses (networks) Source: www.iana.org/assignments/ipv6-unicast-address-assignments/ipv6-unicast-address-assignments.xhtml
ISP	_____	_____ site addresses (networks)
Site (Company)	_____	_____ LANs (networks)
Site (Home)	/56	256 (2^8) LANs (networks)
LAN Segment (Network)	_____	_____ addresses per LAN
Device	/128	One IPv6 address

Step 3   Read the following article from ARIN's site:

https://teamarin.net/2016/07/19/learning-ipv6-puts-step-ahead-career/

What are your biggest takeaways from the article?

_____

_____

Step 4   Open RFC 2460, "Internet Protocol, Version 6 (IPv6)," at www.ietf.org/rfc/rfc2460.txt and record some of the information from the introduction. How many bits long is an IPv6 address compared to an IPv4 address? Click the Obsoletes: 1883 and Obsoleted by: 8200 links for other versions of this RFC.

_____

_____

Step 5   Open RFC 4291, "IP Version 6 Addressing Architecture," at https://tools.ietf.org/html/rfc4291. This RFC defines the various addresses available in IPv6, such as unicast addresses, anycast addresses, and multicast addresses. Take a moment and read the definition of an *anycast address*. Explain what an anycast address is.

_____

_____

Step 6   Visit the following Web sites. Which stats are the most mind-boggling to you regarding the IPv6 address space?

https://itsnobody.wordpress.com/2012/02/17/how-many-addresses-can-ipv6-hold/

http://itknowledgeexchange.techtarget.com/whatis/ipv6-addresses-how-many-is-that-in-numbers/

www.edn.com/electronics-blogs/other/4306822/IPV6-How-Many-IP-Addresses-Can-Dance-on-the-Head-of-a-Pin-

_____

_____

 15 MINUTES

Lab Exercise 12.02: IPv6 Terminology

Half the battle of becoming proficient in technology is developing an understanding of it. You'll have to learn the terminology in order to develop the skills to configure the technology. In this lab you will review IPv6 terminology.

Learning Objectives

At the completion of this lab, you will be able to

- Understand key terminology associated with IPv6

Lab Materials and Setup

The materials you'll need for this lab exercise are

- *Mike Meyers' CompTIA Network+ Guide to Managing and Troubleshooting Networks* textbook

- Pen or pencil

- Paper

Getting Down to Business

Peter, a co-worker of yours at JSW, has been working with a client to implement IPv6 throughout his office. He is having some trouble because the protocol is quite different from IPv4. Peter asks you to help him identify some of the terminology and concepts introduced with the IPv6 protocol. To ensure that you are familiar with the IPv6 terminology before you take the CompTIA Network+ exam, you agree to help Peter, knowing this exercise will help you remember the terms!

✖ Cross-Reference

Before attacking this Lab Exercise, you may want to review the concepts of IPv6 covered in Chapter 12 of the *Mike Meyers' CompTIA Network+ Guide to Managing and Troubleshooting Networks* textbook.

Using the knowledge of IPv6 that you have learned from reading the *Mike Meyers' CompTIA Network+ Guide to Managing and Troubleshooting Networks* textbook and other resources, complete the following matching exercise:

A. ::1	_____ The IPv6 term for LAN, network, or subnet.
B. Link-local address	_____ The IPv6 term for a public IP address.
C. Prefix length	_____ An address type that is assigned to multiple nodes. Any one of the nodes could receive data destined for that address, but it is the node closest to the sending node that will receive the data.
D. Link	_____ Sending IPv6 packets inside of IPv4 packets.
E. Global unicast address	_____ The IPv6 equivalent of an APIPA address.
F. Stateful DHCPv6	_____ New terms for IPv4's Network ID, Host ID.
G. Stateless DHCPv6	_____ An IPv6 DHCP server that only assigns additional TCP/IP settings.
H. Anycast address	_____ The IPv6 loopback address.
I. Prefix, Interface ID	_____ An IPv6 DHCP server that automatically assigns an IP address, subnet mask, and additional TCP/IP settings.
J. Tunneling	_____ The IPv6 term for subnet mask.

 15 MINUTES

Lab Exercise 12.03: IPv6 Address Notation Shortcuts

As you have learned, the IPv6 address is a 128-bit address displayed as eight groups of four hexadecimal numbers, such as 2001:0470:b8f9:0001:020c:29ff:fe53:45ca.

In this lab exercise, you will practice using the notation shortcut method to convert various IPv6 addresses between their long forms and their short forms.

Learning Objectives

In this lab, you'll practice converting IPv6 addresses between long-form notation and short-form notation using the shortcuts introduced in the *Mike Meyers' CompTIA Network+ Guide to Managing and Troubleshooting Networks* textbook. At the end of this lab you will be able to

- Convert IPv6 addresses from long-form notation to short form-notation

- Convert IPv6 addresses from short-form notation to long-form notation

Lab Materials and Setup

The materials you'll need for this lab exercise are

- *Mike Meyers' CompTIA Network+ Guide to Managing and Troubleshooting Networks* textbook

- Pen or pencil

- Paper

Getting Down to Business

One of the new clients JSW has taken on is implementing IPv6 exclusively. Jonathan asks Scott to explore the various IPv6 addresses and their notation. As usual, Scott asks you if you would like to work with him to gain the experience. You heartily agree and quickly begin to tackle the problems together.

✖ Cross-Reference

Please use the shortcuts introduced in the "IPv6 Address Notation" section in Chapter 12 of the *Mike Meyers' CompTIA Network+ Guide to Managing and Troubleshooting Networks* textbook.

Step 1   Using the shortcuts, convert the following IPv6 addresses from their long-form notation into their short-form notation:

    a.   Long Form – 2001:0000:0000:3210:0800:200c:00cf:1234

        Short Form – _____

    b.   Long Form – fe80:0000:0000:0000:020c:000f:0000:fe53

        Short Form – _____

    c.   Long Form – ff02:0000:0000:0000:0000:0000:0000:0001

        Short Form – _____

    d.   Long Form – 2001:0000:0000:0001:0200:000e:ffc8:0010

        Short Form – _____

    e.   Long Form – fe80:0000:0000:0000:205c:2194:3f57:fd71

        Short Form – _____

Step 2   Now using the same shortcuts, convert the following IPv6 addresses from their short-form notation into their long-form notation:

    a.   Short Form – ::1

        Long Form – _____

    b.   Short Form – fe80::a:0:53

        Long Form – _____

    c.   Short Form – ff02::2

        Long Form – _____

    d.   Short Form – 2001::6:e00:9:ffc8:11

        Long Form – _____

    e.   Short Form – fe80::205c:2194:3f57:fd71

        Long Form – _____

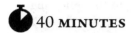 40 MINUTES

Lab Exercise 12.04: IPv6 Configuration and Communication

The time has come to send and receive some actual IPv6 traffic. In this lab, you're going to send and receive traffic using two different types of IPv6 addresses: ULA (unique local address) and link-local address.

Learning Objectives

In this lab, you'll again work with the TCP/IP settings on your Windows machines. You will configure and explore your IPv6 address information. At the end of this lab you will be able to

- Verify your IPv6 settings

- Configure IPv6 ULAs (unique local addresses)

- Test and verify IPv6 connectivity with both a ULA and link-local address

Lab Materials and Setup

The materials you'll need for this lab exercise are

- *Mike Meyers' CompTIA Network+ Guide to Managing and Troubleshooting Networks* textbook

- Two Windows 10 systems connected with a switch

- Cabling

- Pen or pencil

- Paper

Getting Down to Business

Jonathan and Scott come by the network lab and ask how your IPv6 skills are coming along. They have a concept they would like you to explore: an IPv6-native network. They are not able to free up any of the IPv6-capable routers that would enable you to configure your small network with global unicast addresses. Instead, they want you to work with a type of address called ULA (unique local address).

✖ Cross-Reference

You can learn more about the different address types by checking out the "IPv6 Basics" section in Chapter 12 of the *Mike Meyers' CompTIA Network+ Guide to Managing and Troubleshooting Networks* textbook.

Step 1   Begin by generating a random ULA. You can accomplish this by navigating to the following Web site, www.simpledns.com/private-ipv6.aspx, and randomly generating a ULA.

✔ **Tech Tip**

The parameters for the ULA are set forth in RFC 4193: "Unique Local IPv6 Unicast Addresses."

Step 2   If you haven't already done so, disable all Windows firewalls and enable IPv6 on the Windows 10 systems.

Step 3   In the Windows 10 search box, type **sharing**, click Manage Advanced Sharing Settings, click Network And Sharing Center from address bar at the top, right-click the NIC you're using, select Properties, scroll down until you see Internet Protocol Version 6 (TCP/IPv6), select Internet Protocol Version 6 (TCP/IPv6), and click the Properties button.

Configure each Windows 10 system with an IPv6 ULA address and subnet prefix length (leave the rest blank) in the window shown in Figure 12-1. Make sure to give each system an address on the same link (subnet) as the other

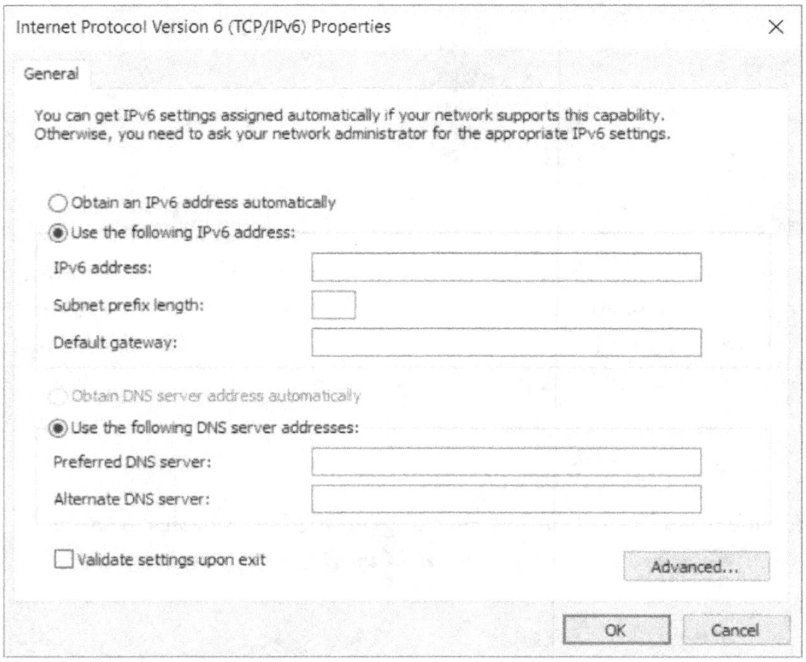

FIGURE 12-1 Windows 10 IPv6 configuration

Step 4 As you have learned by reading Chapter 12 of the *Mike Meyers' CompTIA Network+ Guide to Managing and Troubleshooting Networks* textbook, a unique local address is a private address in IPv6 used for local communication, like the RFC 1918 addresses (10.0.0.0/8, 172.16-31.0.0/16, 192.168.0-255.0/24) are used in IPv4. To access the IPv6 Internet, your system will need an IPv6 global unicast address.

After you have configured both Windows 10 systems, on each system, open a command prompt and run `ipconfig /all`. Record the IPv6 ULA addresses here:

First Windows 10 system's ULA _____

Second Windows 10 system's ULA _____

Step 5 As you have also learned by reading Chapter 12 of the *Mike Meyers' CompTIA Network+ Guide to Managing and Troubleshooting Networks* textbook, all IPv6 hosts use a link-local address (fe80::/10) for traffic on the same link (subnet). Record the link-local addresses for both Windows 10 systems here:

First Windows 10 system's link-local address _____

Second Windows 10 system's link-local address _____

Step 6 Open up Wireshark and filter by **icmpv6**. Send a ping from one Windows 10 machine to the other's ULA. Was the ping successful? What did you see in Wireshark?

_____

_____

Now send a ping from one Windows 10 machine to the other's link-local address. Was the ping successful? What did you see in Wireshark?

_____

_____

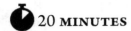20 MINUTES

Lab Exercise 12.05: IPv6 Tunnel Broker

Hurricane Electric Internet Services provides an IPv6 tunnel broker service. Tunnel brokers provide an IPv6 tunneling protocol that enables you to access IPv6 resources on the Internet. The reason the tunneling protocol is needed is that although you have IPv6 installed on your system, and the Internet resources you are accessing have IPv6 running, the routers on the Internet that are between your system and the IPv6 resources you are accessing do not have IPv6 capability. Hurricane Electric provides a 6in4 tunneling protocol that enables IPv6 connectivity through IPv4 devices.

> ✖ **Cross-Reference**
>
> **To learn more about tunnels, 6in4, and tunnel brokers, check out the "Moving to IPv6" section in Chapter 12 of the** *Mike Meyers' CompTIA Network+ Guide to Managing and Troubleshooting Networks* **textbook.**

Learning Objectives

In this lab, you will set up a free account with the tunnel broker, Hurricane Electric. You'll then use `netsh`, the network shell programming environment, to configure and enable the tunnel. When you have completed this lab, you will be able to

- Enable an IPv6 tunnel
- Test IPv6 connectivity

Lab Materials and Setup

The materials you'll need for this lab exercise are

- *Mike Meyers' CompTIA Network+ Guide to Managing and Troubleshooting Networks* textbook
- Windows 10 system with Internet access
- Valid e-mail address
- Pen or pencil
- Paper

Getting Down to Business

JSW's client has finally decided to implement IPv6 office-wide, only to find out that communication over the Internet with native IPv6 is not fully implemented. Jonathan and the client discuss some of the solutions and decide to use one of the commercial tunnel brokers. After doing some research on the various ones, they select Hurricane Electric. Jonathan invites you to tag along as he creates an account and configures the tunneling protocol.

Step 1   In the following space, briefly describe why a 6in4 tunneling protocol, provided by a tunnel broker, is needed.

_____

_____

Step 2   On your Windows 10 system, launch a browser, and enter the URL **ipv6.google.com** in the address bar. Were you able to reach the site?

_____

_____

Step 3   Now navigate to Hurricane Electric at www.tunnelbroker.net. The IPv6 tunnel broker home page is a wealth of information in and of itself. Take a moment and read the introduction. Hurricane Electric offers a free tunnel broker service, but you will have to register, provide personal information and an e-mail address, and create an account. Click the blue Register button on the top left. Fill out the form and click the gray Register button on the bottom. You'll get an e-mail to verify the account. After you do so, log in with your credentials.

➜ **Note**

> If you are performing this lab exercise as part of a class in a college or training center, please follow the instructor's directions. You may be restricted in creating a tunnel through the school's or company's Internet connection. As with any service that you sign up with on the Internet, please read the terms and services before you provide your personal information. Even if you decide not to use the tunnel broker, follow along with the lab exercise steps. You will learn about IPv6, tunnel brokers, and even how to use the `netsh` environment to set up the interface.

Step 4   On the left, under User Functions, click Create Regular Tunnel. You will provide your external IPv4 address that you received from your ISP. You will see the public IPv4 address you're using by You Are Viewing From:. Simply copy and paste that address into the IPv4 Endpoint (Your Side):. You should see the message "IP is a potential tunnel endpoint." Then select one of the radio buttons from Available Tunnel Servers:.

→ **Note**

You may encounter the message "IP is not ICMP pingable. Please make sure ICMP is not blocked. If you are blocking ICMP, please allow 66.220.2.74 through your firewall."

If this occurs at home, you'll need to change the settings on your router's firewall. In most cases, this involves disabling IPv4 SPI Firewall Protection and disabling Filter Anonymous Internet Requests (names will vary from device to device).

If you're doing this at a college or a training center, you won't be able to make any changes to the router's firewall. Read through the rest of the lab anyway, and perform the lab when you get home.

Click the Create Tunnel button. This will create the tunnel and bring you to the summary page. Note the IPv6 tunnel configuration information. Record the information found under IPv6 Tunnel Endpoints.

Server IPv4 Address: _____

Server IPv6 Address: _____

Client IPv4 Address: _____

Client IPv6 Address: _____

Step 5   On the Hurricane Electric Web site, click the Example Configurations tab under Tunnel Details. In the Select Your OS dropdown, pick your operating system (Windows 10). Launch a command prompt with Administrative privileges, and copy and paste the commands from Example Configurations to complete the client-side configuration. If you are behind a NAT, you must substitute your private inside address for your public IPv4 address that appears in the second line of the configuration commands after `localaddress=` (get your private IP address from ipconfig).

The following message, displayed under the configuration commands, is very important:

With the KB3081448, KB3081449, and KB3081452 updates applied, the above configuration should apply properly. You may also need to set an IPv6 DNS server. You can do this under Network and Sharing Center / Change Adapter Settings, select your NIC and right click for Properties, double click Internet Protocol Version 6, and enter an IPv6 DNS server, such as 2001:470:20::2.

As instructed here, for the physical NIC you're currently using, add Hurricane Electric's 2001:470:20::2 DNS server IP address as your preferred DNS server and Google's 2001:4860:4860::8888 Public DNS server IP address as your alternate DNS server, as shown in Figure 12-2.

✔ Tech Tip

The copied commands use the network shell (`netsh`) utility. The `netsh` commands can be entered as one long string of syntax and run from the `C:\>` prompt. For example:

```
C:\>netsh interface teredo set state disabled.
```

You can also drill down to subcontexts by entering the commands one at a time. For example:

```
C:\>netsh
netsh>interface
netsh interface>teredo
netsh interface teredo>set state disabled
```

Either method will work as long as you pay attention to which context you are working within.

FIGURE 12-2 IPv6 DNS servers added

If everything worked as expected, you should have a working IPv6 tunnel and be able to communicate with IPv6-only sites. Run this `netsh` command to verify connectivity. Your results should resemble those shown in Figure 12-3.

```
netsh interface ipv6 show interfaces
```

Step 6 On your Windows 10 system, launch a browser, and enter the URL **ipv6.google.com** in the address bar, as you did earlier. Were you able to reach the site now?

_____

_____

If you've configured your tunnel server to one of the servers outside of the United States, you'll notice a different look to your Google searches now. Since the Google server thinks you're coming from that location of the world (because your tunnel server's DNS server is issuing the query), you're going to get a location-specific Google page. For example, if you selected Tokyo, JP earlier, you'll see Japanese through your Google searches. It's like you're searching from Japan!

For even more fun, check out the location-specific YouTube pages that display, with location-specific videos! If you're getting the U.S. versions, the browser is switching over to IPv4 because of latency. If this is the case, try a different browser to see the location-specific pages through IPv6.

Step 7 While sniffing with Wireshark, in the command-line interface on your Windows 10 system, execute the following command: `ping ipv6.google.com`. What did you see in Wireshark? Which address was used as the source IP address and why?

_____

_____

```
Command Prompt                                                    —   □   ×
Microsoft Windows [Version 10.0.16299.309]
(c) 2017 Microsoft Corporation. All rights reserved.

C:\Users\jswics>netsh interface ipv6 show interfaces

Idx     Met         MTU          State                Name
---  ----------  ----------  ------------  ---------------------------
 10          45        1500  connected     Wi-Fi
  7          45        1280  connected     IP6Tunnel
  1          75  4294967295  connected     Loopback Pseudo-Interface 1
  4           5        1500  disconnected  Ethernet
  8          25        1500  disconnected  Local Area Connection* 1
 17          65        1500  disconnected  Bluetooth Network Connection


C:\Users\jswics>
```

FIGURE 12-3 Connected and disconnected IPv6 interfaces

Step 8   Execute the following commands, and explain the difference in results:

```
ping www.google.com
ping -4 www.google.com
ping -6 www.google.com
```

_____

_____

_____

_____

_____

Step 9   If you have completed all of the previous steps, you should now have an IPv6 tunnel broker enabling you to access IPv6-only Web sites. Point your browser to **test-ipv6.com**. What are the displayed results?

_____

_____

_____

_____

Step 10   If you don't want to keep this tunnel for future use, execute the following two commands from the command prompt, which will delete the tunnel and reset IPv6 settings back to their defaults:

```
netsh int ipv6 delete interface "IP6Tunnel"
netsh int ipv6 reset
```

_____

_____

Lab Analysis

1. Arnel is studying for the CompTIA Network+ exam. While reading about IPv6, he asks, "What is a link-local address and how can I recognize this address type?" Explain it to him.

    _____

    _____

2. Steve wants to know how a system running IPv6 gets a global unicast address. Explain it to him.

    _____

    _____

3. Neal keeps hearing some fellow techs talking about an IPv6 anycast address. Can you help him understand what this is and how it is used?

    _____

    _____

4. Cain wants you to help him understand some of the different multicast addresses supported by IPv6. What will you tell him?

    _____

    _____

5. Ross asks you to explain to him some of the rules for the IPv6 address notation. Break down the format of an IPv6 address for him.

    _____

    _____

    _____

    _____

Key Term Quiz

Use the vocabulary terms from the list provided to complete the sentences that follow.

Extended Unique Identifier (EUI)

global unicast address

link-local address

tunneling

tunnel broker

1. To get on the Internet with IPv6, you will need to have a(n) _____.

2. On an IPv4 network, to access IPv6 resources, you need a(n) _____ protocol.

3. Hurricane Electric is a(n) _____.

4. When each IPv6 system starts up, it will assign itself a(n) _____.

5. In certain cases, the last 64 bits of an IPv6 address are known as the _____.

Chapter 13

Remote Connectivity

Lab Exercises

In many of the lab exercises you have performed thus far, you have integrated both LANs (local area networks) and WANs (wide area networks) as you worked through the lab exercise steps. Now, you will delve specifically into the technologies associated with remote connections. Most networks today have at least one router connected to a WAN environment. A large organization might connect to the outside world through a dedicated line, for example. An individual might connect to a high-speed Internet link.

In these labs, you'll examine the different technologies used for remote connectivity. These labs will include a review of WAN technologies and speeds, a closer look at the technologies that provide the "last mile" of connectivity, and exercises to configure a remote desktop to enable someone to administer a system remotely. You'll finish up by lending a helping hand using Windows Remote Assistant.

Now's the time to jump in and get started!

 20 MINUTES

Lab Exercise 13.01: Identifying WAN Technologies

Network technicians have the responsibility of configuring, managing, and troubleshooting the various methods of connecting LANs to WANs. These connections provide Internet access to the clients on the LAN, and access to the LAN by authorized remote clients from outside the LAN.

As a network technician, you need to understand the terminology used to describe the popular WAN-related technologies, such as PSTN, T1, SONET, Frame Relay, and ATM, as well as define the various speeds associated with these WAN technologies.

Learning Objectives

At the completion of this lab, you will be able to

- Define the speeds of popular WAN technologies
- Identify key WAN-related terms

Lab Materials and Setup

The materials you'll need for this lab exercise are

- *Mike Meyers' CompTIA Network+ Guide to Managing and Troubleshooting Networks* textbook

- Internet access

- Pen or pencil

- Paper

Getting Down to Business

Jonathan and Scott been very supportive of your pursuit of the CompTIA Network+ certification. The network lab continues to be an excellent resource for installing, configuring, and troubleshooting various networking scenarios. They know that it is sometimes difficult to simulate all of the WAN technologies that you should be familiar with, so they recommend that you hit the books and review the different WAN technologies you'll need to understand to pass the CompTIA Network+ exam. They put together the following mix-and-match exercises to help you review WAN technologies and their associated speeds.

Step 1 There are basically three transmission media in use today for dedicated point-to-point services: T-carrier over copper, Optical Carrier over fiber, and Ethernet over copper or fiber. The transmission methods may vary, but the speed of the media remains fairly constant. For each of the media types listed following, place the correct letter beside the corresponding definition for the media type and speed.

A. DS0 Channel	_____ A fiber carrier that achieves a speed of 51.85 Mbps
B. DS1	_____ A copper carrier that uses 32 DS0 channels providing a speed of 2.048 Mbps
C. T1 Line	_____ A fiber carrier that achieves a speed of 622.08 Mbps
D. E1 Line	_____ A fiber carrier that achieves a speed of 9.955 Gbps
E. T3 Line	_____ The basic digital signaling rate of 64 Kbps
F. E3 Line	_____ A fiber carrier that achieves a speed of 39.82 Gbps
G. OC-1	_____ A type of media capable of providing 1000 Mbps–10 Gbps performance
H. OC-3	_____ A fiber carrier that achieves a speed of 2.488 Gbps
I. OC-12	_____ A copper carrier that uses 24 DS0 channels providing a speed of 1.544 Mbps
J. OC-24	_____ A fiber carrier that achieves a speed of 13.22 Gbps
K. OC-48	_____ The logical bit pattern sent across T1 lines
L. OC-192	_____ A copper carrier that uses 672 DS0 channels providing a speed of 44.736 (45) Mbps
M. OC-256	_____ A fiber carrier that achieves a speed of 1.244 Gbps
N. OC-768	_____ A fiber carrier that achieves a speed of 155.52 Mbps
O. Ethernet	_____ A copper carrier that uses 512 DS0 channels providing a speed of 34.368 (34) Mbps

Step 2 Place the correct letter beside the corresponding definition for the following WAN technologies.

A. CSU/DSU	_____ A packet-switching standard designed for T-carrier lines such as a T1
B. ATM	_____ The European specification for the long-distance, high-speed, fiber-optic transmission defined by the International Telecommunications Union (ITU)
C. DWDM	_____ Connects a copper carrier such as a T1 line to your router
D. Frame Relay	_____ The point in a building where the ISP/telephony company's responsibility ends and the organization's responsibility begins
E. Demarc	_____ Label-switching technology that inserts a label between the Layer 2 header and the Layer 3 information
F. MPLS	_____ Allows one single-mode fiber cable to carry approximately 150 simultaneous signals
G. SDH	_____ The primary standard for long-distance, high-speed, fiber-optic transmission
H. SONET	_____ Integrates voice, video, and data over a single link that uses a fixed-size 53-byte cell

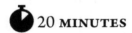 20 MINUTES

Lab Exercise 13.02: Explore the "Last Mile"

Individuals and SOHOs use numerous methods to connect to the digital outside world. For these individuals and smaller organizations, this is the connection to the central office (CO) and is known as the "last mile." In the early days, this connection was primarily analog telephone lines. Today, you will see high-speed cable, fiber, or cellular technologies providing connectivity to residential dwellings.

You have used some form of connection to the Internet in many of the prior lab exercises, so you have some knowledge of one or two of these "last mile" technologies already. To answer some of the questions that you will encounter on the CompTIA Network+ exam comfortably, you should review these connection methods.

Learning Objectives

At the completion of this lab, you will be able to

- Define the "last mile" technologies

- Detail key specifications and features of each connection technology

Lab Materials and Setup

The materials you'll need for this lab exercise are

- *Mike Meyers' CompTIA Network+ Guide to Managing and Troubleshooting Networks* textbook
- Internet access
- Pen or pencil
- Paper

Getting Down to Business

You already have some experience with one or two of the SOHO connection methods. If you have used dial-up, DSL, cable, or fiber, you have used a "last mile" technology. Scott will be presenting a report to Jonathan on the various connection technologies that JSW will recommend to their clients. Since your clients are from all types of locales (rural farms to urban apartments), Scott wants to cover all available technologies. He asks you to help with the preliminary information gathering.

Using the Internet and the textbook, research and review the various SOHO connection technologies and provide a definition and short summary of each.

Step 1 Start with the old standard, dial-up. Cover some of the details and requirements for both PSTN/POTS and ISDN.

_____

_____

_____

_____

Step 2 Next you will explore DSL. Make sure to include information about ADSL, SDSL, and VDSL.

_____

_____

_____

_____

Step 3   Cable Internet connectivity has been popular for a number of years and continues to vie for the highest speeds for residential and commercial service. Discuss some of the characteristics of cable Internet service.

_____

_____

_____

_____

Step 4   In rural areas, satellite Internet connectivity may be the most attractive option. What are some of the features of satellite Internet?

_____

_____

_____

_____

Step 5   With the explosive use of portable smart devices (smartphones), the cellular WAN has become the de facto standard for Internet connectivity on the go. Discuss both mobile data services and IEEE 802.16.

_____

_____

_____

_____

Step 6   The most serious competitor for cable Internet services is delivered by fiber to the home (FTTH). Record some of the features of fiber Internet connectivity.

_____

_____

_____

_____

30 MINUTES

Lab Exercise 13.03: Using Remote Desktop Connection

Most businesses today support users working at remote locations or from home, and with the increase in the use of virtual servers (see Chapter 15), it is not uncommon to manage those servers from a remote client machine. To set up this capability, you can configure the remote system to enable you to use client software to connect remotely to that system when the need arises.

There are a number of remote management software solutions that you can use. One of the popular solutions is to enable Remote Desktop on Windows systems, so that you can then use the Remote Desktop Connection client to initiate a remote session with the system. Once a Remote Desktop session is established, you can then fully administer the system as if you were sitting at the computer.

✖ Cross-Reference

> Before tackling this lab, read over the "Remote Terminal" section in Chapter 13 of the *Mike Meyers' CompTIA Network+ Guide to Managing and Troubleshooting Networks* textbook.

Learning Objectives

In this lab, you will enable Remote Desktop on a Windows server so that you can then administer it remotely. Keep in mind that you can enable Remote Desktop on any Windows system, but the instructions for this lab are specific for Windows 10. At the end of this lab, you will be able to

- Enable Remote Desktop
- Remotely connect to a system using the Windows Remote Desktop Connection client

Lab Materials and Setup

The materials you'll need for this lab exercise are

- *Mike Meyers' CompTIA Network+ Guide to Managing and Troubleshooting Networks* textbook

- Two Windows 10 systems

- Network switch

- Cabling

- Pen or pencil

- Paper

Getting Down to Business

JSW has a number of customers located in remote cities. JSW techs will occasionally travel to the customer site when the customer has a need for server changes. In a discussion with Dan, he tells you that the growing trend is to manage client servers from the JSW office. He recommends that you explore the features of the Remote Desktop program that is built into Windows and configure a remote session in the JSW networking lab.

✔ **Tech Tip**

> **Working with your instructor, take a few moments to review the configuration of your networking lab setup. Components and configurations may have changed over time with multiple groups using the equipment, or some of the systems may still be configured for specific lab exercises. Review Administrator names and passwords and log in to the systems. Check the cabling. Explore the basic TCP/IP configuration and verify that the client systems, servers, and switches (VLANs) are all on the same network. Run some basic utilities and validate connectivity. Performing this routine now will assist in making the future lab exercises run more smoothly.**

Step 1   Ensure that the system you plan to remote into is powered on, and then log on with an account that has Administrator privileges.

Step 2   In the Windows 10 search box, type **This PC**, right-click This PC, and select Properties. In the pane on the left select Remote Settings. The System Properties window with the Remote tab selected should appear, as shown in Figure 13-1.

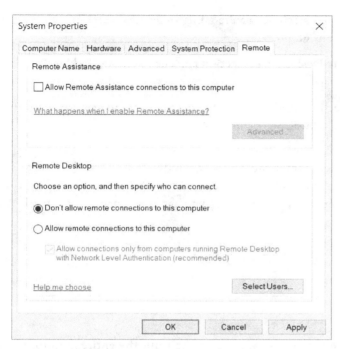

FIGURE 13-1 The Windows 10 Remote tab of the System
Properties window

Step 3 Enable the Remote Desktop option by choosing Allow Remote Connections To This computer. Make sure there is no check in the box underneath dealing with Network Level Authentication.

Step 4 If you want to allow users to use Remote Desktop to connect to the system, click the Select Users button and add the users to the list. When you give users the capability to use Remote Desktop to connect to the system in this manner, you add them to a built-in group that has the permission to use Remote Desktop to connect to the server. What is the name of this built-in group?

_____

_____

_____

Choose OK to close the System Properties window.

Step 5   Now log on to the second Windows 10 machine. You're going to use this machine to connect to the first Windows 10 machine that you just configured.

In the Windows 10 search box type **Remote Desktop Connection** and click Remote Desktop Connection.

This will open the Remote Desktop Connection window. Type the IP address of the first Windows 10 machine you configured earlier, and then click Connect. See Figure 13-2.

Step 6   When queried to enter your credentials, enter the user name and password for the machine you are remoting into. Now you can navigate all of the applications and utilities of the target machine as if you logged on locally. Look at the System Properties to verify that you are connected to the target. What are the results?

_____

_____

Step 7   Notice that the Remote Desktop Connection window by default fills the entire monitor screen. In typical use, you would click Start | Log Off to log off the target machine and close the Remote Desktop Connection. You could also choose Start | Shut Down to perform a remote shutdown of the remote machine. This would be useful if you received a notice that the location where your server resides lost power and you would like to shut down the system gracefully before the UPS battery backup runs out. Go ahead and shut down the remote system. What is the warning message that you receive?

_____

_____

FIGURE 13-2 Remote Desktop Connection window

Step 8   If your target machine was running a server operating system, like Windows Server 2016, you should have noticed a warning stating that "Remote Desktop Firewall exception will be enabled." If the firewall between the Remote Desktop client and the Remote Desktop server is enabled, how would this exception allow the Remote Desktop client to connect to the server?

_____

_____

 30 MINUTES

Lab Exercise 13.04: Using Windows Remote Assistance

Remote Desktop is a great solution when you want to take control of a remote machine, but what if you would like to help someone configure his desktop settings? What can you do to help troubleshoot problems when a remote user calls for help? One of the methods you can use is to have the user invite you to "share" control of his desktop, guiding him in the steps required to resolve his issue.

Microsoft offers a great solution, known as Windows Remote Assistance. Windows Remote Assistance enables a user to invite a technician to connect to a system remotely and then share pointer movement and keystrokes of that system with the tech. This method gives you (the tech) complete access to the remote machine, but at the same time, the user can view and contribute to the session.

Windows Remote Assistance differs therefore from Remote Desktop because Windows Remote Assistance continues the user's currently running session. The user doesn't have to log off at all. When you log in with Remote Desktop, in contrast, you start a completely new session. However, if you're using Remote Desktop to remotely connect to a session with a user name/password combination that's currently logged into that machine, you'll actually intercept that session on the remote machine. For example, let's say you left your office at work with your computer on and different windows and programs open. If you remotely connected to that machine from home, you'd see your desktop as you left it when you were in your office at work.

Learning Objectives

In this lab, you will negotiate a Windows Remote Assistance session on two Windows 10 systems. At the end of this lab, you will be able to

- Initiate a Windows Remote Assistance session
- Remotely assist a Windows 10 client

Lab Materials and Setup

The materials you'll need for this lab exercise are

- Two Windows 10 machines
- Network switch and appropriate cabling to connect the small network
- Pen or pencil
- Paper

Getting Down to Business

Jonathan has you wrap up your exploration of remote connectivity applications with the configuration, initiation, and use of the Microsoft Windows Remote Assistance feature.

Step 1 Power up the two Windows 10 machines, and make sure that they are configured to communicate with each other in the small network lab. Log on to both machines with an administrative account. For the purposes of this lab exercise, consider one machine the Office Tech machine and the other the Remote Client machine.

Step 2 Start the preparation for this lab exercise on the Office Tech machine. Windows Remote Assistance begins the session by having the remote client send an e-mail request to the office tech. On the Remote Client machine, perform the steps to configure the user to accept Remote Assistance and create an invitation:

a. In the Windows 10 search box, type **This PC**, right-click This PC, and select Properties. In the pane on the left select Remote Settings. The System Properties window with the Remote tab selected should appear, as shown earlier in Figure 13-1.

b. Under Remote Assistance, check the box next to Allow Remote Assistance Connections To This Computer. Click the Advanced button. What are the default settings?

_____

_____

_____

_____

c. Close the Remote Assistance settings by clicking OK or Cancel for the Remote Assistance Settings window and then OK for the System Properties window.

d. To begin the process of requesting Remote Assistance, perform the tasks in the following steps:

   i. In the Windows 10 search box type **Remote Assistance** and select Invite Someone To Connect To Your PC And Help You, Or Offer To Help Someone.

   ii. In the Windows Remote Assistance window, select Invite Someone You Trust To Help You, as shown in Figure 13-3.

   iii. Select Save This Invitation As A File and save it to the desktop.

   iv. This will create a password, open a Windows Remote Assistance window, and prompt you to Give Your Helper The Invitation File And Password. See Figure 13-4.

   v. Using a Web-based e-mail provider, send an e-mail to yourself containing the invitation file as an attachment and the password as text copied and pasted into the body of the e-mail.

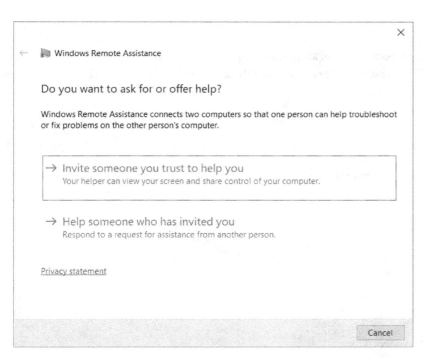

FIGURE 13-3 Inviting a tech you trust to help with system configuration or troubleshooting

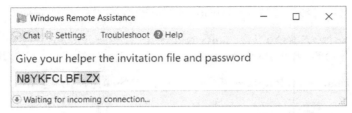

FIGURE 13-4 Windows Remote Assistance waiting for an
incoming connection and displaying the invitation password

Step 3   To complete the invitation process and connect using Remote Assistance, you will now perform
steps on both the Office Tech system and the Remote Client system.

a.   On the Office Tech machine, open up the e-mail you just sent yourself, download the invitation file,
and double-click it. This will open the Windows Remote Assistance window and prompt you to
enter the password. Copy and paste the password from the e-mail body into the dialog box, as shown
in Figure 13-5. Click OK, and then switch over to the Remote Client machine.

b.   On the Remote Client machine, click the Yes button to allow the office tech to view the remote client
desktop. See Figure 13-6. At this point, what is the office tech able to do?

_____

_____

c.   Now switch to the Office Tech machine and select Request Control in the upper lefthand corner of
the menu bar. This will request the ability to control the keyboard and mouse of the Remote Client
machine.

FIGURE 13-5 Entering the password to
connect to the remote computer

FIGURE 13-6 Would you allow Jonathan S. Weissman to connect to your computer?

d. Back on the Remote Client machine, click Allow %username% To Respond To User Account Control Prompts, where %username% is the name of the Office Tech user account. Click Yes to allow.

e. Now the Office Tech and the Remote Client should have co-control of the Remote Client machine's keyboard and mouse functions. Verify that the Office Tech can do something on the Remote Client.

f. Once you've verified capability, click the Close button to close the Windows Remote Assistance window and end the Remote Assistance session.

→ **Note**

A newer version of Windows Remote Assistance, the Quick Assist app, was included in the Windows 10 Anniversary Update. Its usage, however, requires signing in to a Microsoft account.

Lab Analysis

1. Tim is running a small graphic arts business out of his home. He often transfers high-resolution images to a drop box on the Internet for his customers to access these images. What are the different types of DSL, and which would you suggest he use for his business?

_____

_____

2. Many routers offer modules or interface cards that directly support CSU/DSU connections. Amy asks you to explain what a CSU/DSU is and what it is used for.

_____

_____

3. Claire has been reading up on long-distance, high-speed WAN technologies and has noticed various terms like SONET, OC-1, OC-3, STS-256, and STS-768. What can you tell her about these terms?

_____

_____

4. Rachel wants to know when to use Remote Desktop, and Laura wants to know when to use Remote Assistance. What will you tell them?

_____

_____

Key Term Quiz

Use the vocabulary terms from the list provided to complete the sentences that follow.

asymmetric DSL (ADSL)

fiber to the home (FTTH)

Remote Desktop Protocol (RDP)

T1

Windows Remote Assistance

1. A(n) _____ connection uses separate download and upload speeds over the phone lines.

2. A(n) _____ connection has a transfer rate of 1.544 Mbps.

3. ISP customers would switch to _____ cable for greater speeds.

4. Remote Desktop uses _____ to send screen information to the remote user.

5. The _____ tool enables a technician to troubleshoot a remote computer, with the user able to observe and interact at the same time.

Chapter 14

Wireless Networking

Lab Exercises

Wireless networking is the solution to, and the cause of, many network technicians' headaches. Wireless networking is being adopted at a phenomenal rate in all corners of the globe, from small home and office networks to school campuses, local libraries, and large corporate enterprises. You'll also find wireless networking in hotels, airports, cafes, fast-food restaurants, and donut shops. As a networking solution, wireless is an exciting evolution that provides flexibility, scalability, and ever-increasing throughput speeds. On the downside, wireless networks can be finicky to configure, prone to interference, and insecure.

I say "can be" because there are a number of things you, the network tech, can do to overcome the weaknesses of wireless networking to make it a robust, secure, and available solution. The CompTIA Network+ exam expects you to be competent in all aspects of wireless networking. In this chapter, you're going to install, configure, and manage Wi-Fi wireless technology and security. You will explore the basic facts and figures of each wireless technology, the accepted industry standards that apply to them, and how to implement and troubleshoot these technologies. Welcome to wireless networking!

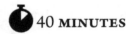 40 MINUTES

Lab Exercise 14.01: Wireless Standards and Security

Understanding the various specifications, operating ranges, speeds, compatibility issues, security methods, and so on enables you to make informed decisions when planning a wireless network rollout.

Learning Objectives

In this lab, you will review the specifications of the various flavors of the IEEE 802.11 wireless networking technologies. When you have completed this lab, you will be able to

- Define the important specifications of wireless networking technologies

Lab Materials and Setup

The materials you'll need for this lab exercise are

- *Mike Meyers' CompTIA Network+ Guide to Managing and Troubleshooting Networks* textbook

- Internet access

- Pen or pencil

- Paper

Getting Down to Business

Remember Jonathan's excitement when he was talking about the wireless connectivity that JSW's client is implementing in all of the rest stops along the interstates and autobahns? Well, now it is time to install these sites and make sure that they will function well into the future. Jonathan asks you to research the current offerings in the world of Wi-Fi and make your recommendations on the technologies to use in each of the installments.

Step 1   Your first step is to research the specifications and features of the devices that meet the various Wi-Fi standards. Using the *Mike Meyers' CompTIA Network+ Guide to Managing and Troubleshooting Networks* textbook and the Internet, research and record the specifications for the IEEE 802.11 standards in the following table.

✖ Cross-Reference

To assist in your review of the specifications, functions, and security associated with wireless networking, consult the "Wi-Fi Standards" section of Chapter 14 in the *Mike Meyers' CompTIA Network+ Guide to Managing and Troubleshooting Networks* textbook.

Standard	Frequency	Modulation	Maximum Speed	Maximum Range	Backward Compatibility
802.11					
802.11a					
802.11b					
802.11g					
802.11n					
802.11ac					

Step 2   Due to the actual architecture of wireless networking, it would be impractical to use carrier sense multiple access with collision detection (CSMA/CD). Wireless networks use carrier sense multiple access with collision avoidance (CSMA/CA) to enable nodes to communicate with each other without interfering with each other's broadcasts and corrupting data. Explain why the CSMA/CD access method wouldn't work with wireless technology, and describe how the CSMA/CA access method functions.

_____

_____

Step 3   Provide an appropriate description for the following components of security associated with Wi-Fi technology:

Security Component	Description
WPA	
WPA2	
TKIP-RC4	
CCMP-AES	
EAP	
Preshared key	
MAC filtering	
Geofencing	

✖ Cross-Reference

Many of the wireless security measures may be found in the "Wi-Fi Security" section of Chapter 14 in the *Mike Meyers' CompTIA Network+ Guide to Managing and Troubleshooting Networks* textbook. Additionally, detailed specifications may be found by conducting Internet searches on the named security components.

✔ **Exam Tip**

The CompTIA Network+ certification exam objectives include MAC filtering (more commonly known as MAC address filtering) as one of the appropriate wireless security measures. Though MAC filtering will deter the casual uninvited user from leeching a connection to the Internet, it should not be considered a viable security measure to protect a wireless network from being hacked, as MAC addresses can be spoofed.

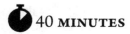 40 MINUTES

Lab Exercise 14.02: Planning the Wireless Network

Now, armed with knowledge of Wi-Fi standards and security, you can look at the requirements for the rest stops. You will want to plan for future growth—including both increased traffic as population and travel continue to expand, and performance as technology improves.

Wireless networking is becoming increasingly important to individuals in their homes as well as businesses that cater to the public. It provides instant connectivity and is the solution to many wired network physical barriers.

Learning Objectives

In this lab, you will analyze the basic information of how wireless networks function to make recommendations for the implementation of wireless networks in the highway rest stops. When you have completed this lab, you'll be able to

- Recommend wireless technology based on application

- Design appropriate wireless models based on usage

- Devise a plan to implement wireless connectivity in highway rest stops

Lab Materials and Setup

The materials you'll need for this lab exercise are

- Pen or pencil

- Paper

Getting Down to Business

The various rest stops along the most traveled highways have facilities that are fairly standard in size and the number of travelers they support per hour. There is usually one building with a number of restaurants and fast-food eateries around the edges of the space with a large common area in the center with tables and chairs. Most of the common areas are wide open with a minimum of obstacles, but they can span hundreds of feet from wall to wall. The general goals for each rest stop are as follows:

- The network should be able to support from 20 to 60 devices at one time.

- The network must be secure against unauthorized wireless access, but also allow authorized visitors to join without issues.

- The network should use industry-standard technology that is widely available.

Step 1   Explain the basic hardware and software required to implement wireless networking.

_____

_____

Step 2   Explain the differences between ad hoc and infrastructure modes.

_____

_____

Step 3   Describe at least two methods to implement security on wireless networks. For a public wireless solution, name two security methods that are not practical.

_____

_____

Step 4   Given the typical size of the rest stops, a standard single wireless access point probably won't provide enough range to cover the entire space. How can you increase the wireless coverage area?

_____

_____

Step 5   Based on the goals listed for the rest stops, describe the wireless networking solution you plan to implement.

_____

_____

Step 6   Explain how you will connect the wireless network nodes to the existing 1000BaseT network and, ultimately, the Internet.

_____

_____

45 MINUTES

Lab Exercise 14.03: Configuring Wireless Networking

With only slight variations, installing and configuring wireless network equipment is much like doing so for a wired network. Since you already know how to install network adapters and network switches, I'll forego a detailed discussion of those procedures here and concentrate on steps for configuring your wireless network nodes to talk to each other in infrastructure mode.

Learning Objectives

In this lab, you will configure PCs for wireless networking. When you have completed this lab, you will be able to

- Configure PCs for Wi-Fi wireless networking in infrastructure mode

- Configure a wireless access point for wireless networking in infrastructure mode

Lab Materials and Setup

The materials you'll need for this lab exercise are

- Two Windows 10 systems equipped with Wi-Fi network adapters

- Wireless access point (802.11ac recommended)

- Pen or pencil

- Paper

Getting Down to Business

After you've delivered a report of your suggested wireless network implementation to Jonathan, he recommends that you build a prototype of the wireless network in the Network Lab. If possible, you should try to model the actual usage that will take place in the rest stops. For instance, many of the travelers will have smartphones, laptops, and tablets. Generally, any of the devices come with integrated wireless network interfaces, so working with various makes and models of wireless network adapters and access points will help prepare you for real-world application.

Step 1   If you have not already done so, install a wireless network adapter into an available slot on your PC, following the manufacturer's instructions. If you're using a PCIe or ExpressCard NIC, this should be a simple matter of inserting the hardware and then, once PnP detects the device, following the prompts to install the hardware drivers. If you're using a USB device, install the hardware drivers before connecting the device to the PC. Once you've successfully installed the device and device drivers, you should see an icon for the wireless network in the Windows 10 notification area. Right-click the icon and select Open Network & Internet Settings, then click Network And Sharing Center, and then, finally, Set Up A New Connection Or Network. The Set Up a Connection or Network wizard is shown in Figure 14-1.

Step 2   Configuring a wireless network to operate in infrastructure mode requires several steps: clear, configure, and then connect.

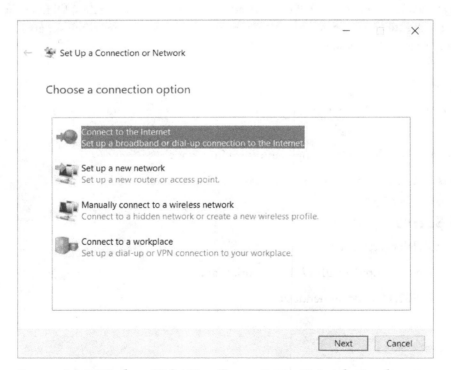

FIGURE 14-1 Windows 10 Set Up a Connection or Network wizard

First, plug the WAP into an electrical outlet. If it's been installed in a network before, you should reset it to factory defaults. That will clear out any sort of configurations, and you'll be able to use the default user name and password to configure it. Almost every WAP has a reset button that you hold for a certain length of time to reset it. If you don't have documentation for the WAP, go for 15 seconds or longer.

Second, plug a computer (laptop or desktop) into the WAP using an Ethernet or USB cable (depending on which connection the WAP has). Most consumer-grade WAPs come bundled with an enabled DHCP server, so as long as the computer you use is set up for DHCP, it will get an IP address that will enable you to access the WAP's Web interface and configure the WAP.

Configuration is done using—you guessed it—a configuration utility supplied by the wireless access point's maker. The utility is usually browser based, and you can simply open your Web browser, point to a special local IP address (such as 192.168.1.1), and enter a password when prompted to access the utility. Some access points require that you install a dedicated configuration utility program. Figure 14-2 shows the configuration utility for a Linksys WAP.

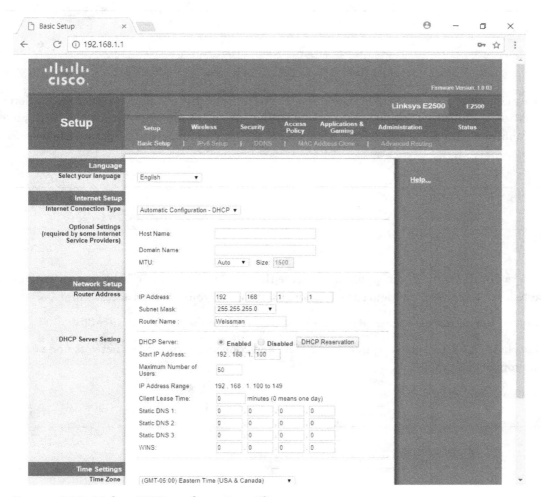

FIGURE 14-2 Linksys WAP configuration utility

As with the wireless network adapter configuration utility, the wireless access point configuration utility may vary in appearance depending on the make and model, but the functions should be practically identical. Launch your access point configuration utility and do the following:

- Configure a unique (nondefault) SSID name, such as TRAVELSTOP.

- If the access point is configured as a DHCP server, disable this setting.

- Change the WAP's IP address so that it fits in the same network ID as your wired network. Be careful not to use an IP address that can be assigned to another device via DHCP.

Save the new configuration settings on the access point.

Finally, connect the WAP to your wired network segment. Installation is a simple matter of connecting it to a network outlet, switch, or patch panel via a patch cable.

What are the results? Are wireless network nodes able to communicate with the access point? Are wireless network nodes able to communicate with each other?

_____

_____

Step 3   Now configure your wireless network nodes with settings that match the new configuration of your wireless access point (SSID, broadcast channel). What are the results? Are wireless network nodes able to communicate with the access point? Are wireless network nodes able to communicate with each other?

_____

_____

Step 4   In a real-world setting, you would never leave the WAP wide open. To bring the security up to an acceptable level, locate and configure the following settings on your wireless access point:

- Change the default user name (if possible) and password for the configuration utility.

- Enable WPA2 Personal encryption on the WAP and configure each wireless network node with the appropriate passphrase.

What are the results?

_____

_____

✔ **Exam Tip**

The CompTIA Network+ exam might ask a question about securing wireless networks that calls for more than encryption and changing the default user name and password. If MAC filtering is one of the other options, select it, even though, as mentioned earlier, it's not security at all.

 30 MINUTES

Lab Exercise 14.04: Troubleshooting Wireless Networks

The famous science fiction writer Arthur C. Clarke coined one of my favorite sayings when he stated in his third law, "Any sufficiently advanced technology is indistinguishable from magic." Wireless networking isn't quite that advanced, but the results are nonetheless quite impressive—when they work correctly. When they don't work correctly, wireless networks afford network techs some unique opportunities to display their troubleshooting acumen.

Learning Objectives

In this lab, you will troubleshoot some common wireless networking issues. When you have completed this lab, you will be able to

- Diagnose common wireless networking problems

- Troubleshoot common wireless networking problems

Lab Materials and Setup

The materials you'll need for this lab exercise are

- Two Windows 10 systems equipped with Wi-Fi network adapters

- Wireless access point (802.11ac or 802.11n recommended)

- Pen or pencil

- Paper

Getting Down to Business

You have successfully installed and configured the wireless network model to be implemented in the highway rest stops. Jonathan now asks you to demonstrate steps for troubleshooting simple problems before you tear down the wireless networking lab.

Step 1   List at least three steps you should take to determine if a loss of wireless connectivity is due to your wireless network adapter's hardware or software configuration.

_____

_____

_____

Step 2   After determining that your wireless network adapter is functioning correctly, how can you find out whether your network node has proper connectivity and signal strength to the wireless network?

_____

_____

Step 3   Name at least three factors that could cause poor signal strength between wireless network nodes.

_____

_____

_____

Step 4   Assuming that a loss of wireless connectivity is not caused by improper hardware or software configuration, excessive distance between wireless network nodes, or environmental factors, what should you check next?

_____

_____

Lab Analysis

1. Chris has just purchased a new 802.11ac AP for his home network. He installs the device and configures the network, and seems to have fewer intermittent drops of connectivity than before with his previous 802.11n router. Explain the types of wireless consumer electronics that may cause interference with a wireless network.

_____

_____

2. Graham has been doing some research on the frequency bands used by 802.11 devices. He asks you to explain the differences between the 2.4 GHz frequency band and the 5.0 GHz frequency band. Which standards are used in each?

_____

_____

3. Marty is using a dual-band 802.11n wireless router. He wants to know if you recommend upgrading it to the newer 802.11ac standard and if doing so would require him to replace all client NICs as well. What do you tell him?

_____

_____

4. Jeremiah has been looking over your proposal for the wireless network implementation for the highway rest stops and would like to know why you do not recommend using MAC address filtering as an added security measure. What is your explanation?

_____

_____

5. Therese is a network administrator for a local university. She is configuring a wireless network to cover the student and faculty common areas. The wireless network will tie into the campus network, so all of the students and faculty will use their existing user names and passwords. How should she configure the wireless authentication?

_____

_____

Key Term Quiz

Use the vocabulary terms from the list below to complete the sentences that follow.

Advanced Encryption Standard (AES)

Extensible Authentication Protocol (EAP)

geofencing

pre-shared key

RADIUS

RC4

Wi-Fi Protected Access 2 (WPA2)

Wired Equivalent Privacy (WEP)

1. The _____ wireless security standard provides a considerable security improvement as compared to the _____ wireless security standard.

2. Configuring client machines with a _____, will allow them to authenticate to a WAP.

3. Authenticating with _____ requires a server that runs _____.

4. _____ replaced _____ as the symmetric encryption algorithm for Wi-Fi security protocols.

5. _____ uses RFID to track mobile devices entering and leaving certain areas.

Chapter 15

Virtualization and Cloud Computing

Lab Exercises

At this point in your studies, you have already worked with virtual environments. You have configured virtual local area networks (VLANs) to organize groups of physical ports on a switch logically, placing the machines connected to those ports into separate networks. You have also worked with virtual private networks (VPNs) to tunnel safely through the Internet, sending traffic from that remote network as if you were physically there.

Now you'll be creating and using virtual machines (VMs)! A major trend in desktops and servers is to use one physical computer, install a host operating system, and then deploy multiple virtual machines on top of the host OS to meet the needs of the users. The ultimate example of virtualization would be the modern data center, where thousands of servers are now hosted on just a few hundred physical machines.

There are various implementations of virtual hardware (NICs, switches, routers, firewalls, etc.) offered by multiple vendors (VMware, Citrix, Microsoft, Oracle, Parallels, etc.). These virtualization technologies set up the environment so that you may install and run various operating systems on the same hardware platform simultaneously. Not only does this promote efficient use of hardware and energy resources, but virtualization also enables you to create images of the virtual machine easily, providing excellent fault tolerance and disaster recovery options. To replicate a VM all you need do is copy the files that make it up. To move a VM from one host to another, all you need do is move the files. The host system can dynamically allocate resources to the VMs, allowing more resources to be dedicated to those that are busy, on the fly. Many training organizations have adopted virtualization to enable swift reconfiguration of systems for specific demonstrations or to implement complex lab exercises.

After four lab exercises that deal with virtualization, the fifth lab exercise will give you some experience with cloud computing through some of Google's Software as a Service (SaaS) offerings.

20 MINUTES

Lab Exercise 15.01: Identifying Virtualization Technologies

Virtualization takes on many aspects of the physical devices used every day in the computing environment. Organizations may choose to install multiple virtual servers on one physical machine to handle DHCP, DNS, Web services, e-mail services, file sharing, and print services, to name a few.

In the lab exercises for this chapter, you will have the opportunity to install one of the most popular virtual machine technologies available today, but this is only one component of virtualization. Before you work with the actual virtualization programs and before you take the CompTIA Network+ certification exam, you will want to explore various technologies associated with virtualization. This lab exercise covers many of them. Time to explore!

Learning Objectives

At the completion of this lab, you will be able to

- Distinguish between different types of hypervisors

- Distinguish between host and guest machines

- Detail the characteristics of virtual routers, switches, and firewalls

- Detail key components and features of cloud computing

Lab Materials and Setup

The materials you'll need for this lab exercise are

- *Mike Meyers' CompTIA Network+ Guide to Managing and Troubleshooting Networks* textbook

- Internet access

- Pen or pencil

- Paper

Getting Down to Business

Before you begin your hands-on exploration of virtualization, it is important that you understand the underlying solutions that virtualization technologies provide. Jonathan collects a list of virtual technologies, and asks you to use your textbook and the Internet to develop a brief description and summary of the characteristics of each of the technologies.

Step 1   Start by researching hypervisors. What are hypervisors? How are Type 1 hypervisors different than Type 2 hypervisors? What is a host operating system? What is a guest operating system? What's the relationship between hypervisors and host and guest operating systems?

_____

_____

_____

_____

Step 2   When we talk about virtualization, what exactly is being virtualized?

_____

_____

_____

_____

Step 3   Based on your answer to the previous question, what is the difference between a virtual machine (VM) and a guest operating system (OS)?

_____

_____

_____

_____

Step 4   A VM can use different networking configurations, including bridged (VMnet0), NAT (VMnet8), and host-only (VMnet1). What are the differences between these configurations? Use the following reference to help formulate your answer: www.vmware.com/support/ws5/doc/ws_net_configurations_common.html.

_____

_____

_____

_____

Step 5   The term *virtual NIC* doesn't just refer to a NIC of a VM. On the host system, virtual NICs are present as well. What are their names and functions on a host system?

_____

_____

_____

_____

Step 6   What is a virtual switch, and why isn't there a virtual NIC on the host for bridged networking (VMnet0)?

_____

_____

_____

_____

Step 7　One of the most popular virtual router/virtual firewall combinations is pfSense. Visit its Web site and list some of your impressions: www.pfsense.org.

_____

_____

_____

_____

 45 MINUTES

Lab Exercise 15.02: Installing and Configuring VMware Workstation Player

VMware is arguably the leader in large-scale, enterprise-wide virtualization. With scalable products, like vSphere and ESXi, which are fully featured solutions for data centers and cloud providers, to VMware Workstation Player, which is free to individuals exploring virtual solutions for their personal PC, VMware offers solutions at every level.

To introduce you to VMware, you will download the hypervisor, VMware Workstation Player, and install it on a Windows 10 host system. Then, you will download, install, and run Ubuntu, a popular Linux distribution, as a guest OS on a VM.

Learning Objectives

In this lab exercise, you will use VMware Workstation Player to install an Ubuntu guest operating system on a VM on a Windows 10 host system. You will then explore a few of the Ubuntu programs and commands. At the end of this lab exercise, you will be able to

　a.　Install and configure VMware Workstation Player on a Windows 10 host system

　b.　Install and run Ubuntu as a guest OS on a VM in the VMware Workstation Player hypervisor

Lab Materials and Setup

The materials you'll need for this lab exercise are

- Windows 10 system with Internet access

- Pen or pencil

- Paper

Getting Down to Business

Jonathan and Scott would like you to take advantage of the network lab yet again. This time they want you to explore virtualization! The network lab offers an excellent environment to work through the idiosyncrasies of virtualization, to see how it works, before deploying it on production systems.

Step 1　At the time of this writing, Ubuntu 16.04.4 LTS seems like a good choice for the guest OS, as it will be supported through April 2021. That's what the LTS stands for: *long-term support*. You can download this free Linux distribution at www.ubuntu.com. Go to https://wiki.ubuntu.com/Releases to see the past, present, and future of Ubuntu releases. Next, go to www.ubuntu.com/download and click Ubuntu Desktop. Click the green Download button next to Ubuntu 16.04.4 LTS (or whatever the current version is at the time you're doing this).

On the next page, unless you want to donate, scroll to the bottom of the page and click Not Now, Take Me To The Download. The ISO image file, ubuntu-16.04.4-desktop-amd64.iso (or a file corresponding to a later release, depending on when you perform this activity), should download to your Downloads folder. Leave it there for now.

Step 2　Launch your browser and navigate to https://my.vmware.com/web/vmware/downloads. Scroll down to the Desktop & End-User Computing section, and click the Download Product link to the right of VMware Workstation Player. Click the Download button next to VMware Workstation 14.1.1 Player for Windows 64-bit Operating Systems (or the current version when you're doing this), as shown in Figure 15-1. The executable installer, VMware-player-14.1.1-7528167.exe (or the current version, depending on when you're doing this), should download to your Downloads folder.

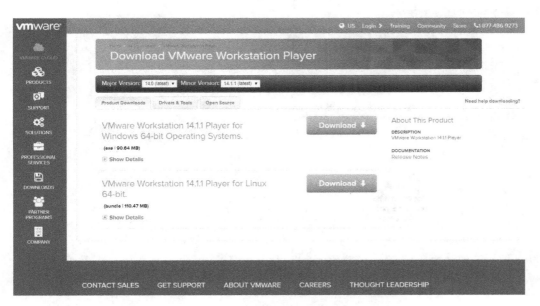

FIGURE 15-1 Downloading the VMware Workstation Player hypervisor

Step 3   Perform the following tasks to install the hypervisor:

    a.   Double-click the file VMware-player-14.1.1-7528167.exe (or the current version, depending on when you're doing this) to launch the installation program. At the Welcome To The VMware Workstation 14 Player Setup Wizard screen (see Figure 15-2), click Next.

    b.   Accept the VMWARE END USER LICENSE AGREEMENT and click Next.

    c.   Put a check in the box for Enhanced Keyboard Driver and click Next.

    d.   Make your selections for the User Experience Settings screen and click Next.

    e.   Leave the checks in the boxes on the Shortcuts screen and click Next.

    f.   On the next screen, click the Install button. VMware Workstation 14 Player Setup will begin the installation.

    g.   Click Finish when the setup wizard completes.

    h.   Click the Yes button, if prompted, to restart your system. When your machine reboots, continue with the next step.

Step 4   Perform the tasks in the following instructions to create a new virtual machine:

    a.   Double-click the VMware Workstation 14 Player icon to launch the application.

    b.   At the VMware Workstation 14 Player screen, click Create A New Virtual Machine. This will launch the New Virtual Machine Wizard.

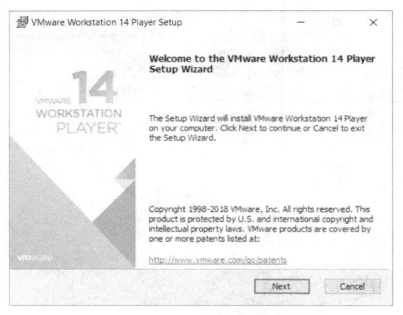

FIGURE 15-2   VMware Workstation Player welcome screen

FIGURE 15-3 New Virtual Machine Wizard

c. Click Browse to locate and select the Ubuntu ISO file you downloaded earlier (see Figure 15-3).
Click Next.

d. Next, set up a user name and password for the Ubuntu guest operating system. Click Next.

e. You will now name the virtual machine and choose the location for the virtual machine folder. You
may use the defaults or change the name and location. Click Next.

f. Specify the disk capacity. The recommended size for Ubuntu is 20 GB. However, you may choose a
smaller disk capacity. Make a choice of either single file (what I would recommend) or multiple files
and click Next.

g. Now you are ready to create the virtual machine. Review the virtual machine settings as shown in
Figure 15-4. If you would like to add more RAM allocated to the VM, click the Customize Hardware
button, and adjust the value on the right of the screen that appears. Click the Close button to return
to the previous screen.

Keep the check in the box next to Power On This Virtual Machine After Creation, and then click
Finish to begin building the virtual machine.

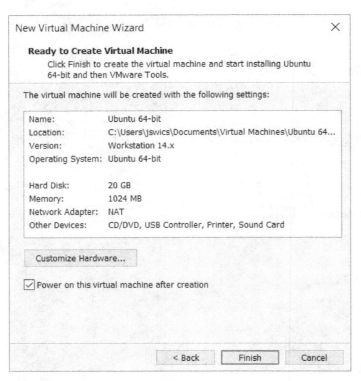

FIGURE 15-4 VMware Workstation Player new virtual machine summary page

➜ **Note**

You may have to enable virtualization in the BIOS. Read more at https://kb.vmware.com/s/article/1003944 and www.howtogeek.com/213795/how-to-enable-intel-vt-x-in-your-computers-bios-or-uefi-firmware/.

h.   As the installation starts, click the Download And Install button in the Software Updates pop-up. VMware Tools For Linux – Version 10.2.0 (current at the time of this writing) should install at the same time. VMware Tools is a suite of utilities that enhances the performance of the virtual machine's guest operating system and improves management of the virtual machine. When the updates finish, click the Close button.

i.   When the VMware Ubuntu virtual machine reboots, you will be prompted for your user name and password. After entering your information, you will have a fully functioning installation of Ubuntu as a guest operating system on top of the host operating system, Windows 10.

 30 MINUTES

Lab Exercise 15.03: Sending Network Traffic Between the Host System and VM

Thus far, you've heard a lot about terms like virtual switch and virtual NIC. You've heard about networking configurations called bridged, NAT, and host-only. You've heard about different types of hypervisors.

Seeing is believing. Talking about host systems and VMs is one thing. Sending traffic between them is something else! Understanding the traffic flow through Wireshark will make the functions of hypervisors crystal clear.

Jonathan is excited, because if you can understand and implement virtualization, JSW can save lots of money in terms of hardware, power, and resources.

Let's get started!

Learning Objectives

At the end of this lab, you will be able to

- Understand the difference between a physical NIC and a virtual NIC

- Understand the difference between bridged networking and NAT networking

- Send traffic to and from the host system and VM

Lab Materials and Setup

The materials you'll need for this lab exercise are

- VMware Workstation Player running on the Windows 10 host OS, with Ubuntu installed as the guest OS, from Lab Exercise 15.02

- Pen or pencil

- Paper

Getting Down to Business

On the Windows 10 host OS, in the Search Box, type **sharing**. Click Manage advanced sharing settings, click Network And Sharing Center in the Address Bar, click Change Adapter Settings on the left, and look at all of your interfaces. Besides your physical interfaces, you now have two new VMware Network Adapters. In bridged networking (VMnet0), the host system and VM are on the same LAN, so no virtual adapter is needed on the host system, since the physical NIC is on the same subnet as the VM.

NAT networking uses a virtual router between the host system and the VM. However, your host system is already configured for a default gateway on a router that doesn't know about another virtual network behind VMware's NAT router. Therefore, to allow the host system to communicate with the VM in NAT networking, a virtual NIC, VMware Network Adapter VMnet8, is created for the host system. This virtual adapter has an IP address on the subnet of the VM running in NAT networking, which allows the host system to send traffic directly to the VM (and vice versa).

Host-only networking, which allows the VM to talk with just the host system, uses the same concept of a virtual NIC on the host system, and this one is called VMware Network Adapter VMnet1. If the host system wants to communicate with the VM in host-only networking, the host system uses the virtual NIC, because again, the default gateway of the host does not know about the existence of this remote network that the VM is on.

This lab helps you understand these differences by observing traffic patterns in both NAT and bridged networking.

Step 1   Log in to the guest OS, as explained at the end of Lab Exercise 15.02. From the VMware menu at the top, click Player | Manage | Virtual Machine Settings and make sure that the Network Adapter is set for NAT. Explore both the Hardware and Options tabs.

Step 2   Click the Search Your Computer button at the top left of the Ubuntu desktop, type **Terminal** in the Search Your Computer box, and then click the Terminal icon. Into the Linux shell known as Bash that opens, type `ip  a`, and then press ENTER. You should see an IP address listed for the ens33 interface (see Figure 15-5).

FIGURE 15-5 ens33 configuration

Step 3 Perform the following substeps:

    a.   Type sudo apt install wireshark.

    b.   Provide the password to your account.

    c.   Type Y and press ENTER.

    d.   Keep the default choice of No by pressing ENTER in the Package Installation screen that pops up.

    e.   Back in the terminal, type sudo wireshark & and press ENTER. The & symbol sends the process to the background, giving you control back in Bash.

    f.   Click OK in the dialog box that pops up.

    g.   Double-click ens33 to start capturing on that interface.

    h.   In the filter box, type ip.addr== followed immediately by (with no white space after the two equals signs) the IP address of the host system (Ethernet or Wi-Fi adapter, whichever one you're using) and press ENTER. If you're not sure what it is, open a Windows command-line interface on the host system and type ipconfig.

Step 4 From the Linux terminal, ping the IP address of your Windows Ethernet or Wi-Fi adapter. When the ping is successful, press CTRL-C to stop the pings. Linux pings don't stop automatically after four like in Windows. Notice the ICMP Echo requests and ICMP Echo replies in Wireshark running on Ubuntu.

The MAC address that was associated with the IP address of the Windows host system in the ICMPs is *not* the MAC address of the Windows Ethernet or Wi-Fi adapter. Which device is this MAC address associated with? What is that device's IP address? What is the function of that device? Use the commands arp -a and route in the terminal of the VM to support your answer.

_____

_____

_____

Step 5 From the Linux terminal, ping the IP address of the VMnet8 adapter on the host system. Use ipconfig /all in the Windows 10 command prompt to get both the IP address and MAC address of the VMnet8 adapter.

When the ping is successful, press CTRL-C to stop the pinging. Notice the ICMP Echo requests and ICMP Echo replies in Wireshark running on Ubuntu.

What are the IP and MAC addresses seen from the pings? How are the pings in this step different than the pings from the previous step?

_____

_____

_____

Step 6   From the Windows command prompt on the host system, ping the IP address of the VM. Notice the ICMP Echo request and ICMP Echo replies in Wireshark running on Ubuntu.

What IP address was used by the host system? What MAC address was associated with that IP address? Why were those IP and MAC addresses used?

_____

_____

_____

Step 7   Now, from the host system, open Wireshark and start a capture on your Ethernet or Wi-Fi adapter. In the filter box, type `icmp` and press ENTER. From the Windows command prompt, ping the IP address of the VM. Then, from the VM, once again, ping the IP address of your host system's Ethernet or Wi-Fi adapter.

Why don't you see _anything_ related to these pings in Wireshark on the host system?

_____

_____

_____

_____

Step 8   Now start sniffing on the VMnet8 Adapter on the host system. Ping from the host system to the VM, and then ping from the VM to the host system.

How do the results differ when sniffing on the VMnet8 adapter as opposed to the Wi-Fi or Ethernet adapter? Why is this the case?

_____

_____

_____

_____

Step 9   Change the Network Adapter settings NAT networking to bridged networking by clicking Player | Manage | Virtual Machine Settings | Network Adapter in VMware Workstation Player. Click the radio button next to Bridged, and check the box next to Replicate Physical Network Connection State. Click the Configure Adapters button, and make sure that every check box is checked. Click OK | OK.

Wait a few seconds, and you'll see a pop-up in the top right of the VM that says Disconnected - You Are Now Offline and another one, right after that, that says Connection Established.

In a terminal, type ip a and press ENTER to see the new IP address assigned to the virtual machine.

From the host system, start a capture on the Ethernet or Wi-Fi adapter. In the filter box, type icmp and press ENTER. Ping the new IP address of the VM. Now you see the ICMPs through the Ethernet or Wi-Fi adapter! Why are they visible now?

_____

_____

_____

_____

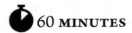

60 MINUTES

Lab Exercise 15.04: Sending Network Traffic from the VM to the Internet

When a frame enters a physical NIC, if the destination MAC address is not the NIC's MAC address, a broadcast, or a multicast, the NIC will drop it. Promiscuous mode is a mode for a wired or wireless NIC that causes the NIC to pass all traffic it receives up the network stack on a machine. Now the NIC will accept, capture, and read frames that are unicast addresses other than the NIC's MAC address. Of course, promiscuous mode is not useful on a switched network because the switch will only send frames to ports associated with destination MAC addresses, as listed in the switch's Media Access Control (MAC) Address Table, also known as Content Addressable Memory (CAM) Table and Source Address Table (SAT).

For a VM running in bridged networking with its own virtual NIC and MAC address, the hypervisor will inject itself through a device driver and force a wired physical NIC to accept a frame with a VM's MAC address, so it can be sent to the VM. Even though the destination MAC address is of the virtual NIC for the VM and not the physical NIC of the host system, the physical NIC is able to take the frame in. The virtual bridge will send the traffic to the VM with the listed destination MAC address.

Hypervisors need to tweak that behavior for wireless traffic because many wireless adapters don't support promiscuous mode; the wireless adapter will automatically drop traffic if the destination MAC address is not the MAC address of the physical wireless NIC. All traffic has to use the MAC address of the host system's wireless adapter. The hypervisor needs to replace the source MAC address in the Layer 2 header of an outgoing packet to the host's MAC address, to make sure the reply will be sent back to the host's MAC address and not the guest's MAC address.

When the hypervisor sees an incoming packet with a destination IP address that belongs to one of the VM's virtual NICs, it replaces the destination MAC address of the host NIC in the Layer 2 header with the VM's virtual NIC's MAC address and sends it on. Layer 2 ARP frames don't have a Layer 3 IP header, so the Target IP address field is parsed by the hypervisor to know which virtual NIC should get the ARP reply. Hypervisors examine ARP and DHCP traffic so they can learn the IP addresses of virtual machines.

Learning Objectives

At the end of this lab, you will be able to

- Understand how physical wired NICs send traffic to VMs

- Understand how physical wireless NICs send traffic to VMs

- Send and analyze network traffic from a VM through a physical wired NIC

- Send and analyze network traffic from a VM through a physical wireless NIC

Lab Materials and Setup

The materials you'll need for this lab exercise are

- VMware Workstation Player running on the Windows 10 host OS, with Ubuntu installed as the guest OS, from Lab Exercise 15.02

- Both a wired and wireless NIC

- Pen or pencil

- Paper

Getting Down to Business

If you've been using a laptop and Wi-Fi for these exercises so far, for Step 1, plug a cable into your Ethernet adapter and use a wired Ethernet connection. Then, in Step 2, take the cable out and resume using a Wi-Fi connection.

If you've been using a desktop to this point, for Step 1, continue as before. For Step 2, if possible, install Ubuntu as a guest OS through VMware Workstation Player on a laptop, and use a Wi-Fi connection.

Step 1 Log in to the guest OS, as explained at the end of Lab Exercise 15.02. From the VMware menu at the top, click Player | Manage | Virtual Machine Settings and make sure that the Network Adapter is set for bridged networking.

Step 2 With your host system using its Ethernet adapter, start sniffing with Wireshark using a display filter of icmp on both the host system and VM.

From the terminal on Ubuntu, send a ping to 8.8.8.8.

What was the MAC address in the ICMP Echo Requests seen through Wireshark on the VM?

What was the MAC address in the ICMP Echo Requests seen through Wireshark on the host system?

_____

_____

_____

_____

Step 3   With your host system using its Wi-Fi adapter, start sniffing with Wireshark, using a display filter of `icmp` on both the host system and VM.

From the Terminal on Ubuntu, send a ping to 8.8.8.8.

What was the MAC address in the ICMP Echo Requests seen through Wireshark on the VM?

What was the MAC address in the ICMP Echo Requests seen through Wireshark on the host system?

_____

_____

_____

_____

 60 MINUTES

Lab Exercise 15.05: Cloud Computing with Google Drive

Remember the days of downloading or going to the store to buy Microsoft Office? Remember having to download and install updates? Then, a few years later, your version of Microsoft Office became obsolete, and you needed a new version! Now, with Microsoft Office 365, you use a browser to access the latest and greatest of the Office suite in the cloud, with security patches applied immediately. Furthermore, you don't have to uninstall the previous version and install the current version. Google's G Suite offers a similar set of cloud tools with Google Docs, Google Sheets, and Google Slides, which are free for consumers; enterprise features, options, tools, and settings, and support come at different pricing levels.

The Software as a Service (SaaS) model provides access to necessary applications wherever you have an Internet connection, often without needing to carry data with you (the data can be stored in the cloud as well) or regularly update software. At the enterprise level, the subscription model of many SaaS providers makes it easier for organizations to budget software expenses and to keep hundreds or thousands of computers up to date with software for office tasks, messaging, payroll processing, database management, business management, and much more.

In exchange for the flexibility of using public, third-party SaaS, you often have to relinquish strict control of your data. Security might not be crucial when someone uses Google Drive to draft a blog post, but many companies are concerned about sensitive intellectual property or business secrets traveling through untrusted networks and residing on servers they don't control.

Specific examples of SaaS include any Web-based e-mail provider (such as Gmail and Yahoo), Dropbox, Box, Slack, Office 365, Google Docs, Google Sheets, and Google Slides.

Learning Objectives

At the end of this lab, you will be able to

- Use Google Drive to store files

- Use Google Docs, Sheets, and Slides

- Use other features of Google's SaaS

Lab Materials and Setup

The materials you'll need for this lab exercise are

- Any operating system

- Any browser

- Internet access

- Pen or pencil

- Paper

Getting Down to Business

You might have carried backups around on floppy disks, a very long time ago. More recently, you might have transported files and programs with flash drives. Cloud computing requires you to carry around nothing, as everything is stored in that proverbial cloud. As the technically inclined like to say, "There is no cloud. It's just someone else's computer."

Step 1 Go to https://drive.google.com and create an account if you don't have one.

Step 2 Click the New button at the top left of the screen. Create and explore each of the following items: Folder, File Upload, Folder Upload, Google Docs, Google Sheets, and Google Slides. If possible, test the ability to access these files and software from any machine with a browser and Internet connection.

Record some of your observations about creating items in Google Drive.

_____

_____

_____

_____

Step 3   Through the More selection, create and explore each of the following items: Google Forms, Google Drawings, Google My Maps, and Google Sites. If possible, test the ability to access your newly created items from any machine with a browser and Internet connection.

Record some of your observations.

_____

_____

_____

_____

Lab Analysis

1. Tamara wants to know why you might create the VM with a single file, as opposed to multiple files (through VMware Workstation Player). Can you answer this question for her?

_____

_____

_____

_____

2. Oren asks you if VMware has other products besides VMware Workstation Player. Using the Web site www.vmware.com, list all the different categories of products that VMware offers.

_____

_____

_____

_____

3. Charlie is planning on upgrading one of his virtual installations of Ubuntu with a major, untested application suite. What steps would you recommend to minimize any problems if the application suite does not meet expectations?

_____

_____

_____

_____

4. Miles wants to know the pros and cons of Software as a Service. What will you tell him?

_____

_____

_____

_____

Key Term Quiz

Use the vocabulary terms from the list provided to complete the sentences that follow.

Bridged

Software as a Service (SaaS)

Type 1

Type 2

virtual router/firewall

1. pfSense is an example of a _____.

2. VMware Workstation Player is a _____ hypervisor.

3. Google Docs, Google Sheets, and Google Slides are all examples of _____.

4. ESXi is a _____ hypervisor.

5. In _____ networking, the host system and VM are on the same LAN.

Chapter 16
Mobile Networking

Lab Exercises

Many ubiquitous mobile technologies today, while being highly convenient, can also be very vulnerable. This is even more concerning when talking about employee-owned mobile devices that are used for work. Attackers will be given many ways to enter the corporate infrastructure through this administrative nightmare known as BYOD (bring your own device).

Furthermore, an amazing number of devices today come with Internet connectivity. Lightbulbs, cameras, thermostats, and even crockpots can be controlled with an app on a phone. Embedded devices that connect to the Internet and enable remote monitoring and controlling are known as *Internet of Things (IoT)*, and their capabilities are extremely similar those of mobile devices.

Jonathan and Scott, therefore, want you to have a solid understanding of these technologies so that you can help protect the corporate infrastructure.

 1 HOUR

Lab Exercise 16.01: Cellular, Bluetooth, and Other Mobile Technologies

Today's mobile devices can support multiple networking technologies and can connect to other mobile devices, as well as nonmobile devices and networks. As the capabilities of these devices get greater and greater, the devices themselves get smaller and smaller.

Let's take a look at mobile networking technologies you need to be familiar with.

Learning Objectives

In this lab, you will develop your knowledge related to mobile networking technologies. When you have completed this lab, you will be able to

- Explain various cellular networking technologies
- Explain what is meant by different generations of technologies
- Understand 802.11 risks
- Understand Bluetooth

Lab Materials and Setup

The materials you'll need for this lab exercise are

- *Mike Meyers' CompTIA Network+ Guide to Managing and Troubleshooting Networks* textbook

- Internet access

- Pen or pencil

- Paper

Getting Down to Business

Used for mobile data services, GSM, EDGE, CDMA, HSPA+, and LTE are all technologies that Jonathan and Scott want you to get more familiar with. Let's jump right into this!

Step 1   Using the *Mike Meyers' CompTIA Network+ Guide to Managing and Troubleshooting Networks* textbook or Google, match each cellular technology with its corresponding definition.

Technologies	Definitions
_____ GSM	1. Used by U.S. carriers, unlike the rest of the world, instead of GSM.
_____ EDGE	2. The final 3G data standard, providing theoretical speeds up to 168 Mbps.
_____ CDMA	3. The first group of networking technologies widely applied to mobile devices, which relied on TDMA (*time-division multiple access*).
_____ HSPA+	4. Marketed as, and now generally accepted as, a true 4G technology, features speeds of up to 300 Mbps for downloading and 75 Mbps for uploading.
_____ LTE	5. Evolution of the GSM standard, which offers data speeds up to 384 Kbps.

Step 2   All this talk about generations (or just G) has you wondering what G, 2G, 3G, and 4G all mean. Research the terms and provide a description of each cellular generation.

G   _____

2G   _____

3G   _____

4G   _____

As this book went to press, 5G wasn't yet deployed but most likely will be by the time you're reading this. So let's cover that one as well.

5G   _____

Step 3   Your friend told you that it's a good idea to use 802.11 on your phone, when available, to avoid cellular WAN data use charges. How do you respond to him? For help, enter the following Google search query (don't put quotation marks around the four words): **never use public wifi**. Read through all links on the first page of results.

_____

_____

_____

_____

Step 4   You've heard of two Bluetooth attacks: Bluejacking and Bluesnarfing. What's the difference between the two?

_____

_____

_____

_____

Step 5   Using the _Mike Meyers' CompTIA Network+ Guide to Managing and Troubleshooting Networks_ textbook or Google, match each of these mobile technologies with its corresponding definition.

Technologies	Definitions
_____ NFC	1. Home automation open standard
_____ RFID	2. Home automation proprietary standard
_____ Infrared	3. Tag and reader span of at least six different radio bands
_____ ANT+	4. Low-speed, short-range technology used for small-value monetary transactions
_____ Z-wave	5. Can be used from some Android phones to control TVs
_____ ZigBee	6. Garmin's low-power/low-speed technology

25 MINUTES

Lab Exercise 16.02: Controlling Users' Mobile Devices

Organizations won't simply purchase devices for each employee. Employees will want to use their devices for work services like e-mail. Take these two facts together, and you have a problem related to users, their devices, and corporate information. This Lab Exercise helps you understand deployment models, including BYOD, COBO, COPE, and CYOD, which help define how organizations approach mobile devices, as well as general on-boarding and off-boarding actions.

Learning Objectives

In this lab, you will

- Solidify your knowledge of deployment models that organizations use for users and their mobile devices.

- Understand general on-boarding and off-boarding actions

Lab Materials and Setup

The materials you'll need for this lab exercise are

- Internet access

- Pen or pencil

- Paper

Getting Down to Business

Scott tells you about what the JSW company was like when he was first hired many years ago. Work-related tasks were conducted on corporate devices and systems. Now, users are coming in as employees with multiple devices that they want to use for work-related tasks. Jonathan has long since implemented some mechanisms to minimize any potential problems related to users and their mobile devices.

Step 1   Scott asks you to learn about the differences between BYOD (bring your own device) and COBO (corporate-owned business only). What does each concept represent?

_____

_____

_____

_____

Step 2   After learning the basics, Scott now wants you to understand the pros and cons of BYOD and COBO. Can you list them?

_____

_____

_____

_____

Step 3   Scott tells you that JSW is considering two potential hybrids of BYOD and COBO: COPE (company-issued, personally enabled) and CYOD (choose your own device). What do these concepts entail, and which one would you recommend?

_____

_____

Step 4   JSW has recently implemented on-boarding, a method of verifying that new mobile devices appearing in an organization's infrastructure are secure and safe to use within the organization. At the same time, JSW rolled out an off-boarding implementation as well, verifying that devices that were on-boarded no longer store any proprietary applications or data. What are some ways that on-boarding and off-boarding can be carried out?

_____

_____

Step 5 You recall reading an article about a new thing called geofencing, and before possibly recommending it to Jonathan and Scott at JSW, you need to review its purpose again. What can you recall about geofencing?

_____

_____

Step 6 Finally, Scott asks you to look into steps that JSW can take if a user loses a corporate device, potentially filled with private and proprietary information. What would you recommend?

_____

_____

Lab Analysis

1. Rank BYOD, COBO, CYOD, and COPE in order from strictest to least strict.

_____

_____

2. List some other on-boarding processes a new employee should have to go through, unrelated to their mobile devices.

_____

_____

3. Geofencing sounds great, but the technology is still very new. What are some potential problems you might have if you roll it out in its early days?

_____

_____

Key Term Quiz

Using the vocabulary terms from the list provided, complete the sentences that follow.

bring your own device (BYOD)

corporate-owned business only (COBO)

company-issued, personally enabled (COPE)

choose your own device (CYOD)

on-boarding

off-boarding

1. The strictest level of corporate control over devices is _____.

2. Users pick their devices with _____.

3. Users use their own devices with _____.

4. Devices should go through a(n) _____ process when an employee is hired and a(n) _____ process when an employee leaves a company.

5. Users get a white list of applications they can install with _____.

Chapter 17

Building a Real-World Network

Lab Exercises

Documentation is not one of the most glamorous tasks that a networking professional does, but it's definitely one of the most important! Having clear and accurate documentation, both in written and diagram formats, can prove to be indispensable when an administrator needs to fix networking issues, whether they occur as part of the overall troubleshooting process or are the result of something suddenly going wrong.

Incomplete or incorrect documentation can actually be counterproductive to restoring service and dealing with problems as they arise.

In the first lab of this chapter, you'll get great experience with documenting a network. In the second lab, you'll learn more about industrial control systems, devices, and software that monitor and control equipment. These two labs will give you a great glimpse into what it's like in the "real world" as a networking professional. Let's go!

 1 HOUR

Lab Exercise 17.01: Configuration Management Documentation

Configuration and change management documentation is a requirement for all but the smallest SOHO network environments. Network administrators and techs will be responsible for defining and documenting the layout and operation of the network. The physical, logical, and functional aspects of the network and devices will be recorded in both diagrams and written documents. The proper use of technology and the roles and responsibilities of the support staff and end users are defined in personnel documentation.

Once the documentation is in place, managing the changes to that documentation—like updating when a portion of the network is upgraded from 100-Mbps equipment and wiring to Gigabit performance—must be attended to diligently. When changes to the network happen—or worse, some component or system fails—the configuration management documentation is the roadmap and guide to bring the network back to full operation.

Learning Objectives

In this lab, you will develop basic configuration management documentation. When you have completed this lab, you will be able to

- Use Microsoft PowerPoint or Visio to document the network layout

- Analyze configuration management documentation for validity

- Implement change management documentation

Lab Materials and Setup

The materials you'll need for this lab exercise are

- Windows 10 system with Internet access and Microsoft PowerPoint or Google Slides

- Optionally (adhering to the organization's security policy), access to the network configuration of your classroom or department for documentation purposes

→ **Note**

In the following lab steps, the details of a fictitious network are provided. Using this fictitious network, you will create a network diagram and a network map as part of a configuration management documentation process. If your instructor or manager will allow you to have access to the parameters of your classroom or department network, substitute your actual network for the fictitious network.

Getting Down to Business

One of the tasks that can really get ahead of you if you're not careful is that of documenting the network configuration and the changes that occur over time. Good administrators and techs will make a point of staying on top of this critical element, documenting when new Gigabit switches are installed, recording the expansion of new departments in the organization with the new devices, PCs, subnets, and so on.

→ **Note**

Over the years, Cisco has become the leading manufacturer of networking routers and switches. With their leadership, many of the icons that have been developed to document Cisco products have been adopted by the industry when documenting network configurations. You may download these icons for use in PowerPoint or Visio at the following URL: www.cisco.com/web/about/ac50/ac47/2.html.

As throughout this Lab Manual, I caution you that Web sites change often. If you find that the link in the preceding paragraph does not bring you to the Cisco network icons, use a search engine and you should be able to find the current location.

Step 1   Using either PowerPoint or Visio and the Cisco networking symbols and icons, develop both a network diagram and network map to document the following fictitious remote office network. All internal cabling is Cat 6A UTP running at Gbps performance level, and the ISP has provided a 100-Mbps fiber connection to the Internet.

- **Server1**   Server1 is the primary server in this remote office network. It provides storage space for the nine employees and also handles the roles of DHCP server and DNS server. The configuration details are included in the following table.

- **Server2**   Server2 is the network backup server. The configuration details are included in the following table.

- **Printer**   An HP LaserJet network printer with an integrated JetDirect card is configured as a shared printer. The configuration details are included in the following table.

- **Edge router**   A Cisco router has been configured as the gateway to the Internet (through the ISP). The configuration details are included in the following table.

- **Switches**   A Cisco managed switch will be used as the primary switch in the main distribution frame (MDF) where the edge router and two servers are all located. Three workgroup switches will be cascaded off the primary switch to handle multiple clients in each of the three office workspaces.

- **Client computers**   To accommodate the nine employees, six desktop PCs and three laptops are installed. All of the machines are initially configured to receive their configuration information through DHCP. The laptops are also used outside of the office by the employees they are assigned to.

Device	Functions	Internal Interface IP Address	External Interface IP Address	Default Gateway
Server1	Primary Server DHCP scope 172.16.250.51/16– 172.16.250.150/16 Scope Option 003 Router–172.16.1.1 Scope Option 006 DNS Server–172.16.1.254/16	172.16.1.254/16	N/A	172.16.1.1
Server2	Network Backup Server	172.16.1.253/16	N/A	172.16.1.1
Cisco Router	Edge Router	172.16.1.1/16	101.150.36.239/21	101.150.32.1/21
HP LaserJet Printer	Network Printer	172.16.1.192/16	N/A	N/A

Step 2 One of your colleagues, Rafael, has acquired three additional desktop PCs from one of the other branch offices and has installed them for the employees who use the laptops so that they have permanent machines in the office. Rafael updates the configuration management documentation. The updated network map is shown in Figure 17-1.

Now the three employees are complaining that they cannot access any of their files on Server1. They also have no Internet connectivity. Analyze the updated network map, diagnose the problem, and provide a solution to restore the users' connectivity.

_____

_____

_____

_____

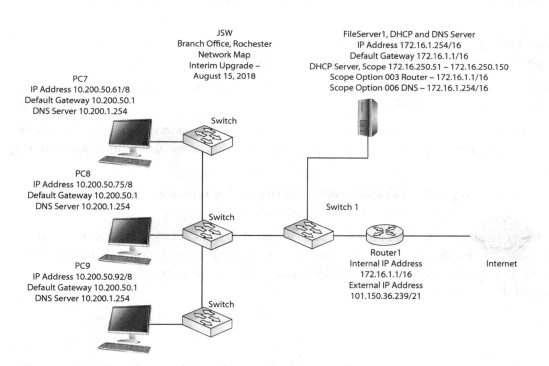

FIGURE 17-1 Partial network map showing three new machines

Step 3   A network configuration management documentation plan is only as good as the most recent update. The term for these updates is *change management documentation*.

> **→ Note**
>
> **Change management documentation includes updates to both network diagrams and network maps. Network diagrams include documentation on the devices such as switches, routers, servers, and PCs, along with their connections, connection speeds, make, model, and firmware revision when available. Network maps include documentation on IP addressing, DHCP servers, DNS servers, Web servers, e-mail servers, DMZs, and the like.**
>
> **When updating the documentation, depending on the modifications, you may only have to update the network diagram or the network map. In the following scenario, you should update both the network diagram and the network map you created in Step 1.**

The branch office has expanded the network, adding a public Web server placed in a demilitarized zone (DMZ), a Cisco firewall, and a wireless access point. The detailed specifications are provided in the following list:

- **WebServer1**   A public Web server for up-to-date traffic information. This will be placed in a DMZ with light security. The configuration details are included in the following table.

- **Firewall**   A Cisco Adaptive Security Appliance will be placed at the internal access point to the DMZ, providing a high level of security to the LAN.

- **Edge router**   The Cisco router will need to be reconfigured to continue operating as the gateway to the Internet (through a service provider). The configuration details are included in the following table.

- **Wireless access point**   A Cisco Meraki Access Point will be used to provide wireless access for the three laptop computers when the employees are in the office.

- **Client computers**   The three laptops should be modified in the network diagram and the network map to show that they are now wireless clients. You may want to update the documentation with the three desktop PCs that Rafael added in the prior step. All client machines should be configured to obtain IP settings automatically.

Building on the network diagram and network map you created in Step 1, update the configuration management documentation. Don't forget to record the date and revisions of the network diagram and network map for the change management documentation records.

Device	Functions	Internal Interface IP Address	External Interface IP Address	Default Gateway
WebServer1	Traffic update Web site; public Web server in a lightly protected DMZ	10.200.73.252/19	N/A	10.200.72.2
Cisco ASA	Firewall	172.16.1.1/16	10.200.73.1/19	10.200.72.2
Cisco Router	Edge router	10.200.72.2/19	101.150.36.239/21	101.150.32.1
Cisco Meraki access point	Access point LAN & WLAN DHCP scope 192.168.40.100– 192.168.40.150	WAN Port 172.16.1.3/16	LAN & WLAN 192.168.40.1/24	WAN 172.16.1.1

✔ **Hint**

When building on the network diagram and network map, you will place the public Web servers in the lightly protected area known as the DMZ. One method of creating the DMZ is to place the edge router as the first device between the Internet (WAN) and the internal network (LAN). This will have very light security enabled to facilitate access from the outside world. At the other end of the DMZ, you would place the firewall (Cisco ASA) to secure all of the internal machines from external access, thus creating a lightly protected area between the LAN and WAN where the Web server can be placed.

25 MINUTES

Lab Exercise 17.02: Industrial Control Systems

You might remember from the *Mike Meyers' CompTIA Network+ Guide to Managing and Troubleshooting Networks* textbook that any industry that makes things, changes things, or moves things is filled with equipment to do the job they have to do. From making mousetraps to ice cream, any given industrial plant, power grid, or pipeline is filled with stuff that needs to be monitored and stuff that needs to be controlled.

The following are a few examples of things to monitor:

- Temperature
- Power levels
- Fill quantity
- Illumination
- Mass

And here are a few examples of the things to control:

- Heaters
- Voltage
- Pumps
- Retractable roofs
- Valves

Learning Objectives

In this lab, you will

- Solidify your knowledge of industrial control system (ICS) terms

Lab Materials and Setup

The materials you'll need for this lab exercise are

- *Mike Meyers' CompTIA Network+ Guide to Managing and Troubleshooting Networks* textbook
- Internet access
- Pen or pencil
- Paper

Getting Down to Business

If JSW is to become a global force, and expand its services, you will need to understand the following terms and concepts. Jonathan asks you to complete the following matching exercise to make sure you feel comfortable with ICS terminology.

A. Human machine interface (HMI)	_____ The overall system that monitors and controls machines today.
B. Media Gateway Control Protocol (MGCP)	_____ Three basic components of an ICS.
C. Controller	_____ These monitor things like temperature.
D. Distributed Control System (DCS)	_____ These make changes that modify the temperature.
E. UC device	_____ A sort of computer that knows enough to manage the process, such as "keep the temperature between 50 and 55 degrees Fahrenheit."
F. Industrial control system (ICS)	_____ The monitor that an operator watches.
G. Interface	_____ As computing power went up and costs went down, it made much more sense to put these smaller controllers directly on each machine, to distribute the computing load.
H. Input/output (I/O) functions on the machine, controller, and operator interface	_____ In a modern DCS, where each of the local controllers connects (eventually) to a centralized controller—where global changes can be made managed.
I. ICS server	_____ Controllers that operators interact with through controls or a computer, which is most likely a PC running a custom, touchscreen interface.
J. Actuators	_____ This monitors sensors (like timers and oven temperatures) and tells the machine when to do the next step in the process.
K. UC server	_____ A subset of ICS, designed for large-scale, distributed processes such as power grids, pipelines, and railroads. A DCS using servers, HMIs, sensors, and actuators.
L. Programmable logic controller (PLC)	_____ The classic, multicast-based presentation where one presenter pushes out a stream of video to any number of properly configured and authorized multicast clients. These clients do not normally have a way to respond via video.
M. Supervisory control and data acquisition (SCADA)	_____ Enables bidirectional communication via unicast messages. Real-time video offers both video and audio to communicate.

N. UC gateway	_____ What we used to call the VoIP telephone. In a well-developed UC environment, this handles voice, video, and more.
O. H.323	_____ Typically, this is a dedicated box that supports any UC-provided service. In small organizations this might be a single box, but in larger organizations there will be many of these that connect directly to every UC device on the LAN.
P. Video teleconferencing (VTC)	_____ An edge device, sometime dedicated but often nothing more than a few extra services added to an existing edge router, allowing the router to interface with remote UC gateways, as well as with PSTN systems and services.
Q. Real-time video	_____ The most commonly used video presentation protocol (or codec), which runs on TCP port 1720.
R. Sensors	_____ Designed from the ground up to be a complete VoIP or video presentation connection and session controller.

Lab Analysis

1. Martin wants to know why configuration and change management documentation are so important. Can you explain the reasons to him?

_____

_____

2. Eva wants to know what the difference is between *network diagrams* and *network maps*. Help her understand.

_____

_____

3. Eli knows that SCADA is a subset of an ICS, but needs to know more. What will you tell him?

_____

_____

4. Maxine wants to learn more about some of the terms from Lab 17.02. Pick three that you haven't yet been asked about and explain them to her.

    _____

    _____

Key Term Quiz

Using the vocabulary terms from the list provided, complete the sentences that follow.

Distributed Control System (DCS)

documentation

network diagram

network map

programmable logic controller (PLC)

regulations

1. _____ are the laws governing the proper usage of materials in the workplace to keep both the facilities and the workers safe.

2. A _____ monitors sensors and tells the machine when to do the next step in a process.

3. Change management documentation includes updates to both _____(s) and _____(s).

4. Having clear and accurate _____, both in written and diagram formats, can prove to be indispensable when an administrator needs to fix networking issues.

5. A _____ is a smaller controller on a machine.

Chapter 18

Managing Risk

Lab Exercises

Risk, as far as networks go, represents the likelihood that a vulnerability will be exploited as well as any related consequences. There's no foolproof design to network security. Threat agents (which carry out threats, which in turn exploit vulnerabilities) include insiders, outsiders, and even Mother Nature. The threat agents need just one mere vulnerability to exploit, but the security team needs to constantly defend against all possible attack vectors. It's not a fair game by any stretch of the imagination!

The more preventive security implementations there are in place from the start, the easier it will be to mitigate a security violation. Humans have always been, and will always continue to be, the weakest link in any security system. Therefore, any security plan must begin with a solid education plan for employees.

In this chapter's first lab, you will write a security policy that will be read by employees, clearly delineating what they can and cannot do. The next lab takes user education to the next level. Making sure users read the policies is one thing. Making sure that they understand them is something else. Finally, the last lab deals with two important entities that need to be in place should an attack happen: disaster recovery and business continuity.

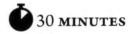 30 **MINUTES**

Lab Exercise 18.01: Security Policies

Policies are the cornerstone of an organization's IT security. Policies help define what equipment they use, how they organize data, and what actions people take to ensure the security of an organization. Policies tell an organization how to handle almost any situation that might arise (such as disaster recovery, covered later in this chapter).

A security policy is a written document that defines how an organization will protect its IT infrastructure.

Learning Objectives

In this lab, you'll learn how to

- Write a security policy
- Research other security policies

Lab Materials and Setup

The materials you'll need for this lab exercise are

- *Mike Meyers' CompTIA Network+ Guide to Managing and Troubleshooting Networks* textbook
- Windows 10 system with Internet access
- Pen or pencil
- Paper

Getting Down to Business

The acceptable use policy (AUP) defines what is and what is not acceptable to do on an organization's computers. It's arguably the most famous of all security policies, as this is one document that pretty much everyone who works for any organization is required to read, and in many cases sign, before they can start work.

For this lab exercise, assume that you are writing an acceptable use policy for your organization.

Step 1   Expand on this statement in your AUP dealing with ownership: Equipment and any proprietary information stored on the organization's computers are the property of the organization.

_____

_____

Step 2   Expand on this statement in your AUP dealing with network access: Users will only access information they are authorized to access.

_____

_____

Step 3   Expand on this statement in your AUP dealing with privacy/consent to monitoring: Anything users do on the organization's computers is not private. The organization will monitor what is being done on computers at any time.

_____

_____

Step 4   Expand on this statement in your AUP dealing with illegal use: No one may use an organization's computers for anything that breaks a law. (This is usually broken down into many subheadings, such as Introducing Malware, Hacking, Scanning, Spamming, and so forth.)

_____

_____

 30 MINUTES

Lab Exercise 18.02: User Training

Users are probably the primary source of security problems for any organization. To mitigate this, training users is a critical piece of managing risk. While a formal course is preferred, it's typically up to the IT department to do what it can to make sure users have an understanding of certain security risks.

Learning Objectives

In this lab, you'll learn how to

- Create a presentation for user training
- Give the presentation to a live audience

Lab Materials and Setup

The materials you'll need for this lab exercise are

- *Mike Meyers' CompTIA Network+ Guide to Managing and Troubleshooting Networks* textbook
- Windows 10 system with Internet access and Microsoft PowerPoint or Google Slides
- Pen or pencil
- Paper

Getting Down to Business

Using Microsoft PowerPoint or Google Slides, make slides for a formal presentation for user training. You will then deliver the presentation to an audience, which can be your classmates, other students, or even family and friends.

In each of the following steps, make two to three slides dealing with the following concepts.

Step 1   Add slides dealing with security policies: Users need to read, understand, and, when necessary, sign all pertinent security policies.

_____

_____

Step 2   Add slides dealing with passwords: Make sure users understand basic password skills, such as sufficient length.

_____

_____

Step 3   Add slides dealing with social engineering: Users need to recognize typical social engineering tactics and know how to counter them.

_____

_____

Step 4   Add slides dealing with malware: Teach users to recognize malware attacks and train them to deal with them.

_____

_____

Step 5   Deliver the presentation to your classmates, other students, or family and friends. Ask for feedback on both content and delivery, and note what they say.

_____

_____

 30 **MINUTES**

Lab Exercise 18.03: Disaster Recovery and Business Continuity

Fault tolerance should not be the end-all of data security. In keeping with the philosophy that the most important part of a network is the data, a comprehensive backup strategy is the point of last defense, and should be one of the linchpins of the administrator's network management routines. When RAID arrays fail, when users accidentally delete that critical database, or when viruses corrupt your file server, the ability to restore the systems to their most recent state will allow the organization to recover from the disaster gracefully.

Numerous technologies are available to implement quality system backups, especially cloud backups and network attached storage (NAS), to protect the data when disaster strikes. Mission-critical organizations such as world financial institutions, government agencies, and national security operations will even employ entire alternate locations that will have some level of network infrastructure ready to go in case of a complete failure of the primary location.

Although the terms are sometimes blurred, disaster recovery deals with recovering your primary infrastructure from disaster, and business continuity seeks to keep your business going at alternate locations if the primary location cannot be used.

Data backup technology, techniques, and strategies are tools that you can apply immediately from the smallest of organizations to large enterprise networks. Along with preparing for the CompTIA Network+ exam and honing your skills as a network administrator or tech, you can also adopt these techniques to keep your precious photos and music safe from disaster!

Learning Objectives

In this lab, you'll learn how to

- Identify members for a disaster recovery team
- Plan backup methods
- Calculate time needed to restore backups
- Understand the differences between hot sites, warm sites, and cold sites

Lab Materials and Setup

The materials you'll need for this lab exercise are

- Windows 10 system with Internet access

- Pen or pencil

- Paper

Getting Down to Business

You have almost completed your studies for the Network+ exam! Along the way, you have developed a deep understanding of networking concepts and applied these skills to daily responsibilities in your position as a desktop support specialist. Now a Network Tech, Level 1 position has opened up at JSW, and you would like to apply for the position.

Jonathan is confident of your capabilities and agrees to be one of your professional references. He recommends that you focus on one last area of network management before your interview: disaster recovery and business continuity. He explains that no organization can ever prepare "too much" to avoid the devastating results of a poorly planned backup and recovery strategy. In this lab exercise, you will develop a disaster recovery plan.

Step 1 Form a disaster recovery team. Do some research and find out which employees in specific roles might be good choices for membership on this team.

_____

_____

Step 2 Plan your backups. Do some research, and decide on a proper plan on backup for your essential and non-essential data.

_____

_____

Step 3   Jonathan tells Scott about your current research adventure. Scott wants to help, and tells you that he used to work for a large trading company that was involved in multimillion-dollar online transactions. He mentions that they had a complete hot backup site for the transaction servers. If the system were to go down for more than a few hours or so, they could lose millions of dollars. Conduct an Internet search and provide the definitions for hot, warm, and cold backup sites.

_____

_____

Step 4   Compare the following two disaster recovery/business continuity vendors, and make a recommendation, with explanation, to Jonathan for your favorite.

www.mindshift.com (Search for "backup" using the site's search bar to view its offerings.)

www.castlesys.com

_____

_____

_____

Lab Analysis

1.   Brandyn has just finished an exhilarating game of *Counter-Strike* when his supervisor steps into his cubicle and gives him a verbal warning concerning gaming during business hours. She explains to Brandyn that there is a company policy that defines what is allowed and not allowed in the workplace. After his supervisor leaves, Brandyn asks you what she is talking about. What do you tell Brandyn?

_____

_____

2.   Aidan wants to know why everyone around the office talks about social engineering. Tell him why it's of utmost importance.

_____

_____

3. Doug thinks the disaster recovery plan kicks in before the business continuity plan. Charles thinks it's the other way around. Who's right, and why?

_____

_____

Key Term Quiz

Use the vocabulary terms from the list provided to complete the sentences that follow.

acceptable use policy (AUP)

cold site

hot site

warm site

1. A(n) _____ is the most expensive offsite backup option but requires very little to get up and running.

2. A(n) _____ combines the benefits of the two other offsite backup models.

3. A(n) _____ is the cheapest offsite backup option but requires the most configuration to get up and running.

4. _____ defines what can and can't be done on an organization's computers.

Chapter 19
Protecting Your Network

Lab Exercises

Network protection covers many different security aspects. You have probably already explored the various antivirus, anti-spyware, and anti-adware programs (or simply, anti-malware) that fight against the infections of malware (especially if you are a CompTIA A+ certified technician). Likewise, the topic of RAID (redundant array of inexpensive disks) should be familiar from your prior studies. You have worked with encryption in Chapter 10 and VPNs in Chapter 11. Now it's time to review some of these components and some new concepts too, because they apply to the protection of both computer networks and critical data.

Given the many options available, these labs concentrate on a number of fundamental concepts and components that demonstrate technology and techniques for protecting your network. In the first lab, you will identify some of the common types of threats that could possibly affect your network and corrupt or destroy the important data. Next, you will implement password policies in Windows, to implement and manage user authentication. The third lab explores firewalls—but shows how even this fairly narrow topic can manifest itself in both hardware devices (usually combined with other protective mechanisms) and software implementations. Finally, the fourth lab involves configuring Windows Defender Firewall, putting what you learned to good use.

 30 **MINUTES**

Lab Exercise 19.01: Identifying Common Threats

As briefly described in the opening paragraphs of this chapter, there are countless threats, malicious or otherwise, that can affect the security of a network and therefore the data contained within. These threats range from the simple but possibly time-consuming loss of data from a hard drive or server crash to the devastating results of information stolen through a mismanaged administrative account or a Trojan horse.

Effective protection of the network (and the data) requires due diligence on the part of the network administrator when it comes to analyzing these threats and warding them off or planning contingency measures. Employers (and the CompTIA Network+ exam) expect the network tech to have a working knowledge of the various threats that are waiting to pounce on the unsuspecting network.

Learning Objectives

In this lab, you will review the common threats you may encounter when working as a network technician. When you have completed this lab, you will be able to

- List and detail the various forms of malware

- Explain the concept of social engineering

- Define man-in-the-middle attacks

- Provide the definition of a denial of service (DoS) attack

- Identify attacks on wireless connections

- Understand recent attacks (WannaCry, NotPetya)

- Identify the weakest link in any security implementation

Lab Materials and Setup

The materials you'll need for this lab exercise are

- *Mike Meyers' CompTIA Network+ Guide to Managing and Troubleshooting Networks* textbook

- Internet access

- Pen or pencil

- Paper

Getting Down to Business

Now that you are progressing well through your studies and are almost ready to sit the CompTIA Network+ exam, Jonathan has a request. It has been a while since the department has provided an update to the business managers on the security measures in place to protect the network and corporate data. He asks you to conduct a study of the most common threats affecting networks today (from small home networks to large corporate enterprises) and present a report as part of the team's presentation to management.

Use both the textbook and the Internet for your research. Work through the following steps and further refine your knowledge of threats to the network.

Step 1   Provide an appropriate definition for each of the listed types of malware:

Malware	Definition
Virus	
Worm	
Logic bomb	
Trojan horse	
Rootkit	
Ransomware	

Step 2   Define the method and purpose of social engineering.

_____

_____

Step 3   What is the difference between phishing, spearphishing, and whaling?

_____

_____

Step 4   Provide a scenario depicting a man-in-the-middle attack.

_____

_____

Step 5   Document a denial of service (DoS) attack.

_____

_____

Step 6 Explain the factors that might lead to network intrusion through wireless connections.

_____

_____

Step 7 Describe a cybersecurity attack or data breach that affected you personally.

_____

_____

_____

_____

_____

Step 8 Describe the WannaCry attack from May 2017.

_____

_____

_____

_____

_____

Step 9   Describe the NotPetya attack from June 2017.

_____

_____

_____

_____

_____

_____

Step 10   What will always be the weakest link in any security implementation? Why?

_____

_____

 30 MINUTES

Lab Exercise 19.02: Implementing and Managing User Authentication

One of the most important safeguards against unwanted access to corporate client PCs and servers (and therefore, the network) is a strong password. Passwords are the most common form of authentication, which is proving who you say you are. Microsoft Windows systems include security policies that allow you to configure various settings that control how a user's password can be formulated.

Your part of the job that includes managing users and security will have you address account passwords, ensuring that only the people who should have access to the particular system they are trying to access actually do have access.

Learning Objectives

In this lab, you will configure computer security and develop a template for assigning a strong password. When you have completed this lab, you will be able to

- Create a password policy

- Edit account security settings

- Log on to a system with a valid account and change the password to meet strong password requirements

Lab Materials and Setup

The materials you'll need for this lab exercise are

- Windows 10 system

- Pen or pencil

- Paper

Getting Down to Business

Scott has been asked to set up a group policy structure for the marketing department of a new client. He invites you to tag along as he defines and tests the user account password policy that he will implement.

→ **Note**

> **In a corporate environment such as JSW and many of their clients, the password policy would be configured for the various departments and all of the users on a global basis. If the corporation is using a Microsoft architecture, the corporate network will be defined by Active Directory Domains, various Organizational Units, and Group Policy Objects. Typically, the actual configuration of system settings will take place on a Windows Server 2016 Domain Controller using the Active Directory Group Policy Object editor.**

> **For the purposes of the lab exercise, the exploration and configuration of the password policy can be completely facilitated on a PC running Windows 10.**

Step 1 Log on to the Windows 10 machine with an Administrator account. In the Windows search box, type **Local Security Policy,** and click Local Security Policy. In the pane on the left, expand Account Policies and select Password Policy.

Step 2   In the Password Policy settings in the right pane (see Figure 19-1), set the following values for the various password policy security settings:

Enforce password history	10
Maximum password age	30
Minimum password age	0
Minimum password length	8
Password must meet complexity requirements	Enabled
Store passwords using reversible encryption	Disabled

Step 3   In the Windows search box type **Computer Management** and select Computer Management. This opens the Computer Management Console. Expand Local Users And Groups, right-click Users, and select New User.

Create a new user named **DavidBanner** and attempt to use the following password (see Figure 19-2):

hulk

What are the results? Are they similar to the message shown in Figure 19-3?

_____

_____

Now, using the same user name, DavidBanner, assign the following password (with User Must Change Password At Next Logon selected):

DsB!hOtTf#Sp81

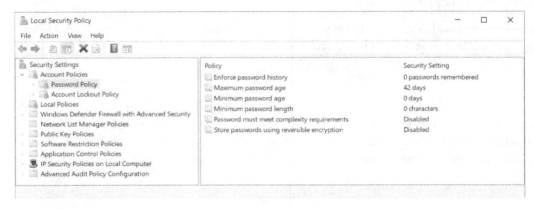

FIGURE 19-1   Configuring the password policy

FIGURE 19-2 Creating a new user

➜ **Note**

Make sure that the password is typed exactly as it appears in the example. The use of both uppercase and lowercase characters, special characters, and numerical characters is imperative to meet password complexity requirements.

A good way to come up with a complex password that's easy to remember is to use the first letter of words from one of your favorite songs and to mix and match case, interspersed with numbers and symbols. See if you can figure out the song I chose for the password provided here. Hint: It will be a fun *Journey*.

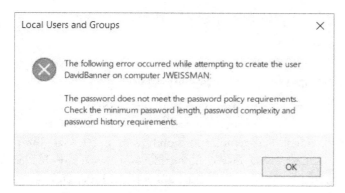

FIGURE 19-3 Local Users And Groups error message

→ **Note**

The length of a password is proportional to its strength, as longer passwords are more resistant to brute-force attacks. Keep in mind, however, that two other recommendations of the past, complexity (using different character sets) and regularly changing passwords, were moved into the "don't" category by NIST (National Institute of Standards and Technology) in 2017. They've actually been proven to be counterproductive, causing users to write down, store, and make passwords far more accessible than they should be, because they're too hard to remember and keep track of. Read the new NIST password guidelines here: https://pages.nist.gov/800-63-3/.

Step 4 Log off, and log back on as DavidBanner. When prompted to change the password, enter the same password and click OK. What are the results?

_____

_____

Step 5 Now come up with a new password that will be accepted, based on the changes to the password policy made earlier. What are the results?

_____

_____

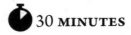 30 MINUTES

Lab Exercise 19.03: Exploring Hardware Firewalls

With the proliferation of the Internet and the wonderful communication capabilities it affords comes the proliferation of dishonest people and programs attempting to exploit that communications capability for illicit gain. There is no question that educating individuals and organizations on how to practice safe Internet usage is the first step toward protecting the network from these unscrupulous thieves. However, sophisticated infiltration programs require sophisticated intrusion protection to keep the network safe. Enter *firewalls*!

Firewalls are devices that protect networks and computers by filtering network traffic. There are many companies offering firewall products, most of which fall into two categories. The first type is a network-based firewall. This is a firewall that is incorporated into another device such as a router or a dedicated stand-alone firewall. Along with some other features, the firewall works to keep harmful traffic off the network, as well as preventing the exit of harmful traffic from inside the network. Since the router is a physical device (and, of course, a stand-alone device is as well), this type of firewall is often called a *hardware firewall*. The second type is a host-based firewall. This firewall protects individual computers from harmful traffic. This host-based firewall is also known as a *software firewall* because there is no special hardware; it is just another program on your computer.

You will work with a software firewall in Lab Exercise 19.04. For now, you are going to research hardware firewalls to understand them better.

Learning Objectives

In this lab, you'll explore firewalls. When you have completed this lab, you'll be able to

- Identify various firewalls provided by various manufacturers
- Define the components that typically make up a hardware firewall

Lab Materials and Setup

The materials you'll need for this lab exercise are

- *Mike Meyers' CompTIA Network+ Guide to Managing and Troubleshooting Networks* textbook
- Internet access
- Pen or pencil
- Paper

Getting Down to Business

Hardware firewalls, by design, are physical devices with a collection of features designed to protect your network from the unwanted entry of programs or people from the outside world. They also prevent any malicious traffic from leaving your network. These devices can be dedicated security sentry devices, robust edge routers, or simple SOHO wireless routers with various components to ward off uninvited access.

The distinction between "hardware" and "software" firewalls really comes down to where the firewall software resides. If it is on a dedicated device such as a Cisco Adaptive Security Appliance (ASA) or a router, it is considered a hardware firewall. If it is host-based (on an individual computer), it is considered a software firewall.

Step 1   Research the current offerings in the hardware firewall market. Identify the make, model, and key features of at least three devices.

1. _____

2. _____

3. _____

Step 2   One of the benefits of using a hardware firewall device is that the traditional firewall protection (usually the Stateful Packet Inspection [SPI] component is considered to be the actual firewall) is not the only protection included. Define some of the other features that are offered by hardware firewalls.

_____

_____

_____

_____

 20 MINUTES

Lab Exercise 19.04: Configuring Windows Defender Firewall

The Windows software firewall was renamed from Windows Firewall to Windows Defender Firewall with Windows 10 version 1709 in September 2017.

Learning Objectives

In this lab, you'll work with a software firewall. When you have completed this lab, you'll be able to

- Understand how software firewalls work.

- Create rules to permit or deny traffic.

Lab Materials and Setup

The materials you'll need for this lab exercise are

- Windows 10 system and any other type of device that can send pings to the Windows 10 system
- Pen or pencil
- Paper

Getting Down to Business

As you learned in the last exercise, the distinction between "hardware" and "software" firewalls really comes down to where the firewall software resides. The Microsoft Windows Defender Firewall is a host-based (on an individual computer) firewall and therefore considered a software firewall. You can't go wrong with enabling Windows Defender Firewall. Even if you have a wireless router with a firewall, you'll just end up enhancing the security.

Step 1 In the Windows search box type **Firewall** and select Windows Defender Firewall. What is your current Windows Defender Firewall status? (See Figure 19-4.) Keep this window open for future steps.

_____

_____

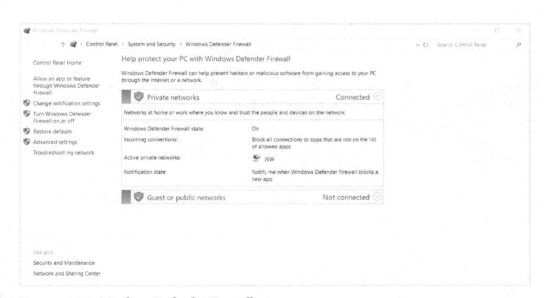

FIGURE 19-4 Windows Defender Firewall

Step 2   As you have learned, Windows Defender Firewall is a host-based, software firewall. Using the Internet, determine if the Windows Defender Firewall is of the Stateful Packet Inspection (SPI) type. Provide a short definition of SPI.

_____

_____

_____

_____

Step 3   In the pane at the left of the Windows Defender Firewall window (opened earlier), click Turn Windows Defender Firewall On Or Off. For each network location, select Turn Off Windows Defender Firewall (Not Recommended). Click OK. Keep this window open for future steps.

_____

_____

_____

_____

Step 4   Determine what IP address is assigned to the Windows 10 machine, and from a different device, ping the Windows 10 machine. (Make sure a firewall is not in effect on the other device.) Did the ICMP Echo requests get ICMP Echo replies?

_____

_____

_____

_____

Step 5 In the pane at the left of the Windows Defender Firewall window (opened earlier), click the Use Recommended Settings button. The red colors will turn green. In the pane on the left, click Restore Defaults, then the Restore Defaults button, and then Yes. Keep this window open for future steps.

_____

_____

_____

_____

Step 6 From a different device, ping the Windows 10 machine. Did the ICMP Echo requests get ICMP Echo replies?

_____

_____

_____

_____

Step 7 In the pane at the left of the Windows Defender Firewall window (opened earlier), click Advanced Settings. In the left pane of the new window (see Figure 19-5), click Inbound Rules. In the right pane, there will be some rules called File And Printer Sharing (Echo Request – ICMPv4-In) (see Figure 19-6). Right click each of them, and select Enable Rule.

_____

_____

_____

_____

FIGURE 19-5 Windows Defender Firewall with Advanced Security

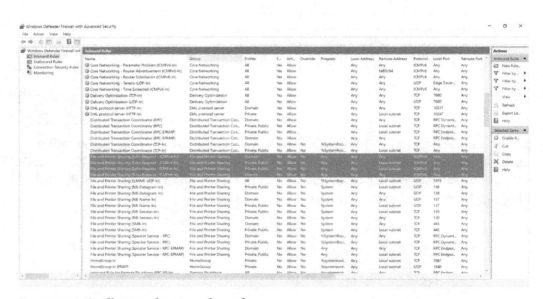

FIGURE 19-6 Allowing the pings through

Step 8   From a different device, ping the Windows 10 machine. Did the ICMP Echo requests get ICMP Echo replies?

_____

_____

_____

_____

Lab Analysis

1.   In Lab Activity 19.04, you performed three separate pings in Steps 4, 6, and 8. Dovid wants to know why each step got those particular results. Can you explain this to him?

_____

_____

2.   Chany is working in her cubicle one day when the phone rings. She answers it and is surprised to hear that it is one of the network administrators from the IT department. The gentleman identifies himself as Yossi and says that he needs to verify Chany's user name and password. Chany hesitates, leans over her cubicle wall, and tells you what's happening. What would you recommend Chany do?

_____

_____

3.   Shmuel has been attempting to get on the company Web site for over a half an hour and has not been able to connect. He calls the helpdesk and they tell him that the company network is under a DDoS attack. Shmuel would like to know what this is. How would you explain a DDoS attack to him?

_____

_____

4. Laivy is using Windows 10 in his apartment and has implemented Windows Defender Firewall to protect his computer. It works great, and he wonders why network administrators at his company spend so much money on dedicated firewall devices. His company hosts a couple of Web servers and has about 100 employees. What would you tell Laivy?

_____

_____

Key Term Quiz

Use the vocabulary terms from the list provided to complete the sentences that follow.

firewall

humans

longer

ransomware

social engineering

1. The WannaCry attack of May 2017 involved _____.

2. Someone posing as an IT support person and calling a user to get her user name and password is an example of _____.

3. Passwords that are _____ offer the best protection against brute-force attacks.

4. Any device that filters TCP/IP traffic based on IP address or port number, among other things, is by definition a _____.

5. _____ are the weakest link in any security implementation.

Chapter 20
Network Monitoring

Lab Exercises

Setting up a network, establishing connectivity, and sharing resources is not the end of the list of responsibilities for network administrators. You can't just put a network on autopilot. Just like a human body requires monitoring by doctors, dentists, and other entities, like scales and mirrors, a network needs to be constantly analyzed, scrutinized, and tweaked to ensure security and efficiency.

What traffic is entering the network? What traffic is leaving the network? How should firewalls that are either too permissive or too restrictive be modified? Is there anything malicious going on inside the network? Without proper monitoring, none of these questions can be answered.

In the following lab exercises, you'll examine different ways a network can be monitored. First, you'll examine the de facto network management protocol, Simple Network Management Protocol (SNMP). Then, you'll get some hands-on experience with Windows' Performance Monitor tool, which will help you establish a baseline of your network performance. Finally, you'll explore an instance of security information and event management (SIEM), services that incorporate security information management (SIM) and security event management (SEM) that offer analysis of security alerts generated by devices and software in real time.

The CompTIA Network+ exam expects you to be familiar with the different troubleshooting tools used by network professionals—so put some time into these lab exercises, and don't forget to reference Chapter 20, "Network Monitoring," in the *Mike Meyers' CompTIA Network+ Guide to Managing and Troubleshooting Networks* textbook.

20 MINUTES

Lab Exercise 20.01: Understanding SNMP

The Simple Network Management Protocol (SNMP) is the de facto network management protocol for TCP/IP networks. But just using SNMP without understanding the differences in versions can lead to problems because each version adds something new. SNMP has evolved substantially since its initial version.

In this lab exercise, you'll look closely at the differences between versions of SNMP.

Learning Objectives

In this lab, you will

- Research the differences between the different versions on SNMP

Lab Materials and Setup

The materials you'll need for this lab exercise are

- Internet access
- Pen or pencil
- Paper

Getting Down to Business

Protocols evolve over time for many reasons. Sometimes, they evolve for efficiency purposes. Other times, they evolve for security purposes. Networks and their uses are constantly changing over time. A version of a protocol that was used many years ago might not be robust enough for modern networks today.

Let's take a look at the official RFCs and learn how SNMP has evolved over the years.

Step 1 Open up a browser, and head to www.snmp.com/protocol/snmp_rfcs.shtml for a full hyperlinked list of RFCs for the various versions of SNMP. Use the RFCs to answer the following questions.

Step 2 What is the biggest weakness of SNMPv1?

_____

_____

_____

_____

Step 3   What did SNMPv2 add to its predecessor?

_____

_____

_____

_____

Step 4   Why should SNMPv3 be the only version used today?

_____

_____

_____

_____

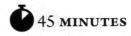 45 MINUTES

Lab Exercise 20.02: Monitoring Performance and Connectivity

Along with staying on top of the network documentation, technology, and network applications such as e-mail and Internet, it is the responsibility of the network team (often the entry-level network tech) to ensure the continued performance of network components and connectivity. Is the Internet connectivity slowing to a crawl when all of the users are accessing Web sites to complete their tasks? Can upper management use the video conferencing system without experiencing lags in both video and audio data?

Obviously, the initial design of the network must take into account the needs of the users as well as the business application being serviced. If you are designing a system for an organization that provides a search engine, the network design should take into account concurrent connections, load balancing, and overall bandwidth. Even small network installations can benefit from careful design and monitoring of the network's performance.

After the initial design is complete, the network tech should establish a baseline of the performance under "normal load," that is, the normal daily use of the network when the business is performing normal operating procedures. The network should then be measured under times of extreme usage to determine bottlenecks, the devices that will hold back the performance when driven to their operating capacities. Is one server being overused? Is the T1 line too small for the organization when it is in full swing?

Various tools are included with most of the popular operating systems as well as benchmark test engines from third-party developers. As usual, Microsoft provides many utilities as part of their various operating systems. You are now going to explore two of these tools in Windows 10: Performance Monitor and Event Viewer.

Learning Objectives

In this lab, you will

- Create a baseline of a system under normal load

- Stress a system and record the change in performance

- Explore the various logs created in Event Viewer

Lab Materials and Setup

The materials you'll need for this lab exercise are

- Windows 10 system

- Pen or pencil

- Paper

Getting Down to Business

To develop a baseline for the performance of an entire organization, you will monitor and record all of the critical devices during a time of "normal load," or normal operation. Then, during times of increased activity, you can capture additional data on these devices, store the information in log reports, and compare the data captured during normal load to that of the high-stress load. This will help you identify bottlenecks, providing direction on where the next equipment updates are needed.

Jonathan knows the importance of guaranteeing performance to the network users (this is actually one of his responsibilities). He recommends that you use the network lab to experiment with the Performance Monitor tool that is included with every version of the Windows operating system.

→ **Note**

Over the years, Microsoft has called the performance monitoring tool by many names; System Monitor, Performance Monitor, Reliability and Performance Monitor, and just Performance have all seen the light of day. Depending on the version of Windows you are using, there will be slight differences in implementation, but all versions will allow you to create a log of various objects and counters.

Step 1   In the Windows search box, type **perfmon**, and then press ENTER to open the Performance Monitor utility in Windows 10.

Step 2   Performance Monitor can show and record statistics about almost anything happening inside the computer. Select Performance Monitor under the Monitoring Tools. You can customize the collection of counters by clicking the green + symbol in the main pane or pressing CTRL-N to add a counter (see Figure 20-1). Using either method, add the following objects and counters (click the down arrow for specific counters for each object):

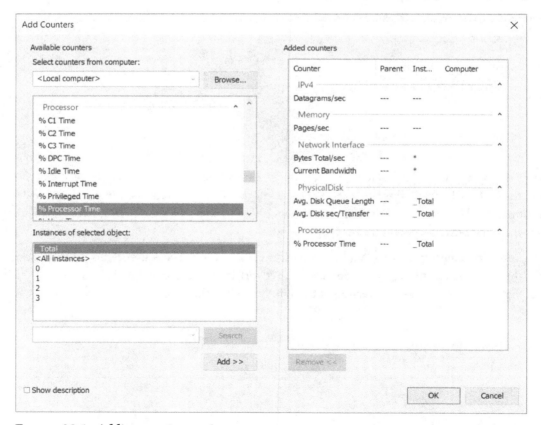

FIGURE 20-1   Adding counters

Object	Instance	Counter
IPv4	N/A	Datagrams/sec
Network Interface	\<All Instances\>	Bytes Total/sec
		Current Bandwidth
Memory	N/A	Pages/sec
Physical Disk	Total	Avg. Disk Queue Length
		Avg. Disk sec/Transfer
Processor	Total	% Processor Time

Once you have added the counters, you should see a graphic representation of the current usage of each of the objects and counters displayed in Performance Monitor, similar to Figure 20-2. What are some of the values for your system?

_____

_____

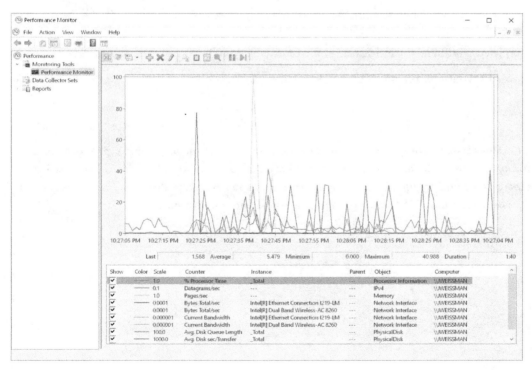

FIGURE 20-2 Performance Monitor

Step 3   Using Performance Monitor to view current transient data is great if you have a specific slowdown that you are trying to diagnose, but if you want to create baselines and peak usage reports, you will have to create a data collector set. This will be used to collect data over an extended period of time, which you can then use to create reports of network usage.

To use the current objects and counters for your data collector set, right-click Performance Monitor in the left-hand pane and select New | Data Collector Set. Name the data collector set **JSW Baseline** and click Next | Next. When prompted, select Start This Data Collector Set Now and click Finish.

Step 4   Allow the data collector set to run for a few minutes, and then in the Data Collector Sets folder, expand User Defined and right-click JSW Baseline. Select Stop from the drop-down menu. This will create a system monitor log under Reports | User Defined | JSW Baseline | System Monitor. You may have to add some of the objects and counters that you captured, such as the Network Interface: Bytes Total/sec, as they may not appear in the default report. Record some of the average performance data in the following space:

_____

_____

Step 5   Create a second data collector set and name it **JSW High Load**. Before you launch the data capture, run the following activities on your system:

- Open www.pandora.com and stream some music that you like.

- Go to www.youtube.com and view a video.

✔ **Tech Tip**

The applications listed in Step 5 really test your Internet connection and may not produce "high load" conditions on the local devices such as the hard disk or network interface. To increase the overall load, you could set up a network share on another machine and download large files across the LAN while watching a DVD and streaming a video from the Internet.

Now start the JSW High Load data collector set and let it run while the applications are performing their duties. After a few minutes, stop the data collection and open the System Monitor log to view the performance during high-load conditions. Again, you may have to add some of the objects and counters that are not displayed in the default report. Record some of the performance data. How does it compare to the baseline?

_____

_____

Step 6   Event Viewer has been around almost as long as Windows and provides standard logs of Application, Security, and System events. Further specialized events such as DHCP, DNS, Active Directory, and more are included with Microsoft Windows Server operating systems.

In the Windows search box type **Event Viewer**, click on Event Viewer, and explore some of the Application, Security, and System logs (see Figure 20-3).

Record a few items from your system's information, warnings, errors, and audit failures in the following space:

_____

_____

FIGURE 20-3   Event Viewer

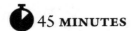 45 MINUTES

Lab Exercise 20.03: Understanding SIEM

Security information and event management (SIEM) represents software products and services that combine security information management (SIM) and security event management (SEM). SIEM technology provides real-time analysis of security alerts generated by network hardware and applications. SIEM is sold as software, appliances, or managed services, and is also used to log security data and generate reports for compliance purposes.

Learning Objectives

In this lab, you will

- Understand how SIEM works
- Understand the need for SIEM
- Explore various components of a SIEM product

Lab Materials and Setup

The materials you'll need for this lab exercise are

- Internet access
- Pen or pencil
- Paper

Getting Down to Business

EventTracker Log Manager is one of many different SIEM solutions. *SC Magazine* named Log Manager the Best Buy product in SIEM for 2014, and awarded it a perfect 5-Star rating in the 2016 UTM-SIEM annual product Group Test review. Therefore, Scott wants you to investigate this product, to both understand the concept of SIEM better and possibly make a recommendation for purchase.

Let's not waste any time! Jump right into it.

Step 1   Head to www.eventtracker.com/solutions/log-manager/ and note your first observations of the product and its Web site.

Step 2 Read the Features section. Explain which feature you consider to be the most important.

_____

_____

Step 3 Mouse over the Solutions tab and click its links. Explain more about this product's solutions.

_____

_____

Step 4 Mouse over the Capabilities tab and click its links. Explain more about this product's capabilities.

_____

_____

Step 5 Explain the solutions and capabilities that make the most sense for JSW. Recall that JSW is a mid-sized IT consulting firm with clients of all sizes.

_____

_____

Lab Analysis

1. Ethan wants you to give him a quick explanation of why SNMP is such a valuable protocol. Explain it to him.

_____

_____

2.   Justin wants to understand why taking baseline measurements is important, even if nothing is wrong with the network. Can you help him understand this?

_____

_____

3.   Brock has been trying to understand the purpose of SIEM but still has some uncertainty. Make it clear for him.

_____

_____

Key Term Quiz

Use the vocabulary terms from the list provided to complete the sentences that follow.

logs

objects

SIEM

SNMPv3

1.   _____ improves upon its predecessors by adding encryption.

2.   _____ combines information management and security event management.

3.   Event Viewer's _____ can be used to analyze certain types of events that occurred on the network.

4.   Processor, Memory, and Physical Disk are considered _____ in Performance Monitor.

Chapter 21
Network Troubleshooting

Lab Exercises

Similar to the discussion back in Chapter 3 concerning the "art of making cables," the skills and processes you will need to learn and refine to troubleshoot networks are also referred to as an "art." The art of troubleshooting can be difficult to master. In order to hone your skills, you need to familiarize yourself with the terms and processes and to practice with the many network troubleshooting tools available (both hardware and software).

In the following lab exercises, you'll examine the different hardware and software tools that are used to help troubleshoot network problems. You will also take time to identify some useful troubleshooting questions that you would ask a user in a troubleshooting situation to help you identify the problem. The CompTIA Network+ exam expects you to be familiar with the different troubleshooting tools used by network professionals—so put some time into these lab exercises, and don't forget to reference Chapter 21 in the *Mike Meyers' CompTIA Network+ Guide to Managing and Troubleshooting Networks* textbook.

20 MINUTES

Lab Exercise 21.01: Identifying the Troubleshooting Process

When troubleshooting any problem, it is important to have a plan of attack to develop a solution to that problem. The CompTIA Network+ certification exam objectives set forth a methodology to troubleshoot networking issues. The Network+ exam expects you to know these steps to troubleshooting network-related issues. As a network tech, you should not only commit these steps to memory but also work to master the art of troubleshooting, gradually applying simple to complex techniques to arrive at a solution.

The key to troubleshooting is to be mentally prepared when a problem arises. As with any skill, the best way to develop a troubleshooting technique is practice, practice, practice.

Learning Objectives

In this lab, you'll review the troubleshooting process. When you have completed this lab, you will be able to

- Identify the steps of the troubleshooting process

- Describe what each process does

- Develop a number of basic probing questions

Lab Materials and Setup

The materials you'll need for this lab exercise are

- *Mike Meyers' CompTIA Network+ Guide to Managing and Troubleshooting Networks* textbook

- Internet access

- Pen or pencil

- Paper

Getting Down to Business

You have now been working with Jonathan and Scott for a number of months. After watching them troubleshoot network issues, you would like to know how they seem to be able to fix problems fairly quickly. Jonathan and Scott explain that it is one thing to know how to use the hardware and software tools, but it is another thing to know when to use them. They explain that troubleshooting network issues is like learning to play a musical instrument—it is much easier if there is a process to follow and you must practice.

✖ Cross-Reference

Before performing this lab exercise, re-read the section titled "The Troubleshooting Process" in Chapter 21 of the *Mike Meyers' CompTIA Network+ Guide to Managing and Troubleshooting Networks* textbook.

Step 1   The following is a list of the steps to properly troubleshoot a problem. Place a number beside each step to indicate the order in which the steps should be performed.

_____   Test the theory to determine the cause.

_____   Document findings, actions, and outcomes.

_____   Identify the problem.

_____   Implement the solution or escalate as necessary.

_____   Establish a theory of probable cause.

_____   Verify full system functionality and, if applicable, implement preventative measures.

_____   Establish a plan of action to resolve the problem and identify potential effects.

Step 2   You have been asked by Jonathan to give a brief explanation of each step in the troubleshooting process. In the space provided, record a brief description of each step in the troubleshooting process.

_____

_____

_____

_____

_____

_____

Step 3   During the "Identify the problem" phase of the troubleshooting process, you will need to be prepared with some questions that you can ask users to help identify the problem. In the space provided, list three or four potential questions you could ask a user after she complains that she does not have Internet access.

✔ **Hint**

The troubleshooting process and basic questioning techniques are not unique to the IT industry or to networking. If you conduct an Internet search, you can augment the basic questions you may find in the textbook. Search on terms like "basic troubleshooting questions."

_____

_____

_____

_____

 20 MINUTES

Lab Exercise 21.02: Identifying Hardware Troubleshooting Tools

When troubleshooting network problems, you will utilize hardware tools to help identify physical issues with the network. The hardware tools will help you identify and correct problems with the physical components of the network, such as network cabling, connectors, and physical connectivity. You will start your study of troubleshooting techniques with a review of the popular tools available to diagnose and correct problems with the physical components of the network.

Learning Objectives

When you have completed this lab, you will be able to

- Identify the various tools used to work with the physical components of a network

- Contrast the different tools you would use to troubleshoot the physical network and the tools you would use to assemble and repair the physical components of the network

Lab Materials and Setup

The materials you'll need for this lab exercise are

- *Mike Meyers' CompTIA Network+ Guide to Managing and Troubleshooting Networks* textbook

- Internet access

- Pen or pencil

- Paper

Getting Down to Business

Monroe, one of the other network techs at JSW, is helping one of his friends outside of work with a small office upgrade. They are upgrading the old cabling to Cat 6A, and running a piece of fiber-optic cable between two buildings. Lee invites you to tag along for the experience. He recommends that you put together a list of some of the tools you should have on hand and asks you to review the function of each of the tools.

Step 1   In the following mix-and-match exercise, identify the description that corresponds with each hardware tool by recording the correct letter.

Tool	Description
A. Time domain reflectometer (TDR)	_____ Used to capture and analyze network traffic
B. Butt set	_____ Can tell you how much voltage is on the line
C. Protocol analyzer	_____ Removes the insulation from a cable, exposing the conductor
D. Certifier	_____ Can identify where a break in copper cable is
E. Temperature monitor	_____ Places UTP wires into a 66- or 110-block
F. Multimeter	_____ Can identify if the cable is handling its rated capacity
G. Punchdown tool	_____ Used to firmly connect RJ-45 connectors to Cat cables
H. Cable tester	_____ Can identify where a break in fiber cable is
I. Toner probe	_____ Can indicate if there is continuity between the two ends of a wire
J. Optical time domain reflectometer	_____ Can tap into a 66- or 110-block to see if a particular line is working
K. Wire stripper	_____ Can help you locate a particular cable
L. Crimping tool	_____ Can be used to monitor and ensure the temperature level

Step 2   Now, utilizing the Internet, conduct a search for each of the tools listed and provide the name of one or two popular manufacturers. Make note of whether the tool is primarily an assembly/repair tool or is typically used to verify/troubleshoot connectivity issues.

Tool	Manufacturer/Product	Typical Use
Time domain reflectometer (TDR)		
Butt set		
Protocol analyzer		
Certifier		
Temperature monitor		
Multimeter		
Punchdown tool		
Cable tester		
Toner probe		
Optical time domain reflectometer		
Wire stripper		
Crimping tool		

 30 MINUTES

Lab Exercise 21.03: Using Software Troubleshooting Tools

When troubleshooting network problems, you first check the hardware aspects of the network—for example, making sure that everything is connected. After verifying that everything is connected, you then look to the visual indicators, such as the link light on the network card or the "online" light on the printer. What do you do after verifying that everything is physically in place and appears to be working?

The next step is to jump into the operating system and use some of the useful commands that you have learned that allow you to troubleshoot network problems!

Learning Objectives

In this lab, you'll review the different Windows commands that are used to troubleshoot network problems. At the end of this lab, you will be able to

- Verify your IP address
- Verify connectivity to another system
- Verify that DNS name resolution is working
- View systems that are connected to you

Lab Materials and Setup

The materials you'll need for this lab exercise are

- Windows 10 system with Internet access
- Pen or pencil
- Paper

Getting Down to Business

Regis calls you over to his desk and appears to be very frustrated. He can't seem to get on the Internet and needs you to show him some of the tools he can use to verify network connectivity.

You start by verifying the physical network components. You have verified that the network cable is connected to Regis' system and that the link light is on. You are now ready to verify the configuration of his system using some of the software tools available in Windows.

Step 1   In the following space, list some of the utilities you might use to troubleshoot the problem.

_____

_____

_____

_____

What are some of the tools that would be available to you if you were working on a Linux distro such as Ubuntu?

_____

_____

Step 2 You will first verify that the system has an IP address by typing the `ipconfig` command at a Windows command prompt. Record the IP configuration information in the following spaces:

IP address: _____

Subnet mask: _____

Default gateway: _____

→ **Note**

> The `ipconfig` command can be used by itself to view the connection-specific DNS suffix, link-local IPv6 address, IPv4 IP address, subnet mask, and default gateway of a system, or you can use `ipconfig /all` to display all TCP/IP settings, including your DNS servers' IP addresses, DHCP servers' IP addresses, physical MAC address, and more.

Step 3 After verifying that the system has an IP address, you will need to verify that the system is configured with DNS server IP addresses. Type the `ipconfig /all` command and record the following information.

DNS server: _____

Step 4 Once you have recorded the IP address of the default gateway and DNS server, you will verify that they are running by using the `ping` command. Ping the IP address of the default gateway by typing `ping <ip_address_of_default gateway>` and pressing ENTER.

Now ping the IP address of the DNS server by typing `ping <ip_address_of_DNS_server>` and pressing ENTER. Do you get replies from both systems? (Circle your answers on the following lines.)

Default gateway?	Yes	No
DNS server?	Yes	No

Step 5 Along the same lines as the `ping` utility, another TCP/IP utility that allows you to troubleshoot connectivity is known as `traceroute` (`tracert` is the name of the utility in Windows). The `tracert` utility will allow you to record the number of "hops" or routers a packet has to pass through to get from a source computer to a destination computer (usually on a far-removed remote network).

Open a command prompt and type `tracert www.comptia.org`. This will trace the route from your computer to the Web server hosting www.comptia.org. Sometimes, tracert will time out well before reaching the destination host. While this could indicate an actual connectivity problem, it's much more likely that ICMP, which tracert relies on, is being blocked by firewalls or other security measures.

Open a browser and navigate to www.comptia.org. If you are able to open the Web site, there are no connectivity problems or firewalls between your computer and the CompTIA Web site.

Record a few of the hops in the following space.

_____

_____

_____

Step 6   Next you will use the `nslookup` command to troubleshoot DNS. To find out the IP address of the Web server for www.rit.edu, type `nslookup www.rit.edu`. Record both the IPv4 and IPv6 addresses of the Web server in the following space. See Figure 21-1.

_____

_____

Step 7   Now you will try to find out the mail servers for the rit.edu domain using the `nslookup` utility. Type the following commands to find out the mail servers for the rit.edu domain:

```
nslookup
set q=mx
rit.edu
```

Your results should resemble those shown in Figure 21-2. MX records in DNS are used to refer to the mail servers of a domain.

FIGURE 21-1   Output of the `nslookup` command

```
Command Prompt - nslookup                                        —    □    ×

Microsoft Windows [Version 10.0.16299.248]
(c) 2017 Microsoft Corporation. All rights reserved.

C:\Users\jswics>nslookup
Default Server:  dns.quad9.net
Address:  9.9.9.9

> set q=mx
> rit.edu
Server:  dns.quad9.net
Address:  9.9.9.9

Non-authoritative answer:
rit.edu  MX preference = 5, mail exchanger = mx03d-in01r.rit.edu
rit.edu  MX preference = 10, mail exchanger = mx03a-in01r.rit.edu
rit.edu  MX preference = 10, mail exchanger = mx03b-in01r.rit.edu
rit.edu  MX preference = 5, mail exchanger = mx03c-in01r.rit.edu
>
```

FIGURE 21-2 A list of mail exchange (MX) records for google.com

Record the information about the mail servers in the following space.

_____

_____

→ **Note**

The `nslookup` command is used to troubleshoot DNS-related issues. It can be used the way it is presented in the previous step, or you can use it to resolve a single host Web address to IP address by typing `nslookup www.totalsem.com.`

Step 8   You have shown Regis how to verify the TCP/IP settings with the `ipconfig` command and how to verify connectivity with the `ping` command. You have also verified that he can communicate with the DNS server using the `nslookup` command. Next you will show Regis how to use commands to see the active connections to the system. Open a Web browser and navigate to www.totalsem.com.

Step 9   Now open a command prompt, type `netstat -n`, and press ENTER (the `-n` option displays addresses and ports in numerical format). The `netstat` command is used to display current connections, including both connections you initiate and connections initiated by someone else!

In the `netstat` output, record the line of information that is related to your connection to the Total Seminars Web site. Identify what each column in the output is used for. See Figure 21-3.

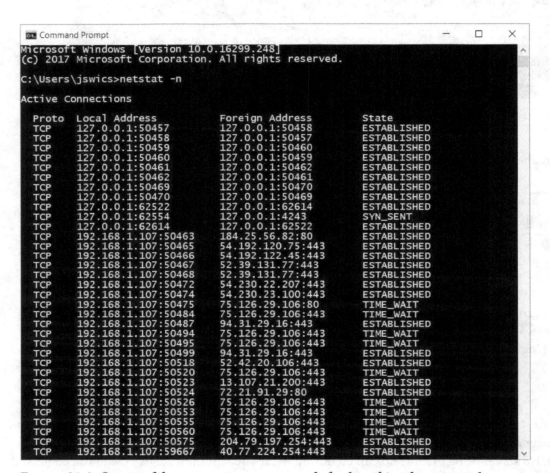

FIGURE 21-3 Output of the `netstat -n` command after launching the www.totalsem .com Web site

45 MINUTES

Lab Exercise 21.04: Exploring Vulnerability Scanners

With the heightened need for cybersecurity, maintaining and troubleshooting the various components that can compromise the network's security will continue to be the focus of the skilled network technician. Nmap (Network Mapper) is a wonderful tool that not only allows you to create a virtual map of the devices on your network but also generates a report listing the host names, MAC addresses, IP addresses, and all of the open ports for each device.

The Nmap suite of tools also includes Zenmap. Zenmap is a GUI front end and results viewer for Nmap. It allows you to scan your network, examine the network map, and view some of the detailed information related to the devices on your network, all from a convenient Windows interface. Zenmap provides an excellent tool to troubleshoot host names, IP addressing, and firewall configuration.

Learning Objectives

In this lab, you'll install and run Nmap/Zenmap. When you've completed this lab, you will be able to

- Install and run the Nmap and Zenmap port scanning applications
- Examine the resultant network map
- Review the port data generated by the scan

Lab Materials and Setup

The materials you'll need for this lab exercise are

- Internet access
- Multiple systems preferably (a mix between clients and servers as well as OSes)
- Network switch
- Cabling
- Pen or pencil
- Paper

Getting Down to Business

Zenmap (the official GUI for Nmap) provides an excellent method to create a network map of all of the systems and devices available on your network. It also provides a detailed report on each of the devices, including operating systems and host names (when available), MAC addresses, IP addresses, and open port information. This information can then be analyzed and used to troubleshoot security holes such as IP addressing schemes, open ports, and firewall issues.

To generate a more realistic scenario, Jonathan and Scott recommend that you use the machines and devices in the Network Lab to construct a simple network consisting of one or two client systems, one or two servers, and a wireless router. You can then run Nmap/Zenmap and use the data to troubleshoot network security.

Take a few moments, build the small network, and then launch Nmap/Zenmap and commence your exploration!

Step 1   To begin your exploration of your network and the Nmap/Zenmap network mapping tool, you will first download the installation files from Nmap's Web site.

  a.   Go to http://nmap.org and click the Download hyperlink on the left.

  b.   On the download page, scroll down to the Microsoft Windows Binaries section and navigate to the Latest Stable Release Self-Installer, and then click the nmap-7.60-setup.exe hyperlink (current at time of writing). The Nmap executable installation file will download to your Downloads folder.

✔ Tech Tip

To provide a richer experience when using Nmap, Jonathan and Scott have recommended that you perform the lab exercise on a small closed local area network. Configure two Windows Server 2016 systems (one as the DNS server), two or more clients, and a wireless router (used as a wired switch/router). Enable the firewalls on all devices. You may choose an IP addressing scheme of your own or use 192.168.1.0/24 as shown in the figures for this lab exercise.

Step 2   Use the following instructions to install Nmap/Zenmap:

  a.   Launch the Nmap Setup program nmap-7.60-setup.exe.

  b.   Select I Agree on the License Agreement screen.

  c.   Verify that all of the components are checked as shown in Figure 21-4, and click Next.

  d.   Select the destination location (the default location is fine) and click Install.

  e.   At the License Agreement for Npcap 0.93 Setup (a separate dialog box will pop up), click Cancel. We're going to use WinPcap instead.

  f.   Nmap Setup will now install all of the files needed to configure and run the Nmap/Zenmap utility. When the installation of the files is complete, click Next.

  g.   Create the shortcuts and click Next.

  h.   When you're finished, Nmap/Zenmap will be installed on your computer. Click Finish.

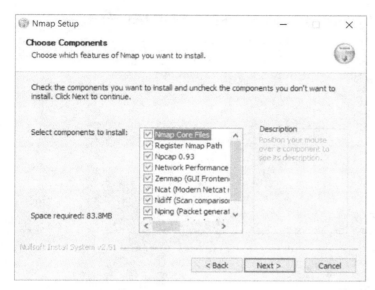

FIGURE 21-4 Choosing components such as Nmap Core Files and Zenmap (GUI front end)

Step 3 Now launch the Nmap/Zenmap application by double-clicking the icon on the Desktop. In the Target dialog box, type the Network ID of the IP address and an * for the Host ID, such as **192.168.1.***. This will scan all hosts on the 192.168.1.0/24 network. Click the Scan button to begin the process, as shown in Figure 21-5.

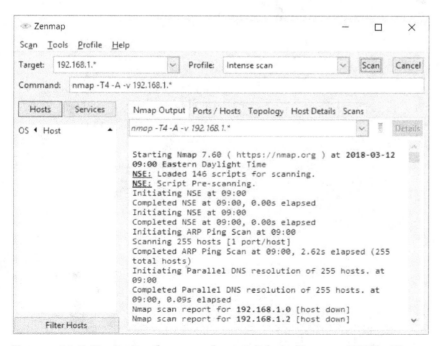

FIGURE 21-5 Beginning the network scan with the Zenmap GUI for Nmap

Step 4   After the scan of your network completes, you should have a list of devices (depending on how many systems you have running) and a large amount of data (scanned addresses, scanned ports, operating system types, and so on). When the scan completes, click the Topology tab and then click the Fisheye tab. Your display should look similar to the network map shown in Figure 21-6.

FIGURE 21-6 Zenmap-generated network map

Using the detailed information discovered during the Nmap/Zenmap scan of your network, record the device names and IP addresses of the various systems in the following space.

_____

_____

_____

_____

Step 5   Next, select one of the remote Windows systems that you are not running Nmap/Zenmap from. This will be the Target machine for the port scans. Configure the firewall to block all incoming connections as follows:

a.   Open the Windows Firewall configuration utility by typing **Firewall** into the Windows search box and selecting Windows Defender Firewall.

b.   Select Turn Windows Defender Firewall On Or Off from the menu items listed on the left-hand side of the window.

c.   Confirm that the Windows Firewall is turned on for both private and public network locations. Check the box Block All Incoming Connections, Including Those In The List Of Allowed Apps, as shown in Figure 21-7.

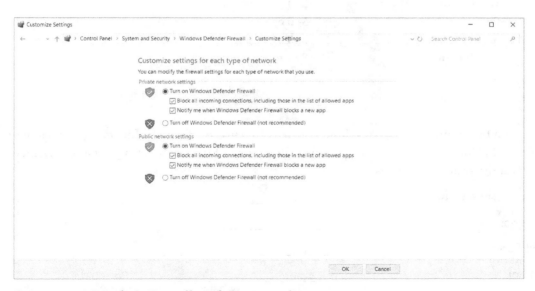

FIGURE 21-7 Windows Firewall configuration utility

Step 6   Now, to scan the specific Windows machine you configured in Step 5 (the target machine), open Nmap/Zenmap on another machine on the same network and complete the following steps:

    a.   Enter the IP address for the machine that you just configured into the Target dialog box.

    b.   Click the Scan button and let the scan complete.

    c.   Select the Host Details tab and record the following information:

Operating System Icon: _____

Open Ports: _____

Filtered Ports: _____

Closed Ports: _____

Security Icon: _____

✔ Hint

The Zenmap GUI front end includes a number of icons to indicate which operating system is installed on the system that has been scanned. Zenmap also includes icons that indicate the status of the security of the system, based on the number of open ports. A full list of the icons along with additional information can be found in the *Zenmap GUI Users' Guide*. This guide can be found at http://nmap.org/book/zenmap-results.html.

The following list is a simple description of the security icons:

Safe Icon:	**0–2 open ports**
Chest Icon:	**3–4 open ports**
Open Box Icon:	**5–6 open ports**
Swiss Cheese Icon:	**7–8 open ports**
Bomb Icon:	**9 or more open ports**

Step 7   Now, on the Windows target machine, uncheck the box for Block All Incoming Connections, Including Those In The List Of Allowed Apps to unfilter some of the ports. Scan the target machine again and record the results as follows:

Operating System Icon: _____

Open Ports: _____

Filtered Ports: _____

Closed Ports: _____

Security Icon: _____

How do your results compare to those shown in Figure 21-8?

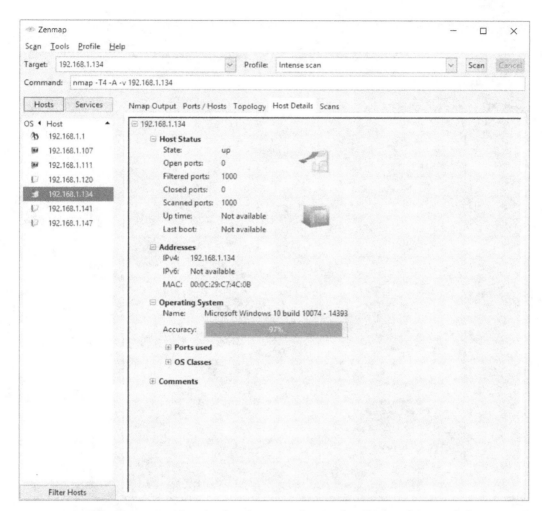

FIGURE 21-8 Zenmap Host details after the scan of a Windows 10 machine with the
Windows Firewall enabled

Step 8   To complete your exploration of port scanning, on the Windows target machine, completely
disable Windows Defender Firewall. Scan the target machine again and record the results as follows:

Operating System Icon: _____

Open Ports: _____

Filtered Ports: _____

Closed Ports: _____

Security Icon: _____

How do your results compare to those shown in Figure 21-9?

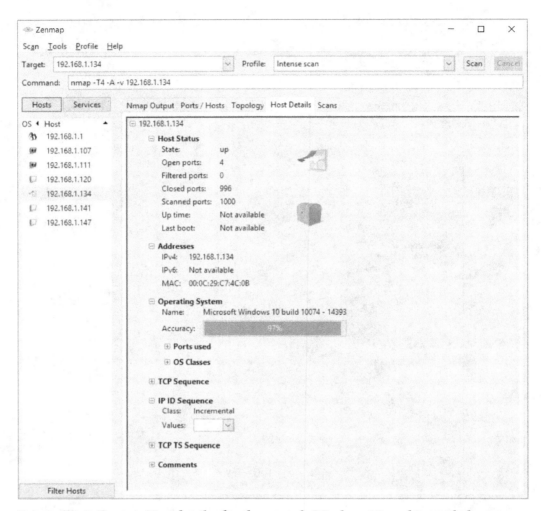

FIGURE 21-9   Zenmap Host details after the scan of a Windows 10 machine with the Windows Firewall disabled

Lab Analysis

1. Kyle has often used a multimeter to check the voltages of a PC's power supply, especially when a component is not working. How can he use a multimeter to help him troubleshoot network problems?

_____

_____

2. Stephen has been studying a number of the command-line utilities used to troubleshoot networks. He asks if you could briefly describe the `netstat` utility.

_____

_____

3. Nicholas is exploring the `nslookup` utility. He would like to know what it's used for. Can you help him out?

_____

_____

4. Dakota is running a monthly security check on the office network. One of the tools he is using is a port scanner. What is the purpose of a port scanner?

_____

_____

5. After studying the steps that CompTIA recommends when troubleshooting networks, Tory wonders if he will actually apply this technique when he is troubleshooting a real problem. Why is it important to know the troubleshooting process?

_____

_____

Key Term Quiz

Use the vocabulary terms from the list provided to complete the sentences that follow.

certifier

ipconfig /all

nslookup

port scanner

tracert

1. _____ is the Windows command that will show your MAC address.

2. On a Windows machine, to see all routers in between you and a destination, you'd use _____ .

3. A _____ is responsible for testing a cable to ensure that it can handle its rated capacity.

4. _____ is used to query DNS servers.

5. If you want to analyze a remote system for open ports that may allow for security breaches, you can use a(n) _____ .

GLOSSARY

3G Third-generation wireless data standard for cell phones and other mobile devices. 3G matured over time until Evolved High-Speed Packet Access (HSPA+) became the final wireless 3G data standard. It transferred at theoretical maximum speeds up to 168 megabits per second (Mbps), although real-world implementations rarely passed 10 Mbps.

4G Most popularly implemented as Long Term Evolution (LTE), a wireless data standard with theoretical download speeds of 300 Mbps and upload speeds of 75 Mbps.

4to6 Internet connectivity technology that encapsulates IPv4 traffic into an IPv6 tunnel to get to an IPv6-capable router.

6in4 An IPv6 tunneling standard that can go through IPv4 Network Address Translation (NAT).

6to4 An IPv6 tunneling protocol that doesn't require a tunnel broker. It is generally used to directly connect two routers because it normally requires a public IPv4 address.

8 position 8 contact (8P8C) Four-pair connector used on the end of network cable. Erroneously referred to as an RJ-45 connector.

10 Gigabit Ethernet (10 GbE) A very fast Ethernet designation, with a number of fiber-optic and copper standards.

10Base2 The last true bus-standard network where nodes connected to a common, shared length of coaxial cable.

10BaseFL Fiber-optic implementation of Ethernet that runs at 10 Mbps using baseband signaling. Maximum segment length is 2 km.

10BaseT An Ethernet LAN designed to run on UTP cabling. Runs at 10 Mbps and uses baseband signaling. Maximum length for the cabling between the NIC and the hub (or the switch, the repeater, and so forth) is 100 m.

10GBaseER/10GBaseEW A 10 GbE standard using 1550-nm single-mode fiber. Maximum cable length up to 40 km.

10GBaseLR/10GBaseLW A 10 GbE standard using 1310-nm single-mode fiber. Maximum cable length up to 10 km.

10GBaseSR/10GBaseSW A 10 GbE standard using 850-nm multimode fiber. Maximum cable length up to 300 m.

10GBaseT A 10 GbE standard designed to run on Cat 6a UTP cabling. Maximum cable length of 100 m.

66 block   Patch panel used in telephone networks; displaced by 110 blocks in networking.

100BaseFX   An Ethernet LAN designed to run on fiber-optic cabling. Runs at 100 Mbps and uses baseband signaling. Maximum cable length is 400 m for half-duplex and 2 km for full-duplex.

100BaseT   An Ethernet LAN designed to run on UTP cabling. Runs at 100 Mbps, uses baseband signaling, and uses two pairs of wires on Cat 5 or better cabling.

100BaseT4   An Ethernet LAN designed to run on UTP cabling. Runs at 100 Mbps and uses four-pair Cat 3 or better cabling. Made obsolete by 100BaseT.

100BaseTX   The technically accurate but little-used name for 100BaseT.

110 block   Also known as a *110-punchdown block,* a connection gridwork used to link UTP and STP cables behind an RJ-45 patch panel.

110-punchdown block   The most common connection used on the back of an RJ-45 jack and patch panels.

110-punchdown tool   *See* punchdown tool.

802 committee   The IEEE committee responsible for all Ethernet standards.

802.1X   A port-authentication network access control mechanism for networks.

802.3 (Ethernet)   *See* Ethernet.

802.3ab   The IEEE standard for 1000BaseT.

802.3z   The umbrella IEEE standard for all versions of Gigabit Ethernet other than 1000BaseT.

802.11   *See* IEEE 802.11.

802.11a   A wireless standard that operates in the frequency range of 5 GHz and offers throughput of up to 54 Mbps.

802.11ac   A wireless standard that operates in the frequency range of 5 GHz and offers throughput of up to 1 Gbps.

802.11a-ht   Along with the corresponding 802.11g-ht standard, technical terms for mixed-mode 802.11a/802.11g operation. In mixed mode, both technologies are simultaneously supported.

802.11b   The first popular wireless standard, operates in the frequency range of 2.4 GHz and offers throughput of up to 11 Mbps.

802.11g   Older wireless standard that operates on the 2.4-GHz band with a maximum throughput of 54 Mbps. Superseded by 802.11n.

802.11g-ht   Along with the corresponding 802.11a-ht standard, technical terms for mixed-mode 802.11a/802.11g operation. In mixed mode, both technologies are simultaneously supported.

802.11i A wireless standard that added security features.

802.11n An 802.11 standard that increases transfer speeds and adds support for multiple in/multiple out (MIMO) by using multiple antennas. 802.11n can operate on either the 2.4- or 5-GHz frequency band and has a maximum throughput of 400 Mbps. Superseded by 802.11ac.

802.16 *See* IEEE 802.16.

1000BaseCX A Gigabit Ethernet standard using unique copper cabling, with a 25-m maximum cable distance.

1000BaseLX A Gigabit Ethernet standard using single-mode fiber cabling, with a 5-km maximum cable distance.

1000BaseSX A Gigabit Ethernet standard using multimode fiber cabling, with a 220- to 500-m maximum cable distance.

1000BaseT A Gigabit Ethernet standard using Cat 5e/6 UTP cabling, with a 100-m maximum cable distance.

1000BaseTX Short-lived gigabit-over-UTP standard from TIA/EIA. Considered a competitor to 1000BaseT, it was simpler to implement but required the use of Cat 6 cable.

1000BaseX An umbrella Gigabit Ethernet standard. Also known as *802.3z*. Comprises all Gigabit standards with the exception of 1000BaseT, which is under the 802.3ab standard.

A records DNS records that map host names to their IPv4 addresses.

AAA (Authentication, Authorization, and Accounting) *See* Authentication, Authorization, and Accounting (AAA).

AAAA records DNS records that map host names to their IPv6 addresses.

absorption Quality of some building materials (such as brick, sheetrock, and wood) to reduce or eliminate a Wi-Fi signal.

acceptable use policy A document that defines what a person may and may not do on an organization's computers and networks.

access control All-encompassing term that defines the degree of permission granted to use a particular resource. That resource may be anything from a switch port to a particular file to a physical door within a building.

access control list (ACL) A clearly defined list of permissions that specifies what actions an authenticated user may perform on a shared resource.

Access Control Server (ACS) Cisco program/process/server that makes the decision to admit or deny a node based on posture assessment. From there, the ACS directs the edge access device to allow a connection or to implement a denial or redirect.

access port Regular port in a switch that has been configured as part of a VLAN. Access ports are ports that hosts connect to. They are the opposite of a trunk port, which is only connected to a trunk port on another switch.

Active Directory A form of directory service used in networks with Windows servers. Creates an organization of related computers that share one or more Windows domains.

activity light An LED on a NIC, hub, or switch that blinks rapidly to show data transfers over the network.

ad hoc mode A wireless networking mode where each node is in direct contact with every other node in a decentralized free-for-all. Ad hoc mode is similar to the *mesh topology*.

Adaptive Network Technology (ANT+) A low-speed, low-power networking technology; used in place of Bluetooth for connecting devices, such as smart phones and exercise machines.

Address Resolution Protocol (ARP) A protocol in the TCP/IP suite used with the command-line utility of the same name to determine the MAC address that corresponds to a particular IP address.

administrative accounts Specialized user accounts that have been granted sufficient access rights and authority to manage specified administrative tasks. Some administrative accounts exist as a default of the system and have all authority throughout the system. Others must be explicitly assigned the necessary powers to administer given resources.

ADSL (asymmetric digital subscriber line) *See* asymmetric digital subscriber line (ADSL).

Advanced Encryption Standard (AES) A block cipher created in the late 1990s that uses a 128-bit block size and a 128-, 192-, or 256-bit key size. Practically uncrackable.

adware A program that monitors the types of Web sites you frequent and uses that information to generate targeted advertisements, usually pop-up windows.

agent In terms of posture assessment, refers to software that runs within a client and reports the client's security characteristics to an access control server to be approved or denied entry to a system.

agent-less In terms of posture assessment, refers to a client that has its posture checked and presented by non-permanent software, such as a Web app program, that executes as part of the connection process. Agent-less software does not run directly within the client but is run on behalf of the client.

aggregation A router hierarchy in which every router underneath a higher router always uses a subnet of that router's existing routes.

air gap The act of physically separating a network from every other network.

Aircrack-ng An open source tool for penetration testing many aspects of wireless networks.

alert Proactive message sent from an SNMP manager as a result of a trap issued by an agent. Alerts may be sent as e-mail, SMS message, voicemail, or another avenue.

algorithm A set of rules for solving a problem in a given number of steps.

allow Permission for data or communication to pass through or to access a resource. Specific allowances through a firewall are called *exceptions*.

American Registry for Internet Numbers (ARIN) A Regional Internet Registry (RIR) that parcels out IP addresses to large ISPs and major corporations in North America.

amplification The aspect of a DoS attack that makes a server do a lot of processing and responding.

amplified DoS attack The type of DoS attack that sends a small amount of traffic to a server, which produces a much larger response from the server that is sent to a spoofed IP address, overwhelming a victim machine.

Angled Physical Contact (APC) Fiber-optic connector that makes physical contact between two fiber-optic cables. It specifies an 8-degree angle to the curved end, lowering signal loss. APC connectors have less connection degradation from multiple insertions compared to other connectors.

anti-malware program Software that attempts to block several types of threats to a client including viruses, Trojan horses, worms, and other unapproved software installation and execution.

antivirus Software that attempts to prevent viruses from installing or executing on a client. Some antivirus software may also attempt to remove the virus or eradicate the effects of a virus after an infection.

anycast A method of addressing groups of computers as though they were a single computer. Anycasting starts by giving a number of computers (or clusters of computers) the same IP address. Advanced routers then send incoming packets to the closest of the computers.

Apache HTTP Server An open source HTTP server program that runs on a wide variety of operating systems.

Application layer *See* Open Systems Interconnection (OSI) seven-layer model.

application log Tracks application events, such as when an application opens or closes. Different types of application logs record different events.

Application Programming Interface (API) Shared functions, subroutines, and libraries that allow programs on a machine to communicate with the OS and other programs.

application/context aware Advanced feature of some stateful firewalls where the content of the data is inspected to ensure it comes from, or is destined for, an appropriate application. Context-aware firewalls look both deeply and more broadly to ensure that the data content and other aspects of the packet are appropriate to the data transfer being conducted. Packets that fall outside these awareness criteria are denied by the firewall.

approval process One or more decision makers consider a proposed change and the impact of the change, including funding. If the change, the impact, and the funding are acceptable, the change is permitted.

archive The creation and storage of retrievable copies of electronic data for legal and functional purposes.

archive bit An attribute of a file that shows whether the file has been backed up since the last change. Each time a file is opened, changed, or saved, the archive bit is turned on. Some types of backups turn off the archive bit to indicate that a good backup of the file exists on tape.

Area ID Address assigned to routers in an OSPF network to prevent flooding beyond the routers in that particular network. *See also* Open Shortest Path First (OSPF).

areas Groups of logically associated OSPF routers designed to maximize routing efficiency while keeping the amount of broadcast traffic well managed. Areas are assigned a 32-bit value that manifests as an integer between 0 and 4294967295 or can take a form similar to an IP address, for example, "0.0.0.0."

ARP *See* Address Resolution Protocol (ARP).

ARP cache poisoning A man-in-the-middle attack, where the attacker associates his MAC address with someone else's IP address (almost always the router), so all traffic will be sent to him first. The attacker sends out unsolicited ARPs, which can either be requests or replies.

arping A command used to discover hosts on a network, similar to ping, but that relies on ARP rather than ICMP. The arping command won't cross any routers, so it will only work within a broadcast domain. *See also* Address Resolution Protocol (ARP) *and* ping.

asset disposal Reusing, repurposing, or recycling computing devices that follows system life cycle policies in many organizations.

asset management Managing each aspect of a network, from documentation to performance to hardware.

asymmetric digital subscriber line (ADSL) A fully digital, dedicated connection to the telephone system that provides download speeds of up to 9 Mbps and upload speeds of up to 1 Mbps.

asymmetric-key algorithm An encryption method in which the key used to encrypt a message and the key used to decrypt it are different, or asymmetrical.

Asynchronous Transfer Mode (ATM) A network technology that runs at speeds between 25 and 622 Mbps using fiber-optic cabling or Cat 5 or better UTP.

attenuation The degradation of signal over distance for a networking cable.

authentication A process that proves good data traffic truly came from where it says it originated by verifying the sending and receiving users and computers.

Authentication, Authorization, and Accounting (AAA) A security philosophy wherein a computer trying to connect to a network must first present some form of credential in order to be authenticated and then must have limitable permissions within the network. The authenticating server should also record session information about the client.

Authentication Server (AS) In Kerberos, a system that hands out Ticket-Granting Tickets to clients after comparing the client hash to its own. *See also* Ticket-Granting Ticket (TGT).

authoritative DNS servers DNS servers that hold the IP addresses and names of systems for a particular domain or domains in special storage areas called *forward lookup zones*. They also have *reverse lookup zones*.

authoritative name servers Another name for authoritative DNS servers. *See* authoritative DNS servers.

authorization A step in the AAA philosophy during which a client's permissions are decided upon. *See also* Authentication, Authorization, and Accounting (AAA).

Automatic Private IP Addressing (APIPA) A networking feature in operating systems that enables DHCP clients to self-configure an IP address and subnet mask automatically when a DHCP server isn't available.

Autonomous System (AS) One or more networks that are governed by a single protocol, which provides routing for the Internet backbone.

back up To save important data in a secondary location as a safety precaution against the loss of the primary data.

backup Archive of important data that the disaster recovery team can retrieve in case of some disaster.

backup designated router (BDR) A second router set to take over if the designated router fails. *See also* designated router (DR).

backup generator An onsite generator that provides electricity if the power utility fails.

badge A card-shaped device used for authentication; something you have, a possession factor.

bandwidth A piece of the spectrum occupied by some form of signal, whether it is television, voice, fax data, and so forth. Signals require a certain size and location of bandwidth to be transmitted. The higher the bandwidth, the faster the signal transmission, thus allowing for a more complex signal such as audio or video. Because bandwidth is a limited space, when one user is occupying it, others must wait their turn. Bandwidth is also the capacity of a network to transmit a given amount of data during a given period.

bandwidth saturation When the frequency of a band is filled to capacity due to the large number of devices using the same bandwidth.

bandwidth speed tester Web sites for measuring an Internet connection throughput, both download and upload speeds.

banner grabbing When a malicious user gains access to an open port and uses it to probe a host to gain information and access, as well as learn details about running services.

baseband Digital signaling that has only one signal (a single signal) on the cable at a time. The signals must be in one of three states: one, zero, or idle.

baseline Static image of a system's (or network's) performance when all elements are known to be working properly.

basic NAT A simple form of NAT that translates a computer's private or internal IP address to a global IP address on a one-to-one basis.

Basic Rate Interface (BRI) The basic ISDN configuration, which consists of two *B* channels (which can carry voice or data at a rate of 64 Kbps) and one *D* channel (which carries setup and configuration information, as well as data, at 16 Kbps).

Basic Service Set (BSS) In wireless networking, a single access point servicing a given area.

Basic Service Set Identifier (BSSID) Naming scheme in wireless networks.

baud One analog cycle on a telephone line.

baud rate The number of bauds per second. In the early days of telephone data transmission, the baud rate was often analogous to bits per second. Due to advanced modulation of baud cycles as well as data compression, this is no longer true.

Bearer channel (B channel) A type of ISDN channel that carries data and voice information using standard DS0 channels at 64 Kbps.

bidirectional (BiDi) transceiver Full-duplex fiber-optic connector that relies on wave division multiplexing (WDM) to differentiate wave signals on a single fiber, creating single-strand fiber transmission.

biometric Human physical characteristic that can be measured and saved to be compared as authentication in granting the user access to a network or resource. Common biometrics include fingerprints, facial scans, retinal scans, voice pattern recognition, and others.

biometric devices Devices that scan fingerprints, retinas, or even the sound of the user's voice to provide a foolproof replacement for both passwords and smart devices.

Bit Error Rate Test (BERT) An end-to-end test that verifies a T-carrier connection.

block Access that is denied to or from a resource. A block may be implemented in a firewall, access control server, or other secure gateway. *See also* allow.

block cipher An encryption algorithm in which data is encrypted in "chunks" of a certain length at a time. Popular in wired networks.

blocks Contiguous ranges of IP addresses that are assigned to organizations and end users by IANA. Also called *network blocks*.

Bluejacking The process of sending unsolicited messages to another Bluetooth device.

Bluesnarfing Use of weaknesses in the Bluetooth standard to steal information from other Bluetooth devices.

BNC connector A connector used for 10Base2 coaxial cable. All BNC connectors have to be locked into place by turning the locking ring 90 degrees.

BNC coupler Passive connector used to join two segments of coaxial cables that are terminated with BNC connectors.

bonding Two or more NICs in a system working together to act as a single NIC to increase performance.

Bootstrap Protocol (BOOTP) A component of TCP/IP that allows computers to discover and receive an IP address from a DHCP server prior to booting the OS. Other items that may be discovered during the BOOTP process are the IP address of the default gateway for the subnet and the IP addresses of any name servers.

Border Gateway Protocol (BGP-4) An exterior gateway routing protocol that enables groups of routers to share routing information so that efficient, loop-free routes can be established.

botnet A group of computers under the control of one operator, used for malicious purposes. *See also* zombie.

bottleneck A spot on a network where traffic slows precipitously.

bounce A signal sent by one device taking many different paths to get to the receiving systems.

bps (bits per second) A measurement of how fast data is moved across a transmission medium. A Gigabit Ethernet connection moves 1,000,000,000 bps.

bridge A device that connects two networks and passes traffic between them based only on the node address, so that traffic between nodes on one network does not appear on the other network. For example, an Ethernet bridge only looks at the MAC address. Bridges filter and forward frames based on MAC addresses and operate at Layer 2 (Data Link layer) of the OSI seven-layer model.

bridge loop A negative situation in which bridging devices (usually switches) are installed in a loop configuration, causing frames to loop continuously. Switches using Spanning Tree Protocol (STP) prevent bridge loops by automatically turning off looping ports.

bridged connection An early type of DSL connection that made the DSL line function the same as if you snapped an Ethernet cable into your NIC.

bridging loop A physical wiring of a circuitous path between two or more switches, causing frames to loop continuously. Implementing Spanning Tree Protocol (STP) in these devices will discover and block looped paths.

bring your own device (BYOD) A trend wherein users bring their own network-enabled devices to the work environment. These cell phones, tablets, notebooks, and other mobile devices must be easily and securely integrated and released from corporate network environments using on-boarding and off-boarding technologies.

broadband Analog signaling that sends multiple signals over the cable at the same time. The best example of broadband signaling is cable television. The zero, one, and idle states exist on multiple channels on the same cable. *See also* baseband.

broadcast A frame or packet addressed to all machines, almost always limited to a broadcast domain.

broadcast address The address a NIC attaches to a frame when it wants every other NIC on the network to read it. In TCP/IP, the general broadcast address is 255.255.255.255. In Ethernet, the broadcast MAC address is FF-FF-FF-FF-FF-FF.

broadcast domain A network of computers that will hear each other's broadcasts. The older term *collision domain* is the same but rarely used today.

broadcast storm The result of one or more devices sending a nonstop flurry of broadcast frames on the network.

browser A software program specifically designed to retrieve, interpret, and display Web pages.

brute force A type of attack wherein every permutation of some form of data is tried in an attempt to discover protected information. Most commonly used on password cracking.

buffer A component of a fiber-optic cable that adds strength to the cable.

building entrance Location where all the cables from the outside world (telephone lines, cables from other buildings, and so on) come into a building.

bus topology A network topology that uses a single bus cable that connects all of the computers in a line. Bus topology networks must be terminated to prevent signal reflection.

business continuity planning (BCP) The process of defining the steps to be taken in the event of a physical corporate crisis to continue operations. Includes the creation of documents to specify facilities, equipment, resources, personnel, and their roles.

butt set Device that can tap into a 66- or 110-punchdown block to see if a particular line is working.

byte Eight contiguous bits, the fundamental data unit of personal computers. Storing the equivalent of one character, the byte is also the basic unit of measurement for computer storage. Bytes are counted in powers of two.

CAB files Short for "cabinet files." These files are compressed and most commonly used during Microsoft operating system installation to store many smaller files, such as device drivers.

cable certifier A very powerful cable testing device used by professional installers to test the electrical characteristics of a cable and then generate a certification report, proving that cable runs pass TIA/EIA standards.

cable drop Location where the cable comes out of the wall at the workstation location.

cable modem A bridge device that interconnects the cable company's DOCSIS service to the user's Ethernet network. In most locations, the cable modem is the demarc.

cable stripper Device that enables the creation of UTP cables.

cable tester A generic name for a device that tests cables. Some common tests are continuity, electrical shorts, crossed wires, or other electrical characteristics.

cable tray A device for organizing cable runs in a drop ceiling.

cache A special area of RAM that stores frequently accessed data. In a network there are a number of applications that take advantage of cache in some way.

cached lookup The list kept by a DNS server of IP addresses it has already resolved, so it won't have to re-resolve an FQDN it has already checked.

cache-only DNS servers (caching-only DNS servers) DNS servers that do not have any forward lookup zones. They resolve names of systems on the Internet for the network, but are not responsible for telling other DNS servers the names of any clients.

caching engine A server dedicated to storing cache information on your network. These servers can reduce overall network traffic dramatically.

Cacti Popular network graphing program.

campus area network (CAN) A network installed in a medium-sized space spanning multiple buildings.

canonical name (CNAME) Less common type of DNS record that acts as a computer's alias.

captive portal A Wi-Fi network implementation used in some public facilities that directs attempts to connect to the network to an internal Web page for that facility; generally used to force terms of service on users.

capture file A file in which the collected packets from a packet sniffer program are stored.

capturing a printer A process by which a printer uses a local LPT port that connects to a networked printer. This is usually only done to support older programs that are not smart enough to know how to print directly to a UNC-named printer; it's quite rare today.

card Generic term for anything that you can snap into an expansion slot.

carrier sense multiple access with collision avoidance (CSMA/CA) *See* CSMA/CA (Carrier Sense Multiple access with Collision avoidance).

carrier sense multiple access with collision detection (CSMA/CD) *See* CSMA/CD (carrier sense multiple access with collision detection).

Cat 3 Category 3 wire, a TIA/EIA standard for UTP wiring that can operate at up to 16 Mbps.

Cat 4 Category 4 wire, a TIA/EIA standard for UTP wiring that can operate at up to 20 Mbps. This wire is not widely used, except in older Token Ring networks.

Cat 5 Category 5 wire, a TIA/EIA standard for UTP wiring that can operate at up to 100 Mbps.

Cat 5e Category 5e wire, a TIA/EIA standard for UTP wiring with improved support for 100 Mbps using two pairs and support for 1000 Mbps using four pairs.

Cat 6 Category 6 wire, a TIA/EIA standard for UTP wiring with improved support for 1000 Mbps; supports 10 Gbps up to 55 meters.

Cat 6a Category 6a wire, a TIA/EIA standard for UTP wiring with support for 10 Gbps up to 100 meters.

Cat 7 Category 7 wire, a standard (unrecognized by TIA) for UTP wiring with support for 10+ Gbps at 600 MHz max. frequency.

category (Cat) rating A grade assigned to cable to help network installers get the right cable for the right network technology. Cat ratings are officially rated in megahertz (MHz), indicating the highest-frequency bandwidth the cable can handle.

CCITT (Comité Consutatif Internationale Téléphonique et Télégraphique) European standards body that established the V standards for modems.

CCMP-AES A 128-bit block cipher used in the IEEE 802.11i standard.

central office Building that houses local exchanges and a location where individual voice circuits come together.

certificate A public encryption key signed with the digital signature from a trusted third party called a *certificate authority (CA)*. This key serves to validate the identity of its holder when that person or company sends data to other parties.

certifier A device that tests a cable to ensure that it can handle its rated amount of capacity.

chain of custody A document used to track the collection, handling, and transfer of evidence.

Challenge Handshake Authentication Protocol (CHAP) A remote access authentication protocol. It has the serving system challenge the remote client, which must provide an encrypted password.

Challenge-Response Authentication Mechanism-Message Digest 5 (CRAM-MD5) A tool for server authentication in SMTP servers.

change management The process of initiating, approving, funding, implementing, and documenting significant changes to the network.

change management documentation A set of documents that defines procedures for changes to the network.

change management team Personnel who collect change requests, evaluate the change, work with decision makers for approval, plan and implement approved changes, and document the changes.

change request A formal or informal document suggesting a modification to some aspect of the network or computing environment.

channel A portion of the wireless spectrum on which a particular wireless network operates. Setting wireless networks to different channels enables separation of the networks.

channel bonding Wireless technology that enables wireless access points (WAPs) to use two channels for transmission.

channel overlap Drawback of 2.4-GHz wireless networks where channels shared some bandwidth with other channels. This is why only three 2.4-GHz channels can be used in the United States (1, 6, and 11).

Channel Service Unit/Digital Service Unit (CSU/DSU) *See* CSU/DSU (Channel Service Unit/Data Service Unit).

chat A multiparty, real-time text conversation. The Internet's most popular version is known as Internet Relay Chat (IRC), which many groups use to converse in real time with each other.

checksum A simple error-detection method that adds a numerical value to each data packet, based on the number of data bits in the packet. The receiving node applies the same formula to the data and verifies that the numerical value is the same; if not, the data has been corrupted and must be re-sent.

choose your own device (CYOD) Deployment model where corporate employees select among a catalog of approved mobile devices.

cipher A series of complex and hard-to-reverse mathematics run on a string of ones and zeroes in order to make a new set of seemingly meaningless ones and zeroes.

cipher lock A door unlocking system that uses a door handle, a latch, and a sequence of mechanical push buttons.

ciphertext The output when cleartext is run through a cipher algorithm using a key.

circuit switching The process for connecting two phones together on one circuit.

Cisco IOS Cisco's proprietary operating system.

cladding The part of a fiber-optic cable that makes the light reflect down the fiber.

class license Contiguous chunk of IP addresses passed out by the Internet Assigned Numbers Authority (IANA).

class of service (CoS) A prioritization value used to apply to services, ports, or whatever a quality of service (QoS) device might use.

classful Obsolete IPv4 addressing scheme that relied on the original class blocks, such as Class A, Class B, and Class C.

classless IPv4 addressing scheme that does not rely on the original class blocks, such as Class A, Class B, and Class C.

Classless Inter-Domain Routing (CIDR) The basis of allocating and routing classless addresses, not restricting subnet masks to /8, /16, or /24, which classful addressing did. *See also* subnetting.

classless subnet A subnet that does not fall into the common categories such as Class A, Class B, and Class C.

cleartext *See* plaintext.

cleartext credentials Any login process conducted over a network where account names, passwords, or other authentication elements are sent from the client or server in an unencrypted fashion.

client A computer program that uses the services of another computer program; software that extracts information from a server. Your autodial phone is a client, and the phone company is its server. Also, a machine that accesses shared resources on a server.

client/server A relationship in which client software obtains services from a server on behalf of a user.

client/server application An application that performs some or all of its processing on an application server rather than on the client. The client usually only receives the result of the processing.

client/server network A network that has dedicated server machines and client machines.

client-to-site A type of VPN connection where a single computer logs into a remote network and becomes, for all intents and purposes, a member of that network.

closed-circuit television (CCTV) A self-contained, closed system in which video cameras feed their signal to specific, dedicated monitors and storage devices.

cloud computing Using the Internet to store files and run applications. For example, Google Docs is a cloud computing application that enables you to run productivity applications over the Internet from your Web browser.

cloud/server based Remote storage and access of software, especially anti-malware software, where it can be singularly updated. This central storage allows users to access and run current versions of software easily, with the disadvantage of it not running automatically on the local client. The client must initiate access to and launching of the software.

cloud/server-based anti-malware Remote storage and access of software designed to protect against malicious software where it can be singularly updated.

clustering Multiple pieces of equipment, such as servers, connected, which appear to the user and the network as one logical device, providing data and services to the organization for both redundancy and fault tolerance.

coarse wavelength division multiplexing (CWDM) An optical multiplexing technology in which a few signals of different optical wavelength could be combined to travel a fairly short distance.

coaxial cable A type of cable that contains a central conductor wire surrounded by an insulating material, which in turn is surrounded by a braided metal shield. It is called coaxial because the center wire and the braided metal shield share a common axis or centerline.

code-division multiple access (CDMA) Early cellular telephone technology that used spread-spectrum transmission. Obsolete.

cold site A location that consists of a building, facilities, desks, toilets, parking, and everything that a business needs except computers.

collision The result of two nodes transmitting at the same time on a multiple access network such as Ethernet. Both frames may be lost or partial frames may result.

collision domain *See* broadcast domain.

collision light A light on some older NICs that flickers when a network collision is detected.

command A request, typed from a terminal or embedded in a file, to perform an operation or to execute a particular program.

Common Internet File System (CIFS) The protocol that NetBIOS used to share folders and printers. Still very common, even on UNIX/Linux systems.

community cloud A private cloud paid for and used by more than one organization.

compatibility issue When different pieces of hardware or software don't work together correctly.

compatibility requirements With respect to network installations and upgrades, requirements that deal with how well the new technology integrates with older or existing technologies.

complete algorithm A cipher and the methods used to implement that cipher.

computer forensics The science of gathering, preserving, and presenting evidence stored on a computer or any form of digital media that is presentable in a court of law.

concentrator A device that brings together, at a common center, connections to a particular kind of network (such as Ethernet) and implements that network internally.

configuration management A set of documents, policies, and procedures designed to help you maintain and update your network in a logical, orderly fashion.

configuration management documentation Documents that define the configuration of a network. These would include wiring diagrams, network diagrams, baselines, and policy/procedure/configuration documentation.

configurations The settings stored in devices that define how they are to operate.

connection A term used to refer to communication between two computers.

connectionless A type of communication characterized by sending packets that are not acknowledged by the destination host. UDP is the quintessential connectionless protocol in the TCP/IP suite.

connectionless communication A protocol that does not establish and verify a connection between the hosts before sending data; it just sends the data and hopes for the best. This is faster than connection-oriented protocols. UDP is an example of a connectionless protocol.

connection-oriented Network communication between two hosts that includes negotiation between the hosts to establish a communication session. Data segments are then transferred between hosts, with each segment being acknowledged before a subsequent segment can be sent. Orderly closure of the communication is conducted at the end of the data transfer or in the event of a communication failure. TCP is the only connection-oriented protocol in the TCP/IP suite.

connection-oriented communication A protocol that establishes a connection between two hosts before transmitting data and verifies receipt before closing the connection between the hosts. TCP is an example of a connection-oriented protocol.

console port Connection jack in a switch used exclusively to connect a computer that will manage the switch.

content filter An advanced networking device that implements content filtering, enabling administrators to filter traffic based on specific signatures or keywords (such as profane language).

content switch Advanced networking device that works at least at Layer 7 (Application layer) and hides servers behind a single IP.

contingency plan Documents that set out how to limit damage and recover quickly from an incident.

contingency planning The process of creating documents that set out how to limit damage and recover quickly from an incident.

continuity The physical connection of wires in a network.

continuity tester Inexpensive network tester that can only test for continuity on a line.

convergence Point at which the routing tables for all routers in a network are updated.

copy backup A type of backup similar to normal or full, in that all selected files on a system are backed up. This type of backup does *not* change the archive bit of the files being backed up.

core The central glass of the fiber-optic cable that carries the light signal.

corporate-owned business only (COBO) Deployment model where the corporation owns all the mobile devices issued to employees. Employees have a whitelist of preapproved applications they can install.

cost An arbitrary metric value assigned to a network route with OSFP-capable routers.

counter A predefined event that is recorded to a log file.

CRC (cyclic redundancy check) A mathematical method used to check for errors in long streams of transmitted data with high accuracy.

crimper Also called a *crimping tool*, the tool used to secure a crimp (or an RJ-45 connector) onto the end of a cable.

crossover cable A specially terminated UTP cable used to interconnect routers or switches, or to connect network cards without a switch. Crossover cables reverse the sending and receiving wire pairs from one end to the other.

cross-platform support Standards created to enable terminals (and now operating systems) from different companies to interact with one another.

crosstalk Electrical signal interference between two cables that are in close proximity to each other.

crypto-malware Malicious software that uses some form of encryption to lock a user out of a system. *See also* ransomware.

CSMA/CA (carrier sense multiple access with collision avoidance) Access method used only on wireless networks. Before hosts send out data, they first listen for traffic. If the network is free, they send out a signal that reserves a certain amount of time to make sure the network is free of other signals. If data is detected in the air, the hosts wait a random time period before trying again. If there are no other wireless signals, the data is sent out.

CSMA/CD (carrier sense multiple access with collision detection) Obsolete access method that older Ethernet systems used in wired LAN technologies, enabling frames of data to flow through the network and ultimately reach address locations. Hosts on CSMA/CD networks first listened to hear if there is any data on the wire. If there was none, they sent out data. If a collision occurred, then both hosts waited a random time period before retransmitting the data. Full-duplex Ethernet completely eliminated CSMA/CD.

CSU/DSU (Channel Service Unit/Data Service Unit) A piece of equipment that connects a T-carrier leased line from the telephone company to a customer's equipment (such as a router). It performs line encoding and conditioning functions, and it often has a loopback function for testing.

customer-premises equipment (CPE) The primary distribution box and customer-owned/managed equipment that exists on the customer side of the demarc.

cyclic redundancy check (CRC) *See* CRC (cyclic redundancy check).

daily backup Also called a *daily copy backup*, makes a copy of all files that have been changed on that day without changing the archive bits of those files.

daisy-chain A method of connecting together several devices along a bus and managing the signals for each device.

data backup The process of creating extra copies of data to be used in case the primary data source fails.

Data Encryption Standard (DES) A symmetric-key algorithm developed by the U.S. government in the 1970s and formerly in use in a variety of TCP/IP applications. DES used a 64-bit block and a 56-bit key. Over time, the 56-bit key made DES susceptible to brute-force attacks.

Data Link layer *See* Open Systems Interconnection (OSI) seven-layer model.

Data Over Cable Service Interface Specification (DOCSIS) The unique protocol used by cable modem networks.

datagram A connectionless transfer unit created with User Datagram Protocol designed for quick transfers over a packet-switched network.

datagram TLS (DTLS) VPN A virtual private network solution that optimizes connections for delay-sensitive applications, such as voice and video.

DB-9 A 9-pin, D-shaped subminiature connector, often used in serial port connections.

DB-25 A 25-pin, D-shaped subminiature connector, typically used in parallel and older serial port connections.

dead spot A place that should be covered by the network signal but where devices get no signal.

deauthentication (deauth) attack A form of DoS attack that targets 802.11 Wi-Fi networks specifically by sending out a frame that kicks a wireless client off its current WAP connection. A rogue WAP nearby presents a stronger signal, which the client will prefer. The rogue WAP connects the client to the Internet and then proceeds to intercept communications to and from that client.

decibel (dB) A measurement of the quality of a signal.

dedicated circuit A circuit that runs from a breaker box to specific outlets.

dedicated line A telephone line that is an always open, or connected, circuit. Dedicated telephone lines usually do not have telephone numbers.

dedicated server A machine that does not use any client functions, only server functions.

de-encapsulation The process of stripping all the extra header information from a packet as the data moves up a protocol stack.

default A software function or operation that occurs automatically unless the user specifies something else.

default gateway In a TCP/IP network, the IP address of the router that interconnects the LAN to a wider network, usually the Internet. This router's IP address is part of the necessary TCP/IP configuration for communicating with multiple networks using IP.

Delta channel (D channel) A type of ISDN line that transfers data at 16 Kbps.

demarc A device that marks the dividing line of responsibility for the functioning of a network between internal users and upstream service providers. Also, *demarcation point.*

demarc extension Any cabling that runs from the network interface to whatever box is used by the customer as a demarc.

demilitarized zone (DMZ) A lightly protected or unprotected subnet network positioned between an outer firewall and an organization's highly protected internal network. DMZs are used mainly to host public address servers (such as Web servers).

demultiplexer Device that can extract and distribute individual streams of data that have been combined together to travel along a single shared network cable.

denial of service (DoS) An effort to prevent users from gaining normal use of a resource. *See also* denial of service (DoS) attack.

denial of service (DoS) attack An attack that floods a networked server with so many requests that it becomes overwhelmed and ceases functioning.

dense wavelength division multiplexing (DWDM) An optical multiplexing technology in which a large number of optical signals of different optical wavelength could be combined to travel over relatively long fiber cables.

designated router (DR) The main router in an OSPF network that relays information to all other routers in the area.

destination port A fixed, predetermined number that defines the function or session type in a TCP/IP network.

device driver A subprogram to control communications between the computer and some peripheral hardware.

device ID The last six digits of a MAC address, identifying the manufacturer's unique serial number for that NIC.

device types/requirements With respect to installing and upgrading networks, these determine what equipment is needed to build the network and how the network should be organized.

DHCP four-way handshake (DORA) DHCP process in which a client gets a lease for an IPv4 address—Discover, Offer, Request, and Ack.

DHCP lease Created by the DHCP server to allow a system requesting DHCP IP information to use that information for a certain amount of time.

DHCP relay A router process that, when enabled, passes DHCP requests and responses across router interfaces. In common terms, DHCP communications can cross from one network to another within a router that has DHCP relay enabled and configured.

DHCP scope The pool of IP addresses that a DHCP server may allocate to clients requesting IP addresses or other IP information like DNS server addresses.

DHCP snooping Switch process that monitors DHCP traffic, filtering out DHCP messages from untrusted sources. Typically used to block attacks that use a rogue DHCP server.

dial-up lines Telephone lines with telephone numbers; they must dial to make a connection, as opposed to a dedicated line.

differential backup Similar to an incremental backup in that it backs up the files that have been changed since the last backup. This type of backup does not change the state of the archive bit.

differentiated services (DiffServ) The underlying architecture that makes quality of service (QoS) work.

dig (domain information groper) *See* domain information groper (dig).

digital signal 1 (DS1) The signaling method used by T1 lines, which uses a relatively simple frame consisting of 25 pieces: a framing bit and 24 channels. Each DS1 channel holds a single 8-bit DS0 data sample. The framing bit and data channels combine to make 193 bits per DS1 frame. These frames are transmitted 8000 times/sec, making a total throughput of 1.544 Mbps.

digital signal processor (DSP) *See* DSP (digital signal processor).

digital signature An encrypted hash of a private encryption key that verifies a sender's identity to those who receive encrypted data or messages.

digital subscriber line (DSL) A high-speed Internet connection technology that uses a regular telephone line for connectivity. DSL comes in several varieties, including asymmetric (ADSL) and symmetric (SDSL), and many speeds. Typical home-user DSL connections are ADSL with a download speed of up to 9 Mbps and an upload speed of up to 1 Kbps.

dipole antenna The standard straight-wire antenna that provides most omnidirectional function.

direct current (DC) A type of electric circuit where the flow of electrons is in a complete circle.

directional antenna An antenna that focuses its signal more toward a specific direction; as compared to an omnidirectional antenna that radiates its signal in all directions equally.

direct-sequence spread-spectrum (DSSS) A spread-spectrum broadcasting method defined in the 802.11 standard that sends data out on different frequencies at the same time.

disaster recovery The means and methods to recover primary infrastructure from a disaster. Disaster recovery starts with a plan and includes data backups.

discretionary access control (DAC) Authorization method based on the idea that there is an owner of a resource who may at his or her discretion assign access to that resource. DAC is considered much more flexible than mandatory access control (MAC).

disk mirroring Process by which data is written simultaneously to two or more disk drives. Read and write speed is decreased but redundancy, in case of catastrophe, is increased. Also known as *RAID level 1*. *See also* duplexing.

disk striping Process by which data is spread among multiple (at least two) drives. It increases speed for both reads and writes of data, but provides no fault tolerance. Also known as *RAID level 0*.

disk striping with parity Process by which data is spread among multiple (at least three) drives, with parity information as well to provide fault tolerance. The most commonly implemented type is RAID 5, where the data and parity information is spread across three or more drives.

dispersion Diffusion over distance of light propagating down fiber cable.

distance vector Set of routing protocols that calculates the total cost to get to a particular network ID and compares that cost to the total cost of all the other routes to get to that same network ID.

distributed control system (DCS) A small controller added directly to a machine used to distribute the computing load.

Distributed Coordination Function (DCF) One of two methods of collision avoidance defined by the 802.11 standard and the only one currently implemented. DCF specifies strict rules for sending data onto the network media. *See also* Point Coordination Function (PCF).

distributed denial of service (DDoS) Multicomputer assault on a network resource that attempts, with sheer overwhelming quantity of requests, to prevent regular users from receiving services from the resource. Can also be used to crash systems.

distributed switching The centralized installation, configuration, and handling of every switch in a virtualized network.

DLL (dynamic link library) A file of executable functions or data that can be used by a Windows application. Typically, a DLL provides one or more particular functions, and a program accesses the functions by creating links to the DLL.

DNS cache poisoning An attack that adds or changes information in a DNS server to point host names to incorrect IP addresses, under the attacker's control. When a client requests an IP address from this DNS server for a Web site, the poisoned server hands out an IP address of an attacker, not the legitimate site. When the client subsequently visits the attacker site, malware is installed.

DNS domain A specific branch of the DNS name space. Top-level DNS domains include .com, .gov, and .edu.

DNS forwarding DNS server configuration that sends (forwards) DNS requests to another DNS server.

DNS resolver cache A cache used by Windows DNS clients to keep track of DNS information.

DNS root servers The highest in the hierarchy of DNS servers running the Internet.

DNS server A system that runs a special DNS server program.

DNS tree A hierarchy of DNS domains and individual computer names organized into a tree-like structure, the top of which is the root.

document A medium and the data recorded on it for human use; for example, a report sheet or book. By extension, any record that has permanence and that can be read by a human or a machine.

documentation A collection of organized documents or the information recorded in documents. Also, instructional material specifying the inputs, operations, and outputs of a computer program or system.

domain A term used to describe a grouping of users, computers, and/or networks. In Microsoft networking, a domain is a group of computers and users that shares a common account database and a common security policy. For the Internet, a domain is a group of computers that shares a common element in their DNS hierarchical name.

domain controller A Microsoft Windows Server system specifically configured to store user and server account information for its domain. Often abbreviated as "DC." Windows domain controllers store all account and security information in the *Active Directory* domain service.

domain information groper (dig) Command-line tool in non-Windows systems used to diagnose DNS problems.

Domain Name System (DNS) A TCP/IP name resolution system that resolves host names to IP addresses, IP addresses to host names, and other bindings, like DNS servers and mail servers for a domain.

domain users and groups Users and groups that are defined across an entire network domain.

door access controls Methodology to grant permission or to deny passage through a doorway. The method may be computer-controlled, human-controlled, token-oriented, or many other means.

dotted decimal notation Shorthand method for discussing and configuring binary IP addresses.

download The transfer of information from a remote computer system to the user's system. Opposite of *upload*.

drive duplexing *See* duplexing.

drive mirroring The process of writing identical data to two hard drives on the same controller at the same time to provide data redundancy.

DS0 The digital signal rate created by converting analog sound into 8-bit chunks 8000 times a second, with a data stream of 64 Kbps. This is the simplest data stream (and the slowest rate) of the digital part of the phone system.

DS1 The signaling method used by T1 lines, which uses a relatively simple frame consisting of 25 pieces: a framing bit and 24 channels. Each DS1 channel holds a single 8-bit DS0 data sample. The framing bit and data channels combine to make 193 bits per DS1 frame. These frames are transmitted 8000 times/sec, making a total throughput of 1.544 Mbps.

DSL Access Multiplexer (DSLAM) A device located in a telephone company's central office that connects multiple customers to the Internet.

DSL modem A device that enables customers to connect to the Internet using a DSL connection. A DSL modem isn't really a modem—it's more like an ISDN terminal adapter—but the term stuck, and even the manufacturers of the devices now call them DSL modems.

DSP (digital signal processor) A specialized microprocessor-like device that processes digital signals at the expense of other capabilities, much as the floating-point unit (FPU) is optimized for math functions. DSPs are used in such specialized hardware as high-speed modems, multimedia sound cards, MIDI equipment, and real-time video capture and compression.

dual stack Networking device, such as a router or PC, that runs both IPv4 and IPv6.

duplexing Also called *disk duplexing* or *drive duplexing*, similar to mirroring in that data is written to and read from two physical drives for fault tolerance. In addition, separate controllers are used for each drive, for both additional fault tolerance and additional speed. Considered RAID level 1. *See also* disk mirroring.

dynamic addressing A way for a computer to receive IP information automatically from a server program. *See also* Dynamic Host Configuration Protocol (DHCP).

Dynamic ARP Inspection (DAI) Cisco process that updates a database of trusted systems. DAI then watches for false or suspicious ARPs and ignores them to prevent ARP cache poisoning and other malevolent efforts.

Dynamic DNS (DDNS) A protocol that enables DNS servers to get automatic updates of IP addresses of computers in their forward lookup zones, mainly by talking to the local DHCP server.

Dynamic Host Configuration Protocol (DHCP) A protocol that enables a DHCP server to set TCP/IP settings automatically for a DHCP client.

dynamic link library (DLL) *See* DLL (dynamic link library).

dynamic multipoint VPN (DMVPN) A virtual private network solution optimized for connections between multiple locations directly.

dynamic NAT (DNAT) Type of Network Address Translation (NAT) in which many computers can share a pool of routable IP addresses that number fewer than the computers.

dynamic port numbers Port numbers 49152–65535, recommended by the IANA to be used as ephemeral port numbers.

dynamic routing Process by which routers in an internetwork automatically exchange information with other routers. Requires a dynamic routing protocol, such as OSPF or RIP.

dynamic routing protocol A protocol that supports the building of automatic routing tables, such as OSPF or RIP.

E1 The European counterpart of a T1 connection that carries 32 channels at 64 Kbps for a total of 2.048 Mbps—making it slightly faster than a T1.

E3   The European counterpart of a T3 line that carries 16 E1 lines (512 channels), for a total bandwidth of 34.368 Mbps—making it a little bit slower than an American T3.

EAP-TLS (Extensible Authentication Protocol with Transport Layer Security)   A protocol that defines the use of a RADIUS server as well as mutual authentication, requiring certificates on both the server and every client.

EAP-TTLS (Extensible Authentication Protocol with Tunneled Transport Layer Security)   A protocol similar to *EAP-TLS* but only uses a single server-side certificate.

edge device   A hardware device that has been optimized to perform a task in coordination with other edge devices and controllers.

edge router   Router that connects one Autonomous System (AS) to another.

effective permissions   The permissions of all groups combined in any network operating system.

electromagnetic interference (EMI)   Interference from one device to another, resulting in poor performance in the device's capabilities. This is similar to having static on your TV while running a hair dryer, or placing two monitors too close together and getting a "shaky" screen.

electronic discovery   The process of requesting and providing electronic and stored data and evidence in a legal way.

electrostatic discharge (ESD)   *See* ESD (electrostatic discharge).

e-mail (electronic mail)   Messages, usually text, sent from one person to another via computer. E-mail can also be sent automatically to a large number of addresses, known as a *mailing list*.

e-mail alert   Notification sent by e-mail as a result of an event. A typical use is a notification sent from an SNMP manager as a result of an out-of-tolerance condition in an SNMP managed device.

e-mail client   Program that runs on a computer and enables a user to send, receive, and organize e-mail.

e-mail server   Also known as a *mail server*, a server that accepts incoming e-mail, sorts the e-mail for recipients into mailboxes, and sends e-mail to other servers using SMTP.

emulator   Software or hardware that converts the commands to and from the host machine to an entirely different platform. For example, a program that enables you to run Nintendo games on your PC.

encapsulation   The process of putting the packets from one protocol inside the packets of another protocol. An example of this is TCP/IP encapsulation in Ethernet, which places TCP/IP packets inside Ethernet frames.

encryption   A method of securing messages by scrambling and encoding each packet as it is sent across an unsecured medium, such as the Internet. Each encryption level provides multiple standards and options.

endpoint   In the TCP/IP world, the session information stored in RAM. *See also* socket.

endpoints Correct term to use when discussing the data each computer stores about the connection between two computers' TCP/IP applications. *See also* socket pairs.

end-to-end principle Early network concept that originally meant that applications and work should happen only at the endpoints in a network, such as in a single client and a single server.

Enhanced Data rates for GSM Evolution (EDGE) Early cellular telephone technology that used a SIM card; obsolete.

Enhanced Interior Gateway Routing Protocol (EIGRP) Cisco's proprietary hybrid protocol that has elements of both distance vector and link state routing.

enhanced small form-factor pluggable (SFP+) Fiber-optic connector used in 10 GbE networks.

environment limitations With respect to building and upgrading networks, refers to the degree of access to facilities and physical access to physical infrastructure. The type of building or buildings must be considered. Access to the walls and ceilings will factor in the construction of the network.

environmental monitor Device used in telecommunications rooms that keeps track of humidity, temperature, and more.

ephemeral port In TCP/IP communication, an arbitrary number generated by a sending computer that the receiving computer uses as a destination address when sending a return packet.

ephemeral port number *See* ephemeral port.

equipment limitations With respect to installing and upgrading networks, the degree of usage of any existing equipment, applications, or cabling.

equipment rack A metal structure used in equipment rooms to secure network hardware devices and patch panels. Most racks are 19 inches wide. Devices designed to fit in such a rack use a height measurement called *units*, or simply *U*.

ESD (electrostatic discharge) The movement of electrons from one body to another. ESD is a real menace to PCs because it can cause permanent damage to semiconductors.

Ethernet Name coined by Xerox for the first standard of network cabling and protocols. Ethernet is based on a bus topology. The IEEE 802.3 subcommittee defines the current Ethernet specifications.

Ethernet over Power (EoP) The IEEE 1901 standard, also known as *HomePlug HD-PLC*, provides high-speed home networking through the building's existing power infrastructure.

evil twin An attack that lures people into logging into a rogue access point that looks similar to a legitimate access point.

Evolved High-Speed Packet Access (HSPA+) The final wireless 3G data standard, transferring theoretical maximum speeds up to 168 Mbps, although real-world implementations rarely passed 10 Mbps.

executable viruses Viruses that are literally extensions of executables and that are unable to exist by themselves. Once an infected executable file is run, the virus loads into memory, adding copies of itself to other EXEs that are subsequently run.

Exim E-mail server for every major platform; fast and efficient.

exit plan Documents and diagrams that identify the best way out of a building in the event of an emergency. It may also define other procedures to follow.

Extended Service Set (ESS) A single wireless access point servicing a given area that has been extended by adding more access points.

Extended Service Set Identifier (ESSID) An SSID applied to an Extended Service Set as a network naming convention.

Extended Unique Identifier, 48-bit (EUI-48) The IEEE term for the 48-bit MAC address assigned to a network interface. The first 24 bits of the EUI-48 are assigned by the IEEE as the organizationally unique identifier (OUI).

Extended Unique Identifier, 64-bit (EUI-64) The last 64 bits of the IPv6 address, which are determined based on a calculation based on a device's 48-bit MAC address.

Extensible Authentication Protocol (EAP) Authentication wrapper that EAP-compliant applications can use to accept one of many types of authentication. While EAP is a general-purpose authentication wrapper, its only substantial use is in wireless networks.

external connections A network's connections to the wider Internet. Also a major concern when setting up a SOHO network.

external data bus (EDB) The primary data highway of all computers. Everything in your computer is tied either directly or indirectly to the EDB.

external firewall The firewall that sits between the perimeter network and the Internet and is responsible for bearing the brunt of the attacks from the Internet.

external network address A number added to the MAC address of every computer on an IPX/SPX network that defines every computer on the network; this is often referred to as a *network number*.

external threats Threats to your network through external means; examples include virus attacks and the exploitation of users, security holes in the OS, or weaknesses of the network hardware itself.

fail close Defines the condition of doors and locks in the event of an emergency, indicating that the doors should close and lock.

fail open Defines the condition of doors and locks in the event of an emergency, indicating that the doors should be open and unlocked.

FAQ (frequently asked questions) Common abbreviation coined by BBS users and spread to Usenet and the Internet. This is a list of questions and answers that pertains to a particular topic, maintained so that users new to the group don't all bombard the group with similar questions. Examples are "What is the name of the actor who plays *X* on this show, and was he in anything else?" or "Can anyone list all of the books by this author in the order that they were published so that I can read them in that order?" The common answer to this type of question is "Read the FAQ!"

far-end crosstalk (FEXT) Crosstalk on the opposite end of a cable from the signal's source.

Fast Ethernet Nickname for the 100-Mbps Ethernet standards. Originally applied to 100BaseT.

fault tolerance The capability of any system to continue functioning after some part of the system has failed. RAID is an example of a hardware device that provides fault tolerance for hard drives.

F-connector A screw-on connector used to terminate small-diameter coaxial cable such as RG-6 and RG-59 cables.

FDDI (Fiber Distributed Data Interface) *See* Fiber Distributed Data Interface (FDDI).

Federal Communications Commission (FCC) In the United States, regulates public airwaves and rates PCs and other equipment according to the amount of radiation emitted.

Fiber Distributed Data Interface (FDDI) Older technology fiber-optic network used in campus-sized installations. It transfers data at 100 Mbps and uses a token bus network protocol over a ring topology.

fiber-optic cable A high-speed physical medium for transmitting data that uses light rather than electricity to transmit data and is made of high-purity glass fibers sealed within a flexible opaque tube. Much faster than conventional copper wire.

Fibre Channel (FC) A self-contained, high-speed storage environment with its own storage arrays, cables, protocols, cables, and switches. Fibre Channel is a critical part of storage area networks (SANs).

file hashing When the download provider hashes the contents of a file and publishes the resulting message digest.

file server A computer designated to store software, courseware, administrative tools, and other data on a local or wide area network (WAN). It "serves" this information to other computers via the network when users enter their personal access codes.

File Transfer Protocol (FTP) A set of rules that allows two computers to talk to one another as a file transfer is carried out. This is the protocol used when you transfer a file from one computer to another across the Internet.

fire ratings Ratings developed by Underwriters Laboratories (UL) and the National Electrical Code (NEC) to define the risk of network cables burning and creating noxious fumes and smoke.

firewall A device that restricts traffic between a local network and the Internet.

FireWire An IEEE 1394 standard to send wide-band signals over a thin connector system that plugs into TVs, VCRs, TV cameras, PCs, and so forth. This serial bus developed by Apple and Texas Instruments enables connection of 60 devices at speeds ranging from 100 to 800 Mbps.

first responder The person or robot whose job is to react to the notification of a possible computer crime by determining the severity of the situation, collecting information, documenting findings and actions, and providing the information to the proper authorities.

flat name space A naming convention that gives each device only one name that must be unique. NetBIOS uses a flat name space. TCP/IP's DNS uses a hierarchical name space.

flat-surface connector Early fiber-optic connector that resulted in a small gap between fiber-optic junctions due to the flat grind faces of the fibers. It was replaced by Angled Physical Contact (APC) connectors.

flood guard Technology in modern switches that can detect and block excessive traffic.

flow A stream of packets from one specific place to another.

flow cache Stores sets of flows for interpretation and analysis. *See also* flow.

forensics report A document that describes the details of gathering, securing, transporting, and investigating evidence.

forward lookup zone The storage area in a DNS server to store the IP addresses and names of systems for a particular domain or domains.

forward proxy server Server that acts as middleman between clients and servers, making requests to network servers on behalf of clients. Results are sent to the proxy server, which then passes them to the original client. The network servers are isolated from the clients by the forward proxy server.

FQDN (fully qualified domain name) *See* fully qualified domain name (FQDN).

fractional T1 access A service provided by many telephone companies wherein customers can purchase a number of individual channels in a T1 line in order to save money.

frame A defined series of binary data that is the basic container for a discrete amount of data moving across a network. Frames are created at Layer 2 of the OSI model.

frame check sequence (FCS) A sequence of bits placed in a frame that is used to check the primary data for errors.

Frame Relay An extremely efficient data transmission technique used to send digital information such as voice, data, LAN, and WAN traffic quickly and cost-efficiently to many destinations from one port.

FreeRADIUS Free RADIUS server software for UNIX/Linux systems.

freeware Software that is distributed for free with no license fee.

frequency division multiplexing (FDM) A process of keeping individual phone calls separate by adding a different frequency multiplier to each phone call, making it possible to separate phone calls by their unique frequency range.

frequency mismatch Problem in older wireless networks with manual settings where the WAP transmitted on one channel and a wireless client was set to access on a different channel.

frequency-hopping spread-spectrum (FHSS) A spread-spectrum broadcasting method defined in the 802.11 standard that sends data on one frequency at a time, constantly shifting (or *hopping*) frequencies.

frequently asked questions (FAQ) *See* FAQ (frequently asked questions).

FUBAR Fouled Up Beyond All Recognition.

full backup Archive created where every file selected is backed up, and the archive bit is turned off for every file backed up.

full-duplex Any device that can send and receive data simultaneously.

fully meshed topology A mesh network where every node is directly connected to every other node.

fully qualified domain name (FQDN) The complete DNS name of a system, from its host name to the top-level domain name. Textual nomenclature to a domain-organized resource. It is written left to right, with the host name on the left, followed by any hierarchical subdomains within the top-level domain on the right. Each level is separated from any preceding or following layer by a dot (.).

gain The strengthening and focusing of radio frequency output from a wireless access point (WAP).

gateway router A router that acts as a default gateway in a TCP/IP network.

general logs Logs that record updates to applications.

geofencing The process of using a mobile device's built-in GPS capabilities and mobile networking capabilities to set geographical constraints on where the mobile device can be used.

Get (SNMP) A query from an SNMP manager sent to the agent of a managed device for the status of a management information base (MIB) object.

giga The prefix that generally refers to the quantity 1,073,741,824. One gigabyte is 1,073,741,824 bytes. With frequencies, in contrast, giga- often refers to one billion. One gigahertz is 1,000,000,000 hertz.

Gigabit Ethernet *See* 1000BaseT.

gigabit interface converter (GBIC) Modular port that supports a standardized, wide variety of gigabit interface modules.

gigabyte 1024 megabytes.

global routing prefix The first 48 bits of an IPv6 unicast address, used to get a packet to its destination. *See also* network ID.

Global System for Mobile (GSM) Early cellular telephone networking standard; obsolete.

global unicast address A second IPv6 address that every system needs in order to get on the Internet.

grandfather, father, son (GFS) A tape rotation strategy used in data backups.

graphing Type of software that creates visual representations and graphs of data collected by SNMP managers.

greenfield mode One of three modes used with 802.11n wireless networks wherein everything is running at higher speed.

ground loop A voltage differential that exists between two different grounding points.

Group Policy A feature of Windows Active Directory that allows an administrator to apply policy settings to network users *en masse*.

Group Policy Object (GPO) Enables network administrators to define multiple rights and permissions to entire sets of users all at one time.

groups Collections of network users who share similar tasks and need similar permissions; defined to make administration tasks easier.

guest In terms of virtualization, an operating system running as a virtual machine inside a hypervisor.

guest network A network that can contain or allow access to any resource that management deems acceptable to be used by insecure hosts that attach to the guest network.

H.320 A standard that uses multiple ISDN channels to transport video teleconferencing (VTC) over a network.

H.323 A VoIP standard that handles the initiation, setup, and delivery of VoIP sessions.

hackers People who break into computer systems. Those with malicious intent are sometimes considered *black hat* hackers and those who do so with a positive intent (such as vulnerability testing) are regularly referred to as *white hat* hackers. Of course, there are middle-ground hackers: *gray hats*.

half-duplex Any device that can only send or receive data at any given moment.

hardening Applying security hardware, software, and processes to your network to prevent bad things from happening.

hardware appliance Physical network device, typically a "box" that implements and runs software or firmware to perform one or a multitude of tasks. Could be a firewall, a switch, a router, a print server, or one of many other devices.

hardware tools   Tools such as cable testers, TDRs, OTDRs, certifiers, voltage event recorders, protocol analyzers, cable strippers, multimeters, tone probes/generators, butt sets, and punchdown tools used to configure and troubleshoot a network.

hash   A mathematical function used in cryptography that is run on a string of binary digits of any length that results in a value of some fixed length.

HDMI Ethernet Channel (HEC)   Ethernet-enabled HDMI ports that combine video, audio, and data on a single cable.

header   First section of a frame, packet, segment, or datagram.

heating, ventilation, and air conditioning (HVAC)   All of the equipment involved in heating and cooling the environments within a facility. These items include boilers, furnaces, air conditioners and ducts, plenums, and air passages.

hex (hexadecimal)   Hex symbols based on a numbering system of 16 (computer shorthand for binary numbers), using 10 digits and 6 letters to condense zeroes and ones to binary numbers. Hex is represented by digits 0 through 9 and alpha *A* through *F*, so that 09h has a value of 9, and 0Ah has a value of 10.

hierarchical name space   A naming scheme where the full name of each object includes its position within the hierarchy. An example of a hierarchical name is www.totalseminars.com, which includes not only the host name, but also the domain name. DNS uses a hierarchical name space scheme for fully qualified domain names (FQDNs).

high availability (HA)   A collection of technologies and procedures that work together to keep an application available at all times.

high-speed WAN Internet cards   A type of router expansion card that enables connection to two different ISPs.

history logs   Logs that track the history of how a user or users access network resources, or how network resources are accessed throughout the network.

home automation   The process of remotely controlling household devices, such as lights, thermostats, cameras, and washers and dryers.

home page   Either the Web page that your browser is set to use when it starts up or the main Web page for a business, organization, or person. Also, the main page in any collection of Web pages.

honeynet   The network created by a honeypot in order to lure in hackers.

honeypot   An area of a network that an administrator sets up for the express purpose of attracting a computer hacker. If a hacker takes the bait, the network's important resources are unharmed and network personnel can analyze the attack to predict and protect against future attacks, making the network more secure.

hop   The passage of a packet through a router.

hop count An older metric used by RIP routers. The number of routers that a packet must cross to get from a router to a given network. Hop counts were tracked and entered into the routing table within a router so the router could decide which interface was the best one to forward a packet.

horizontal cabling Cabling that connects the equipment room to the work areas.

host A single device (usually a computer) on a TCP/IP network that has an IP address; any device that can be the source or destination of a data packet. Also, a computer running multiple virtualized operating systems.

host ID The portion of an IP address that defines a specific machine in a subnet.

host name An individual computer name in the DNS naming convention.

host-based anti-malware Anti-malware software that is installed on individual systems, as opposed to the network at large.

host-based firewall A software firewall installed on a "host" that provides firewall services for just that machine, such as Windows Firewall.

hostname Command-line tool that returns the host name of the computer it is run on.

hosts file The predecessor to DNS, a static text file that resides on a computer and is used to resolve DNS host names to IP addresses. Automatically mapped to a host's DNS resolver cache in modern systems. The hosts file has no extension.

host-to-host Type of VPN connection in which a single host establishes a link with a remote, single host.

host-to-site Type of VPN connection where a host logs into a remote network as if it were any other local resource of that network.

hot site A complete backup facility to continue business operations. It is considered "hot" because it has all resources in place, including computers, network infrastructure, and current backups, so that operations can commence within hours after occupation.

hotspot A wireless access point that is connected to a cellular data network, typically 4G. The device can route Wi-Fi to and from the Internet. Hotspots can be permanent installations or portable. Many cellular telephones have the capability to become a hotspot.

HTML (Hypertext Markup Language) An ASCII-based script-like language for creating hypertext documents like those on the World Wide Web.

HTTP over SSL (HTTPS) A secure form of HTTP in which hypertext is encrypted by Transport Layer Security (TLS) before being sent onto the network. It is commonly used for Internet business transactions or any time where a secure connection is required. The name reflects the predecessor technology to TLS called Secure Sockets Layer (SSL). *See also* Hypertext Transfer Protocol (HTTP) *and* Secure Sockets Layer (SSL).

hub An electronic device that sits at the center of a star topology network, providing a common point for the connection of network devices. In a 10BaseT Ethernet network, the hub contains the electronic equivalent of a properly terminated bus cable. Hubs are rare today and have been replaced by switches.

human machine interface (HMI) In a distributed control system (DCS), a computer or set of controls that exists between a controller and a human operator. The human operates the HMI, which in turn interacts with the controller.

hybrid cloud A conglomeration of public and private cloud resources, connected to achieve some target result. There is no clear line that defines how much of a hybrid cloud infrastructure is private and how much is public.

hybrid topology A mix or blend of two different topologies. A star-bus topology is a hybrid of the star and bus topologies.

hypertext A document that has been marked up to enable a user to select words or pictures within the document, click them, and connect to further information. The basis of the World Wide Web.

Hypertext Markup Language (HTML) *See* HTML (Hypertext Markup Language).

Hypertext Transfer Protocol (HTTP) Extremely fast protocol used for network file transfers on the World Wide Web.

Hypertext Transfer Protocol over SSL (HTTPS) Protocol to transfer hypertext from a Web server to a client in a secure and encrypted fashion. Uses Transport Layer Security (TLS) rather than Secure Sockets Layer (SSL) to establish a secure communication connection between hosts. It then encrypts the hypertext before sending it from the Web server and decrypts it when it enters the client. HTTPS uses port 443.

hypervisor In virtualization, a layer of programming that creates, supports, and manages a virtual machine. Also known as a *virtual machine manager (VMM)*.

ICS (industrial control system) A centralized controller where the local controllers of a distributed control system (DCS) meet in order for global changes to be made.

ICS (Internet Connection Sharing) Also known simply as *Internet sharing*, the technique of enabling more than one computer to access the Internet simultaneously using a single Internet connection. When you use Internet sharing, you connect an entire LAN to the Internet using a single public IP address.

ICS server Unit in a distributed control system (DCS) that can be used to manage global changes to the controllers.

IEEE (Institute of Electrical and Electronics Engineers) The leading standards-setting group in the United States.

IEEE 802.2 IEEE subcommittee that defined the standards for Logical Link Control (LLC).

IEEE 802.3 IEEE subcommittee that defined the standards for CSMA/CD (a.k.a. *Ethernet*).

IEEE 802.11 IEEE subcommittee that defined the standards for wireless.

IEEE 802.14 IEEE subcommittee that defined the standards for cable modems.

IEEE 802.16 A wireless standard (also known as *WiMAX*) with a range of up to 30 miles.

IEEE 1284 The IEEE standard for the now obsolete parallel communication.

IEEE 1394 IEEE standard for FireWire communication.

IEEE 1905.1 Standard that integrates Ethernet, Wi-Fi, Ethernet over power lines, and Multimedia over Coax (MoCA).

IETF (Internet Engineering Task Force) The primary standards organization for the Internet.

ifconfig A command-line utility for Linux servers and workstations that displays the current TCP/IP configuration of the machine, similar to ipconfig for Windows systems. The newer command-line utility, ip, is replacing ifconfig on most systems.

IMAP (Internet Message Access Protocol) An alternative to POP3. Currently in its fourth revision, IMAP4 retrieves e-mail from an e-mail server like POP3, but has a number of features that make it a more popular e-mail tool. IMAP4 supports users creating folders on the e-mail server, for example, and allows multiple clients to access a single mailbox. IMAP uses TCP port 143.

impedance The amount of resistance to an electrical signal on a wire. It is used as a relative measure of the amount of data a cable can handle.

implicit deny The blocking of access to any entity that has not been specifically granted access. May also be known as *implicit deny any*. An example might be a whitelist ACL. Any station that is not in the whitelist is implicitly denied access.

in-band management Technology that enables managed devices such as a switch or router to be managed by any authorized host that is connected to that network.

inbound traffic Packets coming in from outside the network.

incident Any negative situation that takes place within an organization.

incident response Reaction to any negative situations that take place within an organization that can be stopped, contained, and remediated without outside resources.

incremental backup Backs up all files that have their archive bits turned on, meaning they have been changed since the last backup. This type of backup turns the archive bits off after the files have been backed up.

Independent Basic Service Set (IBSS) A basic unit of organization in wireless networks formed by two or more wireless nodes communicating in ad hoc mode.

Independent Computing Architecture (ICA) Citrix technology that defined communication between client and server in remote terminal programs.

industrial control system (ICS) *See* ICS (industrial control system).

infrared (IR) Line-of-sight networking technology that uses light pulses on the non-visible (to humans) spectrum.

Infrastructure as a Service (IaaS) Providing servers, switches, and routers to customers for a set rate. IaaS is commonly done by large-scale, global providers that use virtualization to minimize idle hardware, protect against data loss and downtime, and respond to spikes in demand. *See also* cloud computing.

infrastructure mode Mode in which wireless networks use one or more wireless access points to connect the wireless network nodes centrally. This configuration is similar to the *star topology* of a wired network.

inheritance A method of assigning user permissions, in which folder permissions flow downward into subfolders.

insider threats Potential for attacks on a system by people who work in the organization.

Institute of Electrical and Electronics Engineers (IEEE) *See* IEEE (Institute of Electrical and Electronics Engineers).

insulating jacket The external plastic covering of a fiber-optic cable.

Integrated Services Digital Network (ISDN) *See* ISDN (Integrated Services Digital Network).

integrity Network process that ensures data sent to a recipient is unchanged when it is received at the destination host.

interface identifier (interface ID) The second half (64 bits) of an IPv6 address, unique to a host.

interface monitor A program that tracks the bandwidth and utilization of one or more interfaces on one or more devices in order to monitor traffic on a network.

interframe gap (IFG) A short, predefined silence originally defined for CSMA/CD; also used in CSMA/CA. Also known as an *interframe space (IFS)*.

interframe space (IFS) *See* interframe gap (IFG).

intermediate distribution frame (IDF) The room where all the horizontal runs from all the work areas on a given floor in a building come together.

Intermediate System to Intermediate System (IS-IS) Protocol similar to, but not as popular as, OSPF, but with support for IPv6 since inception.

internal connections The connections between computers in a network.

internal firewall The firewall that sits between the perimeter network and the trusted network that houses all the organization's private servers and workstations.

internal network A private LAN, with a unique network ID, that resides behind a router.

internal threats All the things that a network's own users do to create problems on the network. Examples include accidental deletion of files, accidental damage to hardware devices or cabling, and abuse of rights and permissions.

Internet Assigned Numbers Authority (IANA) The organization originally responsible for assigning public IP addresses. IANA no longer directly assigns IP addresses, having delegated this to the five Regional Internet Registries. *See also* Regional Internet Registries (RIRs).

Internet Authentication Service (IAS) Popular RADIUS server for Microsoft environments.

Internet Connection Sharing (ICS) *See* ICS (Internet Connection Sharing).

Internet Control Message Protocol (ICMP) A TCP/IP protocol used to handle many low-level functions such as error reporting. ICMP messages are usually request and response pairs such as echo requests and responses, router solicitations and responses, and traceroute requests and responses. There are also unsolicited "responses" (advertisements) which consist of single packets. ICMP messages are connectionless.

Internet Corporation for Assigned Names and Numbers (ICANN) Entity that sits at the very top of the Internet hierarchy, with the authority to create new top-level domains (TLDs) for use on the Internet.

Internet Engineering Task Force (IETF) *See* IETF (Internet Engineering Task Force).

Internet Group Management Protocol (IGMP) Protocol that routers use to communicate with hosts to determine a "group" membership in order to determine which computers want to receive a multicast. Once a multicast has started, IGMP is responsible for maintaining the multicast as well as terminating at completion.

Internet Information Services (IIS) Microsoft's Web server program for managing Web servers.

Internet layer In the TCP/IP model, the layer that deals with the Internet Protocol, including IP addressing and routers.

Internet Message Access Protocol Version 4 (IMAP4) *See* IMAP (Internet Message Access Protocol).

Internet of Things (IoT) The billions of everyday objects that can communicating with each other, specifically over the Internet. These include smart home appliances, automobiles, video surveillance systems, and more.

Internet Protocol (IP) The Internet standard protocol that handles the logical naming for the TCP/IP protocol using IP addresses.

Internet Protocol Security (IPsec) Network layer encryption protocol.

Internet Protocol version 4 (IPv4) Protocol in which addresses consist of four sets of numbers, each number being a value between 0 and 255, using a period to separate the numbers (often called *dotted decimal* format). No IPv4 address may be all 0s or all 255s. Examples include 192.168.0.1 and 64.176.19.164.

Internet Protocol version 6 (IPv6) Protocol in which addresses consist of eight sets of four hexadecimal numbers, each number being a value between 0000 and ffff, using a colon to separate the numbers. No IP address may be all 0s or all ffffs. An example is fe80:ba98:7654:3210:0800:200c:00cf:1234.

Internet Small Computer System Interface (iSCSI) A protocol that enables the SCSI command set to be transported over a TCP/IP network from a client to an iSCSI-based storage system. iSCSI is popular with storage area network (SAN) systems.

interVLAN routing A feature on some switches to provide routing between VLANs.

intranet A private TCP/IP network inside a company or organization.

Intra-Site Automatic Tunnel Addressing Protocol (ISATAP) An IPv6 tunneling protocol that adds the IPv4 address to an IPv6 prefix.

intrusion detection system (IDS)/intrusion prevention system (IPS) An application (often running on a dedicated IDS box) that inspects incoming packets, looking for active intrusions. The difference between an IDS and an IPS is that an IPS can react to an attack.

ip Linux terminal command that displays the current TCP/IP configuration of the machine; similar to Windows' ipconfig and macOS's ifconfig.

IP *See* Internet Protocol (IP).

IP address The numeric address of a computer connected to a TCP/IP network, such as the Internet. IPv4 addresses are 32 bits long, written as four octets of 8-bit binary. IPv6 addresses are 128 bits long, written as eight sets of four hexadecimal characters. IP addresses must be matched with a valid subnet mask, which identifies the part of the IP address that is the network ID and the part that is the host ID.

IP Address Management (IPAM) Software that includes at a minimum a DHCP server and a DNS server that are specially designed to work together to administer IP addresses for a network.

IP addressing The processes of assigning IP addresses to networks and hosts.

IP camera Still-frame or video camera with a network interface and TCP/IP transport protocols to send output to a network resource or destination.

IP filtering A method of blocking packets based on IP addresses.

IP helper Command used in Cisco switches and routers to enable, disable, and manage internetwork forwarding of certain protocols such as DHCP, TFTP, Time Service, TACACS, DNS, NetBIOS, and others. The command is technically `ip helperaddress`.

ipconfig A command-line utility for Windows that displays the current TCP/IP configuration of the machine; similar to macOS's ifconfig and UNIX/Linux's ip.

IPsec VPN A virtual private networking technology that uses IPsec tunneling for security.

IRC (Internet Relay Chat) An online group discussion. Also called *chat*.

ISDN (Integrated Services Digital Network) The CCITT (Comité Consutatif Internationale Téléphonique et Télégraphique) standard that defines a digital method for telephone communications. Originally designed to replace the current analog telephone systems. ISDN lines have telephone numbers and support up to 128-Kbps transfer rates. ISDN also allows data and voice to share a common phone line. Never very popular, ISDN is now relegated to specialized niches.

ISP (Internet service provider) An institution that provides access to the Internet in some form, usually for a fee.

IT (information technology) The business of computers, electronic communications, and electronic commerce.

Java A network-oriented programming language invented by Sun Microsystems (acquired by Oracle) and specifically designed for writing programs that can be safely downloaded to your computer through the Internet and immediately run without fear of viruses or other harm to your computer or files. Using small Java programs (called *applets*), Web pages can include functions such as animations, calculators, and other fancy tricks.

jitter A delay in completing a transmission of all the frames in a message; caused by excessive machines on a network.

jumbo frames Usually 9000 bytes long, though technically anything over 1500 bytes qualifies, these frames make large data transfer easier and more efficient than using the standard frame size.

just a bunch of disks (JBOD) An array of hard drives that are simply connected with no RAID implementations.

K Most commonly refers to the binary quantity 1024. For instance, 640K means 640 × 1024, or 655,360. Just to add some extra confusion to the IT industry, *K* is often misspoken as "kilo," the metric value for 1000. For example, 10KB, spoken as "10 kilobytes," means 10,240 bytes rather than 10,000 bytes. Finally, when discussing frequencies, K means 1000. So, 1 KHz = 1000 kilohertz.

kbps (kilobits per second) Data transfer rate.

Kerberos An authentication standard designed to allow different operating systems and applications to authenticate each other.

Key Distribution Center (KDC) System for granting authentication in Kerberos.

key fob Small device that can be easily carried in a pocket or purse or attached to a key ring. This device is used to identify the person possessing it for the purpose of granting or denying access to resources such as electronic doors.

key pair Name for the two keys generated in asymmetric-key algorithm systems.

keypad The device in which an alphanumeric code or password that is assigned to a specific individual for a particular asset can be entered.

kilohertz (KHz) A unit of measure that equals a frequency of 1000 cycles per second.

LAN (local area network) A group of PCs connected together via cabling, radio, or infrared that use this connectivity to share resources such as printers and mass storage.

last mile The connection between a central office and individual users in a telephone system.

latency A measure of a signal's delay.

layer A grouping of related tasks involving the transfer of information. Also, a particular level of the OSI seven-layer model, for example, Physical layer, Data Link layer, and so forth.

Layer 2 switch Any device that filters and forwards frames based on the MAC addresses of the sending and receiving machines. What is normally called a "switch" is actually a "Layer 2 switch."

Layer 2 Tunneling Protocol (L2TP) A VPN protocol developed by Cisco that can be run on almost any connection imaginable. LT2P has no authentication or encryption but uses IPsec for all its security needs.

Layer 3 switch Also known as a *router*, filters and forwards data packets based on the IP addresses of the sending and receiving machines.

LC (local connector) A duplex type of small form factor (SFF) fiber connector, designed to accept two fiber cables. *See also* local connector (LC).

LED (light emitting diode) Solid-state device that vibrates at luminous frequencies when current is applied.

leeching Using another person's wireless connection to the Internet without that person's permission.

legacy mode One of three modes used with 802.11n wireless networks where the wireless access point (WAP) sends out separate packets just for legacy devices.

legal hold The process of an organization preserving and organizing data in anticipation of or in reaction to a pending legal issue.

light leakage The type of interference caused by bending a piece of fiber-optic cable past its maximum bend radius. Light bleeds through the cladding, causing signal distortion and loss.

light meter An optical power meter used by technicians to measure the amount of light lost through light leakage in a fiber cable.

lights-out management Special "computer within a computer" features built into better servers, designed to give you access to a server even when the server itself is shut off.

Lightweight Access Point Protocol (LWAPP) Protocol used in wireless networks that enables interoperability between thin and thick clients and WAPs.

Lightweight Directory Access Protocol (LDAP) A protocol used to query and change a database used by the network. LDAP uses TCP port 389 by default.

Lightweight Extensible Authentication Protocol (LEAP) A proprietary EAP authentication used almost exclusively by Cisco wireless products. LEAP is an interesting combination of MS-CHAP authentication between a wireless client and a RADIUS server.

line tester A device used by technicians to check the integrity of telephone wiring. Can be used on a twisted-pair line to see if it is good, dead, or reverse wired, or if there is AC voltage on the line.

link aggregation Connecting multiple NICs in tandem to increase bandwidth in smaller increments. *See also* NIC teaming.

Link Aggregation Control Protocol (LACP) IEEE specification of certain features and options to automate the negotiation, management, load balancing, and failure modes of aggregated ports.

Link layer In the TCP/IP model, any part of the network that deals with complete frames.

link light An LED on NICs, hubs, and switches that lights up to show good connection between the devices. Called the *network connection LED status indicator* on the CompTIA Network+ exam.

link segments Segments that link other segments together but are unpopulated or have no computers directly attached to them.

link state Type of dynamic routing protocol that announces only changes to routing tables, as opposed to entire routing tables. Compare to distance vector routing protocols. *See also* distance vector.

link status A network analyzer report on how good the connection is between two systems.

link-local address The address that a computer running IPv6 gives itself after first booting. The first 64 bits of a link-local address are always FE80::/64.

Linux The popular open source operating system, derived from UNIX.

list of requirements A list of all the things you'll need to do to set up your SOHO network, as well as the desired capabilities of the network.

listening port A socket that is prepared to respond to any IP packets destined for that socket's port number.

LMHOSTS file A static text file that resides on a computer and is used to resolve NetBIOS names to IP addresses. The LMHOSTS file is checked before the machine sends a name resolution request to a WINS name server. The LMHOSTS file has no extension.

load balancing The process of taking several servers and making them look like a single server, spreading processing and supporting bandwidth needs.

local Refers to the computer(s), server(s), and/or LAN that a user is physically using or that is in the same room or building.

local area network (LAN) *See* LAN (local area network).

local authentication A login screen prompting a user to enter a user name and password to log into a Windows, macOS, or Linux computer.

local connector (LC) One popular type of small form factor (SFF) connector, considered by many to be the predominant fiber connector. While there are several labels ascribed to the "LC" term, it is most commonly referred to as a *local connector. See also* LC (local connector).

Local Exchange Carrier (LEC) A company that provides local telephone service to individual customers.

local user accounts The accounts unique to a single Windows system. Stored in the local system's registry.

localhost The hosts file alias for the loopback address of 127.0.0.1, referring to the current machine.

lock In this context, a physical device that prevents access to essential assets of an organization, such as servers, without a key.

log Information about the performance of some particular aspect of a system that is stored for future reference. Logs are also called *counters* in Performance Monitor or *facilities* in syslog.

log management The process of providing proper security and maintenance for log files to ensure the files are organized and safe.

logic bomb Code written to execute when certain conditions are met, usually with malicious intent.

logical address A programmable network address, unlike a physical address that is burned into ROM.

logical addressing As opposed to physical addressing, the process of assigning organized blocks of logically associated network addresses to create smaller manageable networks called subnets. IP addresses are one example of logical addressing.

Logical Link Control (LLC) The aspect of the NIC that talks to the operating system, places outbound data coming "down" from the upper layers of software into frames, and creates the FCS on each frame. The LLC also deals with incoming frames by processing those addressed to the NIC and erasing ones addressed to other machines on the network.

logical network diagram A document that shows the broadcast domains and individual IP addresses for all devices on the network. Only critical switches and routers are shown.

logical topology A network topology defined by signal paths as opposed to the physical layout of the cables. *See also* physical topology.

Long Term Evolution (LTE) Better known as 4G, a wireless data standard with theoretical download speeds of 300 Mbps and upload speeds of 75 Mbps.

looking glass site Web site that enables a technician to run various diagnostic tools from outside their network.

loopback adapter *See* loopback plug.

loopback address Sometimes called the localhost, a reserved IP address used for internal testing: 127.0.0.1.

loopback plug Network connector that connects back into itself, used to connect loopback tests.

loopback test A special test often included in diagnostic software that sends data out of the NIC and checks to see if it comes back.

MAC (media access control) address Unique 48-bit address assigned to each network card. IEEE assigns blocks of possible addresses to various NIC manufacturers to help ensure that each address is unique. The Data Link layer of the OSI seven-layer model uses MAC addresses for locating machines.

MAC address filtering A method of limiting access to a wireless network based on the physical addresses of wireless NICs.

MAC filtering *See* MAC address filtering.

MAC reservation IP address assigned to a specific MAC address in a DHCP server.

MAC-48 The unique 48-bit address assigned to a network interface card. This is also known as the *MAC address* or the *EUI-48*.

macro A specially written application macro (collection of commands) that performs the same functions as a virus. These macros normally autostart when the application is run and then make copies of themselves, often propagating across networks.

mailbox Special holding area on an e-mail server that separates out e-mail for each user.

main distribution frame (MDF) The room in a building that stores the demarc, telephone cross-connects, and LAN cross-connects.

maintenance window The time it takes to implement and thoroughly test a network change.

malicious user A user who consciously attempts to access, steal, or damage resources.

malware Any program or code (macro, script, and so on) that's designed to do something on a system or network that you don't want to have happen.

man in the middle A hacking attack where a person inserts him- or herself into a conversation between two others, covertly intercepting traffic thought to be only between those other people.

managed device   Networking devices, such as routers and advanced switches, that must be configured to use.

managed network   Network that is monitored by the SNMP protocol consisting of SNMP managed devices, management information base (MIB) items, and SNMP manager(s).

managed switch   *See* managed device.

management information base (MIB)   SNMP's version of a server. *See* Simple Network Management Protocol (SNMP).

mandatory access control (MAC)   A security model in which every resource is assigned a label that defines its security level. If the user lacks that security level, they do not get access.

mantrap   An entryway with two successive locked doors and a small space between them providing one-way entry or exit. This is a security measure taken to prevent tailgating.

manual tunnel   A simple point-to-point connection between two IPv6 networks. As a tunnel, it uses IPsec encryption.

material safety data sheet (MSDS)   Document that describes the safe handling procedures for any potentially hazardous, toxic, or unsafe material.

maximum transmission unit (MTU)   Specifies the largest size of a data unit in a communications protocol, such as Ethernet.

MB (megabyte)   1,048,576 bytes.

MD5 (Message-Digest Algorithm Version 5)   A popular hashing function.

mean time between failures (MTBF)   A factor typically applied to a hardware component that represents the manufacturer's best guess (based on historical data) regarding how much time will pass between major failures of that component.

mean time to recovery (MTTR)   The estimated amount of time it takes to recover from a hardware component failure.

Mechanical Transfer Registered Jack (MT-RJ)   The first type of small form factor (SFF) fiber connector, still in common use.

Media Access Control (MAC)   The part of a NIC that remembers the NIC's own MAC address and attaches that address to outgoing frames.

media converter   A device that lets you interconnect different types of Ethernet cable.

Media Gateway Control Protocol (MGCP)   A protocol that is designed to be a complete VoIP or video presentation connection and session controller. MGCP uses TCP ports 2427 and 2727.

medianet A network of far-flung routers and servers that provides sufficient bandwidth for video teleconferencing (VTC) via quality of service (QoS) and other tools.

mega- A prefix that usually stands for the binary quantity 1,048,576. One megabyte is 1,048,576 bytes. One megahertz, however, is 1,000,000 hertz. Sometimes shortened to *meg*, as in "a 286 has an address space of 16 megs."

memorandum of understanding (MOU) A document that defines an agreement between two parties in situations where a legal contract is not appropriate.

mesh topology Topology in which each computer has a direct or indirect connection to every other computer in a network. Any node on the network can forward traffic to other nodes. Popular in cellular and many wireless networks.

Metasploit A unique tool that enables a penetration tester to use a massive library of attacks as well as tweak those attacks for unique penetrations.

metric Relative value that defines the "cost" of using a particular route.

metro Ethernet A metropolitan area network (MAN) based on the Ethernet standard.

metropolitan area network (MAN) Multiple computers connected via cabling, radio, leased phone lines, or infrared that are within the same city. A perfect example of a MAN is the Tennessee city Chattanooga's gigabit network available to all citizens, the Chattanooga Gig.

MHz (megahertz) A unit of measure that equals a frequency of 1 million cycles per second.

Microsoft Baseline Security Analyzer (MBSA) Microsoft-designed tool to test individual Windows-based PCs for vulnerabilities.

MIME (Multipurpose Internet Mail Extensions) A standard for attaching binary files, such as executables and images, to the Internet's text-based mail (24-Kbps packet size).

Miredo An open source implementation of Teredo for Linux and some other UNIX-based systems. It is a NAT-traversal IPv6 tunneling protocol.

mirroring Also called *drive mirroring*, reading and writing data at the same time to two drives for fault-tolerance purposes. Considered *RAID level 1*.

mixed mode Also called *high-throughput*, or *802.11a-ht/802.11g-ht*, one of three modes used with 802.11n wireless networks wherein the wireless access point (WAP) sends special packets that support older standards yet can also improve the speed of those standards via 802.

modal distortion A light distortion problem unique to multimode fiber-optic cable.

model A simplified representation of a real object or process. In the case of networking, models represent logical tasks and subtasks that are required to perform network communication.

modem (modulator-demodulator) A device that converts both digital bit streams into analog signals (modulation) and incoming analog signals back into digital signals (demodulation). Most commonly used to interconnect telephone lines to computers.

modulation techniques The various multiplexing and demultiplexing technologies and protocols, both analog and digital.

modulator-demodulator (modem) *See* modem (modulator-demodulator).

monlist A query that asks an NTP server about the traffic going on between itself and peers.

motion detection system A feature of some video surveillance systems that starts and stops recordings based on actions caught by the camera(s).

mounting bracket Bracket that acts as a holder for a faceplate in cable installations.

MS-CHAP Microsoft's dominant variation of the CHAP protocol, uses a slightly more advanced encryption protocol.

MTU (maximum transmission unit) *See* maximum transmission unit (MTU).

MTU black hole When a router's firewall features block ICMP requests, making MTU worthless.

MTU mismatch The situation when your network's packets are so large that they must be fragmented to fit into your ISP's packets.

multicast Method of sending a packet in which the sending computer sends it to a group of interested computers.

multicast addresses A set of reserved addresses designed to go from one system to any system using one of the reserved addresses.

multifactor authentication A form of authentication where a user must use two or more factors to prove his or her identity—for example, some sort of physical token that, when inserted, prompts for a password.

multilayer switch A switch that has functions that operate at multiple layers of the OSI seven-layer model.

multilink PPP A communications protocol that logically joins multiple PPP connections, such as a modem connection, to aggregate the throughput of the links.

multimeter A tool for testing voltage (AC and DC), resistance, and continuity.

multimode Type of fiber-optic cable with a large-diameter core that supports multiple modes of propagation. The large diameter simplifies connections, but has drawbacks related to distance.

multimode fiber (MMF) Type of fiber-optic cable that uses LEDs.

multiple in/multiple out (MIMO) A feature in 802.11 WAPs that enables them to make multiple simultaneous connections.

multiplexer A device that merges information from multiple input channels to a single output channel.

Multiprotocol Label Switching (MPLS) A router feature that labels certain data to use a desired connection. It works with any type of packet switching (even Ethernet) to force certain types of data to use a certain path.

multisource agreement (MSA) A document that details the interoperability of network hardware from a variety of manufacturers.

multiuser MIMO (MU-MIMO) Feature of 802.11ac networking that enables a WAP to broadcast to multiple users simultaneously.

MX records Records within DNS servers that are used by SMTP servers to determine where to send mail.

My Traceroute (mtr) Terminal command in Linux that dynamically displays the route a packet is taking. Similar to traceroute.

name resolution A method that enables one computer on the network to locate another to establish a session. All network protocols perform name resolution in one of two ways: either via *broadcast* or by providing some form of *name server*.

name server A computer whose job is to know the name of every other computer on the network.

NAT (Network Address Translation) *See* Network Address Translation (NAT).

NAT translation table Special database in a NAT router that stores destination IP addresses and ephemeral source ports from outgoing packets and compares them against returning packets.

NAT64 A transition mechanism that embeds IPv4 packets into IPv6 packets for network traversal.

native VLAN The specified VLAN designation that will be assigned to all untagged frames entering a trunk port in a switch.

nbtstat A command-line utility used to check the current NetBIOS name cache on a particular machine. The utility compares NetBIOS names to their corresponding IP addresses.

near field communication (NFC) A low-speed, short-range networking technology designed for (among other things) small-value monetary transactions.

near-end crosstalk (NEXT) Crosstalk at the same end of a cable from which the signal is being generated.

neighbor advertisement IPv6 packet sent in response to a multicast neighbor solicitation packet.

neighbor discovery *See* Neighbor Discovery Protocol (NDP).

Neighbor Discovery Protocol (NDP) IPv6 protocol that enables hosts to configure automatically their own IPv6 addresses and get configuration information like routers and DNS servers.

neighbor solicitation IPv6 process of finding a MAC address of a local host, given its IPv6 address.

Nessus Popular and extremely comprehensive vulnerability testing tool.

NetBEUI (NetBIOS Extended User Interface) Microsoft's first networking protocol, designed to work with NetBIOS. NetBEUI is long obsolesced by TCP/IP. NetBEUI did not support routing.

NetBIOS (Network Basic Input/Output System) A protocol that operates at the Session layer of the OSI seven-layer model. This protocol creates and manages connections based on the names of the computers involved.

NetBIOS name A computer name that identifies both the specific machine and the functions that machine performs. A NetBIOS name consists of 16 characters: the first 15 are an alphanumeric name, and the 16th is a special suffix that identifies the role the machine plays.

NetBIOS over TCP/IP (NetBT) A Microsoft-created protocol that enables NetBIOS naming information to be transported over TCP/IP networks. The result is that Microsoft naming services can operate on a TCP/IP network without the need for DNS services.

NetBIOS/NetBEUI *See* NetBEUI; *see also* NetBIOS.

NetFlow The primary tool used to monitor packet flow on a network.

NetFlow collector Component process of NetFlow that captures and saves data from a NetFlow-enabled device's cache for future NetFlow analysis.

netstat A universal command-line utility used to examine the TCP/IP connections open on a given host.

network A collection of two or more devices interconnected by telephone lines, coaxial cables, satellite links, radio, and/or some other communication technique. A computer *network* is a group of computers that are connected together and communicate with one another for a common purpose. Computer networks support "people and organization" networks, users who also share a common purpose for communicating.

network access control (NAC) Control over information, people, access, machines, and everything in between.

network access policy Rules that define who can access the network, how it can be accessed, and what resources of the network can be used.

network access server (NAS) System that controls the modems in a RADIUS network.

Network Address Translation (NAT) A means of translating a system's IP address into another IP address before sending it out to a larger network. NAT manifests itself by a NAT program that runs on a system or a router. A network using NAT provides the systems on the network with private IP addresses. The system running the NAT software has two interfaces: one connected to the network and the other connected to the larger network.

The NAT program takes packets from the client systems bound for the larger network and translates their internal private IP addresses to its own public IP address, enabling many systems to share a single IP address.

network appliance Feature-packed network box that incorporates numerous processes such as routing, Network Address Translation (NAT), switching, intrusion detection systems, firewall, and more.

Network as a Service (NaaS) The act of renting virtual server space over the Internet. *See also* cloud computing.

network attached storage (NAS) A dedicated file server that has its own file system and typically uses hardware and software designed for serving and storing files.

network blocks Also called *blocks*, contiguous ranges of IP addresses that are assigned to organizations and end users by IANA.

network closet An equipment room that holds servers, switches, routers, and other network gear.

network design The process of gathering together and planning the layout for the equipment needed to create a network.

network diagram An illustration that shows devices on a network and how they connect.

network ID A number used in IP networks to identify the network on which a device or machine exists.

network interface A device by which a system accesses a network. In most cases, this is a NIC or a modem.

network interface card (NIC) Traditionally, an expansion card that enables a PC to link physically to a network. Modern computers now use built-in NICs, no longer requiring physical cards, but the term "NIC" is still very common.

network interface unit (NIU) Another name for a demarc. *See* demarc.

Network layer Layer 3 of the OSI seven-layer model. *See also* Open Systems Interconnection (OSI) seven-layer model.

Network Management Software (NMS) Tools that enable you to describe, visualize, and configure an entire network.

network management station (NMS) SNMP console computer that runs the SNMP manager software.

network map A highly detailed illustration of a network, down to the individual computers. A network map will show IP addresses, ports, protocols, and more.

network name Another name for the *Service Set Identifier (SSID)*.

network operations center (NOC) A centralized location for techs and administrators to manage all aspects of a network.

network prefix The first 64 bits of an IPv6 address that identifies the network.

network protocol Special software that exists in every network-capable operating system that acts to create unique identifiers for each system. It also creates a set of communication rules for issues like how to handle data chopped up into multiple packets and how to deal with routers. TCP/IP is the dominant network protocol today.

network segmentation Separating network assets through various means, such as with VLANs or with a DMZ, to protect against access by malicious actors.

network share A shared resource on a network.

network technology The techniques, components, and practices involved in creating and operating computer-to-computer links.

network threat Any number of things that share one essential feature: the potential to damage network data, machines, or users.

Network Time Protocol (NTP) Protocol that gives the current time.

network topology Refers to the way that cables and other pieces of hardware connect to one another.

network-based anti-malware A single source server that holds current anti-malware software. Multiple systems can access and run the software from that server. The single site makes the software easier to update and administer than anti-malware installed on individual systems.

network-based firewall Firewall, perhaps implemented in a gateway router or as a proxy server, through which all network traffic must pass inspection to be allowed or blocked.

newsgroup The name for a discussion group on Usenet.

next hop The next router a packet should go to at any given point.

next-generation firewall (NGFW) Network protection device that functions at multiple layers of the OSI model to tackle traffic no traditional firewall can filter alone.

NFS (Network File System) A TCP/IP file system–sharing protocol that enables systems to treat files on a remote machine as though they were local files. NFS uses TCP port 2049, but many users choose alternative port numbers. Though still somewhat popular and heavily supported, NFS has been largely replaced by Samba/CIFS. *See also* Samba *and* Common Internet File System (CIFS).

NIC teaming Connecting multiple NICs in tandem to increase bandwidth in smaller increments. *See also* link aggregation.

Nmap A network utility designed to scan a network and create a map. Frequently used as a vulnerability scanner.

node A member of a network or a point where one or more functional units interconnect transmission lines.

noise   Undesirable signals bearing no desired information and frequently capable of introducing errors into the communication process.

non-discovery mode   A setting for Bluetooth devices that effectively hides them from other Bluetooth devices.

non-persistent agent   Software used in posture assessment that does not stay resident in client station memory. It is executed prior to login and may stay resident during the login session but is removed from client RAM when the login or session is complete. The agent presents the security characteristics to the access control server, which then decides to allow, deny, or redirect the connection.

nonrepudiation   Not being able to deny having sent a message.

normal backup   A full backup of every selected file on a system. This type of backup turns off the archive bit after the backup.

ns (nanosecond)   A billionth of a second. Light travels a little over 11 inches in 1 ns.

NS records   Records that list the authoritative DNS servers for a domain.

nslookup   A very handy tool that advanced techs use to query DNS servers.

NTFS (NT File System)   A file system for hard drives that enables object-level security, long filename support, compression, and encryption. NTFS 4.0 debuted with Windows NT 4.0. Later Windows versions continue to update NTFS.

NTFS permissions   Groupings of what Microsoft calls special permissions that have names like Execute, Read, and Write, and that allow or disallow users certain access to files.

NTLDR   A Windows NT/2000/XP/2003 boot file. Launched by the MBR or MFT, NTLDR looks at the BOOT.INI configuration file for any installed operating systems.

ntpdc   A command that puts the NTP server into interactive mode in order to submit queries.

object   A group of related counters used in Windows logging utilities.

OEM (Original Equipment Manufacturer)   Contrary to the name, does not create original hardware, but rather purchases components from manufacturers and puts them together in systems under its own brand name. Dell, Inc. and Gateway, Inc., for example, are for the most part OEMs. Apple, Inc., which manufactures most of the components for its own Mac-branded machines, is not an OEM. Also known as *value-added resellers (VARs)*.

off-boarding   The process of confirming that mobile devices leaving the control of the organization do not store any proprietary applications or data.

offsite   The term for a virtual computer accessed and stored remotely.

Ohm rating   Electronic measurement of a cable's or an electronic component's impedance.

omnidirectional antenna   Technology used in most WAPs that send wireless signals in all directions equally.

on-boarding The process of verifying that new mobile devices appearing in the organization's infrastructure are secure and safe to use within the organization.

onsite The term for a virtual computer stored at your location.

open port *See* listening port.

Open Shortest Path First (OSPF) An interior gateway routing protocol developed for IP networks based on the shortest path first or *link state algorithm.*

open source Applications and operating systems that offer access to their source code; this enables developers to modify applications and operating systems easily to meet their specific needs.

Open Systems Interconnection (OSI) An international standard suite of protocols defined by the International Organization for Standardization (ISO) that implements the OSI seven-layer model for network communications between computers.

Open Systems Interconnection (OSI) seven-layer model An architecture model based on the OSI protocol suite, which defines and standardizes the flow of data between computers. The following lists the seven layers:

- **Layer 1** The *Physical layer* defines hardware connections and turns binary into physical pulses (electrical or light). Cables operate at the Physical layer.

- **Layer 2** The *Data Link layer* identifies devices on the Physical layer. MAC addresses are part of the Data Link layer. Switches operate at the Data Link layer.

- **Layer 3** The *Network layer* moves packets between computers on different networks. Routers operate at the Network layer. IP operates at the Network layer.

- **Layer 4** The *Transport layer* breaks data down into manageable chunks with TCP, at this layer. UDP also operates at the Transport layer.

- **Layer 5** The *Session layer* manages connections between machines. Sockets operate at the Session layer.

- **Layer 6** The *Presentation layer,* which can also manage data encryption, hides the differences among various types of computer systems.

- **Layer 7** The *Application layer* provides tools for programs to use to access the network (and the lower layers). HTTP, SSL/TLS, FTP, SMTP, DNS, DHCP, and IMAP are all examples of protocols that operate at the Application layer.

OpenSSH A series of secure programs developed by the OpenBSD organization to fix the limitation of Secure Shell (SSH) of only being able to handle one session per tunnel.

operating system (OS) The set of programming that enables a program to interact with the computer and provides an interface between the PC and the user. Examples are Microsoft Windows 10, Apple macOS, and SUSE Linux.

operator In a distributed control system, the operator is a human who runs the computer-controlled resources through a human machine interface. *See also* human machine interface (HMI).

Optical Carrier (OC) Specification used to denote the optical data carrying capacity (in Mbps) of fiber-optic cables in networks conforming to the SONET standard. The OC standard is an escalating series of speeds, designed to meet the needs of medium-to-large corporations. SONET establishes OCs from 51.8 Mbps (OC-1) to 39.8 Gbps (OC-768).

optical power meter Device that measures light intensity of light pulses within or at the terminal ends of fiber-optic cables.

optical time domain reflectometer (OTDR) Tester for fiber-optic cable that determines continuity and reports the location of cable breaks.

organizationally unique identifier (OUI) The first 24 bits of a MAC address, assigned to the NIC manufacturer by the IEEE.

orthogonal frequency-division multiplexing (OFDM) A spread-spectrum broadcasting method that combines the multiple frequencies of DSSS with FHSS's hopping capability.

OS (operating system) *See* operating system (OS).

oscilloscope A device that gives a graphical/visual representation of signal levels over a period of time.

OSPF (Open Shortest Path First) *See* Open Shortest Path First (OSPF).

outbound traffic Packets leaving the network from within it.

out-of-band management Method to connect to and administer a managed device such as a switch or router that does not use a standard network-connected host as the administrative console. A computer connected to the console port of a switch is an example of out-of-band management.

overlay tunnel Enables two IPv6 networks to connect over an IPv4 network by encapsulating the IPv6 packets within IPv4 headers, transporting them across the IPv4 network, then de-encapsulating the IPv6 data.

packet Basic component of communication over a network. A group of bits of fixed maximum size and well-defined format that is switched and transmitted as a complete whole through a network. It contains source and destination address, data, and control information. *See also* frame.

packet analyzer A program that reads the capture files from packet sniffers and analyzes them based on monitoring needs.

packet filtering A mechanism that blocks any incoming or outgoing packet from a particular IP address or range of IP addresses. Also known as *IP filtering*.

packet sniffer A tool that intercepts and logs network packets.

pad Extra data added to an Ethernet frame to bring the data up to the minimum required size of 64 bytes.

partially meshed topology A mesh topology in which not all of the nodes are directly connected.

passive optical network (PON) A fiber architecture that uses a single fiber to the neighborhood switch and then individual fiber runs to each final destination.

password A series of characters that enables a user to gain access to a file, a folder, a PC, or a program.

Password Authentication Protocol (PAP) The oldest and most basic form of authentication and also the least safe because it sends all passwords in cleartext.

patch antenna Flat, plate-shaped antenna that generates a half-sphere beam; used for broadcasting to a select area.

patch cables Short (2 to 5 foot) UTP cables that connect patch panels to switches.

patch management The process of regularly updating operating systems and applications to avoid security threats.

patch panel A panel containing a row of female connectors (ports) that terminate the horizontal cabling in the equipment room. Patch panels facilitate cabling organization and provide protection to horizontal cabling. *See also* vertical cross-connect.

Path MTU Discovery (PMTU) A method for determining the best MTU setting that works by adding a new feature called the "Don't Fragment (DF) flag" to the IP packet.

path vector Routing protocol in which routers maintain path information. This information gets updated dynamically. *See* Border Gateway Protocol (BGP-4).

pathping Command-line tool that combines the features of the ping command and the tracert/traceroute commands.

payload The primary data that is sent from a source network device to a destination network device.

PBX (private branch exchange) A private phone system used within an organization.

peer-to-peer (P2P) A network in which each machine can act as either a client or a server.

peer-to-peer mode *See* ad hoc mode.

penetration testing (pentesting) An authorized, network hacking process that will identify real-world weaknesses in network security and document the findings.

Performance Monitor (PerfMon) The Windows logging utility.

peripherals Noncomputer devices on a network; for example, fax machines, printers, or scanners.

permanent DoS (PDoS) An attack that damages a targeted machine, such as a router or server, and renders that machine inoperable.

permissions Sets of attributes that network administrators assign to users and groups that define what they can do to resources.

persistent agent In network access control systems, a small scanning program that, once installed on the computer, stays installed and runs every time the computer boots up. Composed of modules that perform a thorough inventory of each security-oriented element in the computer.

persistent connection A connection to a shared folder or drive that the computer immediately reconnects to at logon.

personal area network (PAN) The network created among Bluetooth devices such as smartphones, tablets, printers, keyboards, mice, and so on.

phishing A social engineering technique where the attacker poses as a trusted source in order to obtain sensitive information.

physical address An address burned into a ROM chip on a NIC. A MAC address is an example of a physical address.

Physical Contact (PC) connector Family of fiber-optic connectors that enforces direct physical contact between two optical fibers being connected.

Physical layer *See* Open Systems Interconnection (OSI) seven-layer model.

physical network diagram A document that shows all of the physical connections on a network. Cabling type, protocol, and speed are also listed for each connection.

physical topology The manner in which the physical components of a network are arranged.

ping (packet internet groper) A small network message sent by a computer to check for the presence and response of another system. Also, a command-line utility to check the "up/down" status of an IP addressed host. A ping uses ICMP packets. *See also* Internet Control Message Protocol (ICMP).

ping –6 A command-line utility to check the "up/down" status of an IP addressed host. The "–6" switch included on the command line, using the Windows version of ping, specifies that the host under test has an IPv6 address.

ping6 Linux command-line utility specifically designed to ping hosts with an IPv6 address.

plain old telephone service (POTS) *See* public switched telephone network (PSTN).

plaintext Also called *cleartext*, unencrypted data in an accessible format that can be read without special utilities.

platform Hardware environment that supports the running of a computer system.

Platform as a Service (PaaS) A complete deployment and management system that gives programmers all the tools they need to administer and maintain a Web application. *See also* cloud computing.

plenum Usually a space between a building's false ceiling and the floor above it. Most of the wiring for networks is located in this space. Plenum is also a fire rating for network cabling.

plenum-rated cable Network cable type that resists burning and does not give off excessive smoke or noxious fumes when burned.

Point Coordination Function (PCF) A method of collision avoidance defined by the 802.11 standard but has yet to be implemented. *See also* Distributed Coordination Function (DCF).

point-to-multipoint topology Topology in which one device communicates with more than one other device on a network.

Point-to-Point Protocol (PPP) A protocol that enables a computer to connect to the Internet through a dial-in connection and to enjoy most of the benefits of a direct connection. PPP is considered to be superior to the Serial Line Internet Protocol (SLIP) because of its error detection and data compression features, which SLIP lacks, and the capability to use dynamic IP addresses.

Point-to-Point Protocol over Ethernet (PPPoE) A protocol that was originally designed to encapsulate PPP frames into Ethernet frames. Used by DSL providers to force customers to log into their DSL connections instead of simply connecting automatically.

point-to-point topology Network topology in which two computers are directly connected to each other without any other intervening connection components such as hubs or switches.

Point-to-Point Tunneling Protocol (PPTP) A protocol that works with PPP to provide a secure data link between computers using encryption.

pointer record (PTR) A record that points IP addresses to host names. *See also* reverse lookup zone.

polyvinyl chloride (PVC) A material used for the outside insulation and jacketing of most cables. Also a fire rating for a type of cable that has no significant fire protection.

port (logical connection) In TCP/IP, 16-bit numbers between 0 and 65535 assigned to a particular TCP/IP process or application. For example, Web servers use port 80 (HTTP) to transfer Web pages to clients. The first 1024 ports are called *well-known ports*. They have been pre-assigned and generally refer to TCP/IP processes and applications that have been around for a long time.

port (physical connector) In general, the portion of a computer through which a peripheral device may communicate, such as video, USB, serial, and network ports. In the context of networking, the jacks found in computers, switches, routers, and network-enabled peripherals into which network cables are plugged.

Port Address Translation (PAT) The most commonly used form of Network Address Translation, where the NAT uses the outgoing IP addresses and port numbers (collectively known as a socket) to map traffic from specific machines in the network. *See also* Network Address Translation (NAT).

port aggregation A method for joining two or more switch ports logically to increase bandwidth.

port authentication Function of many advanced networking devices that authenticates a connecting device at the point of connection.

port blocking Preventing the passage of any TCP segments or UDP datagrams through any ports other than the ones prescribed by the system administrator.

port bonding The logical joining of multiple redundant ports and links between two network devices such as a switch and storage array.

port filtering *See* port blocking.

port forwarding Preventing the passage of any IP packets through any ports other than the ones prescribed by the system administrator.

port mirroring The capability of many advanced switches to mirror data from any or all physical ports on a switch to a single physical port. Useful for any type of situation where an administrator needs to inspect packets coming to or from certain computers.

port number Number used to identify the requested service (such as SMTP or FTP) when connecting to a TCP/IP host. Some example server port numbers include 80 (HTTP), 21 (FTP), 25 (SMTP), 53 (DNS), and 67 (DHCP).

port scanner A program that probes ports on another system, logging the state of the scanned ports.

port scanning The process of querying individual nodes, looking for open or vulnerable ports and creating a report.

Post Office Protocol Version 3 (POP3) One of the two protocols that receive e-mail from SMTP servers. POP3 uses TCP port 110. Old and obsolete, this protocol was replaced by IMAP.

PostScript A language defined by Adobe Systems, Inc., for describing how to create an image on a page. The description is independent of the resolution of the device that will create the image. It includes a technology for defining the shape of a font and creating a raster image at many different resolutions and sizes.

posture assessment Process by which a client presents its security characteristics via an agent or agent-less interface to an access control server. The server checks the characteristics and decides whether to grant a connection, deny a connection, or redirect the connection depending on the security compliance invoked.

power converter Device that changes AC power to DC power.

Power over Ethernet (PoE) A standard that enables wireless access points (WAPs) to receive their power from the same Ethernet cables that transfer their data.

power redundancy Secondary source of power in the event that primary power fails. The most common redundant power source is an uninterruptible power supply (UPS).

power users A user account that has the capability to do many, but not all, of the basic administrator functions.

PPP (Point-to-Point Protocol) *See* Point-to-Point Protocol (PPP).

PPPoE (PPP over Ethernet) *See* Point-to-Point Protocol over Ethernet (PPPoE).

preamble A 7-byte series of alternating ones and zeroes followed by a 1-byte *start frame delimiter*, always precedes a frame. The preamble gives a receiving NIC time to realize a frame is coming and to know exactly where the frame starts.

prefix delegation An IPv6 router configuration that enables it to request an IPv6 address block from an upstream source, then to disseminate it to local clients.

prefix length The IPv6 term for subnet mask. In most cases, it's /64.

Presentation layer *See* Open Systems Interconnection (OSI) seven-layer model.

primary (master) DNS server The name server where records are added, deleted, and modified. The primary DNS server sends copies of this zone file to secondary (slave) DNS servers in a process known as a zone transfer.

primary lookup zone A *forward lookup zone* stored in a text file. *See also* forward lookup zone.

Primary Rate Interface (PRI) A type of ISDN that is actually just a full T1 line carrying 23 B channels.

primary zone A *forward lookup zone* that is managed within and by the authoritative DNS server.

private cloud Software, platforms, and infrastructure that are delivered via the Internet and are made available to the general public.

private IP addresses Groups of IP addresses set aside for internal networks; Internet routers block these addresses, such as 10.*x.x.x* /8, 172.(16–31).*x.x* /16, and 192.168.(0–255).*x* /24.

private port numbers *See* dynamic port numbers.

program A set of actions or instructions that a machine is capable of interpreting and executing. Used as a verb, it means to design, write, and test such instructions.

programmable logic controller (PLC) A computer that controls a machine according to a set of ordered steps.

promiscuous mode A mode of operation for a NIC in which the NIC processes all frames that it sees on the cable.

prompt A character or message provided by an operating system or program to indicate that it is ready to accept input.

proprietary Term used to describe technology that is unique to, and owned by, a particular vendor.

Protected Extensible Authentication Protocol (PEAP) An authentication protocol that uses a password function based on MS-CHAPv2 with the addition of an encrypted TLS tunnel similar to *EAP-TLS*.

protocol An agreement that governs the procedures used to exchange information between cooperating entities; usually includes how much information is to be sent, how often it is sent, how to recover from transmission errors, and who is to receive the information.

protocol analyzer A tool that monitors the different protocols running at different layers on the network and that can give Application, Session, Network, and Data Link layer information on every frame going through a network.

protocol data unit (PDU) Specialized type of command and control packet found in SNMP management systems (and others).

protocol stack The actual software that implements the protocol suite on a particular operating system.

protocol suite A set of protocols that are commonly used together and operate at different levels of the OSI seven-layer model.

proximity reader Sensor that detects and reads a token that comes within range. The polled information is used to determine the access level of the person carrying the token.

proxy ARP The process of making remotely connected computers act as though they are on the same LAN as local computers.

proxy server A device that fetches Internet resources for a client without exposing that client directly to the Internet. Most proxy servers accept requests for HTTP, FTP, POP3, and SMTP resources. The proxy server often caches, or stores, a copy of the requested resource for later use.

PSTN (public switched telephone network) *See* public switched telephone network (PSTN).

public cloud Software, platforms, and infrastructure delivered through networks that the general public can use.

public switched telephone network (PSTN) Also known as *plain old telephone service (POTS)*, the most common type of phone connection, which takes your sounds, translated into an analog waveform by the microphone, and transmits them to another phone.

public-key cryptography A method of encryption and decryption that uses two different keys: a public key for encryption and a private key for decryption.

public-key infrastructure (PKI) The system for creating and distributing digital certificates using sites like Comodo, DigiCert, or GoDaddy.

punchdown tool A specialized tool for connecting UTP wires to a 110-block. Also called a *110-punchdown tool*.

PVC-rated cable Type of network cable that offers no special fire protection; burning produces excessive smoke and noxious fumes.

quad small form-factor pluggable (QSFP) BiDi fiber-optic connector used in 40GBase networks.

quality of service (QoS) Policies that control how much bandwidth a protocol, PC, user, VLAN, or IP address may use.

quarantine network Safe network to which are directed stations that either do not require or should not have access to protected resources.

raceway Cable organizing device that adheres to walls, making for a much simpler, though less neat, installation than running cables in the walls.

rack monitoring system Set of sensors in an equipment closet or rack-mounted gear that can monitor and alert when an out-of-tolerance condition occurs in power, temperature, and/or other environmental aspects.

radio frequency interference (RFI) The phenomenon where a Wi-Fi signal is disrupted by a radio signal from another device.

Radio Grade (RG) ratings Ratings developed by the U.S. military to provide a quick reference for the different types of coaxial cables.

RADIUS server A system that enables remote users to connect to a network service.

ransomware Crypto-malware that uses some form of encryption to lock a user out of a system. Once the crypto-malware encrypts the computer, usually encrypting the boot drive, in most cases the malware then forces the user to pay money to get the system decrypted.

real-time processing The processing of transactions as they occur, rather than batching them. Pertaining to an application, processing in which response to input is fast enough to affect subsequent inputs and guide the process, and in which records are updated immediately. The lag from input time to output time must be sufficiently small for acceptable timeliness. Timeliness is a function of the total system: missile guidance requires output within a few milliseconds of input, whereas scheduling of steamships requires a response time in days. Real-time systems are those with a response time of milliseconds; interactive systems respond in seconds; and batch systems may respond in hours or days.

Real-time Transport Protocol (RTP) Protocol that defines the type of packets used on the Internet to move voice or data from a server to clients. The vast majority of VoIP solutions available today use RTP.

real-time video Communication that offers both audio and video via unicast messages.

reassembly The process where a receiving system verifies and puts together packets into coherent data.

recovery point objective (RPO) The state of the backup when the data is recovered. It is an evaluation of how much data is lost from the time of the last backup to the point that a recovery was required.

recovery time objective (RTO) The amount of time needed to restore full functionality from when the organization ceases to function.

Reddit hug of death The massive influx of traffic on a small or lesser-known Web site when it is suddenly made popular by a reference from the media. *See also* Slashdotting.

redundant array of independent [or inexpensive] disks [or devices] (RAID) A way to create a fault-tolerant storage system. RAID has six levels. Level 0 uses byte-level striping and provides no fault tolerance. Level 1 uses mirroring or duplexing. Level 2 uses bit-level striping. Level 3 stores error-correcting information (such as parity) on a separate disk and data striping on the remaining drives. Level 4 is level 3 with block-level striping. Level 5 uses block-level and parity data striping.

reflection Used in DDoS attacks, requests are sent to normal servers as if they had come from the target server. The response from the normal servers are reflected to the target server, overwhelming it without identifying the true initiator.

reflective DDoS *See* reflection.

refraction Bending of radio waves when transmitted through glass.

regedit.exe A program used to edit the Windows registry.

Regional Internet Registries (RIRs) Entities under the oversight of the Internet Assigned Numbers Authority (IANA), which parcels out IP addresses.

registered jack (RJ) Type of connector used on the end of telephone and networking cables. *See* RJ-11 *and* RJ-45, *respectively.*

registered ports Port numbers from 1024 to 49151. The IANA assigns these ports for anyone to use for their applications.

regulations Rules of law or policy that govern behavior in the workplace, such as what to do when a particular event occurs.

remote Refers to the computer(s), server(s), and/or LAN that cannot be physically used due to its distance from the user.

remote access The capability to access a computer from outside a building in which it is housed. Remote access requires communications hardware, software, and actual physical links.

remote access server (RAS) Refers to both the hardware component (servers built to handle the unique stresses of a large number of clients calling in) and the software component (programs that work with the operating system to allow remote access to the network) of a remote access solution.

Remote Authentication Dial-In User Service (RADIUS) An AAA standard created to support ISPs with hundreds if not thousands of modems in hundreds of computers to connect to a single central database. RADIUS consists of three devices: the RADIUS server that has access to a database of user names and passwords, a number of network access servers (NASs) that control the modems, and a group of systems that dial into the network.

Remote Copy Protocol (RCP) Provides the capability to copy files to and from the remote server without the need to resort to FTP or Network File System (NFS, a UNIX form of folder sharing). RCP can also be used in scripts and shares TCP port 514 with RSH.

Remote Desktop Protocol (RDP) A Microsoft-created remote terminal protocol.

Remote Installation Services (RIS) A tool introduced with Windows 2000 that can be used to initiate either a scripted installation or an installation of an image of an operating system onto a PC.

remote login (rlogin) Program in UNIX that enables you to log into a server remotely. Unlike Telnet, rlogin can be configured to log in automatically.

remote shell (RSH) Allows you to send single commands to the remote server. Whereas rlogin is designed to be used interactively, RSH can be easily integrated into a script.

remote terminal A connection on a faraway computer that enables you to control that computer as if you were sitting in front of it and logged in. Remote terminal programs all require a server and a client. The server is the computer to be controlled. The client is the computer from which you do the controlling.

remote terminal unit (RTU) In a SCADA environment, has the same functions as a controller plus additional autonomy to deal with connection loss. It is also designed to take advantage of some form of long-distance communication.

repeater A device that takes all of the frames it receives on one Ethernet segment and re-creates them on another Ethernet segment. Repeaters operate at Layer 1 (Physical) of the OSI seven-layer model. They do not check the integrity of the Layer 2 (Data Link) frame so they may repeat incorrectly formed frames. They were replaced in the early 1980s by bridges which perform frame integrity checking before repeating a frame.

replication A process where multiple computers might share complete copies of a database and constantly update each other.

resistance The tendency for a physical medium to impede electron flow. It is classically measured in a unit called *ohms*. *See also* impedance.

resource Anything that exists on another computer that a person wants to use without going to that computer. Also an online information set or an online interactive option. An online library catalog and the local school lunch menu are examples of information sets. Online menus or graphical user interfaces, Internet e-mail, online conferences, Telnet, FTP, and Gopher are examples of interactive options.

Response Answer from an agent upon receiving a Get protocol data unit (PDU) from an SNMP manager.

reverse lookup zone A DNS setting that resolves IP addresses to FQDNs. In other words, it does exactly the reverse of what DNS normally accomplishes using forward lookup zones.

reverse proxy server A connectivity solution that gathers information from its associated servers and shares that information to clients. The clients don't know about the servers behind the scenes. The reverse proxy server is the only machine with which they interact.

RF emanation The transmission, intended or unintended, of radio frequencies. These transmissions may come from components that are intended to transmit RF, such as a Wi-Fi network card, or something less expected, such as a motherboard or keyboard. These emanations may be detected and intercepted, posing a potential threat to security.

RG-6 A grade of coaxial cable used for cable television and modern cable modem Internet connections. RG-6 has a characteristic impedance of 75 ohms.

RG-58 A grade of small-diameter coaxial cable used in 10Base2 Ethernet networks. RG-58 has a characteristic impedance of 50 ohms.

RG-59 A grade of coaxial cable used for cable television and early cable modem Internet connections. RG-59 has a characteristic impedance of 75 ohms.

ring topology A network topology in which all the computers on the network attach to a central ring of cable.

RIP (Routing Information Protocol) The first version of RIP, which had several shortcomings, such as a maximum hop count of 15 and a routing table update interval of 30 seconds, which was a problem because every router on a network would send out its table at the same time.

RIPv2 The second version of RIP. It fixed many problems of RIP, but the maximum hop count of 15 still applies.

riser Fire rating that designates the proper cabling to use for vertical runs between floors of a building.

risk management The process of how organizations evaluate, protect, and recover from threats and attacks that take place on their networks.

Rivest Cipher 4 (RC4) A streaming symmetric-key algorithm.

Rivest, Shamir, Adleman (RSA) *See* RSA (Rivest, Shamir, Adleman).

RJ (registered jack) Connectors used for UTP cable on both telephone and network connections.

RJ-11 Type of connector with four-wire UTP connections; usually found in telephone connections.

RJ-45 Type of connector with eight-wire UTP connections; usually found in network connections and used for 10/100/1000BaseT networking.

roaming A process where clients seamlessly change wireless access point (WAP) connections, depending on whichever WAP has the strongest signal covered by the broadcast area.

rogue access point (rogue AP) An unauthorized wireless access point (WAP) installed in a computer network.

rogue DHCP server An unauthorized DHCP server installed in a computer network.

role-based access control (RBAC) The most popular authentication model used in file sharing, defines a user's access to a resource based on the roles the user plays in the network environment. This leads to the idea of creation of groups. A group in most networks is nothing more than a name that has clearly defined accesses to different resources. User accounts are placed into various groups.

rollback The process of downgrading—undoing—a recently applied patch or updated.

ROM (read-only memory) The generic term for nonvolatile memory that can be read from but not written to. This means that code and data stored in ROM cannot be corrupted by accidental erasure. Additionally, ROM retains its data when power is removed, which makes it the perfect medium for storing BIOS data or information such as scientific constants.

root directory The directory that contains all other directories.

rootkit A Trojan horse that takes advantage of very low-level operating system functions to hide itself from all but the most aggressive of anti-malware tools.

route A command that enables a user to display and edit the local system's routing table.

route redistribution Occurs in a multiprotocol router. A multiprotocol router learns route information using one routing protocol and disseminates that information using another routing protocol.

router A device that connects separate networks and forwards a packet from one network to another based only on the network address for the protocol being used. For example, an IP router looks only at the IP network number. Routers operate at Layer 3 (Network) of the OSI seven-layer model.

router advertisement A router's response to a client's router solicitation, also sent at regular intervals, that gives the client information to configure itself (prefix, prefix length, and more).

router solicitation In IPv6, a query from a host to find routers and get information to configure itself.

Routing and Remote Access Service (RRAS) A special remote access server program, originally only available on Windows Server, on which a PPTP endpoint is placed in Microsoft networks.

Routing Information Protocol (RIP) *See* RIP (Routing Information Protocol) *and* RIPv1.

routing loop A situation where interconnected routers loop traffic, causing the routers to respond slowly or not respond at all.

routing table A list of paths to various networks required by routers. This table can be built either manually or automatically.

RS-232 The recommended standard (RS) upon which all serial communication takes place on a PC.

RSA (Rivest, Shamir, Adleman) An improved asymmetric cryptography algorithm that enables secure digital signatures.

run A single piece of installed horizontal cabling.

Samba An application that enables UNIX systems to communicate using Server Message Blocks (SMBs). This, in turn, enables them to act as Microsoft clients and servers on the network.

SC connector Fiber-optic connector used to terminate single-mode and multimode fiber. It is characterized by its push-pull, snap mechanical coupling, known as "stick and click." Commonly referred to as *subscriber connector*, *standard connector*, and sometimes, *square connector*.

scalability The capability to support network growth.

scanner A device that senses alterations of light and dark. It enables the user to import photographs, other physical images, and text into the computer in digital form.

secondary (slave) DNS server Authoritative DNS server for a domain. Unlike a primary (master) DNS server, no additions, deletions, or modifications can be made to the zones on a secondary DNS server, which always gets all information from the primary DNS server in a process known as a zone transfer.

secondary lookup zone A backup lookup zone stored on another DNS server. *See also* forward lookup zone.

secondary zone A backup of a primary zone. It is used to provide fault tolerance and load balancing. It gets its information from the primary zone and is considered authoritative. *See also* primary zone.

Secure Copy Protocol (SCP) One of the first SSH-enabled programs to appear after the introduction of SSH. SCP was one of the first protocols used to transfer data securely between two hosts and thus might have replaced FTP. SCP works well but lacks features such as a directory listing.

Secure Hash Algorithm (SHA) A popular cryptographic hash.

Secure Shell (SSH) A terminal emulation program that looks exactly like Telnet but encrypts the data. SSH has replaced Telnet on the Internet.

Secure Sockets Layer (SSL) A protocol developed by Netscape for transmitting private documents over the Internet. SSL worked by using a public key to encrypt sensitive data. This encrypted data was sent over an SSL connection and then decrypted at the receiving end using a private key. Deprecated in favor of TLS.

security A network's resilience against unwanted access or attack.

security considerations In network design and construction, planning how to keep data protected from unapproved access. Security of physical computers and network resources is also considered.

security guard Person responsible for controlling access to physical resources such as buildings, secure rooms, and other physical assets.

security information and event management (SIEM) A two-part process consisting of security event monitoring (SEM), which performs real-time monitoring of security events, and security information management (SIM), where the monitoring log files are reviewed and analyzed by automated and human interpreters.

security log A log that tracks anything that affects security, such as successful and failed logons and logoffs.

security policy A set of procedures defining actions employees should perform to protect the network's security.

segment The bus cable to which the computers on an Ethernet network connect.

segmentation In a TCP/IP network, the process of chopping requested data into chunks that will fit into a packet (and eventually into the NIC's frame), organizing the packets for the benefit of the receiving system, and handing them to the NIC for sending.

sequential A method of storing and retrieving information that requires data to be written and read sequentially. Accessing any portion of the data requires reading all the preceding data.

server A computer that shares its resources, such as printers and files, with other computers on the network. An example of this is a Network File System server that shares its disk space with a workstation that has no disk drive of its own.

Server Message Block (SMB) *See* SMB (Server Message Block).

server-based network A network in which one or more systems function as dedicated file, print, or application servers, but do not function as clients.

service level agreement (SLA) A document between a customer and a service provider that defines the scope, quality, and terms of the service to be provided.

Service Set Identifier (SSID) A 32-bit identification string, sometimes called a *network name*, that's inserted into the header of each data packet processed by a wireless access point.

services Background programs in an operating system that do the behind-the-scenes grunt work that users don't need to interact with on a regular basis.

session A networking term used to refer to the logical stream of data flowing between two programs and being communicated over a network. Many different sessions may be emanating from any one node on a network.

session hijacking The interception of a valid computer session to get authentication information.

Session Initiation Protocol (SIP) A signaling protocol for controlling voice and video calls over IP. SIP competes with H.323 for VoIP dominance.

Session layer *See* Open Systems Interconnection (OSI) seven-layer model.

session software Handles the process of differentiating among various types of connections on a PC.

Set The PDU with which a network management station commands an agent to make a change to a management information base (MIB) object.

share level security A security system in which each resource has a password assigned to it; access to the resource is based on knowing the password.

share permissions Permissions that only control the access of other users on the network with whom you share your resource. They have no impact on you (or anyone else) sitting at the computer whose resource is being shared.

shareware Software that is protected by copyright, but the copyright holder allows (encourages!) you to make and distribute copies, under the condition that those who adopt the software after preview pay a fee. Derivative works are not allowed, and you may make an archival copy.

shell Generally refers to the user interface of an operating system. A shell is the command processor that is the actual interface between the kernel and the user.

shielded twisted pair (STP) A cabling for networks composed of pairs of wires twisted around each other at specific intervals. The twists serve to reduce interference (also called *crosstalk*). The more twists, the less interference. The cable has metallic shielding to protect the wires from external interference. *See also* unshielded twisted pair (UTP) *for the more commonly used cable type in modern networks.*

short circuit Allows electricity to pass between two conductive elements that weren't designed to interact together. Also called a *short*.

Short Message Service (SMS) alert A proactive message regarding an out-of-tolerance condition of an SNMP managed device sent as an SMS text.

Shortest Path First Networking algorithm for directing router traffic. *See also* Open Shortest Path First (OSPF).

signal strength A measurement of how well your wireless device is connecting to other devices.

signaling topology Another name for logical topology. *See* logical topology.

signature Specific pattern of bits or bytes that is unique to a particular virus. Virus scanning software maintains a library of signatures and compares the contents of scanned files against this library to detect infected files.

SIM card *See* subscriber identity module (SIM) card.

Simple Mail Transfer Protocol (SMTP) The main protocol used to send electronic mail on the Internet.

Simple Network Management Protocol (SNMP) A set of standards for communication with network devices (switches, routers, WAPs) connected to a TCP/IP network. Used for network management.

single point of failure One component or system that, if it fails, will bring down an entire process, workflow, or organization.

single sign-on A process whereby a client performs a one-time login to a gateway system. That system, in turn, takes care of the client's authentication to any other connected systems for which the client is authorized to access.

single-mode fiber (SMF) Fiber-optic cables that use lasers.

site survey A process that enables you to determine any obstacles to creating the wireless network you want.

site-to-site A type of VPN connection using two Cisco VPN concentrators to connect two separate LANs permanently.

Slashdotting The massive influx of traffic on a small or lesser-known Web site when it is suddenly made popular by a reference from the media. *See also* Reddit hug of death.

small form factor (SFF) A description of later-generation, fiber-optic connectors designed to be much smaller than the first iterations of connectors. *See also* local connector (LC) *and* Mechanical Transfer Registered Jack (MT-RJ).

small form-factor pluggable (SFP) A Cisco module that enables you to add additional features to its routers.

small office/home office (SOHO) *See* SOHO (small office/home office).

smart card Device (such as a credit card) that you insert into your PC or use on a door pad for authentication.

smart device Device (such as a credit card, USB key, etc.) that you insert into your PC in lieu of entering a password.

smart jack Type of network interface unit (NIU) that enables ISPs or telephone companies to test for faults in a network, such as disconnections and loopbacks.

SMB (Server Message Block) Protocol used by Microsoft clients and servers to share file and print resources.

SMTP (Simple Mail Transfer Protocol) *See* Simple Mail Transfer Protocol (SMTP).

smurf A type of hacking attack in which an attacker floods a network with ping packets sent to the broadcast address. The trick that makes this attack special is that the return address of the pings is spoofed to that of the intended victim. When all the computers on the network respond to the initial ping, they send their response to the intended victim.

smurf attack *See* smurf.

snap-ins Small utilities that can be used with the Microsoft Management Console.

snapshot A tool that enables you to save an extra copy of a virtual machine as it is exactly at the moment the snapshot is taken.

sneakernet Saving a file on a portable medium and walking it over to another computer.

sniffer Diagnostic program that can order a NIC to run in promiscuous mode. *See also* promiscuous mode.

snip *See* cable stripper.

SNMP (Simple Network Management Protocol) *See* Simple Network Management Protocol (SNMP).

SNMP manager Software and station that communicates with SNMP agents to monitor and manage management information base (MIB) objects.

snmpwalk SNMP manager PDU that collects management information base (MIB) information in a tree-oriented hierarchy of a MIB object and any of its subordinate objects. The snmpwalk command queries the object and then automatically queries all of the objects that are subordinated to the root object being queried.

social engineering The process of using or manipulating people inside the networking environment to gain access to that network from the outside.

socket A combination of a port number and an IP address that uniquely identifies a connection.

socket pairs *See* endpoints.

software Programming instructions or data stored on some type of binary storage device.

Software as a Service (SaaS) Centralized applications that are accessed over a network. *See also* cloud computing.

software defined networking (SDN) Programming that allows a master controller to determine how network components will move traffic through the network. Used in virtualization.

SOHO (small office/home office) Refers to a classification of networking equipment, usually marketed to consumers or small businesses, which focuses on low price and ease of configuration. SOHO networks differ from enterprise networks, which focus on flexibility and maximum performance.

SOHO firewall Firewall, typically simple, that is built into the firmware of a SOHO router.

solid core A cable that uses a single solid wire to transmit signals.

SONET (Synchronous Optical Network) An American fiber carrier standard for connecting fiber-optic transmission systems. SONET was proposed in the mid-1980s and is now an ANSI standard. SONET defines interface standards at the Physical layer of the OSI seven-layer model.

Source Address Table (SAT) A table stored by a switch, listing the MAC addresses and port of each connected device.

Spanning Tree Protocol (STP) A protocol that enables switches to detect and prevent bridge loops automatically.

speed-test site A Web site used to check an Internet connection's throughput, such as www.speakeasy.net/speedtest.

split pair A condition that occurs when signals on a pair of wires within a UTP cable interfere with the signals on another wire pair within that same cable.

spoofing A security threat where an attacker makes some data seem as though it came from somewhere else, such as sending an e-mail with someone else's e-mail address in the sender field.

spyware Any program that sends information about your system or your actions over the Internet.

SQL (Structured Query Language) A language created by IBM that relies on simple English statements to perform database queries. SQL enables databases from different manufacturers to be queried using a standard syntax.

SRV record A generic DNS record that supports any type of server.

SSH File Transfer Protocol (SFTP) A replacement for FTP released after many of the inadequacies of SCP (such as the inability to see the files on the other computer) were discovered.

SSID broadcast A wireless access point feature that announces the WAP's SSID to make it easy for wireless clients to locate and connect to it. By default, most WAPs regularly announce their SSID. For security purposes, some entities propose disabling this broadcast.

SSL (Secure Sockets Layer) *See* Secure Sockets Layer (SSL).

SSL VPN A type of VPN that uses SSL encryption. Clients connect to the VPN server using a standard Web browser, with the traffic secured using SSL. The two most common types of SSL VPNs are SSL portal VPNs and SSL tunnel VPNs.

ST connector Fiber-optic connector used primarily with 2.5-mm, single-mode fiber. It uses a push on, then twist-to-lock mechanical connection commonly called stick-and-twist although ST actually stands for straight tip.

star topology A network topology in which all computers in the network connect to a central wiring point.

star-bus topology A hybrid of the star and bus topologies that uses a physical star, where all nodes connect to a single wiring point (such as a hub) and a logical bus that maintains the Ethernet standards. One benefit of a star-bus topology is *fault tolerance.*

start frame delimiter (SFD) One-byte section of an Ethernet packet that follows the preamble and precedes the Ethernet frame.

start of authority (SOA) record DNS record that defines the primary name server in charge of the forward lookup zone.

stateful (DHCP) Describes a DHCPv6 server that works very similarly to an IPv4 DHCP server, passing out IPv6 addresses, subnet masks, and default gateways as well as optional items like DNS server addresses.

stateful filtering/stateful inspection A method of filtering in which all packets are examined as a stream. Stateful devices can do more than allow or block; they can track when a stream is disrupted or packets get corrupted and act accordingly.

stateless (DHCP) Describes a DHCPv6 server that only passes out information like DNS servers' IP addresses, but doesn't give clients IPv6 addresses.

stateless filtering/stateless inspection A method of filtering where the device that does the filtering looks at each IP packet individually, checking the packet for IP addresses and port numbers and blocking or allowing accordingly.

statement of work (SOW) A contract that defines the services, products, and time frames for the vendor to achieve.

static addressing The process of assigning IP addresses by manually typing them into client computers.

static NAT (SNAT) A type of Network Address Translation (NAT) that maps a single routable IP address to a single machine, allowing you to access that machine from outside the network.

static routes Entries in a router's routing table that are not updated by any automatic route discovery protocols. Static routes must be added, deleted, or changed by a router administrator. Static routes are the opposite of dynamic routes.

static routing A process by which routers in an internetwork obtain information about paths to other routers. This information must be supplied manually.

storage A device or medium that can retain data for subsequent retrieval.

storage area network (SAN) A server that can take a pool of hard disks and present them over the network as any number of logical disks.

STP (Spanning Tree Protocol) *See* Spanning Tree Protocol (STP).

straight-through cable UTP or STP cable segment that has the wire and pin assignments at one end of the cable match the wire and same pin assignments at the other end. Straight-through cables are used to connect hosts to switches and are the connective opposite of crossover cables.

stranded core A cable that uses a bundle of tiny wire strands to transmit signals. Stranded core is not quite as good a conductor as solid core, but it will stand up to substantial handling without breaking.

stream cipher An encryption method that encrypts a single bit at a time. Popular when data comes in long streams (such as with older wireless networks or cell phones).

stripe set Two or more drives in a group that are used for a striped volume.

structured cabling Standards defined by the Telecommunications Industry Association/Electronic Industries Alliance (TIA/EIA) that define methods of organizing the cables in a network for ease of repair and replacement.

STS overhead Carries the signaling and protocol information in Synchronous Transport Signal (STS).

STS payload Carries data in Synchronous Transport Signal (STS).

subnet Each independent network in a TCP/IP internetwork.

subnet ID Portion of an IP address that identifies bits shared by all hosts on that network.

subnet mask The value used in TCP/IP settings to divide the IP address of a host into its component parts: network ID and host ID.

subnetting Taking a single class of IP addresses and chopping it into multiple smaller groups.

subscriber identity module (SIM) card Small storage device used in cellular phones to identify the phone, enable access to the cellular network, and store information such as contacts.

succession planning The process of identifying people who can take over certain positions (usually on a temporary basis) in case the people holding those critical positions are incapacitated or lost in an incident.

supervisory control and data acquisition (SCADA) A system that has the basic components of a distributed control system (DCS), yet is designed for large-scale, distributed processes and functions with the idea that remote devices may or may not have ongoing communication with the central control.

supplicant A client computer in a RADIUS network.

switch A Layer 2 (Data Link) multiport device that filters and forwards frames based on MAC addresses.

switch port protection Various methods to help modern switches deal with malicious software and other threats. Includes technologies such as flood guards.

switching loop When you connect multiple switches together in a circuit causing a loop to appear. Better switches use Spanning Tree Protocol (STP) to prevent this.

symmetric DSL (SDSL) Type of DSL connection that provides equal upload and download speed and, in theory, provides speeds up to 15 Mbps, although the vast majority of ISPs provide packages ranging from 192 Kbps to 9 Mbps.

symmetric-key algorithm Any encryption method that uses the same key for both encryption and decryption.

synchronous Describes a connection between two electronic devices where neither must acknowledge (ACK) when receiving data.

Synchronous Digital Hierarchy (SDH) European fiber carrier standard equivalent to SONET.

Synchronous Optical Network (SONET) *See* SONET (Synchronous Optical Network).

Synchronous Transport Signal (STS) Signal method used by SONET. It consists of the STS payload and the STS overhead. A number is appended to the end of STS to designate signal speed.

system life cycle Description of typical beginning and end of computing components. Handling such devices at the end includes system life cycle policies and asset disposal.

system log A log file that records issues dealing with the overall system, such as system services, device drivers, or configuration changes.

System Restore A Windows utility that enables you to return your PC to a recent working configuration when something goes wrong. System Restore returns your computer's system settings to the way they were the last time you remember your system working correctly—all without affecting your personal files or e-mail.

T connector A three-sided, tubular connector found in 10Base2 Ethernet networking. The connector is in the shape of a *T* with the "arms" of the *T* ending with a female BNC connector and the "leg" having a male BNC connector. The T connector is used to attach a BNC connector on a host between two cable segments.

T1 A leased-line connection capable of carrying data at 1,544,000 bps.

T1 line The specific, shielded, two-pair cabling that connects the two ends of a T1 connection.

T3 line A leased-line connection capable of carrying data at 44,736,000 bps.

tailgating When an unauthorized person attempts to enter through an already opened door.

tamper detection A feature of modern server chasses that will log in the motherboard's nonvolatile RAM (NVRAM) if the chassis has been opened. The log will show chassis intrusion with a date and time. Alternatively, the special stickers or zip ties that break when a device has been opened.

TCP segment The connection-oriented payload of an IP packet. A TCP segment works on the Transport layer.

TCP three-way handshake A three-packet conversation between TCP hosts to establish and start a data transfer session. The conversation begins with a SYN request by the initiator. The target responds with a SYN response and an ACK to the SYN request. The initiator confirms receipt of the SYN ACK with an ACK. Once this handshake is complete, data transfer can begin.

tcpdump A command-line packet sniffing tool.

TCP/IP model An architecture model based on the TCP/IP protocol suite, which defines and standardizes the flow of data between computers. The following lists the four layers:

- **Layer 1** The *Link layer (Network Interface layer)* is similar to OSI's Data Link and Physical layers. The Link layer consists of any part of the network that deals with frames.

- **Layer 2** The *Internet layer* is the same as OSI's Network layer. Any part of the network that deals with pure IP packets—getting a packet to its destination—is on the Internet layer.

- **Layer 3** The *Transport layer* combines the features of OSI's Transport and Session layers. It is concerned with the assembly and disassembly of data, as well as connection-oriented and connectionless communication.

- **Layer 4** The *Application layer* combines the features of the top three layers of the OSI model. It consists of the processes that applications use to initiate, control, and disconnect from a remote system.

TCP/IP suite The collection of all the protocols and processes that make TCP over IP communication over a network possible.

telecommunications room A central location for computer or telephone equipment and, most importantly, centralized cabling. All cables usually run to the telecommunications room from the rest of the installation.

telephony The science of converting sound into electrical signals, moving those signals from one location to another, and then converting those signals back into sounds. This includes modems, telephone lines, the telephone system, and any products used to create a remote access link between a remote access client and server.

Telnet A program that enables users on the Internet to log onto remote systems from their own host systems.

temperature monitor Device for keeping a telecommunications room at an optimal temperature.

TEMPEST The NSA's security standard that is used to combat radio frequency (RF) emanation by using enclosures, shielding, and even paint.

Temporal Key Integrity Protocol (TKIP) *See* TKIP-RC4.

Teredo A NAT-traversal IPv6 tunneling protocol, built into Microsoft Windows.

Terminal Access Controller Access Control System Plus (TACACS+) A proprietary protocol developed by Cisco to support Authorization, Authentication, and Accounting (AAA) in a network with many routers and switches. It is similar to RADIUS in function, but uses TCP port 49 by default and separates AAA and accounting into different parts.

terminal adapter (TA) The most common interface used to connect a computer to an ISDN line.

terminal emulation Software that enables a PC to communicate with another computer or network as if it were a specific type of hardware terminal.

termination Endpoint in a network segment. *See* demarc.

TFTP (Trivial File Transfer Protocol) *See* Trivial File Transfer Protocol (TFTP).

thick AP A wireless access point that is completely self-contained with a full set of management programs and administrative access ways. Each thick AP is individually managed by an administrator who logs into the WAP, configures it, and logs out.

thin AP A wireless access point with minimal configuration tools installed. Instead, it is managed by a central controller. An administrator can manage a large number of thin APs by logging into the central controller and performing management tasks on any thin APs from there.

Thinnet Trade name for 10Base2 Ethernet technology. Thinnet is characterized by the use of RG-58 coaxial cable segments and BNC T connectors to attach stations to the segments.

threat Any form of potential attack against a network.

TIA/EIA (Telecommunications Industry Association/Electronics Industry Association) The standards body that defines most of the standards for computer network cabling. Many of these standards are defined under the TIA/EIA 568 standard.

TIA/EIA 568A One of two four-pair UTP crimping standards for 10/100/1000BaseT networks. Often shortened to T568A. The other standard is *TIA/EIA 568B*.

TIA/EIA 568B One of two four-pair UTP crimping standards for 10/100/1000BaseT networks. Often shortened to T568B. The other standard is *TIA/EIA 568A*.

TIA/EIA 606 Official methodology for labeling patch panels.

Ticket-Granting Ticket (TGT) Sent by an Authentication Server in a Kerberos setup if a client's hash matches its own, signaling that the client is authenticated but not yet authorized.

time division multiplexing (TDM) The process of having frames that carry a bit of every channel in every frame sent at a regular interval in a T1 connection.

time domain reflectometer (TDR) Advanced cable tester that tests the length of cables and their continuity or discontinuity, and identifies the location of any discontinuity due to a bend, break, unwanted crimp, and so on.

TKIP-RC4 The extra layer of security that Wi-Fi Protected Access (WPA) adds on top of Wired Equivalent Privacy (WEP); uses RC4 for cipher initialization.

TLS (Transport Layer Security) *See* Transport Layer Security (TLS).

tone generator *See* toners.

tone probe *See* toners.

toners Generic term for two devices used together—a tone generator and a tone locator (probe)—to trace cables by sending an electrical signal along a wire at a particular frequency. The tone locator then emits a sound when it distinguishes that frequency. Also referred to as *Fox and Hound*.

top listener Host that receives the most data on a network.

top talker Host that sends the most data on a network.

top-level domain (TLD) names Peak of the hierarchy for naming on the Internet; these include the .com, .org, .net, .edu, .gov, .mil, and .int names, as well as international country codes such as .us, .eu, etc.

top-level domain servers A set of DNS servers—just below the root servers—that handle the top-level domain names, such as .com, .org, .net, and so on.

topology The pattern of interconnections in a communications system among devices, nodes, and associated input and output stations. Also describes how computers connect to each other without regard to how they actually communicate.

tracert (also traceroute) A command-line utility used to follow the path a packet takes between two hosts.

tracert –6 (also traceroute6) A command-line utility that checks a path from the station running the command to a destination host. Adding the –6 switch to the command line specifies that the target host uses an IPv6 address. tracerout6 is a Linux command that performs a traceroute to an IPv6 addressed host.

traffic analysis Tools that chart a network's traffic usage.

traffic shaping Controlling the flow of packets into or out of the network according to the type of packet or other rules.

traffic spike Unusual and usually dramatic increase in the amount of network traffic. Traffic spikes may be the result of normal operations within the organization or may be an indication of something more sinister.

trailer The portion of an Ethernet frame that is the frame check sequence (FCS).

transceiver The device that transmits and receives signals on a cable.

Transmission Control Protocol (TCP) Part of the TCP/IP protocol suite, operates at Layer 4 (Transport) of the OSI seven-layer model. TCP is a connection-oriented protocol.

Transmission Control Protocol/Internet Protocol (TCP/IP) A set of communication protocols developed by the U.S. Department of Defense that enables dissimilar computers to share information over a network.

transmit beamforming A multiple-antenna technology in 802.11n WAPs that helps get rid of dead spots.

Transport layer *See* Open Systems Interconnection (OSI) seven-layer model.

Transport Layer Security (TLS) A robust update to SSL that works with almost any TCP application.

Trap Out-of-tolerance condition in an SNMP managed device.

Trivial File Transfer Protocol (TFTP) A protocol that transfers files between servers and clients. Unlike FTP, TFTP requires no user login. Devices that need an operating system, but have no local hard disk (for example, diskless workstations and routers), often use TFTP to download their operating systems.

Trojan horse A virus that masquerades as a file with a legitimate purpose, so that a user will run it intentionally. The classic example is a file that runs a game, but also causes some type of damage to the player's system.

trunk port A port on a switch configured to carry all data, regardless of VLAN number, between all switches in a LAN.

trunking The process of transferring VLAN data between two or more switches.

trusted user An account that has been granted specific authority to perform certain or all administrative tasks.

tunnel An encrypted link between two programs on two separate computers.

tunnel broker In IPv6, a service that creates the actual tunnel and (usually) offers a custom-made endpoint client for you to use, although more advanced users can often make a manual connection.

Tunnel Information and Control (TIC) protocol One of the protocols that sets up IPv6 tunnels and handles configuration as well as login.

Tunnel Setup Protocol (TSP) One of the protocols that sets up IPv6 tunnels and handles configuration as well as login.

twisted pair Twisted pairs of cables, the most overwhelmingly common type of cabling used in networks. The two types of twisted pair cabling are UTP (unshielded twisted pair) and STP (shielded twisted pair). The twists serve to reduce interference, called *crosstalk*; the more twists, the less crosstalk.

two-factor authentication A method of security authentication that requires two separate means of authentication; for example, some sort of physical token that, when inserted, prompts for a password. Also called *multifactor authentication*.

TXT record Freeform type of DNS record that can be used for anything.

type Part of an Ethernet frame that describes/labels the frame contents.

U (unit) *See* unit (U).

UART (Universal Asynchronous Receiver/Transmitter) *See* Universal Asynchronous Receiver/Transmitter (UART).

UC device One of three components of a UC network, it is used to handle voice, video, and more.

UC gateway One of three components of a UC network, it is an edge device used to add extra services to an edge router.

UC server One of three components of a UC network, it is typically a dedicated box that supports any UC-provided service.

UDP (User Datagram Protocol) *See* User Datagram Protocol (UDP).

UDP datagram A connectionless networking container used in UDP communication.

Ultra Physical Contact (UPC) connector Fiber-optic connector that makes physical contact between two fiber-optic cables. The fibers within a UPC are polished extensively for a superior finish and better junction integrity.

UNC (Universal Naming Convention) Describes any shared resource in a network using the convention *<server name>**<name of shared resource>*.

unencrypted channel Unsecure communication between two hosts that pass data using cleartext. A Telnet connection is a common unencrypted channel.

unicast A message sent from one computer to one other computer.

unicast address A unique IP address that is exclusive to a single system.

unidirectional antenna An antenna that focuses all of its transmission energy in a single, relatively narrow direction. Similarly, its design limits its ability to receive signals that are not aligned with the focused direction.

unified communication (UC) A system that rolls many different network services into one. Instant messaging (IM), telephone service, and video conferencing are a few examples.

unified threat management (UTM) A firewall that is also packaged with a collection of other processes and utilities to detect and prevent a wide variety of threats. These protections include intrusion detection systems, intrusion prevention systems, VPN portals, load balancers, and other threat mitigation apparatus.

unified voice services Complete self-contained Internet services that rely on nothing more than software installed on computers and the computers' microphone/speakers to provide voice telecommunication over the Internet. All of the interconnections to the public switched telephone network (PSTN) are handled in the cloud.

uninterruptible power supply (UPS) A device that supplies continuous clean power to a computer system the whole time the computer is on. Protects against power outages and sags. The term *UPS* is often used mistakenly when people mean stand-by power supply or system (SPS).

unit (U) The unique height measurement used with equipment racks; 1 U equals 1.75 inches.

Universal Asynchronous Receiver Transmitter (UART) A device inside a modem that takes the 8-bit-wide digital data and converts it into 1-bit-wide digital data and hands it to the modem for conversion to analog data. The process is reversed for incoming data.

UNIX A popular computer software operating system used on many Internet host systems.

unsecure protocol Also known as an *insecure protocol*, transfers data between hosts in an unencrypted, clear text format. If these packets are intercepted between the communicating hosts, their data is completely exposed and readable.

unshielded twisted pair (UTP)   A popular cabling for telephone and networks composed of pairs of wires twisted around each other at specific intervals. The twists serve to reduce interference (also called *crosstalk*). The more twists, the less interference. The cable has *no* metallic shielding to protect the wires from external interference, unlike its cousin, *STP*. 10BaseT uses UTP, as do many other networking technologies. UTP is available in a variety of grades, called categories, as defined in the following:

- **Category 1 UTP**   Regular analog phone lines, not used for data communications
- **Category 2 UTP**   Supports speeds up to 4 Mbps
- **Category 3 UTP**   Supports speeds up to 16 Mbps
- **Category 4 UTP**   Supports speeds up to 20 Mbps
- **Category 5 UTP**   Supports speeds up to 100 Mbps
- **Category 5e UTP**   Supports speeds up to 100 Mbps with two pairs and up to 1000 Mbps with four pairs
- **Category 6 UTP**   Improved support for speeds up to 10 Gbps
- **Category 6a UTP**   Extends the length of 10-Gbps communication to the full 100 meters commonly associated with UTP cabling

untrusted user   An account that has been granted no administrative powers.

uplink port   Port on a switch that enables you to connect two switches together using a straight-through cable.

upload   The transfer of information from a user's system to a remote computer system. Opposite of *download*.

URL (uniform resource locator)   An address that defines the type and the location of a resource on the Internet. URLs are used in almost every TCP/IP application. An example HTTP URL is http://www.totalsem.com.

Usenet   The network of UNIX users, generally perceived as informal and made up of loosely coupled nodes, that exchanges mail and messages. Started by Duke University and UNC-Chapel Hill. An information cooperative linking around 16,000 computer sites and millions of people. Usenet provides a series of "news groups" analogous to online conferences.

user   Anyone who uses a computer. You.

user account   A container that identifies a user to the application, operating system, or network, including name, password, user name, groups to which the user belongs, and other information based on the user and the OS or NOS being used. Usually defines the rights and roles a user plays on a system.

User Datagram Protocol (UDP)   A protocol used by some older applications, most prominently TFTP (Trivial FTP), to transfer files. UDP datagrams are both simpler and smaller than TCP segments, and they do most of the behind-the-scenes work in a TCP/IP network.

user profile A collection of settings that corresponds to a specific user account and may follow the user, regardless of the computer at which he or she logs on. These settings enable the user to have customized environment and security settings.

user-level security A security system in which each user has an account, and access to resources is based on user identity.

UTP coupler A simple, passive, double-ended connector with female connectors on both ends. UTP couplers are used to connect two UTP cable segments together to achieve longer length when it is deemed unnecessary or inappropriate to use a single, long cable.

V standards Standards established by CCITT for modem manufacturers to follow (voluntarily) to ensure compatible speeds, compression, and error correction.

V.92 standard The current modem standard, which has a download speed of 57,600 bps and an upload speed of 48 Kbps. V.92 modems have several interesting features, such as Quick Connect and Modem On Hold.

variable Value of an SNMP management information base (MIB) object. That value can be read with a Get PDU or changed with a Set PDU.

variable-length subnet masking (VLSM) *See* Classless Inter-Domain Routing (CIDR).

vertical cross-connect Main patch panel in a telecommunications room. *See also* patch panel.

very-high-bit-rate DSL (VDSL) The latest form of DSL with download and upload speeds of up to 100 Mbps. VDSL was designed to run on copper phone lines, but many VDSL suppliers use fiber-optic cabling to increase effective distances.

video surveillance Security measures that use remotely monitored visual systems that include IP cameras and closed-circuit televisions (CCTVs).

video teleconferencing (VTC) The classic, multicast-based presentation where one presenter pushes out a stream of video to any number of properly configured and properly authorized multicast clients.

View The different displays found in Performance Monitor.

virtual firewall A firewall that is implemented in software within a virtual machine in cases where it would be difficult, costly, or impossible to install a traditional physical firewall.

virtual IP A single IP address shared by multiple systems. This is commonly the single IP address assigned to a home or organization that uses NAT to have multiple IP stations on the private side of the NAT router.

virtual local area network (VLAN) A common feature among managed switches that enables a single switch to support multiple logical broadcast domains. Not only is VLAN support a common feature of managed switches, but VLAN installations take advantage of this feature and are very common today.

virtual machine (VM) A virtual computer accessed through a class of programs called a hypervisor or virtual machine manager. A virtual machine runs *inside* your actual operating system, essentially enabling you to run two or more operating systems at once.

virtual machine manager (VMM) *See* hypervisor.

Virtual Network Computing (VNC) A terminal emulation program.

virtual PBX Software that functionally replaces a physical PBX telephone system.

virtual private network (VPN) A network configuration that enables a remote user to access a private network via the Internet. VPNs employ an encryption methodology called *tunneling*, which protects the data from interception.

virtual router A router that is implemented in software within a virtual machine. The scalability of a virtual machine makes it easy to add capacity to the router when it is needed. Virtual routers are easily managed and are highly scalable without requiring the purchase of additional network hardware.

virtual switch Special software that enables virtual machines (VMs) to communicate with each other without going outside of the host system.

Virtual Trunking Protocol (VTP) A proprietary Cisco protocol used to automate the updating of multiple VLAN switches.

virus A program that can make a copy of itself without your necessarily being aware of it. All viruses carry some payload that may or may not do something malicious.

virus definition or data files Enables the virus protection software to recognize the viruses on your system and clean them. These files should be updated often. Also called *signature files*, depending on the virus protection software in use.

virus shield Anti-malware program that passively monitors a computer's activity, checking for viruses only when certain events occur, such as a program executing or a file being downloaded.

VLAN hopping Older technique to hack a switch to change a normal switch port from an access port to a trunk port. This allows the station attached to the newly created trunk port to access different VLANs. Modern switches have preventative measures to stop this type of abuse.

VLAN pooling Used in wireless networking, a setup where multiple VLANs share a common domain. The multiple VLANs are used to keep broadcast traffic to manageable levels. Wireless clients are randomly assigned to different VLANs. Their common domain enables them all to be centrally managed.

VLAN Trunking Protocol (VTP) Cisco proprietary protocol to automate the updating of multiple VLAN switches.

Voice over IP (VoIP) Using an IP network to conduct voice calls.

VoIP gateway Interface between a traditional switched telephone network and a VoIP service provider.

VoIP PBX A private branch exchange that uses VoIP instead of the traditional switched telephone circuits.

volt (V) Unit of measurement for voltage.

voltage The pressure of the electrons passing through a wire.

voltage quality recorder Tracks voltage over time by plugging into a power outlet.

VPN concentrator The new endpoint of the local LAN in L2TP.

VPN tunnel A connection over the Internet between a client and a server; the VPN tunnel enables the client to access remote resources as if they were local, securely.

vulnerability A potential weakness in an infrastructure that a threat might exploit.

vulnerability management The ongoing process of identifying vulnerabilities and dealing with them.

vulnerability scanner A tool that scans a network for potential attack vectors.

WAN (wide area network) A geographically dispersed network created by linking various computers and LANs over long distances, generally using leased phone lines. There is no firm dividing line between a WAN and a LAN.

warm boot A system restart performed after the system has been powered and operating. This clears and resets the memory, but does not stop and start the hard drive.

warm site Facility with all of the physical resources, computers, and network infrastructure to recover from a primary site disaster. A warm site does not have current backup data and it may take a day or more to recover and install backups before business operations can recommence.

wattage (watts or W) The amount of amps and volts needed by a particular device to function.

wavelength In the context of laser pulses, the distance the signal has to travel before it completes its cyclical oscillation and starts to repeat. Measured in nanometers, wavelength can be loosely associated with colors.

Web server A server that enables access to HTML documents by remote users.

Web services Applications and processes that can be accessed over a network, rather than being accessed locally on the client machine. Web services include things such as Web-based e-mail, network-shareable documents, spreadsheets and databases, and many other types of cloud-based applications.

well-known port numbers Port numbers from 0 to 1204 that are used primarily by client applications to talk to server applications in TCP/IP networks.

wide area network (WAN) *See* WAN (wide area network).

Wi-Fi The most widely adopted wireless networking type in use today. Technically, only wireless devices that conform to the extended versions of the 802.11 standard—802.11a, b, g, n, and ac—are Wi-Fi certified.

Wi-Fi analyzer *See* wireless analyzer.

Wi-Fi Protected Access (WPA) A wireless security protocol that addresses weaknesses and acts as an upgrade to WEP. WPA offers security enhancements such as dynamic encryption key generation (keys are issued on a per-user and per-session basis), an encryption key integrity-checking feature, user authentication through the industry-standard Extensible Authentication Protocol (EAP), and other advanced features that WEP lacks.

Wi-Fi Protected Access 2 (WPA2) An update to the WPA protocol that uses the Advanced Encryption Standard algorithm, making it much harder to crack.

Wi-Fi Protected Setup (WPS) Automated and semi-automated process to connect a wireless device to a WAP. The process can be as simple as pressing a button on the device or pressing the button and then entering a PIN code.

WiMAX *See* 802.16.

Windows domain A group of computers controlled by a computer running Windows Server, which is configured as a domain controller.

Windows Firewall/Windows Defender Firewall The firewall that has been included in Windows operating systems since Windows XP; originally named Internet Connection Firewall (ICF) but renamed in XP Service Pack 2.

Windows Internet Name Service (WINS) A name resolution service that resolves NetBIOS names to IP addresses.

WINS proxy agent A Windows Internet Name Service (WINS) relay agent that forwards WINS broadcasts to a WINS server on the other side of a router to keep older systems from broadcasting in place of registering with the server.

wire scheme *See* wiring diagram.

Wired Equivalent Privacy (WEP) A wireless security protocol that uses a 64-bit encryption algorithm to scramble data packets.

wired/wireless considerations The planning of structured cabling, determining any wireless requirements, and planning access to the Internet when building or upgrading networks.

wireless access point (WAP) Connects wireless network nodes to wireless or wired networks. Many WAPs are combination devices that act as high-speed hubs, switches, bridges, and routers, all rolled into one.

wireless analyzer Any device that finds and documents all wireless networks in the area. Also known as a *Wi-Fi analyzer*.

wireless bridge Device used to connect two wireless network segments together, or to join wireless and wired networks together in the same way that wired bridge devices do.

wireless controller Central controlling device for thin client WAPs.

wireless LAN (WLAN) A complete wireless network infrastructure serving a single physical locale under a single administration.

wireless network *See* Wi-Fi.

wireless survey tool A tool used to discover wireless networks in an area; it also notes signal interferences.

wiremap Extensive network testing using a better cable tester.

Wireshark A popular packet sniffer.

wiring diagram A document, also known as a *wiring schematic*, that usually consists of multiple pages and that shows the following: how the wires in a network connect to switches and other nodes, what types of cables are used, and how patch panels are configured. It usually includes details about each cable run.

wiring schematic *See* wiring diagram.

work area In a basic structured cabling network, often simply an office or cubicle that potentially contains a PC attached to the network.

Workgroup A convenient method of organizing computers under Network/My Network Places in Windows operating systems.

workstation A general-purpose computer that is small and inexpensive enough to reside at a person's work area for his or her exclusive use.

worm A very special form of virus. Unlike other viruses, a worm does not infect other files on the computer. Instead, it replicates by making copies of itself on other systems on a network by taking advantage of security weaknesses in networking protocols.

WPA2-Enterprise A version of WPA2 that uses a RADIUS server for authentication.

WWW (World Wide Web) A vast network of servers and clients communicating through the Hypertext Transfer Protocol (HTTP). Commonly accessed using graphical Web-browsing software such as Microsoft Internet Explorer and Google Chrome.

X.25 The first generation of packet-switching technology, it enables remote devices to communicate with each other across high-speed digital links without the expense of individual leased lines.

Yost cable Cable used to interface with a Cisco device.

zero-configuration networking (zeroconf) Automatically generated IP addresses when a DHCP server is unreachable.

zero-day attack New attack that exploits a vulnerability that has yet to be identified.

Zigbee Wireless home automation control standard.

zombie A single computer under the control of an operator that is used in a botnet attack. *See also* botnet.

Z-Wave Wireless home automation control standard.

Index

Save 10% on CompTIA Exam Vouchers for ANY CompTIA Certification!

Now there's even more reason to get certified. Ready to get started?

1. Visit the CompTIA Marketplace www.comptiastore.com.

2. Select the appropriate exam voucher.

*3. At checkout, apply the coupon code: **MCGRAW10** to receive your 10% discount.*

WHY CERTIFY?

- To prove you have the knowledge and skills for problem solving
- To make you more competitive and employable

- To qualify you for increased compensation and/or promotions
- To open up new career opportunities